TITO
AND THE
STUDENTS

TITO
AND THE
STUDENTS

*The University and the University Student
in Self-Managing Yugoslavia*

RALPH PERVAN

UNIVERSITY OF WESTERN AUSTRALIA PRESS

First published in 1978
By the University of Western Australia Press
Nedlands W.A. 6009

Agents: Eastern states of Australia and New Zealand: Melbourne University Press, Carlton South, Vic. 3053; United Kingdom and Europe: International Scholarly Book Services (Europe), 8 Willian Way, Letchworth, Hertfordshire SG6 2HG, U.K.; U.S.A. and Canada: International Scholarly Book Services, Inc., Box 555, Forest Grove, Oregon 97116
Photoset by the University of Western Australia Press, printed and bound by Frank Daniels Pty Ltd, Perth, Western Australia.

Pervan, Ralph, 1938-
   Tito and the students.

   Index.
   Bibliography.
   ISBN 0 85564 131 2.
      0 85564 120 7 paperback

   1. Yugoslavia — Politics and government — 1945-
   2. Universities and colleges — Yugoslavia.
   3. Student movements — Yugoslavia. 4. Students —
   Yugoslavia — Political activity. I. Title.

354'.497

To my mother and father

CONTENTS

CONTENTS

TABLES

PREFACE

It is customary for an author to tell his readers little or nothing about himself. However, because it is generally acknowledged that an author's perspective is profoundly affected by his background, and because it seems especially important in this particular case, it is a custom which I have decided to breach.

My maternal grandparents migrated to Australia before World War I from the island of Vis, at that time part of the Austro-Hungarian Empire, and now part of Yugoslavia. They were illiterate peasants who came to Australia because even the fear of an unknown, distant and foreign land weighed less than the hopelessness of home. My father migrated to Australia in 1924 at the age of sixteen from a small village which lay between Split and Dubrovnik, but inland from the coastal range. As a child, I learnt from my family and their friends that the Yugoslavia they knew was a country that offered little hope.

A significant number of these migrants, my parents among them, became enthusiastic supporters of the Communist Party. They subscribed to it, I think, not so much because they saw it as holding the key to the solution of problems in Australia, but because they saw it as the only hope for their native land—the only means by which the abject poverty and brutal oppression, which characterized the Yugoslavia they remembered, could be destroyed. I am not saying that they knew or cared little of Australian politics, but rather, that they often seemed to approach Australian politics from the perspective of their Yugoslav background.

These vignerons, market gardeners, miners, timber workers and the like often made what were for them enormous financial sacrifices to assist the Communist Party and the war effort of World War II. Some of my earliest memories are of fund-raising concerts, plays, etc., in the various centres where Yugoslav migrants were concentrated, and of my mother speaking at public meetings and on the radio, lauding the valiant struggle of the Yugoslav partisans against Hitler and his henchmen; a struggle for national independence but also, as they saw it, a struggle for the establishment of a society which would give its peoples opportunity, hope and freedom.

After the war, the new Yugoslav leadership, led by Tito, encouraged Yugoslav migrants to return home—indeed, it was urged that it was their patriotic duty to come to assist in the struggle for socialism. Hundreds of families from all over the world, and dozens from Western

Australia alone, responded. My parents, of course, were among them. Thus, just when they were beginning to find their feet after the rigours of the depression, the dislocation of the war and the burdens of the war effort, they sold their property, paid off their remaining debts and boarded the ships with boxes of household goods and with a few hundred pounds.

The situation which met these so-called 'returnees' in Yugoslavia was one of 'underdevelopment' exacerbated by the ravages of the recent war, and then in 1948, by the economic dislocation caused by the break between Yugoslavia and the Soviet Union. For the most part, they had no particular skills that were needed in the new Yugoslavia, and naturally this mitigated against their finding a niche in the society. And, difficult though life had been in Australia, the living standard they were now forced to accept was lower than that to which they had been accustomed. Their money, which had been converted into Yugoslav currency at official rates, quickly disappeared, and then began the humiliating process of selling their household possessions and personal effects in order to maintain what to them was a reasonable standard of living.

These difficulties, however, scarcely touched me. And when, after some two and a half years, my parents informed me of their decision to return to Australia, I was seriously torn between the natural desire of any twelve year old to be with his parents and the strong feeling that duty demanded that I stay.

For me, at least, Yugoslavia remained an exciting rather than a depressing memory. And my constant feeling, even after I had settled back happily in Australia, was that we had been unlucky to have encountered the new Yugoslavia when it was at its lowest.

I continued to note with satisfaction and pride those reports of developments in Yugoslavia which pointed to rapid economic growth and the development of a system of government far more democratic and humane than that of other communist countries. Yugoslav officials themselves made much of the vitality and virtue of their system and proudly proclaimed it as a viable alternative to both the capitalist and the 'state capitalist' model. Their claims, I observed, were taken seriously by Western scholars who referred approvingly to the Yugoslav experience.

Because of my background, I was eager to examine and evaluate this experiment for myself, and because of my background, I began my formal study of Yugoslav politics with a favourable disposition and high, but, I hope, not unreasonable expectations.

The actual research was commenced in the United States against the backdrop of significant ferment in that society, especially amongst university students. I was interested in understanding the causes and significance of this unrest; that is, I was interested both in the process of political socialization and the phenomenon of political culture. It was natural, then, that my study of Yugoslavia should focus on the significant student disturbances of June 1968: what did these disturbances indicate concerning the past experiences of these young people? And what did the attitudes and beliefs of the protesters signify concerning the future of the system? Both the official and academic views in Yugoslavia seemed unanimous that these protests represented not a fundamental crisis but rather a revitalization of revolutionary enthusiasm. As I began my study, this view seemed persuasive.

ACKNOWLEDGEMENTS

I am extremely grateful to the many Yugoslav university staff and students and Yugoslav officials and citizens who proved so willing to discuss and debate with me the issues covered in this work. I am also grateful for the financial assistance I received from Duke University and from the University of Western Australia which made it possible for me to carry out research in Yugoslavia on two separate occasions.

On this particular manuscript I had the benefit of helpful criticism and advice from several people. I would particularly like to mention Dr Robert F. Miller of the Australian National University who offered very valuable comments on the organization and argument of the work and Richard Harris of the University of Western Australia who made useful suggestions on particular points. As well as continual encouragement and support, my wife Rayma gave many weeks of invaluable help on matters of style, organization and argument, and with the references and bibliography. I also appreciated the cheerful efficiency of Mrs Nancy McKenzie who typed the entire manuscript. My greatest debt, however, is acknowledged in the dedication.

R.P.

ABBREVIATIONS

Borba (Z)	Edition of *Borba* published in Zagreb
CC	Central Committee
FNRJ	Federativna Narodna Republika Jugoslavije (Federal People's Republic of Yugoslavia)
FPRY	Federal People's Republic of Yugoslavia
JTS	*Joint Translation Service*, Belgrade
LC	League of Communists
LCY	League of Communists of Yugoslavia
NOJ	Narodna Omladina Jugoslavije (Yugoslav People's Youth).
SFRJ	Socijalistička Federativna Republika Jugoslavije (Socialist Federal Republic of Yugoslavia)
SFRY	Socialist Federal Republic of Yugoslavia
SOJ	Savez Omladine Jugoslavije (Union of Yugoslav Youth)
SSJ	Savez Studenata Jugoslavije (Yugoslav Union of Students)

Chapter I

INTRODUCTION

Yugoslav officials and scholars have consistently criticized both 'bourgeois' and 'people's' democracies as failing to offer their citizens real democratic rights and have proudly proclaimed the Yugoslav system of self-management as a model for the rest of the world. Their claim is nothing less than that their system provides an example of how democratic values can be realized in modern mass societies and, in particular, of how ordinary citizens can achieve the right to participate in the decisions affecting their lives within a system which harmonizes the interests of individuals, of the particular collectives and organizations, and of the total community.

This is an extraordinarily bold claim, especially coming from a society such as Yugoslavia, whose recent history, according to its own leaders, is one of economic underdevelopment, of widespread illiteracy and poverty, of bitter ethnic rivalry and of political oppression.

Nonetheless, it is not a claim which can be or has been dismissed lightly. Indeed, the Yugoslav model has attracted the interest of serious scholars of democracy around the world. According to Robert A. Dahl, the distinguished political theorist and former President of the American Political Science Association,

> Probably the most radical alternative to the American and Soviet status quo [on the question of industrial democracy] is exemplified by the system of self-management that has been developed in Yugoslavia since 1950. Yugoslavia is the only country in the world where a serious effort has been made to translate the old dream of industrial democracy into reality.[1]

Similarly, Dr Carole Pateman in her important and influential work *Participation and Democratic Theory* insists that 'no discussion of industrial participation and democracy can afford to ignore the Yugoslav system'. After outlining some of the available evidence and some of the difficulties and peculiarities of the Yugoslav situation, she concludes 'that the Yugoslav experience gives us no good reason to suppose that the democratization of industrial authority structures is impossible'.[2]

This question of participation in modern mass societies is being raised increasingly, and not merely by a small, radical fringe. Therefore, in view of its pioneering role in this crucial area, the Yugoslav experiment must be studied, both as it functions within particular enterprises or

1

collectives and as a total system. That is, it is important to study the decision-making process of particular collectives and also how their decisions are integrated into the decisions of the system as a whole.

Of course, the effort to understand the achievements and short-comings of the Yugoslav model inevitably involves the difficult task of assessing the impact of the model's functioning on the political attitudes and beliefs of Yugoslav citizens: how the model operates obviously affects the attitudes and beliefs of the citizenry and, in turn, their attitudes and beliefs largely determine how the model works.

As an area in which to study these twin points, the university system appeared to be both convenient and useful; in numerous respects the university is a microcosm of Yugoslav society with its many, often contradictory goals, pretensions, successes and failures, and the effect of the achievements and failures of the university system within the broader context of Yugoslav society can be studied with respect to the political attitudes and beliefs of a significant group in the Yugoslav community, namely, university students.

A further consideration prompting the decision to make a book-length study of the themes of university development and student beliefs available in English, was that both of these topics have evoked con-siderable interest among world scholars in recent years—it seemed important, therefore, to present something of the Yugoslav experience for purposes of comparison.

As far as universities are concerned, one of the major articles of faith in the post-war world, both in 'developed' and 'developing' societies, seems to have been the desirability, and indeed the necessity, of university expansion. This faith has been so strong that often university expansion has been urged and secured without agreement on or even serious consideration of such questions as the nature and role of the university (and how and by whom this should be determined), the place of the university in the total tertiary education system, the responsibilities of the university to the particular society as against its responsibilities as part of an international community of scholars, the appropriate level of community support of university education and the position and role of students within the university. Increasingly, however, it is being recog-nized that such difficult questions can no longer be avoided. For example, in the United States there has been in recent years very vigorous debate regarding the proper relationship between members of the university community and the state, the responsibilities of the university regarding the solution of particular social problems, whether and to what extent 'reverse discrimination' should be practised both as concerns the enrolment of students and the appointment and promotion of staff, and so on.

It is not suggested that the Yugoslav experience offers the answers to the problems encountered in our own universities; it may be, however, that a consideration of the Yugoslav experience will at least help clarify some of the questions.

The interest of scholars in student protest is even more pronounced.

2

In particular, the wave of student protest which seemed to sweep the world in 1968 evoked a flood of studies which sought to explain the cause and significance of these protests. A noteworthy exception to this concerns the serious Yugoslav disturbances of June 1968. In this case, serious study by local scholars has been virtually stifled by the official explanation, designed, it might be suggested, primarily to minimize the embarrassment of this unrest.

A close examination of these events is useful for at least two major reasons. First, the effort to explain these protests provides a convenient focus for the examination of the achievements and problems of university development in Yugoslavia—many of the complaints of the students related to their immediate university environment. Second, the thrust of the student protests raised questions concerning the nature and stability of the political system as a whole. In this connection, it must be emphasized that the so-called 'June events' stand out as one of the major occurrences in post-war Yugoslavia and as the first major overt sign of unrest and disquiet. There had, of course, been earlier signs such as worker strikes and even some student disturbances, but all these paled into insignificance alongside what President Tito himself described as a serious shock. The protest clearly had a profound effect on those thousands directly involved, as well as an enormous effect on ordinary Yugoslav citizens who watched these developments with great interest, speculating on what might happen next and on the final outcome.

Undoubtedly the most dramatic event of these turbulent days was President Tito's national television and radio address, an address which effectively ended the protests. Tito dismissed the notion that the demonstrations were prompted by a desire simply to emulate the activities of foreign students: the local disturbances resulted from 'our own shortcomings'.[3] As he explained it, the students obviously felt that their urgings for reform had gone unheard; the delays experienced in the solving of various problems had caused a spontaneous outburst. Among the problems awaiting solution Tito listed education reform to help overcome the high failure rate at the university, the provision of adequate employment opportunities for young graduates, the serious material situation of students and the unsatisfactory development of self-management at the universities: 'I understand their dissatisfaction', he said—instead of settling these pressing problems, 'we have been going round in a circle for years'.

Tito pointed out that in the past, discussions among 'people holding leading positions' had shown broad agreement on the policies required to resolve such difficulties, but, he continued, this unity quickly disappeared when it came to the actual implementation of these policies. 'We are resolved to reinforce the unity of our ranks' and to secure 'not formal but real unity'. He expressed confidence that this time matters would be properly settled and pointed out that the Presidium and Executive Committee of the Central Committee of the League of Communists were currently preparing guidelines which would clearly indicate the specific steps to be taken on a broad range of problems within society as a whole. These included improving the situation of the working class, solving the problems relating to the distribution of resources, eliminating the huge differences in pay scales, which 'hurt the eye' and with which 'I by no means agree', as well as tackling particular student problems such as employment. And those communists who refused to work for the full execution of these decisions 'shall have no place among us'.

He emphasized that even before the protests had erupted, the leading elements within the League had recognized the general difficulties stemming from the slow rate of reform; indeed the Presidium and Executive Committee of the Central Committee of the League had resolved to carry out a comprehensive analysis of this matter. Unfortunately, continued Tito, this resolution was only briefly reported and hence the public was left unaware of the significance of this measure. And before this analysis could be concluded and published, the student demonstrations had begun. Tito even raised the question as to whether there were some 'behind all this' who were aware of the efforts to secure change and who then deliberately moved 'to wrench the initiative . . . from our hands'. Having raised this point, he then observed that it was not a topic appropriate for further discussion.

Elsewhere in his address he claimed that certain hostile elements had sought to use the unrest for their own purposes. What began as a spontaneous outburst was infiltrated by various elements 'who do not hold socialist positions, who do not endorse the positions of the Eighth Congress of the League of Communists of Yugoslavia, [and] who are not for the implementation of the economic reform'. According to Tito, there were various tendencies involved, ranging 'from the most reactionary to the most extreme phoney-radical elements, swayed by Mao Tse-tung's theories'. However, he expressed the firm conviction that the vast majority of the students was part of 'our socialist youth'—the students had shown commendable maturity and had refused to follow those who sought to lead them along false paths. (The Congress to which Tito referred, held in 1964, provided for greater economic self-reliance on the part of the various regions and gave further scope to the operation of the market mechanism and economic competition. As such it tended to be opposed by those concerned by the growing gulf between the less and more developed regions and by those who feared the consequences of the diminution of the power of the central authorities.)[4]

The student protest was, he acknowledged, a serious shock, but the task at hand was to look forward rather than back. He appealed to the students to assist him to deal with these problems and he promised that he himself would wholeheartedly urge their settlement. Moreover, 'if I am incapable of solving these problems', it would follow that 'I should no longer be in this place'. He concluded with the advice that students should now concentrate on their studies: it would be a 'pity for you to waste any more time'.[5]

In essence, Tito maintained that the resistance of various individuals and groups to the implementation of League policies was responsible for the real difficulties which existed; the system as a whole, however, and the broad policies and the role of the League, were basically sound. Then, after praising the maturity and socialist commitment of the students, he asked for their support in the vital struggle to overcome the resistance of these various conservative forces.

The impact of all this was staggering—Tito, the hero and symbol of the revolution, had not attacked the protesters but rather had heaped praise on them, had pleaded for their help and had even stated that he would have no right to continue in office if he proved incapable of solving the grave problems highlighted by the students. It is hardly surprising, then, that many at the time were convinced that these events signified a dramatic turning point in Yugoslav history; a massive force was to be mobilized behind Tito to struggle for the attainment of the ideals of the society.

Several important questions immediately come to mind. With the benefit of hindsight, do these events indeed mark a turning point in Yugoslav history or do they merely represent another landmark? Regardless of the answer to that question, there can be no denying the significance of these events. They represented a serious jolt, but also the promise of dramatic change. The extent to which this promise was met would be bound to have an enormous effect.

Another question was whether Tito and the Yugoslav leadership in general were correct in claiming that the system was essentially sound, that only certain difficulties needed to be overcome and that the support of the socialist youth would prove a valuable weapon in that effort. In particular, were the students committed young socialists eager to follow the leadership of the League? That is, was there a reasonable basis for assuming that these disturbances *could* mark a turning point in Yugoslav history? The attempt to answer this question involves an assessment of two major questions: the functioning of the Yugoslav system as seen in an important microcosm of that system, the university, and also the political attitudes and beliefs of the students. This assessment is the major focus of the present work.

If there was little prospect of these events actually becoming a turning point, what then could be said of the tactics of Tito and those around him and what can be said of the nature and functioning of the Yugoslav system? Would it be possible to suggest that the bold rhetoric used on this occasion was merely another example of the penchant of the Yugoslav leadership for drowning a crisis in a flood of oratory? Could it be argued that the vast gulf between the ideals and practice of the self-managing system was on this occasion temporarily obscured by a masterly performance by Tito, but at the long-term cost of further widening this gulf? In other words, could it be suggested that this victory was won only by arousing expectations which were unrealizable, that this victory would inevitably lead to an increase in cynicism, and that this cynicism would make it even less likely that the ideals of self-management, based on assumptions of commitment and cooperation, could be realized? If the judgement implicit in these questions is correct, what then of the future of self-managing Yugoslavia?

THE UNIVERSITY IN POST-WAR YUGOSLAVIA

Two events stand out in recent Yugoslav history: the establishment of a communist system of government after World War II and the break with the Soviet Union in 1948. The present study cannot pretend to consider the full significance of these occurrences but at least as far as the universities themselves are concerned some points must be made. The rhetoric of the new leaders emphasized the overthrow of the old, backward order, and the construction of an advanced, industrialized society which would provide the basis for a new way of life for the Yugoslav people. The university was seen as a vital factor in the struggle for the construction of this new society.

It was explained that in pre-war Yugoslavia the university fulfilled a limited role, serving primarily as a kind of finishing school for the children of the privileged few, and producing the small number of qualified men needed to maintain the narrow professional and administrative stratum in what was essentially a peasant society. This small 'classical' university system was seen as being inappropriate to the demands of the new order. In particular, it was urged that the universities had to be expanded to provide the number of experts needed to help carry out the ambitious programme of socialist development. Thus, new departments were opened and student enrolments soared. However, mere expansion was not enough: the reorientation and transformation of the university was also required. As a Yugoslav student delegate at an international conference held in 1956 explained it, the less developed countries of the world needed people who, while unable perhaps to write a beautiful poem about a daffodil, nevertheless knew what had to be done to secure the goal of economic development.[6] His view, of course, was quite in accord with the persistent official policy regarding university education which urged the deletion of 'unnecessary' material; it was insisted that the new society could afford neither luxury nor waste and hence that each student should be taught the minimum needed to enable him to perform a specific task in the economy or society.[7]

Professional training was to be narrow, specific and, therefore, 'efficient'. However, the graduate should be more than an expert in a certain area. In particular, he was expected to be a *socialist* expert who would have a firm grasp of the essentials of Marxism and who would, under the guidance and inspiration of the League, devote his skill and his life to the construction of the new order. To help attain these ambitious goals was the particular duty of the university staff and of the youth and student organizations. The former were expected to ensure that their teaching was permeated with a Marxist approach, while the youth and student organizations were also to help create an environment in which the young would be guided and inspired towards the adoption of a thorough-going socialist outlook.[8]

The implications of these goals were enormous: almost overnight the small, quiet, 'classical' universities were to become huge institutions turning out a variety of specialists united only by their commitment to socialism. The scope of this development is examined in chapter IV of the present work, but some indication of the enormity of change is illustrated by these simple facts: in 1945/46 there were 21,195 students enrolled in the various Yugoslav universities, and by 1968/69 the number of students had soared to 140,647.[9] That is, in just twenty-three years there was more than a six-fold increase in student numbers.

Obviously this placed an enormous strain on a country with limited resources. In chapters IV and V some indication is given of the great difficulty of providing adequate staff, teaching facilities, student accommodation, scholarships and the like. In these chapters it is maintained that, first, insufficient finance was provided to support this vastly expanded system and, second, that the available finance was not in fact most rationally or fairly allocated. Concerning the latter it is argued, for example, that departments were opened for 'political' reasons and that able students of limited means found that the few, very few, scholarships usually went to those who had the better 'connections'.

Certain important features of the students' immediate environment related, therefore, to what might be termed this 'over-expansion' of the university system. Conditions at the university and conditions of student life were below a reasonable and satisfactory standard, and partly as a consequence of these difficulties the failure rate rose to alarming proportions.

In chapter IV the dismal prospects for the employment of graduates is also considered. While Yugoslav officials frequently bemoaned the fact that those holding important posts in the economy were inadequately qualified, they did little to create openings for the employment of graduates. In this connection it must be remembered that Tito's partisans had been overwhelmingly young peasants and workers, and that after the war many of these partisans were catapulted into positions of authority.[10] Even the twenty-seven-year old of 1945 was by 1968 only fifty years of age; not surprisingly he was scarcely eager to step down in favour of a youngster with higher paper qualifications.

Thus, the impact of the poor conditions at the university was intensified by the student's pessimistic assessment of his prospects for employment. This, in brief, indicates something of the broad context in which the education or, more precisely, the socialist education of the young expert was to take place.

The second major event in recent Yugoslav history was the break between Yugoslavia and the USSR, which occurred in June 1948 and which had a profound impact on the nature, goals and problems of the Yugoslav system.

The events leading up to the rupture are well known. The basic point was that the Yugoslav leaders refused to accept the pattern and role which the Soviet Union sought to impose. These leaders were no mere puppets installed and kept in office by the might of the Soviet Union; rather, they had won power largely because of their leadership of a major guerrilla struggle waged against Axis forces in Yugoslavia, and they had won adherents to their cause largely through nationalist appeals directed against the foreign invader and with the promise of the creation of a new modern Yugoslavia after the war. It was inevitable, therefore, that these leaders should oppose the notion that Yugoslavia remain basically a provider of food and raw materials within an integrated Soviet bloc economy, and it was inevitable that they should resent the controls and supervision by Soviet authorities within Yugoslavia. The tensions which stemmed from this conflict of national interests and pride led to the decision of the organization of communist governments (known as the Cominform) to expel Yugoslavia, or rather, what was termed the 'Tito clique', from the communist camp; this decision, promoted of course by Stalin, reflected Stalin's conviction that his disapproval would lead to the prompt replacement of Tito by leaders more favourable to the Soviet position.[11]

The initial reaction of the Yugoslav leaders was to protest vehemently their loyalty to Stalin, arguing that the dispute derived from misunderstandings rather than from any fundamental, unbridgeable differences. Their reaction reflected the fact that their claim to power was largely built around Stalin and the Communist Party of the Soviet Union; Yugoslav partisans had fought and died with the name of Stalin on their lips.[12] And further, the lives of the Yugoslav leaders themselves were based on a faith in Stalin and the party which he led. Vladimir Dedijer, who was at the time still a member of the Yugoslav inner circle, vividly described the enormous impact on his colleagues of the break with Stalin.[13]

As time passed with only an exacerbation of the dispute and with the Yugoslav leadership still firmly in control, it was no longer sufficient or necessary to maintain that the Soviet leaders had made an unfortunate error in adjudging the Yugoslav leadership to be unworthy; rather, it was necessary to explain how the Soviet leadership could persist in this error. Consequently, the Yugoslav leaders began to assert that the Soviet Union under Stalin's domination had distorted the basic tenets of Marxism and had built a system characterized by the growing, rather than declining, power of the state apparatus; and that this system of 'state capitalism' had led to the development of a basic contradiction between the state bureaucracy and the masses, with the former living off the labour of the latter in an exploitative relationship. Similarly, the relationship between the Soviet state and the other socialist states was described as being essentially a relationship of exploitation rather than mutual benefit.[14]

Thus, as they sought to explain and justify the past, the Yugoslav leaders were forced onto a new path. And, with the passage of time, what began as hesitant and enforced stumbles away from the Stalinist pattern developed into an eloquent and bold statement of an alternative model. The new Yugoslav system was presented as a rejection of the Stalinist-bureaucratic pattern, in favour of a system termed 'self-management'. It was observed that the term 'management' customarily meant that one man, or group of men, dominated other men; the new system of 'self-management' negated this contradiction as man became both worker and manager—all members of a particular collective, regardless of status, were now accorded the right to participate as equals in the process of decision making. Finally, it was claimed that this system, built on the recognition of the worth and dignity of each individual, would enable man to become the master of his own fate rather than the servant of a bureaucratic apparatus, and enable him to help construct a socialist society rather than a system of state capitalism.[15]

The official rhetoric presented the self-management system as desirable, and indeed crucial, to the construction of a truly socialist society; it was asserted that socialism could not be built or imposed from above but rather had to grow from below, from the people themselves. The state apparatus must be permitted to wither away. Thus, a dramatically new model, a new legitimizing myth, was loudly and proudly proclaimed. The actual functioning of this new model was bound to have a profound effect on the political beliefs of all the citizens of Yugoslavia, not least the university student.

Fundamental to this model was the avowed conviction that the separate self-managing collectives would harmonize their particular interests with the interests of other collectives, with the interests of the community as a whole and with the goal of socialism. Sometimes it seemed as though it was believed that the harmonization would occur naturally.[16] Take, for example, the policy of the collective of a factory concerning the provision of scholarships for university students and concerning the employment of young graduates. It was pointed out that the long-term interest of the factory lay, first, in providing scholarships to ensure the availability of appropriately qualified experts, and second, in employing these experts when they had completed their studies. Only in this manner would the productivity of the factory increase with a corresponding rise in the income of the members of the collective. At the same time, the interests of the entire socialist community would be served by such policies which led to an increase in the qualification of the work force and to increased productivity.

However, it was considered that the level of understanding and the degree of socialist consciousness of many members of particular collectives was such that they would not automatically perceive their collective's 'true' long-term interests, but rather would have to be guided and inspired to see beyond their own selfish, short-range goals. Much of this guidance and inspiration was to come from the individual communists within the particular collective and from what was termed the political and moral authority of the League of Communists as a whole. Thus, while it described the 'withering' of the state as a crucial first step, the leadership rejected the notion that the role of the Communist Party should be similarly reduced.

It was maintained that this 'guidance' did not represent an interference with the self-managing rights of the separate collectives; rather, the responsibility of the individual communists in each collective was merely to endeavour to persuade and influence their colleagues to adopt decisions which enabled the full development of self-management, but which accorded with the broader interests of the developing socialist society. To mark the avowedly changed role of the Communist Party from direction to guidance, its name was officially altered in 1952 to the League of Communists of Yugoslavia.[17]

This guidance and inspiration was, therefore, seen as qualitatively different from direction, and, in particular, direction by the organs of the state. Indeed, as has been emphasized, the 'withering' of the state was seen as an essential prerequisite for the development of a self-managing society. Consequently, proposals for legislation in what some saw as areas of common concern were frequently opposed as threatening the self-managing rights of the particular collectives—the role of state legislation was to provide no more than a broad framework within which the separate collectives were to operate. Of course, it was clear that the limits of this framework could not be finally fixed; however, the point is that any efforts to strengthen broad central legislative controls were generally resisted, avowedly on the grounds that they violated the fundamental principles of a self-managing society.

Indeed, the major changes in the economy, culminating in the economic reform of 1964, were aimed at eliminating or at least reducing what were described as harmful political influences and controls. It was argued that in too many instances decisions had been made on political grounds and at great cost to the general well-being; the reduction of political controls would, it was urged, result in healthier and more natural economic development. A related reason advanced for linking the self-managing system to a market, rather than a centrally controlled, economy was to make real the asserted right of particular collectives to decide their own affairs. Further, only with the freest play being given to market forces would it be possible for the members of a particular collective to have the opportunity to enjoy the rewards of their efforts and thus the incentive to increase their production.

In practice then, the model rested on several vital assumptions. First, that the League was capable of giving clear and confident guidance towards the development of socialism and that the League as a whole retained sufficient moral and political authority to ensure that all would give careful attention to its pronouncements. Second, that individual communists within each collective would willingly accept the obligation to work for the full implementation of the spirit of these League pronouncements and especially for the development of the system of self-management. And third, that non-communists within each collective would be ready to accept the guidance of the individual communists within their ranks and ready to accept the policies of the League.

Clearly these various assumptions were closely interwoven and inter-dependent. For example, the willingness of the members of a collective to accept the guidance of League members or of the League as a whole would greatly depend on the League's reputation and authority and, in turn, this depended on how the League and its members were seen to have performed in the past. Clearly, and even more importantly, these three assumptions represented a very tall order.

How did this system, so proudly held up as an example to the rest of the world, work in practice? To return to the example of the policy of the factory collective concerning the provision of scholarships for university students and concerning the employment of young gradu-ates—despite the avowed expectations, the fact was that the factories offered few jobs and fewer scholarships.

As is explained in chapter IV, many students came to feel that self-management was a device through which a small group could preserve its particular privileges and that those holding the better jobs in factories used the argument of self-management to oppose any effort from above to replace them with individuals possessing higher qualifica-tions. The effort to secure change from within through the activity of those communists who were members of the particular collective simi-larly met with little success. The reasons were obvious: often those who were expected to be in the vanguard of the struggle for change were those who had most to lose from any change.

Nor did the self-management system flourish in the university environ-ment. As is noted in chapter III, there was widespread comment that within many departments the decisions made reflected a determination to preserve the *status quo* rather than to advance the interests of the university or the needs of the community. The extent to which the faculty was actually responsible for the persistent difficulties of the universities is elaborated below in chapter IV; at this point it is suffici-ent to mention that the members of staff, and especially the senior staff, were often portrayed in the press and by Yugoslav officials as misusing self-management in order to serve their own particular ends.

Despite all the discussion in society concerning self-management, opportunities for student participation in decision making within the university were minimal. Even within their own organization the mass of students had little opportunity to participate in the decision-making process. Indeed, as is developed in chapter VI, the history of the youth organizations is another illustration of the difficulty of applying the principles of self-management, this time in a socio-political organiza-tion. On the one hand, it was stated that the basic associations of the Union of Students were to be free to adapt their activities to suit the particular interests and needs of their members, because only in this way could there be a real involvement of the students and only in this way could they develop as responsible members of a self-managing community. At the same time, however, it was maintained that many of the young were immature and that there was a danger that they might fall under the influence of 'hostile' forces; hence it was necessary to

11

ensure that they developed in a 'proper' climate. Thus, the work of the basic associations had to be both free and 'correct'. Again it was assumed that these goals were reconcilable but again practice showed otherwise. For the most part the Union officials ensured that the activity of the organization remained 'correct' rather than free and relevant; inevitably, therefore, the organization involved an ever-decreasing number of students until it came to be sarcastically referred to in the press as the 'Union of Student Leaders'.[18]

Thus, although the students heard a great deal about self-management (indeed they studied and were examined on the topic), in practice they had little opportunity to experience it. Much of what they saw of the functioning of self-management bodies, particularly those which affected both their present situation and their future prospects, showed self-management as a device through which particular groups often sought to preserve their privileges regardless of the cost to the community and regardless of the rights and interests of others.

From the point of view of the development of a socialist society, the linking of the self-management system to a market economy was clearly not without some difficulties and dangers. The most notable comments on this point were made by the scholars associated with the journal *Praxis,* which began publication in 1964 in Zagreb but which drew its most significant contributions from both Zagreb and Belgrade. The basic philosophic position of what has been termed the *'Praxis* group' was rooted in what they referred to as the humanism of Marx. As is explained in chapter III, the members of this group were especially concerned with the effect of this particular change on the development of socialist values. They questioned, for example, the official contention that the linking of self-management to the market economy and the profit motive gave greater scope for the development and enjoyment of individual rights. In their view, self-management in this form focussed on only one facet of man's existence and encouraged consideration of one's own personal interest to the neglect of the interests of the socialist community. They considered that the widely acknowledged problems which developed in the aftermath of the economic reforms were in no small part attributable to the logic inherent in this reform.

Amongst these problems were those of 'unjustified earnings' (for example, an enterprise taking advantage of its monopoly or near monopoly position to charge the maximum that the market would bear). Another problem was of the type alluded to earlier concerning the failure of enterprises to provide either scholarships to students or employment to graduates to the extent anticipated. It proved far more difficult in practice than in theory to reconcile the interests of the members of a particular collective with those of individuals outside the collective or with those of the socialist community as a whole; the pressure of market forces in a period of economic difficulty made the enterprise less able and willing to look beyond its own immediate interests.

Further, there was the problem of integrating the decisions of the separate collectives into a coherent plan. For example, no serious attempt was made to prepare a manpower plan because of the apparent belief that this matter was best resolved simply by market forces. The consequence was that overall enrolments and enrolments in particular fields soared without any regard for the needs of the economy or the society as a whole. As is explained in chapter IV, those young people whose parents could afford to support them flocked to the universities and crowded into those departments elastic enough to admit them.

In the opinion of at least some members of the *Praxis* group, this stress on the market as the regulator in investment, pricing, income, distribution and the like was best described as 'anarcho-liberal' rather than socialist. Svetozar Stojanović contended that

> If the concept of monopolistic self-governing groups is substituted for that of the capitalist, we are immediately struck by the analogy between 'socialist' anarcho-liberalism and the ideology of liberal capitalism . . .
> According to 'socialist' anarcho-liberalism, self-managing groups should aspire solely to realize their own interests and to increase their income. The antagonistic interests of self-managing groups nevertheless *spontaneously* mingle harmoniously to form the social interest. The market and income realized on it automatically reproduce socialist social relations.[19]

In the *Praxis* group's view, any effort at planning or coordination by society as a whole, any attempt made to guard against the unjustified accumulation of wealth and any effort to ensure the provision of social needs as against particularist wants was branded by Yugoslav anarcho-liberals as an attack on self-management.[20]

It might be urged that, according to the *Praxis* group, the virtually unchecked operation of market forces had led to the development of a new ideology based on the market; rather than the market being a means to an end (e.g. greater efficiency and productivity), it had become an end in itself. In their view, the market was an important tool but 'in order to preserve a given society's socialist character. . . . [it] must be placed within the framework of serious planning, regulation and coordination'.[21]

This brief account of some of the views of members of the *Praxis* group cannot hope adequately to represent the depth and breadth of their criticisms; the aim here is merely to outline their views concerning the essential nature of the Yugoslav system and concerning the need to develop a theory which would adequately integrate self-management within particular collectives with the development of a socialist community.

It was widely acknowledged, in official speeches and the press for instance, that many difficulties remained within the Yugoslav system. However, what distinguished the *Praxis* group was the argument that many of the difficulties stemmed from weaknesses inherent in the very theory of self-management. Their views are important not only because they constituted the most coherent and persistent ideological criticism of the League leadership, but also because they found expression in the rhetoric of the student demonstrators in June 1968. That is, despite the journal's limited circulation, and despite the campaign of continual attack and harassment directed against it, it apparently succeeded in influencing the views of at least some students.

The broad views expressed in the journal were vigorously condemned as amounting to an attack on socialism, democracy and the working class. Ironically, this campaign, which is considered elsewhere in this work, was initiated and orchestrated by the leadership of the League of Communists which jealously guarded *its* exclusive right to speak in the name of the working class concerning the true interests of socialism; despite all the talk of the democratization of Yugoslav society, the League leadership in practice steadfastly insisted that in the final analysis it alone determined what should and should not be said.

This, then, in very broad terms, is the background against which the significant unrest among the Yugoslav university students in June 1968 must be set. The emphasis in the present study is on factors relating to the entire Yugoslav situation with especial attention being given to the general situation in the two major cities, Belgrade and Zagreb. Inevitably this approach minimizes the significance of regional variations and of ethnic considerations.[22] The important point, however, is that the aims, policies and problems relating to all Yugoslav universities and their students were essentially the same: in Belgrade, on those few eventful days, thousands of students demonstrated, marched, clashed with the militia, chanted slogans and attended protest meetings, while at the other university centres the students held numerous meetings and passed resolutions supporting their Belgrade counterparts.[23]

The questions raised at the end of Part 1 of this chapter now reassert themselves. What did this crisis signify concerning the functioning of the system of self-management? Was Tito's claim that the crisis demonstrated the essential strength of the system a reasonable and justifiable one? Or was it a position dictated primarily by considerations of short-term expediency, a position which in retrospect might be seen not as the successful mobilization of forces for reform but as being designed to flatter and thus calm the students, and to present these embarrassing incidents in the best possible light?

Fundamental to Tito's argument was the claim that these events demonstrated what he termed the maturity and socialist commitment of the mass of students. How accurate was this claim? And if Tito's assessment of the nature of and the reasons for the students' protests was not correct, what other possible explanation might there be?

Chapter II

STUDENT UNREST

POSSIBLE EXPLANATIONS OF THE CAUSES OF THE YUGOSLAV STUDENT DISTURBANCES OF JUNE 1968

As explained earlier, a major aim of this particular study is to understand something of the nature and causes of disaffection among Yugoslav university students, principally in the period until and including 1968, and in this way to try to understand the attitudes and beliefs of the students. In seeking to achieve that aim it will be necessary to study developments within the university, and also, but obviously to a lesser extent, developments within Yugoslav society as a whole. That considerable disaffection existed was abundantly demonstrated by the large student disturbances which occurred at Belgrade in June 1968, and which had significant support from students at other Yugoslav universities.

The Yugoslav case is of particular interest in the study of both political socialization and student unrest since in that system there has been a persistent and deliberate effort to create a new socialist man. This presents a marked contrast to the more incidental and less self-conscious process of political socialization in a society such as our own. It is instructive to endeavour to assess the impact of such a deliberate programme and in particular to seek to discern its efficacy in light of the fact that often the programme of ideological education was unrelated to, and even contradicted by, the realities of contemporary society.

In its highest form it appeared that this new socialist man was to be exemplified in the young intellectual who would combine the courage, sincerity and self-sacrifice of the partisan hero with a mastery of modern knowledge, and who would enthusiastically follow the guidance of the League of Communists in the struggle for the construction of a socialist society.[1] An important question is whether the events of June 1968 signify, as Tito claimed in his major address concerning the protests, considerable progress toward that goal. A consideration of the actual protests, however, suggests that his assessment was only one of several possible conclusions.

For example, it could be suggested that the mass of students exploded in rage and frustration primarily because of their current situation and future prospects. In this regard one might refer to their serious material difficulties, to the problems they faced within the university (most notably the staggering failure rate) and to their dismal prospects for

15

employment. Concerning politics, it might be urged that they were uninterested and cynical rather than active and committed, and, indeed, that most students merely sought to obtain, with the minimum of difficulty or hardship, a piece of paper which would guarantee them a comfortable niche in the Yugoslav establishment. According to this view, the high-sounding rhetoric of the demonstrators might be described as expressing the views of a small minority, but that as far as the majority was concerned, this rhetoric was, at best, a rationalization for their behaviour.

Another explanation might be that these student protests represented a direct attack on the general political and social system and an open challenge to the authority and legitimacy of the ruling élite. In this connection it is worth noting that the Yugoslav press had chosen to describe the student disturbances which had taken place earlier in various foreign countries as revealing the existence of a serious political crisis in those countries, and as indicating the desire for the radical transformation of the particular society. It is significant that the Yugoslav press, in assessing these events among *foreign* students, paid special attention and gave credence to the rhetoric of the student leaders,[2] but when it came to assessing the disturbances in their own country, the press quickly fell into line with the official explanation as stated by Tito. However, it is obvious that the judgement applied to foreign student disturbances might also be applied to the Yugoslav situation, especially if attention is paid to that group among the Yugoslav students who explicitly and directly attacked certain basic features of the system.

On this question of events outside Yugoslavia, it might also be suggested that the local disturbances were sparked off by the desire of students to join. in what seemed to be a world-wide fashion. Not only had there been significant protests in several Western countries (e.g. France and Italy) but there also had been serious student unrest in both Poland and Czechoslovakia. Or it could be argued that official Yugoslav *analyses* of these disturbances in both East and West (rather than the mere description) stimulated a spirit of ferment among the students. These analyses stressed the virtue of the foreign students in confronting the hypocrisy and weaknesses of their particular system and in seeking its transformation. With considerable pride it was stated that the foreign students were seeking a system based on those self-same principles which formed the foundation of the Yugoslav system, and significant efforts were made to organize meetings and demonstrations of support for the foreign protesters.[3] These explanations of foreign events, and in particular the account of the developments of the so-called 'Czechoslovak Spring', therefore brought into the foreground the principles on which the Yugoslav system was avowedly based and served to highlight in the minds of students the disparity between these principles and the reality.

As a further alternative, it might be suggested that the protest resulted from feelings of frustration and resentment on the part of

16

selfish, spoiled and immature adolescents who felt themselves neglected and under-valued in their present situation and who were unable to accept and adjust to the realities of student life.

As Tito's address makes clear, none of these alternative explanations was adopted by the Yugoslav leadership. First, it was denied that the protests were merely an eruption of feeling among relatively non-political students concerned with their particular difficulties. While it was acknowledged that prior to the June events there had been considerable concern regarding the political apathy of the student body, it was now asserted that the demonstrations indicated a healthy student interest in politics and a commitment to communism.[4] And while it was true that the students had emphasized their particular problems (for example, financial aid and employment) it was conceded that many of their complaints were justified and that the solution of these problems would benefit the whole of society. As matters stood, many young people of ability were denied the opportunity to continue their education; and many of those who did manage to enter university found material and academic conditions so poor that they were forced to withdraw or took far longer than scheduled to complete their studies. Society could not afford such waste. Nor could society afford the situation in which unqualified or under-qualified personnel continued to hold responsible positions in the economy and professions, while young graduates were unable to find suitable employment.[5]

It was denied, therefore, that the students were apolitical or that they were concerned primarily with their own affairs. Indeed, it was pointed out that the students also criticized difficulties in society not directly related to their own lot. Most notable was the criticism relating to what was termed the unjustified accumulation of wealth by certain individuals and groups.[6] Did this criticism mean, however, as the second broad explanation suggested, that the students were attacking the essence of the Yugoslav system, and in particular the leadership of the League of Communists? Did the thrust of the student protest amount to a questioning of the efficacy of the present system? Was there a significant minority which openly challenged the authority of the League leadership and which urged a radical alteration in the League's position and role? To express the point at issue in different terms, in what way could the local disturbances be distinguished from those which had occurred in certain foreign countries and which had been described in the Yugoslav press as amounting to an attack on the basic features of these particular systems?

For the Yugoslav leadership the distinction between the local and foreign disturbances was quite clear. One example, albeit relating primarily to student unrest in the West, should suffice to illustrate this distinction. A member of the Executive Committee of the League observed that although student actions in the West were 'often spontaneous' and although student goals were often shrouded in confusion and contradiction, there was discernible a 'basic deep demand' for the establishment of a system of direct democracy.[7] Students in the West attacked the basic principles and values of the political system of which they were a part;[8] by contrast, the Yugoslav students sought to realize the values of the present system, not to overturn it. They attacked only the deviations from the basic principles and values of their political system. And they sought the implementation of the basic policies enunciated by the League leadership, not the implementation of new and opposing policies; the Yugoslav students showed that they did not wish to be 'a new vanguard' of society but rather to be 'a part of the vanguard of the working class'—this was a socialist society and a socialist youth; these protesters were neither apolitical nor opposed to the essential features of the Yugoslav system, rather, they were the allies of the League leadership in the struggle against those bureaucratic and conservative forces within Yugoslav society which hampered the development of socialism.[9]

Of these possible explanations—one official and several plausible alternatives—which most accurately explains the student protests of June 1968? Obviously, each explanation may account for the behaviour of at least some students. And further, despite the manner in which the various explanations were delineated from each other, it is quite possible that the behaviour of many students cannot be accounted for by reference to a single explanation. For example, it is not inconceivable that a student might be prompted to protest because of his particular personal difficulties, but that he found it easier to demonstrate because he could justify his actions to himself, as well as to others, by presenting his complaints in a broader societal context; even in his own mind the two apparently separate explanations may have blended into one.

Again, while the boundary between the explanation that the students were challenging certain basic features of the system and the explanation that they were allies of the League is analytically clear, many students may not have reached a conscious awareness of such a distinction. It was unlikely that all students would have an unequivocal position in the debate between those who urged that the primary task was to secure the actual implementation of League policy which they considered basically sound and those who maintained that the present difficulties were at least partially the consequence of the role and policies of the League itself. The question was whether the existing problems could be overcome merely by prodding certain individuals to make greater efforts within the present framework or whether the framework itself was unsatisfactory. The problem of determining the principal cause of the student unrest was compounded by the skilful tactics adopted by the League leadership during the crisis. Great care was taken not to antagonize the demonstrators and a great effort was made to persuade them that the thrust of their complaints did not, in fact, amount to an attack on the League leadership.

THE JUNE EVENTS

The spark was struck on Sunday evening, 2 June 1968. An open-air, full-dress rehearsal of a musical programme was scheduled to be held in the new section of Belgrade at the settlement of a voluntary work brigade. In addition to those actually working on the construction site, other young people, principally Belgrade university students, planned to attend. On the eve of the performance the sponsors of the programme changed the venue to a small hall and decided to admit only the actual members of the work brigade.[10] Apparently the organizers of the programme wished to limit that night's audience because of plans for subsequent commercial performances.[11] As many as a thousand people, mainly university students, were thus denied admission to the programme, and, shouting angrily, they sought to enter the hall by force. Fighting erupted between students and the members of the work brigade, and numerous windows were smashed. Over forty members of the militia and two fire trucks then arrived on the scene, but the disturbances continued.

What then occurred is described in the report of an official commission, consisting of several members of the Executive Council of the Serbian Assembly and of some student representatives. (It is significant that while the members of this commission were unable to agree on the causes of *later* clashes between students and the militia, there appeared to be broad agreement on the events of this particular occasion.) Their report, published some ten days after the first incident, noted that when members of the militia arrived, the crowd outside the hall threw stones and 'demolished the building'. 'In order to restore order' the members of the militia 'were forced to intervene' using truncheons and water hoses to drive the crowd away and to enable the members of the work brigade to leave in safety. In the course of this struggle the militiamen themselves became the targets of stones thrown by the angry crowd. The false rumour of a student's death in the clash began to spread, accompanied by shouts of 'Beat them . . . they killed our comrade.' The report also noted that students took over one of the fire trucks by force and wrecked its cabin. Not until the members of the work brigade were taken from the scene in buses did the fighting cease. The report then described how a group of students proceeded to the work brigade settlement where they extensively damaged the front of one of the barracks, smashing some 112 windows in all. Again the militia was called to restore order.[12]

The press accounts of these events published at the time did not essentially differ from the description provided by the commission.[13] However, a common and bitter complaint amongst the students was that the media distorted what took place and presented the first clash as an outbreak of student hooliganism.[14] Students maintained that it was the arrival of the militia and the fire trucks on the scene which gave fuel to their anger and led to the extensive destruction.[15]

The following day there were, according to *Borba,* 'new disturbances', in which 'several thousand' students took part. At 8 A.M. on Monday a protest meeting began in the Student City, the area where the student dormitories were situated. The actual events of Sunday night formed

19

only a part of the discussions. For instance, student speakers began to itemize a number of serious and persistent problems (such as living conditions and employment). Further, they began to articulate criticisms of certain basic aspects of the contemporary Yugoslav system. It was particularly emphasized that while broad solutions to a variety of problems had been announced, the implementation of these solutions was often inexcusably slow. Significantly, the report of this meeting contained no reference to the leaders of the official student organization; it described instead the election of an 'Action Committee' from among the general student body to investigate reports of the arrest of some students and to press for the appointment of a commission to investigate the clash with the militia.[16]

After several hours of speeches, by which time, the *Borba* report estimated, the crowd had grown to between two and three thousand, the students decided to march into the main city square in order to demonstrate their determination to secure effective redress of a variety of pressing problems. Student speakers were careful to emphasize the necessity for order, and according to the *Borba* report, the students themselves acted against the small minority who occasionally broke ranks to shout abuse at the militia. Nevertheless, the marchers were soon forced to halt at an underpass beneath the railway line. The way was barred by 'several hundred' militiamen standing in front of several trucks which had been parked so as to block the road. 'Long and tiresome negotiations' began, the students asking for permission to proceed, while the members of the militia stood firm. The students, particularly those in the middle and at the rear of the march, were described as becoming 'increasingly impatient'.

At this point a group of prominent 'socio-political workers' arrived on the scene, including no less a figure than a member of the Executive Committee of the Central Committee of the League, Veljko Vlahović. According to the *Borba* report, his arrival was loudly acclaimed by shouts of 'Veljko!' 'Here comes Veljko!' The article continued with the observation that he was 'obviously very popular among the students' because the moment they saw him angry faces changed to smiles. Vlahović was described as being in 'good humour', as indeed he always was when 'among the young'. From the account given, it is apparent that Vlahović adopted a conciliatory, elder-brother tone. While still at a distance he called, 'What is all this comrades? Come let us have a talk . . .' Another political leader, Miloš Minić, the President of the Assembly of Serbia, suggested that the students choose representatives who would be given the opportunity to present their case to the highest authorities. It was reported that after a brief discussion this suggestion was widely approved.

'Well, do you have any other demands, comrades?' Vlahović asked, to which some students responded by reiterating some of their grievances such as the necessity for a thorough investigation of the previous night's events, for the accurate dissemination of their views by the media and so on.

Vlahović was asked whether the militia would now allow the students to proceed into Belgrade for their planned meeting in the main city square. He replied that it would be preferable for them to return to the university where their demands and requests could be formulated in an atmosphere of 'peace' and 'reason'. One student promptly accused him of not trusting them to act with maturity, but Vlahović denied this: 'Oh no, not at all! We do trust you, but are you sure that some *provocateurs* would not use this inflammable situation? No, no, comrades, you would be taking too great a responsibility upon yourselves.' Clearly, he was anxious to avoid the embarrassment and risk of a major demonstration in the heart of the city. Among the students it was clear that there were some who were equally anxious to proceed with the original plan and some cried out, 'We want to go to Belgrade.'

At this point the militia made what *Borba* termed an unexpected and violent assault and students scattered before their batons and tear gas.[17] The Pro-Rector of Belgrade University later stated he had participated in student demonstrations before the war which had led to clashes with the police but that he had never experienced anything like this.[18] Another professor was reported to have asked some members of the militia, 'Who ordered you to beat children!? Leave them alone; hit me!' Three members of the militia rushed to oblige and knocked him to the ground.[19] The political functionaries were obviously also taken by surprise by this sudden onslaught; the *Borba* account quoted several of their statements which reflected shock and anger. One was described as 'wringing his hands' and demanding of the militiamen: 'Who ordered you to attack . . .?' The goals of the officials appeared to have been two-fold: to disperse the students, and to defuse their anger, but the methods of the militia secured only the first of these.[20]

Subsequently, angry meetings were held at the Student City, and the School of Liberal Arts building was occupied by students from the departments of Philosophy, Philology and Mathematics.[21] Members of staff were reported as having joined in the student protest. At the major meeting, attended by more than one thousand students, demands and criticisms ranging over a broad area were voiced. Some of the problems raised were high unemployment among professionals, increasing social inequality, the slow development of self-management and the need for the extension of democratic rights. Concerning the latter, it is significant that the right of peaceful demonstration was particularly urged as well as the need for the democratization of the League of Communists. In addition, there were strong demands for the dismissal of those responsible for the behaviour of the militia, for the dismissal of the directors of radio and television stations and for the dismissal of the editors-in-chief of the daily newspapers. The militia was condemned for its behaviour in the two principal clashes with students, while the media was attacked for allegedly presenting the behaviour of the students on Sunday evening as hooliganism[22] and for suggesting that the student demands primarily related to their own immediate problems.[23]

The press accounts of the Monday meetings emphasized the general orderliness of the crowd, the frequent chanting of the slogan 'Tito-Party' and the singing of the national anthem. The demonstrations 'lasted almost the whole night' and were conducted under the watchful eye of members of the militia who maintained a tight cordon around the area. Thus ended the first full day of demonstrations.[24]

For the next several days there was an almost continuous programme of meetings, usually in the separate departments. These meetings were attended by hundreds of students and ranged over both the specific and general problems noted earlier, with two major strands of argument emerging. One strand appeared to reflect a desire to prod the system into dealing with some of the most pressing difficulties facing the students, while the other seemed a more basic criticism of the function-ing of the Yugoslav system itself. This latter strand appeared to ask not merely for the solution of particular problems but also for reasons why these problems had not been resolved earlier. That is, there were questions raised concerning the nature and efficacy of the present system. Indeed, certain elements among the students were described as challenging the leadership of the League of Communists.[25]

Of course, it is impossible to measure the strength of each of the two major strands of discussion or even to distinguish clearly between them, but it does seem that from the perspective of the Yugoslav leadership, there was the disturbing possibility that the more basic criticisms might assume the primary significance.

This was even more worrying as the Yugoslav leaders were fully aware of the potential for full-scale demonstrations at other universities. The events at Belgrade University were certainly the most striking, but unrest was not confined to this centre. This can be quickly illustrated by reference to developments at Zagreb University. Here, students held meetings in their particular departments to discuss the situation in Belgrade. Anticipating the danger of events getting out of hand, the University Committee of the League issued a statement expressing broad support for the Belgrade students. An Action Committee of 'revolutionary students' promptly published a rival document, the principal difference between the two documents being that the former insisted that all solutions should be sought within the self-managing system and opposed the holding of demonstrations. Despite the fact that the document of the University Committee of the League was quite a radical statement, newspaper accounts make clear the fact that there was a vigorous struggle between the proponents of the two rival docu-ments before the majority of departments endorsed the League docu-ment. Two departments, Philosophy and Political Science, could not be persuaded, and endorsed instead the statements of the 'revolutionary students'.[26]

At most other university centres it was clear that the atmosphere was also tense. Smaller scale demonstrations were held in Sarajevo[27] and Niš;[28] League leaders in Slovenia spent considerable time at Ljubljana University in discussion with students;[29] at the University of Novi Sad the programme of the Belgrade students was endorsed by meetings held in several of the departments;[30] and at Titograd it was reported that there was support for the Belgrade students.[31] The details of the events at these centres are not the primary concern; the essential point is that the possibility of large-scale student demonstrations spreading to all other universities was not to be discounted.[32]

A further danger was that the demonstrators could be joined by the workers.[33] That many among the latter were less than satisfied with their lot had been shown by the number of work stoppages which had occurred in the preceding months. A middle-aged man among the group of students gathered around Vlahović in front of the subway was reported as saying reproachfully what no doubt was in the minds of many:

> Comrade Veljko, today the students went out into the streets; you can expect the same from the workers because they have reason to demonstrate . . . . I am a proletarian. And you were one—once.[34]

Faced with these risks, what were the most appropriate tactics to adopt? Quite clearly there was division and confusion within the top ranks of the Yugoslav leadership on this question.[35] While some favoured a firm line against the protesters, there were those who appeared to believe that the mood among the protesters and within the community as a whole was such that the protest could not simply be quashed.[36] Those favouring a firm line emphasized that the level of political knowledge among the students was such as to make it possible for them to be led astray by what were described as hostile forces.[37] As the Secretary of the Belgrade League of Communists later commented, there were at the beginning of the protest numerous slogans of a 'destructive political content'.[38] The second broad group among the Yugoslav leadership tended to treat the protesting students with enormous caution; indeed, a *Borba* editorial, published on the day of Tito's address, scoffed at the willingness of 'certain' leaders to concede almost anything demanded by the students.[39]

However, while there was this cleavage, in practice it revealed itself primarily as a difference in emphasis. After the initial confusion, the overwhelming majority of those holding responsible positions chose to use a generally tactful tone. The approach adopted on this occasion differed markedly from that used at the time of the 1959 student demonstrations at Zagreb University. These earlier demonstrations had led Tito to state that the students were playing into the hands of 'our enemies' and that they failed to appreciate all that the community had done for them despite its limited resources.[40]

The fact that the official response to the June events was generally conciliatory no doubt reflected the view that this was the most effective tactic in the present situation; in this manner the student feeling could be defused and the risk of student hostility focussing even more directly on the League leadership could be avoided. At a meeting held on Monday evening, the Presidium and the Executive Committee of the Central Committee of the League of Communists in Serbia endorsed the students' demands for 'a more successful and swifter settlement' of their material problems, as well as of the university problems in general. Further, their demands for reform of the university and for a full and active participation in self-management at the university, were described as 'justified'.[41] In a television and radio address made the same evening, Veljko Vlahović similarly emphasized the need for the more rapid and more resolute settlement of a large number of burning questions raised by the students. And he also referred to the bulk of the student demands as reasonable and justified.[42]

Student feeling concerning the role of the militia appeared to be especially bitter, and hence the authorities hastened to promise that the activities of the militia would be 'carefully investigated' in order to determine whether they had transgressed their powers.[43] It was even agreed that students should directly participate in the inquiry.[44]

Official spokesmen sought to deny that the leading organs had been oblivious to, or uninterested in, the plight of the students. Thus, at the meeting mentioned above, it was stressed that the problems of the students were neither new nor unknown and that action on these problems had been and was being taken.[45] And in his broadcast, Vlahović pointed out that at the recent meeting of the Presidium and Executive Council of the Central Committee of the League, Tito himself had urged immediate attention to these difficulties; the leading bodies of the League had 'raised all these questions' and 'tribute should be paid' to the League for this.[46]

And when, on June 4, the Serbian Executive Council announced new measures relating to the students' material situation, it stoutly denied that it had acted hastily or in response to pressure. According to the Council's Vice-President, a session on this subject had been scheduled for a date prior to the demonstrations and only 'unusual' circumstances had forced its postponement.[47]

Further, it was maintained that the student demands relating to employment, social differentiation, the development of self-management and the like were an integral part of League policy and that the leading organs of the League had frequently 'emphasized the necessity for more effective action' in these areas.[48] Thus the problems in these areas were described as due to the failure of those in responsible positions in the society as a whole to implement League policy, while the students and the League leadership were presented as sharing the desire to prod those recalcitrant individuals to do more than pay lip service to League policy.[49] Official statements praised the idealism and revolutionary spirit of the mass of students. They were described not as the opponents of the Yugoslav model of socialism but rather as the allies of the League leadership in the struggle for its realization; their protests were portrayed as an attack on those forces within the system which stood in the path of progress and certainly not as an attack on the system itself.[50] Clearly the effort was made to stress and to praise what could be presented as positive and to minimize what could only be seen as negative. The aim was to control and win over the demonstrators and not to risk an exacerbation of the situation. To attack the demonstrators as a mass would only have strengthened support for those among the protesters who maintained that fundamental change in the system was necessary.

This official effort to underline the 'positive' side of the protests is also illustrated by the press reports that the students prominently displayed pictures of Marx and Tito,[51] and that they sang the national anthem and chanted 'Tito-Party'.[52] Significantly, however, these reports failed to point up the fact that some of the pictures of Tito dated from the partisan days and showed a lean, guerrilla fighter, or that one of the student slogans, 'Down with the pipe and the poodle', referred to a recent press photograph of Tito showing him smoking a pipe and holding a poodle.[53] This chant and the hanging of an old picture of Tito reflected criticism by some among the students of the soft life enjoyed by certain groups in contemporary Yugoslavia and of the poor example set by Tito himself.

The next and related step was to endeavour to isolate and defeat the most hostile elements among the students without antagonizing the bulk of the student body. To this end a distinction was drawn between the allegedly praiseworthy motives and justifiable demands of the over-whelming majority of students, and the aims and motives of a minority who sought to 'make use of the progressive political movement of the students and to channel it toward their own objectives'. These were 'forces' which did not find their interest in the 'development of socialist democracy, self-management and egalitarianism among nations',[54] and it was these forces which the Yugoslav leadership now set out to discredit. Thus, on behalf of the Presidium of the Belgrade City Assembly, Branko Pešić stated that:

> We consider that nobody can claim the right arbitrarily to declare himself the champion of social progress, and that usurpation of such a right by any group represents an attack on democracy. Who can claim the right to declare himself a member of the ideological vanguard without the consent of those whose interests he allegedly represents?[55]

This comment asserted that only the League of Communists had the consent of the working class to claim to be the ideological vanguard and denied the right of any other group to such a position. Another article published in *Borba* on June 8 roundly condemned these 'self-styled avant-gardists', these 'quasi-revolutionaries' who could do no more than mouth shallow slogans. They claimed to be 'progressive' and to be struggling for 'democracy, justice and humanism' but it was one thing to make such a claim and another thing to justify it. The members of this 'new left' were busily giving lessons concerning self-management, but, the article continued, the level of development of self-management at the university suggested that they might first begin by setting their own house in order.[56]

In a similarly unequivocal manner, other official and press statements urged that further demonstrations were unnecessary and, indeed, were a threat to democracy. For example, the announcement of the Presidium and Executive Council of the Central Committee of the League of Communists of Serbia published on June 6 made the following point:

> Those who use methods of pressure and acts of violence circumvent and ignore the democratic and self-managing organizations of the working people . . . endanger the basic democratic course of the development of our society and everything on which the working people of this country base their faith in socialist progress. The propagation and organization of so-called 'spontaneous action' (by circumventing the League of Communists and other organized socialist forces) is in its substance a political deceit, an attempt to make use of the strivings of the working people who demand and call for more rapid and more consistent implementation of the political course of the League of Communists, for the achievement of . . . destructive purposes.[57]

In particular, this announcement maintained, some sought to exploit the justified demands of the students in an effort to overthrow the basic self-managing system. How else was it possible to explain the fact that some sought to continue public demonstrations even though the justice and validity of the major student demands had been recognized? It must be understood, the announcement continued, that in a self-managing society all questions must be settled in a democratic way rather than through disorder and pressure.[58]

According to Veljko Vlahović, in his broadcast of June 4, those who failed to use what he described as democratic methods were embarking on a path which led to the destruction of the whole system of 'socialist democracy'. In the first place, he claimed, *provocateurs* could exploit the 'inflammable situation' of a street demonstration. Further, this circumvention of democratic procedures played into the hands of 'bureaucratic, étatist and conservative forces'. By this he seemed to imply that members of the latter group within the party could point to this unrest in order to justify their arguments for tighter central controls.[59]

A very strongly worded article in *Borba* on Wednesday June 5 vigorously maintained that the students should have dissociated themselves 'clearly and with greater determination from certain people', from certain slogans and from 'certain moves' by people within their own ranks. It was 'alarming' that despite the general goodwill expressed concerning their basic demands, the students had continued on the present course. Indeed, reference was again made to the existence of an 'inflammable atmosphere'. These arguments were used to justify a decree, issued by the Republican Secretariat for Internal Affairs on Tuesday June 4, banning all demonstrations and meetings in all public places in Belgrade. According to *Borba,* such an order, together with the increased number of militiamen in the streets, was 'bound to alarm every member of a democratic society'; however, if the system of democratic self-management was to develop it must be protected against attempts to use 'force' to secure particular goals.[60]

These arguments glossed over the fact that the students by their words and actions had maintained that working through the 'regular' channels was often fruitless and that the *initial* response of the League leadership had amounted to a virtual endorsement of this view. As even the President of the Union of Youth later observed, the failure to settle the serious material difficulties faced by students was frequently explained by reference to the shortage of funds, and yet when these demonstrations had erupted, money suddenly became available.[61] Further, while the official position was that continued demonstrations played into the hands of bureaucratic elements within the League, the rhetoric of the demonstrators stressed that the very existence of these bureaucratic elements in fact necessitated freedom of assembly and the right to demonstrate;[62] only thus could the power of these elements be checked.

What is apparent in this opposition to continued demonstrations, especially when seen in the context of statements praising the mass of students, was the desire to isolate that small group of students who were not placated by the mere acknowledgement of the validity of the bulk of the student demands. The members of this group sought the continuation of meetings and the critical examination of fundamental aspects of the Yugoslav system. They refused to be fobbed off by such claims as that the present shortcomings stemmed from the failure of certain individuals to implement League policies and they denied that the League leadership could simply assert that it bore no responsibility for contemporary problems. By its attitude, however, the League leadership steadfastly maintained that it alone could distinguish the justified from the unjustified demand, the valid from the erroneous criticism and that which would strengthen socialism from that which might threaten it.

Another facet of the tactics adopted to deal with the student demonstrations was the apparently deliberate effort to accentuate those student demands which related to their particular material difficulties; the explanation of the protest primarily in terms of 'student' concerns made it far easier to deal with. In the first place, instead of their demands being seen as amounting to an attack on certain basic features of the Yugoslav system, they could be presented as requests to which the system could and would respond. Second, it was obvious that the resentments of many students could be assuaged by promises which related primarily to 'student' concerns. Third, by suggesting that the students were chiefly concerned with their own material situation at a time when the workers were carrying the heavy burden of the recent economic reform, the prospect of a worker/student alliance was reduced.[63]

Efforts by students to take their case directly to the workers on the Monday and Tuesday were quashed. Delegates at a meeting of the Belgrade City Assembly, held on Tuesday June 4, reported that the 'workers' at several factories had closed their doors to 'extremist students'.[64] And the President of the Serbian Assembly was quoted as referring to the mass of telegrams from workers' collectives urging the maintenance of public order, the use of proper, democratic channels and so on.[65]

27

One such message was published in *Borba* on June 4. This message, from the workers at a furniture factory, expressed opposition to the methods chosen by the students to advance their claims. The students were asked to prevent disorders and to unmask the 'instigators' and those 'fishing in troubled waters'.

> We the creators of income and direct producers have a right to ask this and believe that you will succeed in finding your way and show your high socialist conscience just as you have shown it so many times before.[66]

Not everyone was convinced that this flood of telegrams and letters was a spontaneous expression of the opinions of the work collectives. Thus, an article in the trade union newspaper *Rad,* published on June 7, reported these many proclamations but added, 'the question of who wrote the proclamations on behalf of the work collectives is, of course, a different matter'. The same article maintained that the widespread failure of the workers' collectives to understand the students' motives was due to the misinformation, distortion and misrepresentation perpetrated by the mass media.[67] In accord with this view, a Yugoslav scholar has recently commented that there was a conscious effort to misinform the workers as to the student demands.[68] Parenthetically, it might be noted that *Rad* was the newspaper most sympathetic to the student claims. Leading trade union officials were quick to dissociate themselves from the paper's stand and several members of its staff were later dismissed.[69]

Thus the revolutionary enthusiasm of the students was praised in so far as it conformed, or could be made to appear to conform, to the basic League stand; and where it deviated from this position, it was condemned as anti-socialist.[70] Any attempt to challenge the pre-eminent position of the League leadership was denounced as the work of extremists and of enemies of socialism.

This official attitude to the demonstrations was developed and expressed over a period of several days in the context of continued student meetings at the various departments at Belgrade University. It is highly significant that these activities were organized by special Action Committees rather than by the existing structures and organizations within the university. The necessity and desire for such bodies indicated a great deal concerning the relationship between the student body and the university 'self-management' apparatus and the university League and student organizations. Clearly these organizations were viewed as a part of the general problem rather than as a means towards its solution.[71]

At these meetings the Belgrade students continued to discuss the issues raised in the first mass meeting and began to move toward the formulation of a statement explaining the essence of their protest. On June 4—that is, after many hours of speeches and discussions—representatives of the several departmental Action Committees met to formulate a common programme. Significantly, the meeting was also attended by the University Committee of the Union of Students and the University

Committee of the League of Communists. The Secretary of the latter subsequently acknowledged that the participation of these organizations represented an effort to inject themselves into the mainstream of events and to prevent the student movement from getting too far out of hand.[72]

The formulation of this Political Action Programme was a critical stage in the crisis since it represented the effort to integrate the various ideas which had been endorsed at the various departmental meetings into a single, broadly acceptable framework.

The first sentence of the Programme placed the thrust of the student activity squarely within the socialist system:

> Measures must be undertaken in the interest of a more rapid and more effective settlement of outstanding and unsettled questions in the construction of our socialist society, as a self-management community of free and equal nations and nationalities.[73]

What is far more striking and significant than the attitude shown by the opening statement is the fact that nowhere in the Programme was there even token obeisance to the League of Communists as the leading and guiding force in society. Certainly this omission cannot be construed as accidental. In the entire document of some thousand words there was but a single reference to the League of Communists and that was by no means laudatory:

> In conformity with the development of self-management relations it is necessary to step up the process of democratization of all socio-political organizations, especially of the League of Communists.

Also of significance in illustrating the attitude toward the notion of the League as the fount of all wisdom was the statement:

> One must strive for the greater influence of . . . the University and students on the formulation of basic positions concerning the paths, forms, and methods of our further social and economic development.

In addition, the Programme urged the 'democratization' of the mass media and the securing of the basic 'freedoms and rights' set out in the Constitution. Presumably the latter referred to the provisions concerning free speech and assembly.

Another significant item of the Programme stressed that the university should be an institution in which 'progressive' ideas could develop freely. The representatives at the mass meeting of students also agreed to add a demand for legislation which would guarantee the autonomy of the university.

Together these demands seemed to amount to nothing less than a forthright denial of the claim of the League leadership to a monopolistic position on questions relating to the basic economic, social and political development of Yugoslav society. These representatives of the university community appeared to be seeking the right to participate freely in the discussion and formulation of basic policies rather than to function in a merely subordinate role and within the limits set by official League policy.

The remainder of the Action Programme referred to more particular aspects of Yugoslav society. There were demands for the adoption of specific and vigorous measures to deal with what were described as serious social inequalities. It was urged that clear criteria of acceptable minimum and maximum personal incomes should be established, and that incomes above this maximum should be subject to the 'severest' tax. Also included were strong demands for the elimination of differences in personal incomes deriving from 'unsocialist, monopolistic and other privileged positions', for energetic action against the 'unsocialist' accumulation of wealth and for the nationalization of property which had been improperly acquired. Other sections of the Programme condemned the development of joint stock companies and the growing speculation in housing, particularly in so far as this involved the construction of luxury apartments.

Concerning employment, the Programme urged a long-term plan of economic development and the adoption of an investments policy to secure its realization. The clear implication was that in the present situation too much responsibility fell to the particular enterprises which formulated their policies with insufficient regard for the broader interests of society. In addition, the Programme requested the prescription of specific measures to ensure that students would have the opportunity to obtain practical experience as part of their training, and the adoption of unambiguous guidelines to stipulate the qualifications needed for particular work. The last proposal aimed at forcing the unqualified and under-qualified to step down from their positions in order to create opportunities for the young graduate. By seeking such measures, the students were demonstrating their irritation with the existing situation in which officials merely talked about the urgent necessity of upgrading the qualifications of the work force.

In relation to the university, the Programme stressed the need to develop genuine self-management, and in particular to involve the students in this process. Effective action to ensure that young cadres would have the opportunity to embark on an academic career were also urged. Measures to secure what was described as genuine equality of opportunity were advocated; these included steps to improve the students' economic situation as well as measures to ensure that the social structure of the student body matched that of society as a whole.

Certainly this Programme was more than a demand for the improvement of the particular situation of students: points were made which touched the very essence of the present system. In particular, the monopoly of the League in the area of policy formulation was challenged and the consequences of League policies were harshly criticized. Clearly, the complaint concerning the 'unsocialist' accumulation of wealth and the failure of the various collectives to adopt policies which showed appropriate concern for the interests of the wider community related directly to the loudly heralded 'economic reforms' of 1964. These reforms were aimed at ensuring greater economic efficiency and rationality by giving greater scope to market forces. In the eyes of at least those drafting the Programme, however, these reforms had consequences which had little to do with socialism.

Significantly, official and press comments on this document failed to assess its full implications; indeed, they reached conclusions which those responsible for the formulation of the Programme had been careful to avoid. Thus a *Borba* article claimed that the Programme, 'as the students pointed out', derived from their desire to implement League policy.[74] In the same vein, Miloš Minić was reported as saying that it contained the demands of the working class and of the League of Communists.[75]

The completed Programme was referred to the students in the separate departments for their consideration and, hopefully, for their approval. However, its endorsement was no mere formality, since a significant minority within the various departments insisted that the tenor and substance of the Programme was too conservative. Indeed, in the Department of Philosophy, the document was decisively rejected. Here the most outspoken critic of the Programme was a Professor Vojin Milić, who maintained that the Programme was too mild, indeed, that it was a document of capitulation. Rather than follow the lead of the other departments by endorsing this document, he argued that this department should assume the role of the 'vanguard of the vanguard'. He vehemently denied that the student activity was, or indeed should be, in conformity with the general policy of the League of Communists, and he appealed directly to the idealism of the assembled students: 'A generation which wishes to win its place in history must suffer sacrifices.'[76] This deliberate challenge to the authority of the League of Communists was described in *Politika* as signifying nothing less than 'another programme' and another movement 'based on other ideological principles'.[77] The rejection of the Action Programme by this meeting demonstrated that some students were convinced that the concessions that had been made by official spokesmen amounted to mere rhetoric or related only to secondary problems; they insisted that the basic questions concerning the functioning of the system and the role of the League had not been settled.

In this manner a week passed. After the violence of the Sunday and Monday, events had settled into a pattern of almost continual meetings. There was no further disorder, largely because of the great care taken by the student body. They organized patrols around their buildings and constantly urged the need to show 'maturity'. This action, at least in part, seemed to reflect the desire to disprove the earlier media accusations of hooligan attitudes among the students. And the constant presence of the militia around the buildings also seemed important.[78] However, probably of most significance in cooling the mood among the students were the careful tactics of the Yugoslav leadership described above.

At this point, the pertinent question was how the 'rebellion' would end. Would the mass of students simply tire of the continual meetings and drift away? On the one hand, many of them felt that much had already been achieved, but on the other hand, a small minority continued to argue that the basic, systemic problems had not been resolved. It is difficult to assess the mood of the students at this point. According to press accounts,[79] increasing numbers of students were becoming bored with the continued meetings. However, from the point of view of the Yugoslav leadership, the risk still remained that an unexpected incident might again galvanize the students onto the streets and into renewed clashes with the militia.

It was at this juncture that Tito broke his week-long public silence with a shrewd address embodying those tactics employed to such advantage by responsible officials and commentators in the preceding week. It will be recalled from the description of Tito's address in chapter I that he sought, in particular, to conciliate the mass of students and to isolate and discredit the more radical element among them.

The students' response to Tito's speech was immediate and favourable. At each university centre throughout Yugoslavia the speech was reportedly received with tremendous enthusiasm. However, it was among Belgrade students that the most enthusiastic response was described. For example, according to *Borba,* the two thousand students and professors gathered in one hall at the Law Department greeted every sentence of Tito's address with 'an explosion of spontaneous applause and prolonged ovations'. And when the speech was concluded, it seemed, continued the report, that the building might collapse from the noise of loud approval. There were tears in the eyes of numerous students, many embraced each other and several slogans were shouted, all including Tito's name.

Throughout the student body, so it was reported, there was joy. Students danced national dances in the street and sang songs; indeed, at one point some ten thousand students gathered to give 'vent to their feelings in the tireless chanting of the slogan "Tito-Party"'. The Secretary of the Belgrade University Committee of the League of Communists delivered a brief speech, which was frequently interrupted by 'shouts of approval' from the vast throng. He particularly emphasized the supreme confidence Tito had shown in the young; Tito had recognized their responsibility and maturity. The text of a telegram to be sent to Tito was approved by 'prolonged applause'. This message, probably drafted by an official of the University Committee of the League, strongly endorsed Tito's opinion that the student objectives were in accord with the policy of the League of Communists. It might even be suggested that the presentation of such a text to the students at this moment of euphoria was a skilful move intended to provide support for Tito's broad interpretation of these events. The telegram concluded with a request for Tito's support in uncovering the truth concerning the events of June 2 and 3.[80]

Indeed, it was only on this point that any student dissatisfaction was noted. In the midst of the reportedly joyful celebration, students requested a report from a student representative on the commission established by the Serbian Executive Council to investigate the confrontation between students and militia. This representative made the sobering statement that the commission had been unable to agree, principally because student representatives refused to accept the accusations contained in the report of the Secretariat of Internal Affairs. In particular, they had denied that on 'that critical day' students had shouted anti-socialist slogans. At the conclusion of the report 'thousands of voices' began to chant, 'We want the truth.'[81]

Nonetheless one thing was clear: as far as the overwhelming majority was concerned, the demonstrations were over!

The guidelines, which Tito had emphasized, were published on June 14, four days after Tito's address.[82] As has been indicated, these guidelines were intended to eliminate the particular problem to which Tito had alluded, namely the failure on the part of responsible individuals to work for the implementation of League policies. The clear implication was that the guidelines would rectify that one aspect of the total system which had failed. They would ensure that nominal unity would become, in Tito's term, 'real unity'.[83] Responsible individuals would no longer be able to pay mere lip service to League policies; rather, they would be obliged to take specific steps toward the implementation of these policies.[84] Although the present study does not focus on the aftermath of the demonstrations, it is instructive to glance at least at these guidelines to discern how the Yugoslav leadership endeavoured to solve the general problem concerning the gulf between what was decided and what was actually accomplished.

The nature of the guidelines can be illustrated by examining those provisions relating to just one of the students' major grievances, the problem of employment. A reading of the relevant sections makes it abundantly clear that the much vaunted guidelines failed to measure up to what was promised. They vaguely called for 'organized and concerted social action . . . at all levels', for 'changing and fully developing the economic structure' and for reorganizing and modernizing social and economic activities. It was also stated that the employment of experts, especially young ones, was one of the 'important conditions' for the 'successful realization' of the economic reforms, and in order to ensure that the young expert would be able to secure appropriate employment it was necessary to 'break all the resistances' stemming from the short-sightedness and 'primitivism' of particular enterprises. Only in this manner could the problem of the existing unsatisfactory level of expertise be tackled.[85]

It is immediately obvious that such guidelines were not qualitatively different from the many previous official statements on the subject. In their Action Programme the students had demanded precise standards or criteria; these guidelines provided none.

Tito himself expressed concern that the guidelines might simply remain empty words.[86] And as a member of the Serbian Central

Committee of the League observed, there was a danger that some would be satisfied simply with the mere statement of concern while others would act only on those aspects which suited them.[87] This appears to be a vital point. If this failure on the part of responsible individuals or groups to implement League policy could not in fact be remedied, it would be difficult for the Yugoslav leadership to continue to maintain that this was only a peripheral problem, one which related not to the total system or to the League leadership, but only to the failure of some individuals or groups within the system. Be that as it may, for the present purposes the key points are that this particular crisis was over and that the Yugoslav leadership, most notably Tito himself, had had considerable success in securing acceptance of its interpretation of the nature and causes of these events.

But was it the correct interpretation? Was the thrust of the student protests indeed an indication of deep commitment to the ideals of the society and the role and policies of the League?

STUDYING THE CAUSES OF STUDENT UNREST

The task of discerning the political beliefs of university students and the significance of their protest is far from easy. This can be readily shown by even a brief review of the literature on a topic with which most of us are familiar: student protest in Western societies.

At one extreme, scholars have condemned student protest on a variety of points: protesters are overwhelmingly an over-indulged and under-disciplined generation who find it difficult to accept the realities and responsibilities of life;[88] the protests are the acts of young people kept overlong in a state of dependence, feeling unwanted and insignificant and trying 'to prove themselves real adults';[89] protesters offer no guidance for the solution of contemporary problems—indeed, in both temperament and impulse they are kin to the Luddites;[90] they fail to recognize that freedom depends on voluntary restraint;[91] the motivation and thrust of student revolt is most aptly described as fascist;[92] it is probably the 'most irrational force in modern history'[93] largely because the student activists are determined 'somehow to destroy, undermine, subjugate or humiliate the older generation';[94] and, protesters are likely to accomplish nothing 'except mischief and ruin'; indeed, if the United States were to fail as the world's centre of liberal democracy the responsibility for that failure would largely lie with the student movement.[95]

At the other extreme a vastly different picture has been presented: rather than being maladjusted, the student protester may in fact be more 'normal' than those who accept the existing situation;[96] rather than being irrational, the protesters sometimes seem to be the only clear-eyed and sane people in our society;[97] far from rejecting the avowed values of society, the protester is often the only one who appears to take those values seriously;[98] those who condemn the 'undemocratic' methods of the protesters often fail to recognize that, given the reality of the contemporary system, protest is the only avenue to recognition and attention;[99] far from threatening the capacity of the system to survive and adapt, this ferment among the young may be our last, best hope for the transformation of 'this disoriented civilization of ours into something a human being can identify as home'.[100]

But there are additional matters on which there is considerable debate. For example, who is the more typical and who is the more significant—the protester or the non-protester? Is the protester the admired model among other students or is he ignored or even scorned? Is it merely a temporary phase in the life of these individual students and, indeed, in the life of the society as a whole? Does the fact that student unrest has broken out in a host of countries, both 'developed' and 'under-developed' and both communist and non-communist, indicate that we are experiencing a world-wide revolt of the young deriving from a common cause or set of causes?

For our present purposes, this last question is worthy of further consideration. The most notable proponent of the view that this revolt stems from a common cause is Lewis Feuer, who insists that the root of student unrest is the inevitable conflict between generations.[101] There may be some merit in Feuer's thesis, but it would appear that there is danger in ascribing too much to a single factor. It does not tell us a great deal simply to assert that the young are naturally rebellious; it is also necessary to explain why this conflict erupts into the open at one time and not another, and why their 'rebellion' took a particular form. For example, the student on a 'panty raid' and the student sitting in the university President's office are both challenging the authority of the older generation but it may be that the motivations behind these acts are quite dissimilar. It is at least plausible to suggest that the former amounts to little more than a final fling before joining adult society, but that essentially the particular student sees his future in terms of the present society; he may be breaking a certain rule but he is not in fact challenging the legitimacy of those in authority. The motivation for the second action may be markedly different—it could be urged that it signifies a questioning and even a rejection of the present authorities and their rules; rather than a simple prank within the context of a broad acceptance of the present system, it could be maintained that it represents a desire to change that society. One might, of course, suggest that even for many of those students involved in the latter action, this also amounts to a final youthful fling before settling down into adult society. However, it seems that a fundamental distinction might be drawn between the young person who accepts the present system with little questioning and the young person who does not like what he feels the future has in store for him and who dreads the thought of having to 'knuckle under'.

Feuer describes the attitudes of the young towards their elders as amounting to bitter and irrational hatred and as seeking their destruction and humiliation; between the old and the young there are no common bonds or aims.[102] But is this, in fact, the case? Is there, as Feuer suggests, a deep gulf between father and son which stems from the struggle for the affections of the mother and which imposes itself on the total complex of societal relations?[103]

Rather than such dramatic explanations, might one not simply comment that the young, because of their particular situation in life, look at society a little differently from the old? In this vein one could suggest that the young have been taught the values of the society and now for the first time they may be beginning to see how these principles are actually implemented; and what a more mature (or cynical?) person may perceive as the usual gulf between rhetoric and reality may tend to arouse feelings of anger in the more principled (or naive?) younger person.[104] So it could be said that while a difference exists between the generations, its roots might be other than what Feuer suggests. Furthermore, this difference need not necessarily lead to a venomous hostility on the part of the young towards the old, but rather there may be sympathy toward, and understanding of, the old. In this connection Kenneth Keniston notes that

> activists are not, on the whole, repudiating or rebelling against explicit parental values or ideologies. On the contrary, there is some evidence that such students are living out their parents' values in practice; . . . thus, any simple concept of 'generational conflict' or 'rebellion against parental authority' is clearly oversimplified as applied to the motivations of most protesters.[105]

Concerning relations between parents and their activist children, Keniston observes that 'what is most impressive is the solidarity of older and younger generations'. And rather than anger towards their parents, Keniston claims that many of the young feel pity, pity that their parents, despite their own former youthful hopes and ideals, were forced to conform to reality.[106]

Feuer does acknowledge that what he considers to be this basic and inevitable conflict only erupts in an acute form in particular circumstances. As he explains it, there must be above all a feeling that the 'older generation' has 'discredited itself and lost its moral standing'. In this situation there occurs what he terms the 'de-authoritization' of the older generation.[107]

That is, Feuer's main thesis amounts to no more than a claim that generational conflict is a constant condition in human society but not a condition sufficient for the outbreak of a student revolt. What seems far more crucial, therefore, is to explain how and why the 'de-authorization of the older generation' occurs in some situations but not in others, to explain why it is that in some situations a significant proportion of the student body seems to be idealistic and enthusiastic but in another situation the prevailing mood is, say, of uninterest or cynicism broken by the occasional eruption of anger. Feuer's thesis tells us nothing concerning these questions.

An earlier effort to discern the basic cause of student unrest was made by S. M. Eisenstadt. He characterized student unrest as the consequence of the breakdown of traditional authority in the process of modernization. The traditional values transmitted through the family were irrelevant and even dysfunctional to participation in the developing system. The students learned new attitudes in the university situation, attitudes which brought them into conflict with the established élites in their society because these élites were not and could not afford to be as receptive to change as the young. In the process of modernization, the accepted political and social values were challenged by the rising generation, which saw these values as a barrier to the establishment of a 'developed' or 'modern' society.[108]

As Richard Flacks has pointed out, this view seemed a viable one until the eruption of similar protests in 'developed' societies.[109] It is possible, however, in Flack's opinion, to see the conflict in 'developed' societies as similar to that in societies undergoing 'rapid transition from traditional to modern culture'. In both cases one can discern the emergence of a sector of the youth population which finds its fundamental values, aspirations, and character structure in sharp conflict with the values and practices which prevail in the larger society.[110]

In other words, one might urge that what is common to all these situations of student protest is the rejection of, and the challenge to, 'normal' authority within the particular political system. That is, there is what might be termed a crisis of authority. Having distilled much of the literature on student protest down to this one basic point it is obvious that very little has actually been said. Clearly, it is not enough merely to talk of the crisis of authority as causing student unrest; rather, one must endeavour to explain why this crisis of authority occurred, and this can only be discerned in the particular situation and not by reference to a single, simple explanation common to all societies.

Such bold explanations as that advanced by Feuer have the attraction of appearing to organize and give meaning to a mass of diverse material. However, as Sidney Hook insists, this search for a single common cause or set of causes to explain student unrest in the different societies in which it has occurred is a 'profound error': 'one may as well argue that an increase in the death rate in many countries proves that the same cause is operating everywhere'.[111]

Students in one society may be children of affluence, while those in another endure conditions of poverty; or students in one society might be preoccupied with the problems of racial tension and with Vietnam, while those in another may only be peripherally affected by these issues; the list is endless, but the simple point is that one must be wary of those who proclaim a single, neat, universal cause, because such claims serve only to obscure the complexity and uniqueness of particular human events.

This does not mean that such an all-encompassing explanation has no value. In particular, it may prompt the analyst of a specific situation to ask questions that he might otherwise have neglected. However, he must guard against the possibility of being drawn to evidence which serves to confirm a particular hypothesis while ignoring that which is to the contrary. Similarly, particular explanations derived from one situation may stimulate new perspectives in another situation; but again there is the danger of blithely and uncritically transferring explanations from one historical situation to another. There may be similarities between one situation and the next, one student revolt may help spark off or justify another, even the rhetoric of the demonstrators might be the same, but the main causes of each student protest must be searched for in its own situation.

The difficulty of this task must not be under-estimated. As Daniel Bell has warned, 'history is always written after the fact', and hence 'it is easy . . . to give some apparently plausible account of "the causes" and "the determing factors" '. As Bell implies, a plausible account is not necessarily the correct one.[112] Further, as Keniston has remarked, there may be as many explanations of student dissent as there are individual dissenters.[113]

In the first place then, it seems necessary to try to catalogue the particular problems faced by the students and to try to assess their significance. This examination of the students' actual situation would help the observer to form an appreciation as to whether the students had reasonable cause to protest, or whether their protest was the act of maladjusted and irresponsible juveniles. Further, an understanding of the students' situation may help in evaluating the opinions expressed by the students to justify their protest. Care must be taken in evaluating the reported demands and statements of the demonstrators since these may not necessarily be a reliable guide to the basic cause of the involvement of students in the protest. Indeed, the individual student may not himself understand,[114] or be able to admit, the principal causes of this frustration; therefore, his endorsement of an attack on some feature of the university or society might stem from his personal anxieties regarding, for example, his present material situation or his prospects for 'suitable' employment. In this regard it must be remembered that the reported demands and statements of the demonstrators for the most part express the views of the more articulate and politically interested minority; thus the rhetoric may refer to 'participatory democracy', but the mass of students may applaud this attack on 'the system' because there is no hot water in the dormitories. How can the 'real' motive be discerned in such a situation? Obviously, it is impossible to be certain. Nevertheless, it is of some value to search for evidence of an actual desire for participation. Did the students avail themselves of the opportunities offered in the past? If not, how do they justify this failure and is their explanation convincing?

There are, then, different forms of evidence concerning the causes of student protest, such as the expressed opinions of the students and their 'actual' situation. However, while for purposes of analysis it is possible to discern these as separate strands it must be remembered that the evidence constitutes a single whole. To return to the question of the students' situation as a cause of student unrest, what must be borne in mind is that it is not merely a matter of how this situation might appear to the outside observer, but rather, how it appears to the students themselves. To students caught up in a mood of revolutionary enthusiasm, a situation of gross overcrowding at the university might seem to be an unavoidable shortcoming; to apathetic or cynical students the same problem might appear as a further demonstration of the inefficacy of the total system.

In other words, in studying the factors affecting the attitudes and beliefs of the students, these attitudes and beliefs must themselves be understood because they help determine how the students will perceive these particular factors; that is, the study is of both the *process* of political socialization and the *results* of that process at a particular point in time.

Chapter III

SELF-MANAGEMENT IN THE YUGOSLAV UNIVERSITY

As outlined in the introduction, Yugoslav officials have proclaimed self-management as a system in which all citizens, regardless of position and qualifications, have equal right and opportunity to help formulate the decisions affecting their daily life and work. Fundamental to this model is the assumption that the separate self-managing collectives would harmonize their own interests with the interests of other groups, with the interests of the community as a whole and with the goal of socialism. This harmonization would be achieved in large part through the inspiration and guidance from individual communists within the particular collective and from what was termed the moral and political authority of the League of Communists as a whole.

How did this ambitious system work in practice? A partial answer to this question can be discerned in the assessments made by Yugoslav officials and scholars of the functioning of self-management within the university. Its functioning here is relevant to an understanding of the achievements and difficulties of the university system and, further, its functioning within the university could be expected to have a significant impact on the political views of the students—after all, this was their immediate environment. This is not to suggest that their perception of the operation of the self-management system outside the university was unimportant as far as the shaping of their attitudes was concerned. The functioning of the self-managing system within the university can, however, be seen as not untypical of the broader situation.

The system applied at the university was one of 'social management' rather than self-management. In simple terms this meant that 'interested citizens' also sat on departmental and university councils alongside the representatives from within the university—education was seen as being too important to be left only to the educators.[1] In chapter IV, consideration is given to the impact of these representatives of society on the university; however, at this point the focus is on relations within the university community itself, that is, with the 'self-management' aspect of 'social management'.

THE ROLE PLAYED BY STAFF AND STUDENTS

Relations Among Members of Staff

At the very least, a self-managing collective was one in which there

40

were comradely and socialist relations. However, according to many official, press and scholarly comments, actual practice within the Yugoslav university fell abysmally short of the ideals of self-management. Indeed, the constant reiteration of these ideals only seemed to highlight the imperfections and abuses in the actual development of the system. The blunt truth seemed to be that many faculty members continued to oppose self-management, sometimes openly, but more often simply by their attitudes and actions.[2]

Those who opposed the principle of self-management argued that a university was unlike a factory, which was manufacturing a particular product to be sold for a specific price. The organization of work was necessarily different, and, furthermore, it was difficult to measure the economic value of the work of the university.[3] The firm official response to this argument was that the university was indeed different from the factory and consequently the systems of management could not be identical; however, there could be no difference between them on the question of the application of the 'fundamental principles'—the university could not be isolated from the general process of democratization of Yugoslav society.[4]

A significant number of faculty members obviously remained unenthusiastic. Even at the close of the period under review some were described as being unconvinced of the desirability of embarking on 'new and unknown waters'.[5] Others maintained that so much time was wasted in the many meetings that little time for 'real work' was left.[6] Another argument was that the goals and functions of the university were such that a system of management based on assumptions of equality of status was inappropriate,[7] and that any participation in self-management must reflect this divergence in competence and responsibility.[8]

For the most part, however, little open opposition to the principles and ideals of self-management was expressed. Indeed, it was frequently observed that support for self-management *seemed* almost universal, but that this commitment and consensus immediately collapsed when it came to the consideration of practical steps towards this avowed goal.[9] Similarly, it was claimed that a small group in each department, while not specifically opposing self-management, often would simply gather power to itself, and retain it. The general conclusion of many observers was that in spite of the dramatic change in forms and despite two decades of socialism, a system of hierarchical and authoritarian, rather than collegial, relations continued to dominate.[10] These comments and judgements give some insight into the lack of progress in the development of the system of self-management at the university and give some indication of the frustration among some faculty members. However, it is difficult to assess the *extent* of such feeling merely on this basis.

A survey covering university schools in Croatia and published in September 1968 gives a more precise indication of general staff attitudes toward the development of self-management. With each question relating to particular aspects of self-management, satisfaction was expressed by only about one-quarter of the teaching assistants and about half of the full professors.[11] Full details are shown in Table 1.

TABLE 1

STAFF OPINION ON THREE QUESTIONS

1. *Do 'fair interpersonal relations' exist among the staff in your department?*

	Yes %	No %	Only partly %
Full professors	52.7	17.8	29.5
Associate professors, lecturers, etc.	39.4	20.6	40.0
Assistants	25.5	27.0	47.5

2. *Are staff members paid according to their work?*

	Yes %	No %	Only partly %
Full professors	45.0	18.8	36.2
Associate professors, lecturers, etc.	33.3	21.1	45.6
Assistants	26.7	23.7	49.6

3. *Do all 'working people' at your particular institution have the opportunity to participate in the process of deciding 'all important questions'?*

	Yes %	No %	Only partly %
Full professors	57.0	12.1	30.9
Associate professors, lecturers, etc.	46.0	14.0	39.2
Assistants	28.9	19.2	51.9

Source: Based on Aleksandar Bazala and Ante Vukasović, 'Sistem samou-pravljanja na sveučilištu' (The system of self-management at the university), *Univerzitet Danas,* vol. ix, no. 7 (1968), pp. 4-6.

In response to an open-ended question, those who felt that all 'working people' had the opportunity to participate, expressed views along the following lines: both in theory and practice, all questions are decided in the workers' councils; all workers have the opportunity to be elected to these bodies; and the elections are conducted in the 'best democratic manner'.[12]

Those who expressed a negative assessment of the situation, that is, those who denied that everyone had the opportunity for meaningful participation or who felt that unfair relations existed at the university expressed their opinions with considerable bitterness.[13]

Some comments made by professors were as follows: 'a small group of people decides everything without concern for the collective interest'; the majority is 'afraid' of this small group and 'simply endorses their decisions'; 'we learn of various decisions when all is completed; our views are never sought'; it is a 'caste' system; there are cases of 'inhuman attitudes towards those . . . lower in the hierarchy'; and rules are 'altered simply to suit the interests of certain individuals in a particular case'.[14]

Among the associate professors and lecturers, the following comments were made: individuals do not 'speak openly' for fear of reprisal or are 'very frequently' obliged to speak in a manner 'recommended' by their superiors; and, the fate of the young academic is subject to the arbitrary whim of his senior professor.[15]

The more disgruntled among the assistants were quoted along the following lines: self-management bodies exist but the decisions are still 'dictated by the same people'; it is very dangerous to disagree with the recommendations of this small group, for the 'usurper' might find himself 'discredited in all fields, political, academic, and moral'; the system of open balloting in the election of faculty makes it impossible for the more junior staff members to vote as they desire; and, the young member of faculty who challenges even slightly the interests of certain professors may find himself a victim of an 'ugly reprisal' when his promotion or re-election is considered.[16]

That relations among the staff fell far short of the assumptions on which the self-management model was predicated can be further illustrated by specific reference to assessments made of the functioning of the system of the election or re-election of staff. Many of these assessments emphasized the abuses in this system and the consequent deleterious effect on the development of collegial, self-managing relations within the university.

The system of 're-election' applied to all faculty below the level of full professor: after a stipulated term of years the individual holding a particular position was obliged to re-apply for it in open competition. The objective was to provide for the removal of those who had failed to live up to earlier promise and to provide the opportunity for younger scholars to test their competence as teachers and scholars in the socialist university.[17]

The general consensus, however, seemed to be that re-election of the incumbent was usually a formality.[18] According to one Yugoslav scholar, the reluctance to upset the *status quo* within a department reflected the pressures of life in a less developed society—primary consideration was given to economic and social security and hence there was an unwillingness to assess objectively the work of one's colleagues.[19] Speaking or voting against the work of a colleague inevitably caused unpleasantness, and was simply thought to be imprudent.[20] In such an atmosphere it was seen as inevitable that 'monopolies' were created in many departments and that performance became almost irrelevant.[21]

It was claimed that frequently the qualifications stipulated in a competition for a university position were tailor-made for a particular individual, and that as a consequence it was extremely rare to have more than one person respond to such an advertisement.[22] It was also asserted that recommendations frequently depended more on personal ties, nationality and politics than on questions of competence,[23] and that no significant efforts were made to establish procedures which might serve to check such abuses.[24]

The extremely few cases where the incumbent failed to secure re-election were described as usually due to factors unrelated to the incumbent's work as either a scholar or a teacher;[25] what might appear as differences of principle among the faculty were seen as deriving, for the most part, from personal disagreements.[26]

Another aspect of this theme was illustrated by the continuing and unresolved debate as to whether the ballot should be secret or open.[27] On the one hand, it was maintained that open voting led to the automatic re-election of the incumbent because of the desire of his colleagues to avoid creating an enemy.[28] On the other hand, it was argued that secret ballots encouraged 'subjectivism' and 'irresponsibility'; those who had offended their colleagues by maintaining a 'principled' stand were often defeated in such ballots.[29]

The commission concerned with appointments, almost invariably consisting of the senior members of the department, had a very great influence on this selection process. Junior faculty rarely opposed its recommendations, since their own futures greatly depended on the attitude of the members of this commission.[30] One article in *Borba* in 1956 referred to an occasion when two young medical doctors presented— as they were entitled to do—objections to a reference written on behalf of a particular candidate. The department concerned established a commission to investigate these objections; however, the only expert consulted was the very professor whose reference was being challenged. Not surprisingly, the departmental commission condemned the critics for harming the reputation and authority of both the department and the referee.[31]

The young—and often not so young—assistants usually bore a substantial part of the work load at the university; some senior faculty were described as 'occasional guests' at the department.[32] The added responsibilities thrust on the assistant meant that he had considerable difficulty in continuing the research on which his promotion or re-election depended,[33] but it was imprudent for him to complain. He was obliged, so the reports indicated, to defer completely to his professor's wishes, for despite the theory of equality of status, it was obvious that the professor had a decisive voice in determining the assistant's future.[34]

Other resentments were described as relating to the inequitable distribution of personal income within the faculty and to the question of 'reprisal' against a younger member of the faculty at the time of his doctoral examination.[35] On this latter point, the Secretary of the Belgrade University Committee of the League in 1966 made the cryptic observation that matters were 'not always as they should be' when it came to assessing doctoral work.[36]

The power of the senior staff over the junior was even seen on the vital question of housing; for example, an assistant bitterly complained in an article in *Univerzitet Danas* that he had waited to no avail to be allocated accommodation through the departmental housing commission while some of his senior colleagues were allocated a second and even a third apartment. (The latest apartment was apparently for the professor and his newest wife; previous wives lived in the other apartments.) This assistant maintained that the commission had no rules governing its work and gave no public explanation for its decisions: for the most part these decisions depended on 'interpersonal relations'.[37] Few people, he concluded, dared to offend powerful forces within the department by criticizing these procedures.[38]

Within university departments, then, relations were seen as being based on personal friendships or groupings, implicit threats and the like. In particular, junior staff members were seen as being greatly dependent on, and dominated by, the more senior members of staff. In this situation it was a hollow joke to talk of the development of collegial, self-managing relations.[39] Of course, one might say that such behaviour and attitudes are not unknown in our own universities or that much could be attributed to the particular circumstances of Yugoslavia in the current stage of economic development and so on. Nevertheless, the basic fact remains that, in the Yugoslav case, enormously ambitious principles were set out and constantly reiterated. In the first place, this served to highlight what might otherwise have been accepted as inevitable and natural shortcomings; and second, it served to arouse unrealizable expectations. The inevitable consequence was bitter disappointment or deep cynicism in the minds of many within the Yugoslav universities—not least, in the minds of the students.

Staff Attitudes as Demonstrated in the Struggle for Education Reform

The public image of university departments as often dominated by a narrow selfish group was reinforced in reports concerning 'education reform'. This reform,[40] advocated by the Yugoslav leadership, had a two-fold objective. First, instead of students receiving a relatively general education, it was urged that the curricula should be revised so that each student would be prepared for a specific task; in this manner the university would be transformed from its traditional role to one described as appropriate to the particular needs of a rapidly developing economy.

These changes would make possible the realization of the second objective: by sparing students much of what was termed obsolete, abstract and irrelevant material, it would be possible for them to graduate on schedule, thus ending the tremendous waste of resources inherent in the present situation.[41] For example, in 1967 it was estimated that only 12 to 13 per cent of all Yugoslav students graduated on schedule, while the equivalent figures for the USSR and the USA were reported as being 90 per cent and 80 per cent respectively.[42] This single example gives some indication of the enormity of the problem of poor results, which is considered in greater detail in chapter IV.

As early as 1949 the Central Committee of the Communist Party had outlined a plan for the reformulation of curricula. Although it was claimed that this plan had received 'broad approval', it was observed that it was not until the beginning of 1951 that serious efforts began towards its implementation. At first it was reported that revisions were merely of a formal character. Subsequently, however, following 'lively discussions' at the departments, significant progress was achieved. Among the participants in these discussions were 'prominent specialists' from outside the university, representatives of the student organization and of the staff party organization. Clearly this indicated an attempt to bring pressure to bear on the staff from a variety of sources. A review of these early efforts, published in *Borba* in July 1952, concluded by commenting that further efforts were still essential: this first effort had succeeded in areas such as the reduction of the number of compulsory courses; however, revisions of the actual content of particular subjects had scarcely begun.[43] Implicit in this account was the view that the staff needed assistance to enable them to perceive their particular work in the broader context of the needs of society.

Gradually, complaints of faculty resistance again became persistent. In fact, at the end of 1954 the Central Board of the Union of Students concluded that in a majority of cases staff bodies and individual professors had failed to implement the necessary reforms. The constituent student organizations were urged to continue their efforts in this struggle and, if necessary, to boycott particular classes.[44] But while occasional indications of progress were reported, it was increasingly maintained that much of the change was more apparent than real.[45]

By 1957 official dissatisfaction was widely evident.[46] It was insisted that the newly outlined programmes for the most part merely represented the 'legalization of the existing state of affairs', rather than an effort to deal with the basic cause of the 'chronic disease' of student failures.[47] It was maintained that many professors failed to give serious attention to this question and failed to understand the needs of the economy; instead of a serious effort to trim the curricula, the more usual practice was simply to add new material to the already overloaded courses.[48] The Secretary of the Serbian Central Committee of the League of Communists impatiently asked 'whether we are going to bring an end to this procrastination'.[49]

In 1959 the Federal People's Assembly reiterated the official view that the volume of material should be reduced to enable students to complete their studies in four years. (The major exception was medicine, which was planned for a five-year period.) The Assembly recommendations asked all universities and departments to make the necessary changes by the next academic year.[50] Some signs of progress were reported, but the old refrain again became the dominant theme. For example, a *Borba* article noted that 'unnecessary' discussions were still taking place on issues such as specialist versus generalist education which, it was claimed, had already been decided.[51] The President of the Serbian Executive Council was similarly forthright. Departments should be required to submit programmes of studies which would be limited to the stipulated period and if any protested that this was impossible, they must be told 'excuse us, but this cannot be so'. He expressed amazement that certain members of the faculty were continuing to state the opinion that it was unlikely that the set goals could be achieved.[52]

46

The general official line was that the proposed reforms had been buried by the university establishment determined to preserve its selfish privileges and it was 'not infrequent' for the university to be described as 'the citadel of conservatism and even of reaction'. It was maintained that many faculty members were apparently afraid that they might become superfluous if significant changes were secured; and that a number of professors set more store by not antagonizing their colleagues than by meeting their responsibilities to society.[53]

The lack of coordination between departments was frequently cited as a clear example of the failure to secure meaningful reform. The same subject was taught in many departments (for example, at Zagreb University, physics was taught in ten different departments, chemistry in eight, mathematics in twelve, and so on) and there was little cooperation between those teaching the same subject in these separate departments. Consequently, teaching, research and the development of the discipline were said to suffer.

Further, the promotion of an individual teaching a certain subject was decided by his departmental colleagues with little or no input from those capable of assessing the candidate's academic work.[54] Efforts to encourage the development of informal ties between these individuals were described as achieving little because of staff uninterest and resistance. A more dramatic proposal made by the Federal Secretariat for Education and Culture in 1965 was similarly buried under staff opposition. This proposal sought to reorganize departments so that all those teaching the one subject would be gathered in a single department.[55] Similarly, the moves to increase the power of the university over the separate departments, as a means of securing more effective cooperation and coordination, were blocked by those described as seeking to preserve their present privileges under the cloak of defending the self-managing rights of their collective;[56] in 1966 the Pro-Rector of Zagreb University maintained that efforts to solve the many common problems were hamstrung by the 'fetish' made of self-management at the departmental level.[57]

For their part, some members of faculty presented the view that improvements in material conditions represented the indispensable first step in a programme of reform,[58] that present proposals risked the danger of producing poorer graduates and weakening scientific work and that narrow specialization might in fact make the graduate less useful in the economy.[59]

These efforts of staff members to contest the value of the planned reforms were often dismissed as attempts to excuse their irresponsible failure to act in accord with the true interests of the community.[60] For example, a member of the Executive Committee of the Central Committee of the League observed in 1965 that constant demands were being made for increased funds, but that no mention was made of the responsibility to make the most effective use of the money provided.[61] In 1966 another League leader objected to the staff blaming inadequate resources for every failure, since such judgements belittled the efforts of

47

the working people and implied that society showed insufficient concern for education.[62]

As detailed in chapter IV of this study, the efforts designed to secure 'education reform' and, in particular, to reduce the enormous waste of resources caused by the high failure rate, were adjudged to have been unsuccessful. In that chapter, some consideration is given to the merits of the case for educational reform; the question has been raised at this point primarily to show the image presented of the staff as a group determined to preserve their own personal privileges regardless of the interests of society.

The Role of Students in the System of Self-Management

The preceding section has emphasized the public image of the faculty and of relations amongst staff members. This image, no doubt, had a direct influence on student beliefs concerning the efficacy of the system but it also related to the question of the extent of student participation in university and departmental management: did they play what they considered to be an appropriate role, were they uninterested or were they frustrated?

Although the self-managing system was ushered in with much fanfare concerning the rights of individuals to participate in the important decisions affecting their life, the role envisaged for students in the *General Law on Universities* of 1954 was exceedingly limited;[63] the students were ceded representation not within the framework of self-management but within the framework of social management; they were seen not as members of the work collective but as 'interested citizens'.[64]

The *Law* made a basic distinction between 'student' and 'university' affairs. Concerning the former, students were accorded some rights to participate in the management of institutions concerned with the health, social activities and material welfare of the students; concerning the latter, the rights of students were much more narrowly defined.[65] They were permitted to elect only a single student representative to the University Council, the highest organ of university government. This Council consisted of the Rector and Pro-Rector of the university, together with representatives of each department and a deliberately unspecified number elected by the People's Assembly of the Republic. The student representative was explicitly barred from voting on the confirmation of the election of staff, the election and removal of members of the disciplinary appeals court for staff members or the formulation of conclusions or recommendations pertaining to teaching plans.[66]

The other organ in university management was the University Board, consisting of the Rector, Pro-Rector and Deans of all the departments. This body had important administrative functions and at the same time functioned as a committee of the University Council by preparing proposals and reports for its consideration. It was stated that student representatives might attend meetings (but without voting rights) when

48

the agenda contained questions regarding the material position of students and what was vaguely described as 'other questions of interest to students'.[67] Apparently, both the framing of the agenda and the issuing of the invitation to the student representative was in the hands of the University Board itself. It is worth noting that in commenting on the draft law, the Central Committee of the Union of Students had urged that there should be greater precision in defining the rights of the student representatives;[68] it was claimed that the role of students should not depend on the whim or goodwill of individual professors but should be a right guaranteed by law.[69]

Within the organs of departmental management, student participation was similarly limited. On the Departmental Council student representation was again limited to one and this single student faced the departmental Dean and Pro-Dean and an unspecified number of members elected by the staff and the Republican People's Assembly of the Republic.[70] The *Law* stipulated that the student was not to vote on questions relating to the appointment of staff or on teaching plans.

The committee of this Council, known as the Departmental Board, also had the important function of preparing reports and proposals for the larger Departmental Council. Student representatives were entitled to attend meetings of the Board only when certain matters were being considered. These were practical questions of teaching and the implementation of the rules of study. These appeared to relate primarily to questions such as the definition of unsatisfactory progress and the number of attempts a student could have at the exam in a particular subject. The Union of Students' proposal that the student representative have the right to attend all meetings of the Board was denied.[71]

In addition, it was provided that a University Assembly should meet at least once a year. This Assembly was to consist of all the full-time staff, a 'designated number of university assistants', and a designated number of student representatives. In both cases the number was to be specified in the university statute which was formulated by the University Council. As later experience was to show, student representation remained small. Similarly, at the end of each academic year, a Departmental Assembly of staff was to be held.[72] The Departmental Board apparently determined student representation at this meeting, and again student representation remained low. Further, it seemed that these bodies 'for the most part' merely provided the opportunity for general discussion.[73]

The revised *General Law on Faculties* [*Departments*] *and Universities* promulgated in 1960 had little effect on the formal role of students.[74] The only significant changes were that student representation on the University Council was increased from one to three members and to 'at least two' members in the Departmental Council.[75]

No mention was made of student representation at the annual Departmental Assembly; however, there was other provision made for meetings of students and staff. These meetings were to be organized for a specific year of study,[76] and were intended primarily to give the opportunity for the exchange of views, but experience was to demonstrate that their effectiveness was limited since they met only briefly and infrequently, and lacked authority to make decisions.[77]

The only significant opportunities for student participation, therefore, were the University Council and Board and the Departmental Council and Board. The role of students in these bodies appeared to be even less significant in practice than the law provided. The consensus voiced by students, scholars and League officials blamed faculty resistance to the concept of student participation.

Many among the faculty were even prepared to state openly their misgivings concerning the value of student participation: the student's concern for the department was only short term and any interest students showed in academic matters was usually related to proposals aimed at reducing their own work load;[78] students lacked the essential understanding of the process of academic research—'one who begins to blow a trumpet does not immediately become . . . a musician and a composer';[79] it made as much sense for students to help decide problems within the university as it did for the apprentice to begin teaching the master,[80] for the patient to advise the doctor,[81] or even for the shoes in a shoe factory to participate in decision making;[82] students often failed to comprehend the important elements of the teaching process and consequently a few 'unsuccessful but vocal students can lead student "public opinion" astray'.[83]

As the Rector of the University of Ljubljana commented in 1963, students could not be described as members of the university's 'work collective'; rather than being in a 'work relationship', they were *preparing* themselves for work.[84] In a similar vein, the report of a staff committee at Sarajevo University, presented in 1967, referred to students as the 'beneficiaries' of services offered in their interests and in the interest of society by the staff; the participation of students in the management of the university must therefore reflect this basic distinction.[85]

The attitudes on which such views were based explain much of the difficulty student representatives experienced. The very first student representative on the Ljubljana University Council noted that 'individual professors' would privately seek to influence him on certain key issues.[86] Others complained that student representatives were 'not always invited' to the meetings of various organs of management, even when the law specifically provided that such invitations must be extended.[87] Others declared that the mere opportunity to be present did not necessarily result in meaningful participation, since staff members tended to denigrate student suggestions.[88] According to one Yugoslav scholar, there was often automatic opposition to student submissions regardless of their merit.[89]

It was maintained that often students were treated as some sort of 'external factor';[90] that is, as something that had to be taken into account when decisions were made, not as people who had the right to participate in the decision-making process. One student bitterly remarked that 'certain professors' thought it sufficient to have a single student representative on each self-managing body whose function would be to act as 'some sort of intelligence agent' and inform the other members of that body what the students were thinking and planning.[91]

The widespread attitude of denigration was generally blamed for rendering the present small representation merely symbolic.[92] This conclusion was supported by the results of a 1968 survey conducted by Krešimir Besić of student representatives on self-managing organs, which revealed that many felt it was imprudent to press their opinion in the face of staff opposition.[93]

The influence of these student representatives in such circumstances was weakened by several additional factors. First, the rights and status of student representatives were unclear; in particular, the topics on which they might speak or vote were never precisely defined.[94] Second, they were handicapped by the fact that there was no permanent student representation on the Departmental and University Boards, yet these were the bodies where most decisions were in fact reached—as a general rule the Departmental or University Council merely endorsed the recommendations of its particular Board.[95] Third and most important, much of their ineffectiveness stemmed from the failure of the Union of Students, described in more detail in chapter VI, to develop forms which would have enabled the representatives to maintain contact with the student body. Lacking such contact, these representatives came to be regarded simply as individuals and were treated accordingly; their impact would have been far greater if they had been seen as being supported and prodded by the mass of students.

In presenting the results of the survey mentioned above, of the opinions of a group of student representatives at various higher institutions in the city of Rijeka in Croatia, Bezić noted that of the seventy-two respondents, just on 32 per cent thought their position was optimal or fairly good, 38 per cent thought they had only 'some' opportunity to participate, while 31 per cent said they had little or no opportunity. The responses to an open-ended question in the same survey further demonstrated that many of these student representatives keenly felt their subordinate status. There were many who claimed that student representatives should be treated as equal members, that their submissions should be treated with respect, and that they should be permitted to be open and critical. In response to another open-ended question, just over *half* of the respondents felt that to be more effective, student representatives ought to be protected from the consequences that might stem from their frankness.[96]

Nevertheless, Bezić sought to use the results of his survey to show that, contrary to what he described as the prevailing opinion, there was basic agreement between staff and students on the question of student participation. He compared his data with that obtained by a colleague, Zvonimir Cviić, who surveyed some sixty-six members of staff.[97] The student representatives surveyed by Bezić were almost unanimous in describing student participation as 'useful' or 'desirable' and, what was more important, this favourable stance was shared by almost 84 per cent of the staff surveyed by Cviić. (Of the remaining staff, just on 15 per cent were neutral and only 1.2 per cent thought student participation harmful.) Bezić's judgement concerning the relatively close agreement between staff and students on the question of student participation was based primarily on the responses to this single question.[98]

However, in proceeding from vague generalities to more specific questions, this apparent agreement quickly disintegrated, at least on several important issues. This was shown by the responses presented in Table 2 to questions in both surveys asking to what extent students should participate in the decision-making process in various significant areas concerning the work of the institution.[99]

TABLE 2

A COMPARISON OF STAFF AND STUDENT ATTITUDES CONCERNING STUDENT PARTICIPATION
IN DECISION MAKING AT THE UNIVERSITY

	Students should help decide %	Students should be consulted %	Students should be able to give opinions %	Students should not participate %
Teaching plans and programmes				
Staff responses	3	5	60	32
Student responses	19	19	55	7
Organization, content, and conduct of exams				
Staff responses	3	6	58	33
Student responses	18	25	46	11
Staff selection and promotion				
Staff responses	8	2	25	65
Student responses	13	20	39	28

Sources: Based on Krešimir Besić, 'Stavovi studenata o vaspitnoj ulozi u samoupravnim organima visokoškolskih ustanova' (Views of students on the educational role of self-managing bodies of schools for higher education), *Univerzitet Danas,* vol. ix, no. 7 (1968), p. 79; and Zvonimir Cviić, 'Stavovi visokoškolskih nastavnika o ulozi studenata u organima samoupravljanja' (Views of teachers in tertiary institutions on the role of students in self-managing bodies), *Univerzitet Danas,* vol. vii, no. 7 (1966), pp. 68, 69.

As was pointed out, the proportion of student representatives seeking to decide or be consulted on these basic questions was 'unexpectedly small';[100] nevertheless, significant differences between faculty and student views clearly existed. On these three selected, central topics, the proportion of student representatives who said either that students should help decide or that they should be consulted was more than three times the proportion of staff; conversely, the proportion of staff opposed to student participation was more than twice the proportion of student representatives. Furthermore, student responses to other questions cited earlier demonstrated their belief that, while the staff might express

52

verbal support of student participation, in practice they failed to accord student representatives their basic right to participate freely and frankly, and without fear of reprisal.

Even in areas not directly touching on faculty prerogatives, such as the administration of student hostels, the actual role of students in self-management was extremely limited. While there was some variation in the organizational framework of student hostels, the prevailing pattern was one in which students had a significant voice only on committees concerned with discipline, admissions, and with social and recreational activities;[101] on the committees concerned with the business side of the hostel, student representatives were in a minority,[102] and the typical manager of a student hostel was frequently described as an absolutist, who dominated decision making on all significant topics.[103] In addition, it was not unknown for some members of the hostel management committee to be brought under the manager's control, through the payment of 'honoraria', the provision of food without charge, and the like.[104]

However, the major problem concerning the development of self-management in the hostels derived principally from the fact that financial exigencies severely limited the scope of decision making.[105] These institutions limped from one financial year to the next, being saved only by external subsidies. Consequently, it was widely acknowledged that it was impossible to talk of 'self' management since the role of the self-managing organs in these straitened financial circumstances was merely to make the best use of limited resources.[106]

This meant that students could do little within the self-managing organs concerning their actual living conditions, except possibly to discipline a noisy occupant,[107] but they did not seem prepared to do even that. For example, a researcher who studied the situation in hostels in the Serbian town of Novi Sad maintained that a collective spirit based on socialist morality was insufficiently developed. A significant group of students had too little regard for the rights of others; some held what was described as a 'liberal, anarchistic view of personal freedom', many were withdrawn, hypocritical, untidy, sceptical, lacking in enthusiasm and the like, and most failed to contribute to efforts to improve matters. In such a situation, he concluded, the efforts of a few individuals to create a better atmosphere inevitably had poor results.[108]

In fairness to the students, however, most hostels were such as to make it unlikely that any efforts of the residents could lead to a significant improvement. Their conditions, as detailed in chapter V, were of gross overcrowding and inadequate or even non-existent recreational or study facilities. Inevitably, life was noisy, congested and frustrating; that is, conditions were not conducive to study, to high morale or to the development of a healthy, collective spirit.

Less than two months before the June events, the Secretary of the Croatian League of Communists expressed the view that students had 'never been in a more inferior position'.[109] An article in *Komunist*, published in May 1968, pointed out that the students studied and were examined in the area of self-management, but in practice they saw very little of it.[110] A few days later, Tito remarked that the young rightly sought their rights in the area of self-management but that 'we have not done much' toward that goal; it was important to make greater efforts to involve the young in 'our social life with . . . full responsibility'.[111]

The consequence of this denial of the right to participate as equals was described as a major cause of the widespread 'passivity and resignation' among the young intellectuals. Indeed, it was observed that students frequently sought to avoid the dubious honour of being chosen as a student representative.[112] Concern was expressed at the ever present risk that the students' attitude might turn from withdrawal to actions which 'would come to be headed (as experience has shown) by negative forces in society'.[113]

The latter clearly alluded to the tendency for students to follow the path of political pressure, through petitions, delegations or threats of demonstrations. As an article in the *Yugoslav Student News,* published in 1958, discreetly noted, there were 'some cases' where problems reached a 'critical' point and were raised by students in a 'very exacerbated way'.[114] In 1959, for example, Zagreb University students greatly embarrassed Yugoslav authorities by their street demonstration protesting poor living conditions.[115] As the President of Union of Students observed just prior to the June events, many regarded the students as 'troublesome', but failed to understand the causes of student disquiet.[116]

Such demands and protests were not directed against the self-managing bodies, but rather were designed to influence the external state and community authorities which had the responsibility of deciding the amount of the subsidy to be paid to the student institutions. The decisions of these bodies rested on their assessment of several interrelated factors: they considered what was justified, what could be afforded and no doubt what was necessary to dampen student unrest. The main point, however, is that the crucial decisions relating to these institutions were not reached by the self-managing organs, but instead, by state and community authorities in response to the needs, requests and implied or actual threats of the student body.

What then can be said of the actual role of students in self-management? According to several observers, self-management was a clear fiction as far as students were concerned; there may have been some student representatives on certain bodies but in practice their influence was extremely limited; indeed, their significance is demonstrated by the fact that the mass of students was scarcely aware of their existence,[117] and when effective action was sought, the avenue used was direct approach to external authorities.

At the same time, however, the student was constantly bombarded with declamations asserting the right of all Yugoslav citizens, including the young, to effective participation; indeed, it could be argued that student frustrations on this matter were not so much a response to their inferior position, but a response to their inferior position as compared with that promised in the rhetoric.

Sometimes the ideal was described as if it were the reality. Thus an article in *Youth Life* in 1965 proclaimed that significant progress in the development of student rights in the self-managing system had been achieved. Student representatives 'enjoy the same status' as other representatives in the University and Departmental Councils of management; and the mass meetings of those students and staff concerned with a particular year of study provided an additional opportunity for professors and students to meet on 'equal terms'.[118]

The importance of student participation was constantly reiterated on a variety of grounds. First, it was of educational value to involve the students in the decision-making process; those who would deny students the opportunity to participate had an outmoded view of the student as merely 'a passive object of cultivation'.[119] Second, participation was seen as being of even greater significance in the process of socialist education. It was a misconception to believe that political education could be successful if kept within the framework of explanation and mere instruction; indeed, participation, as noted earlier, was described as the most effective means of developing a responsible outlook among students, of eliminating certain 'negative' trends, and of preparing the future experts to take their places in the contemporary self-managing society.[120] Third, it was maintained that student participation was valuable for the university as a whole; in particular, student pressure could help overcome the resistance of staff to reform.[121]

Finally, it was insisted that students should be allowed to participate because it was their right—the ideals and the realities of the contemporary society demanded that the students should be treated with respect. The university could not remain as a relic of an earlier age; rather, its internal structure and relationships must accord with developments in the broader society.[122] In this connection it is significant that, during the June events, some claims were made which directly challenged the assumptions on which, for example, the provisions of the university laws of 1955 and 1960 concerning student participation appear to have been based. Hitherto these axioms had scarcely been questioned, but now the demand was not that the students be regarded as some special, temporary, less experienced and less mature category at the university, but that they be regarded as 'workers'.[123] This simple statement had profound implications. It denied the relevance of all arguments against student participation based on their lack of expertise, experience, capacity, and the like. In the realm of self-management in a factory, the basic principle was that all workers, regardless of qualification or rank, had the right to participate as equals in the management of the enterprise. Indeed, the very system of self-management, as applied in the economy, was an effort to ensure the substitution of industrial democracy for the pattern of hierarchical control deriving from notions of variations in the capacity of personnel within the enterprise. Clearly, then, the rhetoric of self-management had the effect of arousing expectations and highlighting the deficiencies of the existing situation.

To this point the present chapter has sought to demonstrate that relations within the faculty fell far short of the high ideals of the system of self-management and that the mass of students was totally excluded from effective participation in the decision-making bodies of the university. Some of the consequences of this on student attitudes have been alluded to, but before any less tentative conclusions can be drawn it is necessary to examine the role of communists within the university. Their attitudes toward self-management, and in particular towards student participation, as well as their own conception of their role as communists, would inevitably have a profound effect on university developments and at the same time on student attitudes towards the system as a whole.

THE ROLE OF FACULTY COMMUNISTS

Faculty Communists and 'Ideological Deviation'

Much of the blame for the unsatisfactory development of self-management was attributed to the members of the League within the university, and particularly to those on the faculty. (The role of communist students will be considered in chapter VI.) With the avowed rejection of the administrative model of socialism in favour of self-management, individual communists were no longer merely to instruct and direct; rather, they were to guide and inspire the members of the various self-managing bodies to follow the path of socialist development. This meant they had the responsibility to press for the development of comradely, self-managing relations and to urge all members of the university community to recognize their responsibilities to the broad, socialist society.

As understood by the League leadership, consideration of society's interests meant in part that individual communists were to fight for effective education reform, to oppose 'hostile' forces, to encourage ideological education, and to ensure that members of the university community appreciated the sacrifices the 'working people' were making to support the university and understood that additional resources could not readily be provided. The implicit general rule was that they were to help secure those changes which the League leadership considered possible and necessary, and to explain why certain other goals were unattainable.[124]

Not surprisingly, the behaviour of many communists was far from what the leadership could regard as exemplary. Many failed to help develop the proper ideological climate. In an address to the 1952 Party Congress, one leader observed that 'numerous Party members' at the university failed to recognize that a vigorous struggle must be waged against the 'enemies of socialism', against the 'saboteurs' of progress. It was impossible to debate with these individuals in an atmosphere of collegiality; rather, they 'must be isolated and beaten ruthlessly'.[125]

According to Djurica Jojkić, Secretary of the Belgrade Committee of the League of Communists in 1955, 'certain' basic League organizations at the university actually resisted programmes for ideological education. Jojkić claimed that some sought to justify their opposition as follows:

> We are training to become artists. Our teaching is organized on a Marxist basis, we absorb Marxism and materialism through our lessons. It is essential for Communists that they should be properly oriented ideologically but we as artists will never find ourselves in the position of having to concern ourselves with current political problems or of having to work in organizations of social administration.[126]

Reportedly, they also expressed the view that the insistence of the University Committee of the League on the organization of lectures on current political and economic problems was senseless. Jojkić bluntly stated that such concepts ran counter to Marxist teachings and to the policy of the League of Communists; the creative worker had obligations to the community and could not separate his socialist convictions from his creative work. Many 'otherwise fine young men' thought it was 'Stalinist' to argue that art should have direction and social content, and despite efforts to explain this matter it was clear that 'some comrades' remained unconvinced. From the perspective of the Yugoslav leadership it was especially serious that the appropriate role was unclear to individual communists, that is, unclear to those responsible for leading the struggle against what were described as negative tendencies within the university.[127]

Similarly, Tito commented in 1956 that 'some' communists were misled and drew incorrect conclusions from the fact that Yugoslav society had chosen a path of democratic development; they interpreted this to mean that they should remain silent when some reactionary 'wrongly and unjustly' criticized contemporary developments. On the contrary, insisted Tito, they must be prepared to speak, and even be prepared to intervene, in what some termed internal matters; interference to expose and correct various negative tendencies was, he stated, a positive and democratic act.[128]

It was also emphasized that 'some' communists mistakenly believed that the youth, simply because they were living in a socialist society, would automatically become imbued with socialist values. This overlooked the fact that there still existed strong hostile forces which could negatively affect the young. The forces of the old regime, primarily because they were finally vanishing and because they felt their approaching demise, offered a tenacious resistance. And, of course, other harmful influences were present. The League, in particular, must strive to protect the young from these negative influences. The present period, therefore, was one in which there was and had to be a vigorous struggle for the affirmation of socialist conceptions in all spheres of life.[129]

A *Borba* article in 1956 praised the work of the 'progressive' forces at Zagreb University, but warned against the 'widespread' tendency among communists to tolerate certain anti-socialist views and other 'non-sense'.[130] At a 1956 meeting of the Slovenian Central Committee of the League, surprise was expressed that 'our Communist intellectuals' provided such little opposition to those within the university who cast doubts on the capacity of workers within the general self-managing system.[131]

The comprehensive and significant Programme of the League of Communists (adopted in 1958) loudly bemoaned the failure of individual communists to struggle against 'attempts to entrench, under the label of freedom of science and art, reactionary and anti-socialist opinions' and attempts to 'undermine the moral political foundations of socialist society'.[132] Elsewhere in the Programme this basic view was reiterated: communists must

> with determination, oppose every conscious or unconscious attempt
> ... to undermine, in the name of abstract formulas of freedom and
> democracy, the concrete endeavours of socialist forces—endeavours
> which through construction of socialism aim at securing [the]
> constant advance of real democracy and [the] constant widening of
> the real freedom and creativeness of man.[133]

In this vein, the Secretary of the Belgrade University Committee of the League in 1964 criticized the tendency for the basic organizations of the League to discuss secondary problems rather than those of primary importance, such as the analysis of the scientific work of professors. He insisted that the view that such work was the individual's exclusive personal concern must be resolutely opposed.[134] Similarly, the Secretary of the Ljubljana University Committee of the League in 1967 urged greater alertness on the part of communists against those elements which sought to mislead 'our insufficiently conscious people'.[135]

Reports of events at Sarajevo University in 1967 also illustrate the attitudes of individual communists at the university concerning their 'responsibilities'. A Dr Muhamed Filipović of the Philosophy Department had written some articles described in the press as chauvinistic and anti-socialist. The basic League organization in the Philosophy Department considered these criticisms, but declined to censure Filipović. As for the University Committee of the League, it simply failed to take any action, despite what the President of the Central Committee of the League for the Republic of Bosnia and Hercegovina described as the 'public reaction' and press comment relating to these articles. Apparently it was only after direct pressure from League authorities outside the university that a session of the University Committee of the League was called. Even then, the meeting had to be delayed until, after some 'difficulty', a quorum was secured.[136] The Committee did, eventually, condemn the basic League organization in the Philosophy Department for its failure to perceive the harmful consequences of the articles in question and described the organization as not being 'ideologically mature'.[137] It was therefore decided to disband this basic organization.[138] The principal effect of this action was that the University Committee could begin a consideration of each member of the former organization to determine whether he or she would be permitted to remain in the League.[139]

The President of the Republican Central Committee of the League observed that 'certain people' considered that the action of the League in this matter was an impermissible interference with academic freedom. However, he was adamant that one should not be intimidated by the label of academic freedom; rather, one had the solemn responsibility to examine carefully the 'political essence' of such work.[140]

As an article in *Oslobodjenje Nedelje* declared, the League had never obstructed 'real science' but rather, had positively encouraged creative activity; indeed, it continued, the League's Programme actually included a provision stating that 'science is its own judge'. At the same time, however, it was imperative that the League should wage a resolute struggle against 'various kinds of unscientific theories' and against the 'misuse of science for political purposes'.[141]

As the preceding suggests, the failure of communists to work enthusiastically for the creation of the 'proper' ideological climate was not the only problem. Besides simply resisting the leadership's notions in this regard, there were also signs of rival ideological positions.

The most serious case of what the Yugoslav leadership saw as ideological deviation was presented by those academics associated with the journal *Praxis*. Their most striking characteristics were their direct questioning of the fundamental assumptions of the Yugoslav system, their reference to some of the more serious faults of contemporary life to bolster their case, and their appeal to the latent idealism of a significant number at the university, particularly among the young. They urged forthright criticism 'of all that exists',[142] but above all, they questioned what amounted to the claim of final authority made by the League leadership. In their view, the leaders could not be exempted from critical appraisal—indeed, because of their power over society and because the Yugoslav system had advanced onto new and difficult paths, it behoved the philosopher to give especial attention to the leaders' work.[143]

According to Professor Rudi Supek, vigorous and free theoretical debate and criticism were essential; those who sought to stifle such debate acted as though it was 'no longer the case of "theory being the guide to action" [but] rather that "action has become the guide to theory"'.[144] However a critical approach was more than merely useful. Another prominent member of the *Praxis* group, Professor Gajo Petrović, asserted that it was one of the essential attributes of a truly 'human' being; among other things, a man is a man to the extent to which he adopts a 'critical attitude toward the society in which he lives, towards other people and towards his very self'. Without such a questioning attitude he exists at the level of 'beasts, machines or robots'.[145]

That is, this group of communists within the university was far from seeing its duty as merely being to implement the policy enunciated by the League leadership. Not surprisingly, the leadership did not welcome such an attitude. In an address to the Central Committee in 1966, Tito remarked that many of the views expressed in *Praxis* 'have nothing in common with the way we look upon things'. There has been, he continued, 'a lack of vigilance on our part' and a failure to fight such deviations.[146] Official spokesmen sought to distinguish between constructive and destructive criticism. The former was described as important and essential, while the latter was of a type which could result in the working people doubting their leaders and in a general demoralization and disorientation.[147] Each member of the League had the duty to accept what were termed the basic principles of League policy and to observe the 'necessary' limits on debate; only in this manner would the League be capable of effective action.[148] As Mika Tripalo explained the matter in 1967, the League 'must be a more centralist organization than is the system of self-management'. It 'cannot be constituted on the basis of self-management, because in that case it would not be necessary at all'. Those who joined the League accepted the obligation to assist in formulation of policy, but at the same time they accepted the responsibility to help implement this policy when it was formulated. Thus, they were individuals who 'are ready to give up one part of their "citizens' rights" because they are ready to comply with the decisions taken by the majority'.[149]

The view of the *Praxis* group, that mere loyalty to the League could in fact be dangerous, was, therefore, denied, and the members of the group were condemned for their failure to observe what was termed the discipline incumbent on members of the League. Their position was described as amounting to the demand to have an opposition within the Yugoslav political system, a demand for more than one party, and a claim to usurp the authority of what was referred to as the 'working class'. *Praxis* criticisms of certain contemporary developments and of certain policies of the League leadership were attacked as demonstrating their contempt for the 'workers' and their desire to wrest power from the working class; those associated with *Praxis* professed a concern for the worker and for freedom and humanism, but, or so it was urged, this apparent concern was designed to mask their doubts concerning the capacity of the 'workers' to rule.[150]

As noted in the introduction, the *Praxis* group was especially concerned regarding the consequences of linking the self-managing system to a market economy. Their stress on the problem of integrating the decisions of the separate collectives into a cohesive plan which had regard for the interests and needs of the community as a whole was described as signifying opposition to the democratization of Yugoslav society and support for a return to the era of administrative socialism where one small group decided all—only instead of a political bureaucracy, they would substitute the rule of philosophers![151] A *Vjesnik* article maintained that even with the best of intentions, this would be more dangerous than the rule of bureaucrats, since the arrogance of intellectuals was untempered by knowledge of practical realities; they were philosophers 'separated from life'.[152] Despite such imputations, it is difficult to perceive in the work of the *Praxis* group an ambition for actual power. Indeed, a basic premise appeared to be an emphasis on the separation of the philosopher/critic from government, that is, a separation of the functions of 'priest' and 'king'.[153]

Their argument that linking self-management to the market economy and to the profit motive involved danger to socialist values was similarly attacked. The *Praxis* group questioned the official contention that this system inevitably made the individual more of a man. Indeed, in their view, the linking of this system to the market economy and to considerations of profit made the individual less of a man. Self-management in this form focussed on only one facet of man's existence and encouraged, despite all the official explanations, consideration of one's own personal interest to the neglect of the interests of the socialist community; indeed, the gross inequalities of wealth in the contemporary society had already begun to erode socialist values.[154] The latter opinion was vigorously condemned as an endeavour to turn valid criticisms of unjustified earnings and 'excessive social inequality in the direction of a primitive levelling' of incomes.[155] With biting sarcasm they were referred to as those who offered the promise of a 'regimented and ascetic communism in which everybody would have his handful of rice',[156] and as the group which had 'poverty as its platform'.[157] The *Praxis* response was to point out that it was not asceticism they sought, but simply a little modesty.[158]

Despite the vigour of the attacks made on it, the *Praxis* group resolutely defended itself. Thus Petrović cited remarks made by Tito concerning freedom of expression: in 1945 Tito had spoken of the right of people to speak openly, and had gone on to emphasize that these were not to be construed as mere empty words; there must be no fear that 'someone might come to you and tell you that you haven't this right and will put you in jail'; anyone who threatens another's basic right to speak freely will himself be punished. Similarly, Petrović pointed to a statement of Tito in 1965 stressing that man was a subject and not an object;[159] indeed, it could be urged that such an attitude was a basic principle of the system of self-management.

Concerning the distinction made between constructive and destructive criticism, Petrović firmly insisted that all criticism was at once constructive and destructive, and that it was therefore impossible to lay down rules which would distinguish one from the other.[160] And he condemned those who maintained that in particular situations a boldly critical outlook was progressive, but who averred that in contemporary Yugoslavia such an outlook had an 'anti-socialist and non-Marxist character'.[161]

With similar frankness, Supek stated that there were those in positions of responsibility who sought to frighten their critics, often by such Stalinist methods as that of 'political insinuation', by the 'hunt for a word or position which can be stretched' to accord with something quite different from what was intended.[162]

For the purpose of the present study, the ideas of the members of this group highlight certain important features of self-management; further, they influenced the views expressed during the June events. A vital question, however, is whether the mass of students saw them primarily as critics of some of society's worst abuses or whether the bulk of the student body appreciated their position concerning the nature of the current policies and role of the League leadership. That is, did they reach the student body in the sense of involving them in their theoretical critique of the present system? The final chapter endeavours to take up these questions.

It is hoped that these examples have demonstrated that communists at the university could not be regarded as a disciplined group resolutely determined to implement League policy. Attention has been given to signs of what was termed local nationalism or chauvinism, to cases of failure to follow the leadership's demand for active opposition to negative influences and even to the case of the criticism of many of the basic principles of the Yugoslav system.

Faculty Communists and the Development of Self-Management

In addition to these differences of opinion on ideological issues, the effectiveness of communists within the university was seriously affected by other factors.

In the first place, many were described as nominal members who often failed even to attend meetings of the League or of self-managing organs. For example, a 1957 report on the activity of communists at Belgrade University indicated that almost one-third failed to attend League meetings.[163] Similarly, in 1964 the Secretary of the Belgrade University Committee of the League complained that most members were passive and failed to learn what had been decided and what had to be done.[164] Another League official at Belgrade University commented in 1968 that the only obligation recognized by many members was the payment of their dues. Indeed, meetings of the League organizations were frequently postponed for lack of a quorum.[165]

Part of this passivity was adjudged to be the consequence of the onerous responsibilities placed on individual communists by the self-managing system.[166] According to an official of the League at Zagreb University, the League 'is not only a League of good people, it is that, but a League of people who wish to change the world and create conditions so that all will be good'.[167] A communist was expected to set an example to his colleagues both as a scholar and a teacher. However, conscientious work in these areas could not excuse inactivity in the socio-political sphere—the duty of a communist was to study the party press and basic works on Marxism[168] and work for the development of a healthy, self-management atmosphere.

Something of the dilemma facing conscientious members of the League can be discerned in a report presented to the Eighth Congress of the League of Communists in 1964 which insisted that the individual communist was required to oppose both bureaucratic and pseudo-liberal views of the role of the League. The former position threatened 'the social role and democratic rights of the working people', while the latter 'underrated and undermined the leading ideological-political and guiding role' of the League. The individual communist no longer simply transmitted party decisions to the non-party organ, but was required to mobilize the 'subjective forces' in the particular organization, in order that it may effect its own development into an independent, self-managing body. At the same time, however, he was required to strengthen feelings of 'responsibility' within the organization.[169] This meant that while the individual communist was obliged to respect the democratic rights of the members of a particular collective, he was also obliged to ensure that the decisions reached by the collective were 'responsible'.

This same report criticized those basic League organizations which merely 'discussed' matters instead of 'formulating precise decisions and organizing concrete action', checking that these decisions were implemented or analysing the causes of failure; at the same time, however, the article condemned those basic organizations which reached decisions in 'more or less closed circles', and which thus sometimes reduced the work of non-League organizations to 'a mere formality'.[170]

Almost the same language was used by a speaker at the Eighth Congress of the League of Communists in Serbia, when he claimed that there existed at the university two extreme and erroneous views concerning the role of the League. At one extreme the 'demobilization' of the League was urged on the grounds that self-management meant that communists 'must not interfere with or hamper self-managing bodies'; the other view was that communists were 'responsible for all decisions and hence that they must keep a firm hand on matters'.[171] Obviously, such vague statements of principle were impossible for individual communists to apply with any confidence.

The task of guiding and inspiring was far more difficult than simply transmitting directives; it involved diligence, imagination, courage, selflessness and constant criticism and self-criticism. As the writer of a 1966 *Komunist* article observed, the high demands of active membership stimulated feelings of inadequacy and self-doubt, and, as a consequence, passivity. To support this conclusion, reference was made to a poll among communists at the University of Ljubljana which demonstrated a considerable lack of self-confidence and a desire for the enunciation of clear, unambiguous directives. Additional evidence for the view was found in the statements of those leaving the ranks of the League of Communists; with increasing frequency individuals were described as expressing doubts concerning their own maturity and ability in regard to the responsibility of League membership.[172]

Another reason for this lack of involvement was the fact that many communists were described as primarily concerned with their own interests rather than the interests of the community. An article in *Borba* in 1966 concluded that such changes as did occur within the university frequently resulted from administrative and legislative decisions made outside the university rather than from the guidance and inspiration of communists within the university.[173] Conscientious activity meant the expenditure of much time, together with the risk of creating bitter enemies among colleagues; often the desire to protect one's own interests and to avoid unpleasantness led to the situation where many discussions and conclusions of the basic League organizations amounted to no more than a meaningless recitation of generalities.[174]

Numerous articles in the press contended that communists avoided becoming involved in discussions of basic questions unless their own particular personal interests were involved.[175] Indeed, those serious differences which did occur within League organizations were described as often relating to the struggle for position and privilege.[176] Rather than setting an example of selflessness, it was observed that individual communists, 'although not sufficiently capable', often demanded promotion as their right. Such demands often led to the withdrawal of 'better candidates' from the competition for a particular post.[177] It was absurd to expect that such organizations would be in the vanguard of the movement towards self-management and difficult to talk of the moral authority of communists.[178] Indeed, instead of pressing for the development of the system of self-management, some communists were described as working to subvert it in order to preserve both their power and status.[179] Instead of functioning solely as an ideological political force, it was maintained that university *aktivs* of the League sought to monopolize administrative authority for their own ends and that as a consequence the work of the self-managing organ was 'sometimes reduced to a mere formality'.[180]

As the principal speaker to the 1964 Conference of the Zagreb University League of Communists emphasized, the achievement of communists at the university left much to be desired:

> Almost invariably our conclusions receive unanimous support. However, when it comes to their implementation in practice . . . when action or even struggle is required to give effect to these stands, when it is a question of action and effort on the part of each individual communist, or when the matter relates to his own personal interests, very little or even nothing is left of that generally agreed on position.[181]

It was also claimed that to preserve their privileged position, communists showed a marked reluctance to admit new members to the basic organizations of the League, although there were many who had 'long ago' proved themselves worthy of membership.[182]

The fact that the young were not 'fully included in the self-management process' was claimed to be in part due to the indifference and even resistance on the part of individual communists.[183] The relationship between staff and student communists further illustrated this—for the most part they were organized in separate rather than integrated organizations,[184] and on the occasions that they came together the faculty members tended to dominate.[185] That is, the organizations of the

League within the university, especially of the staff, tended to reflect the attitudes towards the young typical of the wider university community.

Just prior to the June events, the Secretary of the Belgrade University Committee of the League had noted that frequently the League was by-passed by the spontaneous activity of groups and individuals. The failure of the League to involve itself in the problems of the university meant it was often found at the tail of events rather than playing a leading role. He admitted that there was 'some truth' in the opinion that the League was 'not revolutionary enough'.[186] As an article in *Student* expressed it, in the eyes of many, the communist organization at the university was irrelevant or a hindrance to the process of change, rather than a driving, progressive force.[187]

His successor, Professor Branko Pribićević, commented that the June events showed that communists within the university could not regain the initiative nor have a decisive influence on developments, unless they dealt with basic questions and unless they formulated clear and definite steps toward their goals:[188] communists must lead the struggle against 'inequality, hierarchy and bureaucracy'[189] within the university and help secure for students and all staff a 'decisive influence' on the conditions of their life.[190] In the past, Pribićević continued, there had been many general and 'frequently simply rhetorical statements' concerning the importance and value of reform, but, in concrete terms, little actual progress was apparent and little actual commitment was demonstrated. Following this ringing declaration concerning the right of students, and on the need to seize the initiative by elaborating the steps toward this goal, Pribićević proceeded to warn against 'vulgarizations' in developing new relationships between faculty and students. In particular, 'equality of status' did not mean that their roles within the university organs could be equal.[191]

Pribićević noted that the discussions of change sometimes revealed dramatically differing conceptions, ranging from those who felt that a small change in emphasis was sufficient, to those who totally rejected the present system and denied that it could be reformed.[192] With the latter, Pribićević was apparently referring to those sympathetic to, or directly connected with, the *Praxis* position. 'It is equally unacceptable to us to hide all weaknesses as it is cheap and demagogic to dismiss all that we have achieved in the last two and a half decades.'[193] Therefore, Pribićević urged such reform as would secure radical change in the 'position, structure, function, internal relations and the methods of accomplishing the basic tasks of education', but which would not involve 'rejecting the present system "without a trace"'. What was required was a 'critical, but not a negative', attitude toward the present system; it was necessary to be 'rigorous and critical but at the same time objective and responsible'.[194] The members of the League, he continued, had the 'very responsible' duty to analyse present problems, to formulate concrete goals and to outline the methods by which these goals would be achieved. Once this had been done, it was necessary for all to work in unison for the realization of these decisions.[195]

Obviously, despite Pribićević's avowed hopes, it was unrealistic to expect that the communists within the university could come together and seize the initiative on the complex range of university problems. The basic organizations encompassed members with various motivations and with often sharply divergent views. To return to the question of self-management as an example, it was clear that many communists shared the reservations of many of their non-communist colleagues concerning expanded student participation; indeed, a significant number were opposed to any change in the present pattern of relations at the university. Further, there can be no doubt that Pribićević's guiding principles would be interpreted by various individuals so as to conform to their own particular views and interests. Indeed, his attack on 'simply rhetorical statements' sounded very much like a rhetorical statement itself.

CONCLUSION

The bold concept of self-management formed the basis of the ideological education of the Yugoslav youth. It was proudly taught as the system in which all men would be treated with respect, and in which they would find greater fulfilment, both by having the opportunity to determine their own lives and by being able to join with their fellows in the mutually enriching task of constructing a new society. In its highest form, self-management was the system in which the interests of the individual, the particular group and the broad socialist community could be harmoniously reconciled.

It is scarcely surprising that Yugoslav society failed to attain these high ideals. But, especially from the point of view of the young who had often gained an idealized picture of the system, the gulf between rhetoric and reality was monumental.

With self-management described as the central core of the Yugoslav system, and with such obvious shortcomings in practice, it is only to be expected that much of the student rhetoric during the June events related to this question. This emphasis could lead to the conclusion that this was the vital issue among the student body and that the demonstrations were primarily an expression of the frustration which stemmed from the failure to develop this new form. Indeed, as has been noted, the official explanation was that the denial of student rights in the area of self-management was a major cause of student resentment; the young had been seeking to participate in the processes of self-management but had been consistently frustrated.[196] Further, the official line emphasized that the Yugoslav student unrest differed fundamentally from foreign student disturbances: in those countries the students were seeking to overthrow the prevailing system, whereas in Yugoslavia the students were protesting the slow progress towards the universally accepted goals of the society, of which self-management was the most important.

Further, the usual pattern of passivity noted among students, and their normal lack of interest in the work of their student representatives and in self-management, was explained by some Yugoslav commentators as stemming from the students' conviction that no opportunity existed for what one could term 'meaningful participation'. That is, it was implied that a genuine desire for meaningful participation existed but that it had been stifled by unfavourable circumstances.

On the other hand, it could be maintained that it is important not to exaggerate student concern on this question of self-management since many students may have been primarily preoccupied with their personal affairs rather than with political activity, or were cynical when it came to politics. If this were so, then it might be argued that for most students during the June events, the discussion of the failure of self-management may have been important primarily in that it provided a convenient and respectable framework in which general feelings of frustration, deriving from other student problems, could be articulated. Further consideration is given to this question in the concluding chapter.

Chapter IV

THE ACADEMIC ENVIRONMENT

UNIVERSITY EXPANSION AND ITS RESULTS

Of all the achievements of the communist system in Yugoslavia, one of the most spectacular is the extraordinary growth in the number and size of universities, a growth which to Yugoslav spokesmen is at once the foundation of the new society and a graphic symbol of the destruction of the former backward, static and unequal order. The aim of the present chapter is to outline and assess this achievement.

Officially it was explained that in pre-war Yugoslavia the university served primarily as a kind of finishing school for the children of a privileged few and provided the small number of qualified men needed to maintain the narrow professional and administrative stratum in what was essentially a peasant society; university graduates formed a part of the small, cohesive group which dominated and exploited the mass of the people. This small, 'classical' university system was seen as being inappropriate to the demands of the new order. In particular, it was urged that the universities had to be expanded to provide the number of experts needed for the ambitious programme of development. However, the objective was not merely economic growth; the expansion of educational opportunity was also intended to smash the power of the old élite and replace it with a socialist intelligentsia rooted in the working class.[1]

The desire for university education in the community was awakened or at least greatly stimulated by official statements which emphasized the right of every citizen to enrol under equal conditions, and which presented university studies as the means through which the young could prepare themselves to become useful, indeed vital, members of the new society.[2] These declarations were given practical support by the increase in the number of university places, the opening of new university departments in regional centres throughout the country, the dramatic easing of regulations governing university enrolment, the expansion of scholarship opportunities, the provision of subsidized student housing and restaurants, the development of the secondary school network, and the like.

The statistics shown in Table 3 indicate the success of this policy of university expansion.[3] Taking the first post-war year (1945/46) as the base, the increase in the number of students in the next ten years was almost three-fold, the increase in twenty years was five-fold and the increase in twenty-three years, as the total number of students soared

TABLE 3

UNIVERSITY EXPANSION

	Number of University Departments	Total Students in University Departments
1938/39	18	15,505
1945/46	19	21,195
1955/56	45	60,559
1965/66	96	107,329
1968/69	100	140,647
1974/75	141	238,006

Sources: Federal Council for Statistics, *Jugoslavija 1945-1964, Statistički Pregled* (Yugoslavia 1945-1964, Statistical Review) (Belgrade, [1964]), p. 299; *Statistički Godišnjak* SFRJ, 1969 (statistical Yearbook FPRY, 1969) (Belgrade, 1969), p. 292; and *Statistički Godišnjak SFRJ, 1975* (Belgrade, 1975), p. 330; Miodrag Milenović, 'Dinamika razvoja visokog školstva i zapošljavanja diplomiranih studenata' (The dynamics of the development of higher education and the employment of graduates), *Ideje,* vol. i, no. 2 (1970), pp. 238, 240.

from 21,195 to 140,647, was almost seven-fold. (Incidentally, the figures cited for 1974/75 demonstrate that the rapid rate of expansion has been maintained—in just under thirty years student numbers have increased more than ten times.) This success prompted the proud claim that the proportion of young people at university in Yugoslavia was amongst the highest in the world.[4]

In at least one important area, therefore, the Yugoslav leadership achieved its aim. However, in most other areas it seems clear that the achievements were far less satisfactory. Indeed, a strong case can be made for the view that the expansion was often unplanned and unrestrained, beyond the financial support provided and beyond the capacity of the university system to absorb. Further, the expanded number of students did not lead to a commensurate increase in the number of graduates. In short, the impressive figures regarding growth in student numbers obscure serious weaknesses and failures.

Planning and Financing

Some Yugoslav scholars and officials assert that often university expansion was irrational and arbitrary and that within the total system there was considerable fragmentation, lack of coordination and wasteful duplication. University departments were scattered on separate sites throughout the various cities, and each provided its students with all the subjects needed for the particular degree pattern. As observed in the

69

previous chapter, this meant that the same subject was taught in many different departments (for example, at Zagreb University in 1971, physics was taught in ten separate departments, chemistry in eight, mathematics in twelve and so on) and there was little cooperation between those teaching the same subject in these departments.[5]

New departments were established with seeming abandon. A recent report on Yugoslav higher education referred to the establishment of three textile engineering departments as an example of the 'waste of human material resources' which had occurred. It was doubtful, this report continued, 'whether our society is prepared, or indeed able, to finance such narrowly specialised institutions on such a broad scale. The question is also whether as many textile engineers are needed as these three Faculties [Departments] can produce'.[6] As is noted later, there was little evidence that university development was related to even a broad plan of society's future manpower needs; indeed such a plan did not exist.

Several Yugoslav scholars have recently maintained that part of the reason for the proliferation of universities and other higher education institutions could be attributed primarily to the desire of politicians to build something to their glory and to the desire of every town to have its own status symbol. As one Yugoslav scholar observed, 'the pharoahs built pyramids, kings built castles, churches and monasteries—and politicians . . . build universities'.[7]

Often the vital element in the decision to establish a tertiary body related to the nationality question.[8] While this might have had great 'historical significance' for the particular nationality,[9] there was a tendency to ignore certain harsh realities; often it was very difficult to find staff of an adequate calibre and the finances to maintain the new institution.[10]

There were complaints that new departments were founded and enrolments increased at a rate far greater than the increase in total educational expenditure. Existing buildings had imposed on them 'two to three times and even more' the number of students for which the buildings had been planned.[11] For example, from 1965/66 to 1970/71 the number of students at Belgrade University jumped from 28,353 to 40,480, but not a single new building was opened during this period.[12] Classrooms became overcrowded, laboratory work often degenerated into demonstration lessons, students often had nowhere to study, their living conditions declined drastically and so on.[13] The fate of the 1961 Federal Assembly decision on educational expenditure is a telling illustration of the lag between recognized need and finance provided. The particular decision was to spend 15,000 million dinars over a four-year period to help equip and extend facilities in which the situation was especially acute. It was acknowledged that even this amount was not enough to provide what was regarded as essential, and yet, in the four-year period, a total of only 8,700 million dinars was in fact allocated.[14] Further, despite the continued expansion of enrolments, the expenditure on education expressed as a percentage of national income steadily declined from the peak figure set in 1962,[15] as can be readily seen from Table 4.

TABLE 4

EDUCATION EXPENDITURE AS A PROPORTION OF
GROSS NATIONAL INCOME

%

1961	4.3
1962	5.5
1963	5.2
1964	4.8
1965	4.6
1966	4.4

Source: Institute for Social Research, University of Zagreb, *Innovation in Higher Education: Reforms in Yugoslavia* (Paris: OECD, 1970), p. 148.

In addition, it was maintained that these figures did not accurately reflect the seriousness of the local situation. A report of a committee of the Belgrade University Council asserted that the amount invested in education would be less than half that claimed if calculated on the same basis as that used in the West; further, Yugoslavia's relatively large student population meant that the available finance was spread thinly, and finally, in contrast to the situation in most other countries where considerable basic facilities existed, Yugoslavia's university development began virtually from scratch.[16] Despite this clear evidence of serious financial inadequacy, many spokesmen failed to acknowledge it. Petar Stambolić, a member of the Central Committee of the League, boldly denied in 1966 that education had been neglected, and justified his denial by pointing to the massive increases in departments and students since the war.[17]

In some departments the overcrowding was so severe that it was physically impossible to admit all applicants. This led to fervent apologies from official spokesmen. For example, the responsible minister in 1960 expressed regret that exceptional circumstances had forced the adoption of this 'temporary and extraordinary measure' at certain departments and gave assurances that students would be able to enrol in other departments.[18]

In 1956, when limits were placed on enrolments at several departments for the first time, it was simultaneously announced that the departments of Law and Economics would admit those students unable to enrol in the department of their choice. (Alternatively, students could enrol at other universities where the 'disproportion between the number of students and teaching facilities was much less severe'.) As a result of this policy, almost two-thirds of the freshman class enrolled in economics and law; this marked a dramatic rise from the figure of less than a quarter (22.8 per cent) for the previous year's class. As the Secretary of the University Committee of the League of Communists commented, the current year's high enrolment in these departments was not an accurate reflection of the career preferences of the first year students, nor was it in accord with the needs of society.[19]

Yet there was no serious attempt to limit overall enrolments to accord with the real capacity of the university system. Any mention of the desirability of limiting total enrolments was seen as an undue restriction on the right to education. Indeed, the Yugoslav leadership did all it could to enlarge the pool of potential students by easing the rules governing university enrolment. In 1959, for example, a decision of the Federal Executive Council made it possible for graduates of apprentice schools, schools for practical training and advanced vocational schools to enrol at university. The decision also allowed individuals who had not graduated from any of the secondary schools to enrol (provided they had completed four years in the work force and passed an entrance examination).[20] Also noteworthy was the 1960 decision relating to the graduates of the 'Two Year Post-Secondary' schools. The orientation in these schools was intended to be specific and practical, and until 1960 their graduates could only enrol as freshmen at the university, but in that year it was decided to give them full credit for their work at these schools.[21] According to some, this decision meant the destruction of the distinctive character of these schools: in order to increase their prestige, the staff adopted teaching plans and programmes 'exactly' like those of the first two years at university. This, of course, only strengthened the tendency of the graduates of these schools to go on to university.[22]

The opening of university departments in small regional centres was also encouraged as a means of enlarging the pool of potential students. In 1938/39 there were eighteen university departments in Yugoslavia. Ten years later the number of departments had doubled and in the next twenty years the number of departments grew until there were five times as many as before the war.[23] In 1938/39 only four towns had university departments, but by 1960/61 there were university departments situated at sixteen different locations.[24] It was urged that both children and parents would be encouraged to think of the possibility of the young continuing their education on to the university and more would be able to attend university if they did not have the expense of living away from home.[25]

As a Yugoslav youth leader commented in 1968, the mood at the time when the pattern of university development was laid amounted to nothing less than the 'illusion that the possibilities of our society were such as to enable every young person to acquire university education'.[26] But the result of such policies was that after being urged to study, so as to fit themselves for an important role in society, thousands of young graduates found themselves unwanted. Indeed, although the need for it was often mentioned, there was no official manpower plan which would have provided the basis for a rational programme of university development.[27]

The failure to link enrolments to the opportunities in society is exemplified by statistics prepared for the Presidium of the Union of

Students, showing the number of unemployed graduates and the number of registered vacancies in certain fields as of 30 September 1968.[28] No less than 3,178 graduates were unemployed, a figure of very great significance when it is realized that the total number of graduates in the previous year was only 14,533. But while there was a general 'over-production' of graduates, the statistics indicate that in several disciplines there was a serious 'under-production'. In particular, there had been a failure to develop the Engineering and Economic departments to accord with societal needs. And if these particular disciplines are removed from consideration, the 'over-production' of experts in the majority of disciplines becomes even more apparent. (See Table 5.) On average almost a quarter of those who graduated in these remaining fields had been unable to find employment. It should also be noted that these figures do not include those who had left to seek employment abroad nor do they include those who found employment in areas unrelated to their training or at an inappropriately low level.[29]

TABLE 5

COMPARISON OF THE NUMBER OF GRADUATES, UNEMPLOYED GRADUATES AND VACANCIES
AS AT 30 SEPTEMBER 1968

	No. of graduates in previous year	No. of unemployed graduates	No. of vacancies
Total	14,533	3,178	1,341
Deleting Economics and Engineering	4,006	420	911
	10,527	2,758	430

Source: Based on Miodrag Milenović and Vera Gavanski, 'Razvoj visokog školstva 1939-1968' (The development of tertiary education 1939-1968), paper prepared for the Presidium of YUS, Belgrade, 1969, p. 38 (mimeographed).

The importance of this cannot be exaggerated. It was claimed that employment had become the major worry among students in developing countries and many looked 'with fear on their prospects for employ-ment';[30] according to an article in *Borba,* many Yugoslav students felt that graduation merely meant the loss of student privileges.[31] Just prior to the June events the President of the Union of Youth warned of the 'ideological and political consequences' of this fear among students,[32] and Tito himself urged the necessity for the rapid solution of the problem.[33] As a member of the Executive Committee of the Serbian League of Communists commented shortly after the June protests, without significant progress towards the solution of such problems as unemployment, it was 'in all probability' unlikely that the confidence of the young could be won.[34] Or as a Yugoslav scholar observed, the situation in which the young graduate, after years of study, found it impossible to obtain suitable employment, could lead to 'catastrophic social consequences'.[35] These consequences were exacerbated by the widely known fact that the few vacancies were not filled simply according to ability, but often on the basis of personal or political connections, and even on payment of a bribe.[36]

Again the impact of the particular problem must be seen in the context of the expectations that had been aroused. The tremendous expansion of university enrolments had been based on the assumption that there was an insatiable need for highly qualified experts. Indeed, it was emphasized that there was no cause to fear a surplus of university educated personnel and that the young graduate could expect to play an important and satisfying role in the community. Even in 1968 it was claimed that the widely held view among responsible authorities was that the need for graduates was such that no limits on enrolments should be applied.[37] This failure to adjust enrolments in particular areas to even an approximate estimate of future requirements seemed to contradict official statements concerning the need to eliminate wastage, to prepare experts for specific responsibilities and so on.[38] It was as though a simple increase in enrolments as a whole would ensure the realization of the leaders' avowed aims of economic, social and political development.

Young people also felt pressured to continue their education, as it became increasingly apparent that academic qualification was, at least for the non-partisan generation, the key to membership in the new élite. This élite (and this attitude) developed in spite of the official rhetoric regarding the creation of a new socialist intelligentsia rooted in the working class, and despite the comments which stressed the importance of bridging the gulf between physical and intellectual work, both in terms of status and income.

Many clearly believed that 'in our society' an individual could achieve a 'satisfactory life' only if he continued on to the tertiary level and became a doctor, engineer or the like,[39] and that a high school diploma offered very little in terms of opportunity, salary or prestige.[40] Indeed, the high school graduate had increasing difficulty even in finding employment. In part, this was due to the fact that the curriculum, even at the so-called technical secondary school, was geared toward a general education rather than toward preparation for a particular vocation.[41] Largely, however, it was due to the worsening employment situation: an increasing proportion of secondary school graduates continued their education because they were unable to find employment. This trend is illustrated by figures showing that in 1954/55 only 54.2 per cent of secondary school leavers continued on to the tertiary level; however by 1969/70 this percentage had risen to 70.3.[42]

Thus, as the prestige of being a university student increased and as prospects for 'suitable' employment for the young declined, so university enrolments continued to boom. The already overburdened universities became swamped with students, many of whom had little aptitude for or interest in university studies and who lacked the necessary background. In 1967/68, for example, over a third of the first-year students at Zagreb University were graduates of secondary *vocational* schools.[43]

Almost all who wished to enrol, and could afford to, were able to enter university.

The Decline in Quality of the University Staff

The tremendous expansion of the university inevitably had a deleterious impact on the general calibre of the university staff. In the first place the steep climb in student numbers necessitated an extraordinary increase in the number of staff: as can be seen in Table 6, in 1938/39 there were only 500 staff members above the rank of assistant; however, in each ten-year period from that date the number of faculty approximately doubled.[44] And to obtain this increase the criteria for staff were, in the words of one Yugoslav scholar, 'dangerously lowered'.[45] The Law on Higher Education (1960) required candidates for the position of professor and associate professor to hold a doctor's degree while candidates for appointment as assistant professors 'shall hold a Master's degree' or similar qualification. However, because of the acute shortage of qualified staff, the positions of lecturer and senior lecture were also provided for; according to the law, candidates for these positions were only required to have completed the normal undergraduate course.[46]

TABLE 6
THE NUMBER OF STAFF ABOVE THE RANK OF ASSISTANT

1938-39	500
1948-49	1,123
1958-59	2,276
1968-69	5,447

Source: Miodrag Milenović, 'Dinamika razvoja visokog školstva i zapošljavanja diplomiranih studenata' (The dynamics of the development of higher education and the employment of graduates), Ideje, vol. i, no. 2 (1970), p. 240.

The formal qualifications of the staff were lowest at the newly opened universities. Faculty at existing institutions were reluctant to move to a new one situated in a less developed area. Consequently, the bulk of the staff of new universities was recruited locally, often from among the high school teachers and practising lawyers, doctors and engineers. As one observer remarked, many lacked 'real connection with learning'.[47] The net result was illustrated by figures for the faculty at Sarajevo University in 1968/69. Of those above the rank of assistant, only 44.7 per cent had a doctorate, while 25.3 per cent lacked formal qualification beyond a first degree.[48]

There was the further difficulty that staff were not chosen simply on the basis of academic qualification. In the immediate post-war years there had been an effort to appoint candidates whose primary qualification was that they were 'Marxists' who would dilute the influence of

75

those who held 'incorrect' views.[49] In later periods it was increasingly claimed that the general quality of staff was also affected by the fact that candidates were often chosen on the basis of the desire of older staff to avoid appointing the most promising applicants to junior positions, lest these new applicants later threaten the security and advancement of the older members.[50]

However, the major barrier to securing and retaining qualified staff to serve the needs of the rapidly expanding university network was the relatively low salaries. This relatively low level of remuneration led many to leave the university in favour of other employment, either at home or abroad.[51] At the Seventh Congress of the League of Communists held in 1958, Tito noted that the position of those in education was 'not exactly the best', that generally they were 'very poorly rewarded' and that 'the time has come to solve this problem of the payment of educational staff in a satisfactory manner'.[52] However, little change occurred. For example, comparisons made in 1964 between the salaries of full professors and individuals of equivalent rank in the judiciary or the bureaucracy showed the latter group receiving 40 per cent more than the professors.[53] And the salary scales of university staff slipped even further behind. When the 'economic reforms' were debated there were solemn assurances that education would not suffer, but, according to the Pro-Rector of Belgrade University in 1967, experience showed these assurances to be illusory.[54] The increase in faculty salaries was said to have lagged behind increases in the salaries of those outside the university and behind increases in the cost of living. For example, in one period following these reforms, personal incomes in the field of education in Serbia rose by 10 to 20 per cent while in other fields the minimum increase was 50 to 60 per cent.[55]

As one professor bitterly pleaded in a *Univerzitet Danas* article, the association of university teachers must, at the very least, protect its members from exploitation. University professors must fight to secure incomes comparable to those received by similarly qualified individuals outside the university. He concluded, however, that the current economic difficulties made it unlikely that those in positions of responsibility would show an understanding of the plight of the university staff. Therefore, vigorous action, including demonstrations and strikes, would be necessary in order to publicize faculty demands.[56]

The relatively low level of income therefore compounded the problem of finding competent and conscientious personnel to staff the rapidly expanding university system and not surprisingly there were frequent comments relating to the low level of knowledge among the faculty. For instance, it was observed that many staff members failed to endeavour to remedy the deficiencies in their background, either by completing the requirements for a higher degree[57] or by learning foreign languages in order to remain abreast of world developments in their discipline.[58]

In an address to a meeting in 1962 of the Zagreb University Council, the Rector of the university emphasized the need for vigorous action, since otherwise, he claimed, it would be years before even the old university standards could be regained. He further observed that the circle of candidates for academic positions was continually shrinking since it was difficult to find candidates willing to accept the salary offered, and, 'what is more important, candidates who have an apartment'. (Apparently accommodation was in very short supply and hence the university often lost a potential staff member to an organization able to provide housing.) The Rector concluded with the remark that the circle of potential candidates had shrunk to such an extent that the 'possibility of finding individuals of high quality in that circle is fairly small'.[59] As one professor explained it, there was actually a process of 'negative selection of staff', since the best young graduates simply did not seek employment in the universities.[60] And those very able students who were determined on an academic career were often forced to seek their opportunity in foreign universities.[61]

The relatively low salaries were described as the principal reason why many of the staff spent a large proportion of their time working outside their own department either as consultants or as part-time teachers at other university departments. The extent of their outside involvement, and thus the impact on the performance of their primary task, may be gauged by an estimate that it was not uncommon for individual staff members to receive between half to double the amount of their regular salary for outside work.[62] In defence of this practice it was maintained that they became 'burdened' with this work largely out of financial necessity.[63] And as one professor observed, the failure on the part of the university staff to devote their full attention to the university was most vigorously criticized by those whose regular salaries were significantly higher than those of the faculty.[64] Whatever the justification, the simple fact was that often the burden of teaching was thrust on the inadequately qualified assistant.[65] Further, it was claimed that the assistant was also obliged 'to do all sorts of jobs on the side', often jobs with little connection with scholarship 'in order to make ends meet'.[66]

This decline in the quality and commitment of the university staff coupled with the problem of inadequate facilities meant that less research of significance could be carried out within the university, and this led to the establishment of research organizations separate from the university. This development had two major consequences. First, it led to the further weakening, in some cases even the severing, of the vital links between research and teaching. Second, rather than continue in the difficult situation within the universities, a significant number of staff members chose to move into these research institutions with the result that the calibre of the university staff declined still further.[67]

Many among the staff were described as showing little interest in teaching, the content of their lectures failed to reflect contemporary developments in the discipline, and their methods of instruction often treated the student as an object rather than as a participant.[68]

According to an article in *Univerzitet Danas,* many staff members were without enthusiasm for either their discipline or their role in society; in place of enthusiasm they had only concern for their personal social and material status.[69] In similar vein, an assistant at the University of Sarajevo wrote that, for many, a position at the university meant higher prestige than they could otherwise obtain, the opportunity for lucrative consulting work and the pleasure of long holidays, and instead of intellectual themes they discussed cars, week-end cottages and the problem of finding reliable domestic help.[70]

For a number of reasons, then, the standards and commitment of many of the staff seemed to fall far short of what might be regarded as acceptable.

Results at the Universities

In the light of even this brief description of the situation in the universities it is not surprising to learn that standards reached by students were not considered satisfactory by various observers. Even a Report of the Presidium of the Central Committee of the Union of Students concluded in 1965 that the professional knowledge of graduates was below a 'satisfactory level'.[71] Similarly, an article in a 1970 issue of *Univerzitet Danas* concluded that the quality of graduates was poor and that 'a good number would be unable to cope with a serious test of their knowledge or their practical skill'.[72]

As our own experience indicates, it is difficult to speak with certainty on such questions as whether or to what exent university standards have declined. However, what can be stated firmly is that university results in Yugoslavia, in terms of passes and failures, were appalling. The typical university student simply could not expect to graduate on schedule; rather, he could expect either to take even twice the scheduled time or to leave the university without graduating. The likely impact of this fact on student attitudes needs no emphasis.

A few examples should suffice to indicate something of the colossal consumption of both university facilities and human resources: the law course at Zagreb University was designed to cover four years, but in 1957 it was noted that only 10 per cent managed to graduate even in *five* years.[73] In 1958 it was reported that at the Belgrade School of Electrotechnical Engineering, 2.1 per cent graduated in five years, 21.4 per cent in six, 35.1 per cent in seven, 27.2 per cent in nine, 9.6 per cent in ten, and 1.2 per cent in eleven years. These figures do not, of course, include those who failed to graduate at all.[74] Statistics pertaining to a group of engineering graduates of 1956 show that only 15.8 per cent were under twenty-five years of age while 58.1 per cent were between twenty-six and twenty-nine and 21.3 per cent were between thirty and thirty-four.[75]

If anything, the situation deteriorated during the fifties. For example, statistics concerning departments in Yugoslavia with a five-year curriculum show that the percentage of graduates who took eight years to complete their requirements rose significantly in the period 1952 to 1955. In 1952, 14 per cent of the graduates had taken eight years to complete their degree; the percentage was 30.8 in 1953, 41.8 in 1954, and 47.3 in 1955.[76]

In the late fifties and early sixties both the reported statistics and the assessment of Yugoslav observers seemed to indicate some progress towards reducing the average length of studies. Indeed, one observer claimed in 1959 that a 'turning point' had been reached. At Belgrade University the average length of study was reduced from 7.0 years in 1958/59 to 6.4 years in 1961/62, at Ljubljana the reduction was from 7.2 to 6.6 years, while at Skoplje it was reduced from 7.9 to 7.7 years. As was observed, this decrease could 'hardly be called spectacular, but it was at least a step in the right direction'.[77]

Much of this improvement was attributed to the fact that all those concerned with higher education 'actively supported' the so-called '1958 Recommendation' adopted by the Federal Chamber of the Federal Assembly. This 'Recommendation for the Creation of Better Conditions for Training of Highly Skilled Specialists' particularly emphasized the need to reduce the length of studies to a 'reasonable level'. The observed improvements were explained as reflecting the successful effort of both staff and students. The staff adopted 'new forms' of teaching, 'particularly valuable were [the] regular tutorials during which teachers helped students . . ., guided them through the subject matter and prepared them for examinations'. Greater responsibilities were also placed on the student, in particular, by regulations adopted at various departments which placed some pressure on students to take examinations at the prescribed times.[78]

Nonetheless, the situation remained unsatisfactory. For example, in 1964 it was reported that the period of study for the 'successful' student, that is, for those who graduated, still remained approximately six years.[79] By 1965 it was acknowledged that the situation was again deteriorating, and later that the drop-out rate was increasing.[80]

The gradually worsening situation is most readily, if somewhat crudely, illustrated by comparing the trend in enrolments with the trend in the number of graduates. Overall, the dramatic increase in full-time, first-year enrolments is not matched by a commensurate increase in the number of graduates. Table 7 shows the numerical relationships between first-year enrolments and the number of graduates five and a half to six years later. The selection of this time span is fairly arbitrary; however, whatever time span is chosen the same basic downward trend remains.[81]

Of those who graduated from four-year university courses in 1967 not quite 60 per cent studied for at least an additional two years and almost one-fifth had actually taken at least double the scheduled time to complete their studies. (Again these figures do not include those who failed to graduate at all.)[82]

Failure rates in the first two years of study were, as Table 8 shows, especially high; for example, in 1967/68, on average less than half of the first-year students passed into second year.[83]

One recent study noted that university graduates often did not enter

TABLE 7

THE NUMERICAL RELATIONSHIP BETWEEN ENROLMENTS AND GRADUATIONS

First Year Enrolments		Number of Graduates 5½ to 6 years later		Number of Graduates as a proportion of the first year enrolments of 5½ to 6 years previous %
1957/58	23,236	12,794	(1963)	55.06
1958/59	23,517	12,223	(1964)	51.98
1959/60	24,443	11,958	(1965)	48.92
1960/61	29,150	11,627	(1966)	39.89
1961/62	32,902	11,781	(1967)	35.81
1962/63	32,735	12,071	(1968)	36.87

Sources: Based on Miodrag Milenović, 'Dinamika razvoja visokog školstva i zapošljavanja diplomiranih studenata' (The dynamics of the development of higher education and the employment of graduates), *Ideje*, vol. i, no. 2 (1970), p. 245; and Institute for Social Research, University of Zagreb, *Innovation in Higher Education Reforms in Yugoslavia* (Paris: OECD, 1970), p. 175.

TABLE 8

THE PROPORTION OF STUDENTS PASSING FROM FIRST TO SECOND YEAR AND FROM SECOND TO THIRD YEAR IN 1967/68

University	From I to II %	From II to III %
Belgrade	48	65
Ljubljana	39	52
Niš	46	64
Novi Sad	39	88
Sarajevo	42	42
Skoplje	48	50
Zagreb	50	49

Source: Petar Kobe, 'Efikasnost studiranja na jugoslovenskim univerzitetima' (Efficiency of studying at Yugoslav universities), *Univerzitet Danas,* vol. ix, no. 9/10 (1968), p. 46.

the work force until their very late twenties. Thus, while in many countries graduates began working at twenty-two or twenty-three years of age, their Yugoslav contemporaries usually had several years of study remaining.[84] It was often observed that the Yugoslav community was not so rich as to be able to afford the waste of time and facilities caused by the fact that studies lasted nine, ten or even more years.[85]

Part of the problem of both low standards and poor results was attributed to the poor preparation of entering students. For example, in

1967 it was reported that 40 per cent of the secondary school teachers of history in Serbia were 'unqualified'.[86] Clearly, the secondary school system was also reflecting the problems of rapid expansion. A further point made was that virtually no selection took place in the high school system; almost all who had the desire and means were able to complete high school, and virtually all were oriented to enrol at university. Little was done to guide into employment those students without sufficient aptitude for higher education.[87]

In those departments which were forced to select students because of limited accommodation, it was claimed, not unexpectedly, that both the general level of work and examination results were significantly better. Thus, one researcher noted that, while the general rule was for only approximately 10 per cent of students to graduate on schedule, in those departments where selection was strict, the proportion was as high as 50 per cent.[88] Despite this evidence concerning the benefits of strict selection, its general application was strongly resisted. As noted earlier, it was seen as restricting educational opportunity. In particular, it was urged that entrance examinations were unfair to those students from poorer quality secondary schools.[89] Having regard for the failure to remedy the gross inequalities that existed in other areas, the concern for equality of opportunity demonstrated on this point seems somewhat incongruous.

The system which permitted students to make frequent attempts at a particular examination was also said to affect both the time taken and the final standard reached. Many students failed time after time but eventually completed the formal requirements for a degree. Not surprisingly, some began to question the potential value of such an expert and began to suggest the adoption of measures through which such students could be removed from the university.[90] As one professor remarked, such rules would enable the university to be freed of those who exploited the present rule (which allowed, in some cases, ten or more attempts to pass an oral exam)[91] and who 'brutally exhaust the teacher and finally compel him to capitulate and grant a passing grade'.[92] However, on the part of the students there was often strong resistance to a tightening of these rules. Obviously many of them feared that they would be the ones eliminated and, of course, they were able to argue with considerable justification that their poor results often derived from such 'objective' difficulties as gross overcrowding and the decline in teaching standards.[93]

Basic methods of studying were also criticized. It was observed that in many cases the student had too little opportunity for independent work, having an average of almost five classes per day. Frequently, studying meant simply learning by heart the lecture notes or sections of the basic textbook. Other materials were not easy to obtain and, since they were often in a foreign language, difficult for the average student to use.[94]

The inadequate staff/student ratio and the consequent lack of contact between teachers and students was also described as a major problem.

81

There were frequent references to the dangers of excessive 'verbalism' and the need for smaller classes and more seminars as a means of enabling students to become participants in the process of education rather than remaining mere objects.[95] However, both the limited staff and facilities meant that such statements would remain no more than empty hopes.[96]

It was indeed true, therefore, as Yugoslav spokesmen proudly claimed, that the proportion of young people at university in Yugoslavia was amongst the highest in the world. However, it must be remembered that these numbers were artificially inflated. Poor results meant that a large proportion of graduates remained enrolled in their particular schools far beyond the scheduled time; the average graduate took approximately six years to complete a four-year course.[97] The total enrolments were further inflated by the vast number who dropped out of university without managing to graduate. According to one Yugoslav researcher, the proportion of Yugoslav students who succeeded in graduating from tertiary institutions was amongst the lowest in the world; for example, while only 40 per cent of Yugoslav students managed to graduate, the percentage for the United States was 65, for Italy 63, for Britain 85, for France 57, and for the Soviet Union 86.[98] Enrolments were also boosted by those who might be described virtually as perpetual students and who moved, almost without restriction and regardless of their previous records, from one department to another. For many such individuals, often the children of notoriously indulgent parents, the *status* of student was the major consideration. According to an article in *Studentski List,* it was not unknown for such students to be admitted even to the more selective institutions following behind-the-scenes intervention by some 'very important comrades'.[99]

Education Reform

In the 1950s the Yugoslav leadership began urging the necessity of a programme of radical education reform. However, the major difficulty with this programme was that it appeared to focus on one of the symptoms rather than on the basic causes of the difficulties at the university. As understood by the Yugoslav leadership, education reform simply entailed the pruning of curricula and study programmes to enable students to graduate on schedule. In justification of this, it was insisted that a developing society could not afford to give students a broad background since this provided them with more education than was necessary[100]—as Tito explained it, the responsibility of the education system was to prepare every citizen for 'a certain function' in the further development of Yugoslavia.[101]

Educating all students for what was termed an academic as distinct from a practical career was described by Yugoslav spokesmen as most inefficient; it was essential to distinguish between those who would join the economy on graduation and those few who were being prepared for academic life.[102]

82

To achieve this aim of preparing students for practical tasks in the economy and society, close consultation between the faculty teaching a particular subject and those experts actually working in that area was urged—the needs of the economy must be well understood, for the university was the *basic,* rather than merely an important, force for change; the university could no longer be seen as a desirable and interesting adjunct to society or as something relevant only to the élite. Thus the term 'education reform', as the Yugoslav leadership saw it, implied a constant effort to enable the university to keep abreast of societal developments.[103] It was maintained that this consultation with experts outside the university would help the staff determine the necessary minimum for each course and would help them devise more specialized, practical and relevant programmes.[104] Such consultation was recommended even in the preparation of particular lectures. And, of course, it would be useful if these experts actually gave some lectures themselves. Further, the students should be set practical problems; even dissertation topics could be related to particular developments in production. Not only would this help prepare students for industry, it would also have the advantage that the individual student would have the satisfaction of working to help society.[105]

An article in *Univerzitet Danas* described as exemplary an arrangement between a university department and an enterprise. The situation concerned an electronics factory in the city of Niš which helped the local university establish an electronics department. All of the students in the department held scholarships from the enterprise and had the opportunity to do practical work in it. The industry's particular problems were used as the basis of seminars, as themes for student papers, and for faculty research. Consequently, education was tied to the practical and relevant. Finally, it was observed that the staff in this department had the satisfaction of being the instigators of modernization in this particular industry.[106]

Not only would collaboration with industry help the university adapt to what were described as the real needs of society but it would also help the universities solve their serious financial problems; enterprises would be encouraged to extend financial support if they could perceive the practical benefits of the work being carried out.[107]

However, as explained in chapter III, it was generally agreed that little progress towards this goal of 'education reform' was achieved. For example, an article published in 1972 noted that the 'greatest result' achieved to date at the University of Skoplje was 'merely in the posing of the questions'; apart from this, only peripheral changes had been implemented.[108] The official view blamed faculty resistance; members of staff were described as being more concerned with the preservation of their own particular interests than in furthering the interests of society as a whole. Their objections to the advocated reforms were usually dismissed as mere rationalizations or as indicating their failure to perceive society's true needs.[109]

To the outside observer, however, the objections of certain members of faculty were not without merit. Some among the staff contended that the very objective of having the university act as a direct stimulant to change in the economy might be endangered by the type of close collaboration advocated by official spokesmen. In their view, the university should not merely inculcate its students with the knowledge of contemporary industrial practice; rather, it should acquaint them with contemporary world trends in the particular academic discipline so as to prepare them for an innovative and creative role. That is, university teaching should not be simply linked to contemporary practice, but, rather, it should be in advance of it. Linking education to methods in current use in society and the economy involved the danger that the influence of laymen or even practical experts might stultify creativity in both teaching and research.[110]

The preceding statements basically concerned disagreement as to how the university could best serve the needs of the developing economy; however, at least some academics rejected the notion that the function of the university should be seen primarily in terms of its contribution to the economic development of society. As one scholar argued, to reshape the university as a 'service organization' involved its degradation; practical needs would quickly become the boundaries of research and the university would be enrolled in the service not of knowledge but of political power. He maintained that the Soviet situation as described by Professor Sakharov was most instructive in this regard. Therefore, while he approved of preparing students for their future employment, he insisted that this goal must be subordinated to the primary goal of the university. Finally, he pointed out, work was only a part of life:[111] as other scholars and, indeed, Yugoslav official spokesmen themselves had emphasized, the student also had to be prepared to become a participant in the self-managing social and political system.[112]

A specific measure of 'practical' reform which exemplified the official attitude was introduced at Yugoslav universities following the promulgation of the 1960 *General Law on Faculties and Universities*. The law provided that undergraduate instruction 'may comprise' two 'independent and inter-connected levels of education'. As a general rule, the first level was to last two years and was designed to 'train technicians . . . giving them an entirely systematic training'. The objective was not only to produce needed experts at a particular level but also to give those university students who were currently leaving the university without completing the requirements for the four-year degree, the opportunity to obtain some sort of certification. The second level of instruction was expected to be a continuation of the first level, that is, levels one and two together were to form an integrated course. The expected pattern was that some students would go into industry after two years' study while others would choose to continue for an additional two-year period.[113]

At the universities, objections were raised to the concepts implicit in the planned first level, the main argument being that the type of training envisaged could more appropriately be carried out at technical institutes.[114] In the implementation of the scheme, the major problem faced was the restructuring of the existing programme so as to create an integrated two-year course within an integrated four-year course. Certain subjects previously taught in the later years were said to have been brought forward, sometimes in their entirety, sometimes partially and sometimes superficially; the net result was often to increase the amount and difficulty of the material covered in the first two years and consequently to increase the failure rate in these years.[115] Although in some cases the first level was far too difficult, in other cases, as one professor observed, the scientific work was reduced and the education of students was primarily directed towards practical work: rather than university education, the resultant situation was more appropriately described as a 'fiasco'.[116] A further point was that those students who managed to complete the first level for the most part simply moved on to the second; that is, very few graduates of the first level entered the economy at that stage. Their inclination to continue was strengthened by the fact that enterprises showed very little interest in employing graduates of the first level.[117] The general failure to achieve the desired results led to the eventual abandonment of the scheme.[118]

What appeared to be involved in this debate concerning education reform were two radically different concepts of the university. Many faculty members continued to see university education in the traditional sense and retained a concept of university education which transcended a single historical situation;[119] on the other hand, many among the leadership sought to keep the name 'university' while essentially transforming these institutions into technical colleges.[120] As an advocate of the official view wrote in 1960, a major fault of the existing university was that it suited only a particular type of student and failed to provide for the individual whose talents lay in the solution of practical problems but who might not be able to grasp abstract and theoretical questions.[121]

THE YUGOSLAV LEADERSHIP
AND THE PROBLEMS OF THE UNIVERSITY

At first sight it might have appeared that, in advocating a more practical orientation, the leadership was outlining a realistic and responsible solution to the problems of the university; seen in perspective, however, it is clear that most of the university's problems were the direct consequence of the leadership's own deliberate policies and that the solution now proposed was irrelevant as far as these problems were concerned.

The leadership had thrown open the doors of the university to virtually all comers—the available staff and facilities, particularly in the light of the inadequate preparation of many of the entering students, were not able to cope and hence failure rates soared—the Yugoslav leadership then demanded that the faculty members solve this problem, which was not of their making, by changing the nature of university education. Even when serious difficulties in the university became apparent in the middle and late 1950s, Yugoslav authorities continued to press for the expansion of university schools and enrolments. This was graphically exemplified in the provisions of the important 'Recommendation for the Creation of Better Conditions for the Training of Highly Skilled Specialists' which, as mentioned earlier, was adopted by the Federal Chamber of the Federal Assembly in 1958. This urged the rapid expansion of institutions and of enrolments, but at the same time insisted that serious attention be given to the grave problem of poor results.[122] That is, Yugoslav authorities acted as though the poor results and increasing enrolments were separate, rather than two closely related issues.

Thus, while the League leadership vigorously assailed the university for its failure to implement the so-called education reform, the League itself did little to tackle other problems of the university system which were beyond the powers of the university itself to resolve. It is difficult to avoid the impression that official spokesmen frequently preferred to blame the university for the consequences of official errors and that, while urging the university to take decisive action, they carefully avoided acting within their own sphere of responsibility.[123] That is, they failed to grapple with the problems of excessive and irrational enrolment, the scarcity of jobs for young graduates, the excessive proliferation and fragmentation of the tertiary education system and its under-capitalization.

The pressure on facilities *could* have been eased by restricting enrolment to accord with the capacity of the universities, but as far as dealing with enrolments was concerned, the simple fact was that it was politically inexpedient to take any significant action. In particular, the expansion of tertiary enrolments enabled the Yugoslav leadership to disguise and minimize the short-term effects of the serious lack of employment opportunities for the young.[124] Entrance examinations remained merely a device by which students were diverted from the departments in which overcrowding was most grave to departments which had more room or in which the physical facilities were more elastic.[125]

The employment difficulties of graduates *could* have been alleviated if the responsible authorities had prepared even an approximate estimate of future needs[126] and if decisive action had been taken to induce work collectives to offer employment to those with the appropriate qualifications. Concerning the latter, the President of the Belgrade University Union of Students in 1967[127] urged that minimum qualifications should be specified for certain positions so as to force those with inadequate qualifications who were presently occupying such positions to step down in favour of those with the appropriate education.[128] Nevertheless, despite the many resolutions and speeches, little effective action was taken; unqualified or under-qualified individuals continued to retain positions of responsibility in the society and the economy to the exclusion of those with the appropriate qualifications.[129] For example, a detailed analysis of the situation in 1967 showed that more than one-fifth of the positions in the work force which required special training were in fact held by individuals who lacked the appropriate preparation.[130] Another report in 1967 showed that one in five managers of economic enterprises in Serbia had only completed elementary school.[131]

Many such individuals had obtained their positions in the immediate post-war years and had naturally become accustomed to this way of life. They were now being asked to admit their inability and to surrender their positions to a young expert. An article in *Komunist* in 1967 loftily condemned their selfish attitude and decried the fact that 'such people easily find supporters [in their particular collective] for their own viewpoints which are then . . . disguised as democracy'.[132] That is, the self-managing institutions within an enterprise were allegedly perverted so as to deny the rights of individuals outside the collective to appropriate employment.

When the economic reforms were introduced in 1964 it was acknowledged that this would place pressure on each enterprise to stabilize or even reduce its work force, but it was insisted that this would not operate to the particular disadvantage of the young graduates; each enterprise would have even greater need for expertise if it were to survive in this less well-protected economic environment. Of course, nothing of the sort happened—those who had jobs jealously guarded them. The only action of real significance to deal with the problem of unemployed graduates was to permit their emigration.[133]

According to Krste Crvenkovski, a member of the Federal Executive Council, many young experts went abroad not merely to find employment or to make more money, but also to realize that special satisfaction which stemmed from employment that fully utilized their qualifications and knowledge.[134] Thus, an increasing number within the student body were forced to begin seeing their futures in a sphere other than in the construction of socialist Yugoslavia. Although Yugoslavia may have needed them, it did not want them.

In addition, the limited funds available for university education *could* have been used far more effectively and rationally. One Yugoslav scholar noted the tendency to maintain the existing allocation formulae, which simply perpetuated the present illogical network. Consequently, he contended, those institutions which needed development and modernization usually received less than certain institutions which in fact should be closed down or which were already relatively well provided for.[135] According to another scholar, in 1969 there were more than 120 tertiary educational institutions. He estimated that a reasonable number, having regard for the needs and resources of society, would be between seventy and eighty institutions; the present number meant that available resources were spread too thinly and that there was much wasteful duplication. In his view, until this problem was resolved, there could not be meaningful reform at the university and, further, it could not be resolved without the intervention of authorities outside the particular institutions. Concerning the latter point, the writer emphasized that it could hardly be expected that the staff at these various institutions would through their autonomous procedures decide to close down or contract the activity of their particular institution.[136]

Clearly on one point there was broad agreement: the system of higher education was in desperate straits, but as to who was responsible for the

87

difficulties and how they should be resolved were far more difficult questions.

For its part the League leadership endeavoured to blame the university staff for misusing the institutions of self-management to maintain their particular privileges regardless of the interests of society. If this were indeed the case, it could still be argued that the League itself had to accept final responsibility. In this connection it must be emphasized that the laws pertaining to university governance did not provide for a simple system of self-management by the members of the university collective, but rather, for a system of 'social management'. 'Social management' meant that representatives of economic enterprises and of social organizations had significant representation within the organs of both university and departmental administration. This meant that the League of Communists was in a position to influence the decisions of these bodies through its influence over the nomination of community representatives to University and Departmental Councils. In fact, the justification of 'social management' rather than mere 'self-management' had lain in the argument that the university was too important to be isolated from society or to be freed of responsibility to society for its work.[137]

As mentioned in chapter III, the 1954 *General Law on Universities* provided that the university was to be administered by a University Council, a University Board and the Rector of the university. The University Council was the organ on which non-university personnel were represented.[138]

The council had comprehensive powers. It formulated the statute of the university, gave its opinion on the statutes of the various departments and submitted them to the People's Assembly of the Republic for confirmation, and confirmed the election of staff; it supervised the preparation of the budget, and appointed (and could remove) the members of the tribunal to which appeals could be made concerning decisions of the staff disciplinary court; similarly, it had the power to appoint and remove the members of the appeals tribunal of the disciplinary court for students. It prepared the student disciplinary regulations and confirmed the rules of student associations, and, finally, the University Council had the power to reach conclusions and give recommendations on questions which were described as being of common interest for the administration of the departments and for the organization of teaching and scientific work.[139] The University Board, which consisted of the Rector, Assistant Rector and Deans of all the departments, had the right to appeal against any decision of the University Council. However, it is significant to note that this appeal was decided by an extra-university authority, namely, the Republican Executive Council.[140]

Clearly, the University Council was the key element in university government, at least in terms of the law. The question of the composition of this body is therefore crucial. According to the 1954 *Law,* the University Council consisted of a single student representative, the

Rector and Assistant Rector of the university, a representative from the local city authority, a representative from each of the departments and, finally, representatives elected by the People's Assembly of the Republic. The representatives in the last category were to be elected from among scientific, professional 'and other public workers'. With all but a single category, the number of representatives was fixed; the exception concerned the members chosen by the People's Assembly of the Republic. The law specifically stated that the number of members chosen by the Assembly was to be determined by the Assembly itself. Therefore, at yet another step, provision was made for the assertion of final control by non-university forces.[141]

A similar situation applied at the level of departmental governance. In addition to the department Dean, Pro-Dean and one student, the Departmental Council was to consist of members elected by the faculty and by another group elected by the People's Assembly of the Republic. Again the number to be chosen by the People's Assembly was determined by that body itself at the time when it was choosing its representatives.[142]

Despite this apparent threat to university autonomy, the system of social management was defended as increasing rather than decreasing the rights of the members of the university community. It was emphasized that social management was qualitatively different from the preceding pattern which had been closely modelled on Soviet practice. The basic aim of the new system was described as being to free the university from interference on the part of the state administration. It was contended that in the past the most vital decisions had rested on the relationship between the university Rector and the responsible minister and that inevitably this relationship was one in which the Rector was subordinate. Consequently, the university had been simply a unit within the system of state authority.[143] This law, therefore, was a decisive step in university life which freed the members of the university community from the threat of petty meddling by the state administration and thus gave them greater scope to exercise their own initiative. The university's relations were now with the 'community' and the representative assemblies, rather than with the bureaucratic apparatus. An article in the *Yugoslav Student News* asserted there was general agreement that on the one hand the community should support the university and that, on the other, the university should be accountable to society for the use it made of these funds. Under the old pattern of relations where the state apparatus was the link between the university and society, the subjugation of the university was inevitable; the new system of social management would enable freer, more natural and democratic links to develop between the university and the community.[144]

Those who argued that the mechanisms of social management in fact infringed on university autonomy were vigorously criticized. The first point to note was the sharp distinction Yugoslav authorities made between demands for autonomy in 'old Yugoslavia' and the demands made in the current situation: in the pre-war period the struggle for autonomy was a 'progressive' one; then the progressive forces at the universities had sought independence from the reactionary influence of the bourgeoisie. By contrast, the demand for autonomy in the new socialist society was described as a reactionary concept. As Crvenkovski explained it, 'well intentioned people who have not yet succeeded in overcoming the remnants of the old in their own minds deserve our attention'. He insisted that it was necessary for people outside the university to be engaged in the effort to help solve some of the university problems and to help it adapt to the new situation. It was vehemently denied that the members of the university community had the right to do as they wished, free of any responsibility to the community. The university was not something above society. Indeed, the claim for autonomy was described as a convenient mask behind which to hide, as a slogan which non-progressive elements in the university could use to justify resistance to change and to protect their own privileges regardless of the needs of the community.[145]

It was contended that the educational institution was not like a factory in which the workers created a new value—those who provided the resources for the university had to be in a position to influence their utilization; it would be absurd to argue otherwise.[146] Despite the certainty expressed in such comments, it could be maintained that the right of social control of education need not inevitably follow from the fact that society provided the university's resources. As the Yugoslav leaders themselves admitted, the 'products' of the university were vital to the continued success of the process of development. That is, according to their own statements, it could be declared that the university was indeed creating 'a new value'.

Obviously, the major reason for insisting on final control simply related to the fact that society was far more concerned with the 'products' of the university than of the factory. It was frequently noted that successful socialist development to a large degree depended on how the new generations were educated and shaped, and that the leadership, therefore, could not risk entrusting the governance of the university solely to the members of the teaching collective. Social management was seen as a vital factor in the process of restructuring the bourgeois system of education to accord with the needs of the contemporary, socialist society. Even in the case of a factory it was observed that society retained the right to lay down certain rules governing price or quality in order to protect the community's interest. With educational institutions it was contended that such precise rules could not be drafted; the solutions to these questions depended on the subjective application of general principles to particular problems. In this context, therefore, the direct involvement of the community was necessary.[147]

Indeed, so the argument ran, not merely did society have the right to intervene, but this 'assistance' was in fact desirable, even from the point of view of the faculty. Social management was a system through which the freedom of the university staff would be enhanced rather than diminished. That is, in social management the apparent contradictions between autonomy and accountability, between responsibility and creative freedom, would be harmonized.

The first point stressed was that within the university which functioned according to the old pre-war form of autonomy, true freedom did not exist. To simply permit self-management within the university would be dangerous, since it would strengthen the tendency for the unversity to become a closed body fraught with 'cliquism', personal connections, hierarchical complacency, selfishness and the like. Therefore, far from destroying freedom, social management would lead to its enlargement, since the progressive members of staff would receive the support of forces within the society in their efforts to forge a more creative atmosphere within the university. This assistance, it was declared, should not be interpreted as signifying a lack of confidence in the teaching staff; indeed, this help from persons outside the university, whose perspective was not distorted through the prism of a clique approach, would be welcomed by all teachers who wished for a better future for their profession.[148]

Linked with this argument was the contention that the system of social management would enhance the creative freedom of the university staff by reducing their isolation from the challenges and achievements of the contemporary society. Thus, in contemporary Yugoslavia the university had more than 'mere autonomy': social management united those directly involved in education with those 'toilers' outside education who possessed a broader perspective; this 'happy solution' thus enriched the university atmosphere.[149]

From the first it was insisted that social management did not mean that individuals outside the university would meddle in instruction, give grades or otherwise interfere in the daily work of the teacher.[150] Indeed, the *General Law on Universities* enacted in 1954 specifically provided that the

> questions of carrying out the teaching programmes and scientific work shall be the exclusive jurisdiction of the teaching-scientific collectives.[151]

Another article virtually repeated this promise by guaranteeing freedom of instruction and scientific work at the university.[152]

Thus, it was claimed, social management linked the university to the community while guaranteeing 'full academic freedom'. The old concept of autonomy was disappearing but all that was positive in it was preserved.[153] Despite the confidence of this claim, however, it was clear that the potential for conflict between university staff and the representatives of the community existed.

The problem now is to assess the impact of this arrangement, provided for in the 1954 *General Law on Universities* and confirmed in the 1960 Law. That is, to what extent did these representatives of non-university bodies affect the functioning of the universities?

On the basis of the available evidence, their impact appears surprisingly small. This can be quickly illustrated by the debates concerning rationalization between departments within a single university. It was noted that frequently the university structure was excessively fragmented, that there was insufficient coordination and collaboration between departments and that often there was wasteful duplication. The efforts to remedy these problems were, it was claimed, defeated by the selfish desire of the members of the separate departments to maintain their particular privileges regardless of the interests of society or of the university as a whole.[154] Such attitudes, it was explained, ran counter to the spirit of the entire self-management system. It will be recalled, however, that the League leadership had expected such behaviour from members of staff; the imposition of the system of *social* management had been urged on the grounds that individuals and groups within the university had a narrow and selfish perspective, and, as a consequence, needed the assistance of representatives from outside the university who would take a more objective view. In fact, there is simply no evidence that these representatives played such a role. Indeed, the general consensus was that when it came to university matters both their knowledge and interest were often limited.[155]

Similarly, on the topic of curriculum reform, on which many strong words were spoken, some Yugoslav scholars have commented that the representatives from outside the university gave little direction, and that while they frequently condemned the curricula as being outmoded and irrelevant, they failed to specify actual examples.[156]

In practice, then, it would appear that the League failed to develop and utilize its powers within this system. Again the tendency was observed for the League leadership to stand outside the university and to subject the faculty to vigorous criticism without itself endeavouring to take the action which was within its power.

CONCLUSION

The university experience for many students was obviously not a happy one. The physical facilities were grossly overcrowded, the calibre of staff was often below a satisfactory level, the failure rate was staggeringly high and, to cap the matter, employment opportunities for many graduates were limited.

Throughout this period there was constant reference in official statements and in the press to the grave problems of the university, constant urgings that these problems should be remedied and constant complaints that meaningful change had not been secured. The most likely impact these official and press comments had on the students was to sharpen their perception of their unenviable situation and increase their cynicism and frustration.

Both the objective situation and its analysis served to persuade the student that he was a victim within the university system. But who was the villain? The officials and the press tended to describe the problem primarily in terms of the poor examination results and to attribute the bulk of the blame for this to the staff; in particular, the staff were condemned for their failure to 'reform' the curriculum to ensure that students could graduate on schedule and, at the same time, be prepared for a specific task. In general, it was contended that the faculty misused the device of self-management to preserve their own selfish interests and failed to make the most effective and responsible use of the resources provided by the community.

But was the university staff wholly or even largely to blame for the current difficulties of the university? In the first place, the narrow attitudes allegedly displayed by the faculty were exactly the attitudes ascribed to them when social management (instead of mere self-management) was introduced at the university—official spokesmen had maintained that education could only be reformed if representatives from outside the university were included in university and departmental councils. These representatives, described as having a broader and more responsible perspective, would ensure the transformation of the university to meet the needs of the developing, socialist society. The preceding has demonstrated that, in fact, the expected changes were not achieved. Clearly the representatives had not had the intended effect. But what is of great significance in the official comments on this 'failure' to secure reform, was the resounding silence regarding the role of the representatives from outside the university. Virtually the entire blame was placed on the faculty, who had, at worst, only behaved as predicted.

In the second place, it can be urged that many of the problems of the university were the inevitable consequences of the official policy of rapid expansion. This policy was pursued with little regard for the particular needs of society, or for the background of the entering students, or for the problems of providing adequate facilities and staff. It must be emphasized that consideration of these problems was not the province of a particular university department but rather the province of the League leadership. This flooding of the universities was largely responsible for the staggering failure rate, but rather than deal with the basic causes of this situation, the Yugoslav leadership demanded that the university staff treat the symptom. That is, the university staff was urged to prune the curricula so that the 'average' student would be able to graduate on schedule. The Yugoslav leadership claimed this would eliminate many of the difficulties facing the university and at the same time ensure the graduation of the necessary experts; however, to many among the university staff, this 'reform' meant changing the university into some form of low standard technical college. In this connection it has been suggested that a greater number of graduates may have been produced if the universities had not been so overloaded. That is, simply increasing enrolments did not automatically result in the graduation of a greater number of experts. And further, it has been suggested that, if the resources of the university had not been so diluted, the decline in standards might have been avoided.[157] These suggestions, however, imply that the single aim of the Yugoslav leadership was to make the best use of the university's resources in order to provide the necessary experts; this overlooks the fact that another aim of university expansion seems to have been to absorb some of the army of unemployed so as to enable the leadership to minimize and disguise at least the short-term effects of this serious problem.

Be that as it may, from the point of view of the students the essential points were: the universal agreement concerning the existence of a serious crisis in university education, the agreement that no significant improvement was under way, and the agreement that decisive action to remedy the situation was long overdue.

Chapter   V

THE MATERIAL SITUATION OF STUDENTS

As is indicated in chapter VI, student meetings towards the close of this period gave considerable—indeed, almost exclusive—attention to the question of student living conditions. Concern, bitterness and frustration were all very much in evidence.

The present chapter endeavours to present something of the reality of student life in order to give some indication of the strength of student feelings on this matter. Again, the daily reality must be seen in the context of the expectations aroused by the official oratory which led to the conviction among the students that they had the right to material security.[1]

It was claimed, as explained in chapter I, that university expansion was a means of breaking down privilege to provide opportunity for all. However, the various policies adopted seemed to lead to consequences opposite to those avowedly sought: despite the grandiloquence, the amount and distribution of aid to students was such as to leave those from economically poorer families at a distinct disadvantage in securing a university education.

For example, scholarships were few in number and were frequently offered not on the basis of merit or need but on the basis of 'connections'. Further, the amount paid was nowhere near enough to cover a student's basic living expenses; the recipient of a scholarship was still largely dependent on his parents for financial support.

As for student hostels and restaurants, these, like the universities, were grossly under-financed and thus below a satisfactory standard. The serious overcrowding meant, for example, that study facilities simply did not exist at many hostels—the obvious comment was that this seemed a most short-sighted method of saving. The meagre subsidies merely had the effect of making it a little easier for the less disadvantaged to attend university, but for the children of most workers and peasants this support was too low to be of any consequence.

Of course, the problem of ensuring equality of opportunity could not be solved merely by changes in student aid programmes at the university level. However, it is significant that not even these changes were made. It could be said that it was more expedient to continue the existing system, which favoured the children of bureaucrats, managers, teachers, officers, journalists and the like, rather than to battle for a scheme based on ability and need.

There was much discussion concerning the rights of students to adequate material support and much discussion of the many imperfections in the system and of the urgent need for reform, but little change in fact occurred. The net result seems to have been to highlight the very real difficulties experienced by the students and to evoke cynicism and frustration. In this regard it is worth noting the view and tone of an article published in *Student* in 1967. The writer discussed some of the problems encountered by students, noted the expressions of concern and the promises which he said had remained empty words, and then pointed to the constitutional provision referring to the equal right of all citizens to continue their education. This stated in part that 'citizens shall be entitled, under equal conditions . . . to acquire knowledge and training in any type of school and in any other educational institution . . .' The writer concluded bitterly that 'comment is unnecessary'.[2]

EQUALITY OF OPPORTUNITY

According to the official rhetoric, the new socialist society demanded equal opportunity for all citizens, regardless of family background, to continue their education. As an article in a 1956 issue of the *Yugoslav Student News* observed, in pre-war society university education was limited almost exclusively to the children of wealthy parents; the children of workers and of peasants had to overcome enormous barriers of social position and poverty before they could enrol at university. That era, the article claimed, was now a matter of history.[3] According to the official report of the 1958 Youth Congress, 'thousands and thousands of boys and girls . . . from the furthest mountain villages, from all strata of our population have for the first time the equal opportunity . . . to cross the threshold of the school'.[4] And an article in *Borba* in 1958 proudly reported that the Yugoslav state was fulfilling the obligations contained in the Universal Declaration of Human Rights, especially in the field of education where opportunity was open to all.[5] The previously cited article from the *Yugoslav Student News* confidently maintained that in contemporary society a new intelligentsia drawn from, and rooted in, the masses was being created, an intelligentsia markedly different from the old intellectual élite which stood above and apart from the people.[6]

Partly in order to realize this goal, the number of places at university was greatly increased. However, an effective programme of student aid was also necessary if this expanded opportunity was to become a reality for the children of workers and peasants. One measure of the effectiveness of the system of student aid would be the proportion of university students from worker or peasant backgrounds; it was clear, however, that according to this criterion, the system of student aid failed abjectly. The consensus of both scholars and officials was that entrance to the university in the new, socialist Yugoslavia continued to depend primarily on economic and social criteria rather than on ability.[7] Rather than education being the means through which social inequalities were broken down, education became the means through which social inequalities were perpetuated and strengthened.[8]

Precise data concerning the proportion of students from worker and peasant families is impossible to obtain because of the manner in which the official statistics office has organized and re-organized the pertinent data.[9] However, various scholars and officials have made estimates which give an indication of the situation. One such study concerned student enrolments in tertiary education institutes in Yugoslavia in 1961. The figures, reproduced in Table 9, indicate the 'over-representation' of children of white-collar families among the student body: the white-collar population constituted only 14 per cent of the whole population, yet their children formed fully half of the student population.[10]

TABLE 9

FAMILY BACKGROUND OF TERTIARY STUDENTS IN 1961

	White collar	Worker	Peasant
Approximate percentage of total population	14	35	50
Approximate percentage of tertiary student body	50	19	22*

* No explanation is offered why the figures do not total 100%.

Source: Velimir Tomanović, *Socijalna struktura učenika i studenata u Srbiji* (Social structure of pupils and students in Serbia) (Belgrade: Institut Društvenih Nauka, 1970), cited in Miloš Nikolić, *Omladina i Drustvo* (Youth and Society) (Belgrade: Komunist, 1972), p. 56.

Another researcher, looking at the situation from a different viewpoint, reported that in 1961/62 one-third of the children of white-collar workers were full-time students at the tertiary level, while for the children of workers and peasants the figures were one-twenty-fourth and one-fortieth respectively.[11] It was estimated that, if anything, the opportunity for the children of workers and peasants actually declined during the 1960s.[12]

Yugoslav leaders vigorously and frequently decried what they viewed as a serious and deteriorating situation, but failed to take effective action to deal with the problem. Probably the major weakness was that the greatly expanded enrolment meant that the resources available for student aid were spread so thinly that the amount available to any individual student was not sufficient to provide for even his basic needs. Obviously then, fewer children of workers and peasants were able to afford university education because their parents were less able to bridge the gulf between the amount provided in various forms for student support and the amount needed to cover basic expenses. As early as 1955 an article in *Politika* suggested that a more equitable policy would have been to limit enrolments so that an increased proportion of the student body could secure adequate financial support.[13] In particular, this would have made it possible to increase scholarship payments to a level closer to the cost of living. The actual details concerning both the number and value of scholarships are presented in the next section of this chapter.

Another factor which bore against the child from a poorer family was the fact that fewer scholarships were awarded to new students; if a student could not obtain a scholarship to help cover his first-year expenses it was often of little consequence to him if scholarships were more readily available for later years of study. Those enterprises offering scholarships clearly favoured later-year students, apparently because with these students there was a far greater likelihood of receiving a return on their investment. Thus, at the University of Sarajevo in 1963/64, those receiving scholarships in the first year and in the fourth year numbered 418 and 716 respectively[14]—and, of course, these figures take no account of the fact that the first year class was much larger.

Further discrimination occurred because of the system of general subsidies for student hostels and restaurants—students received the benefits of community support with inadequate regard for either their need or work.[15] Some indication of the extent of this community support is given by 1965 figures for Zagreb students which showed that students paid only three-fifths of the cost of their bed and board.[16] (And again first-year students were discriminated against in that they had greater difficulty securing a place in the subsidized student hostel—relative to their numbers, only a small proportion of the places in the hostels were reserved for new students.)[17]

Of course, the availability of financial aid for university students was not the only factor determining the opportunity for children from families of a lower socio-economic level. For both social and economic reasons the bulk of children from these families failed to complete secondary school, and often even elementary school.[18] In the republic of Bosnia and Hercegovina, for example, 10 per cent of children did not attend school at all and only 59 per cent completed the legally obligatory elementary school programme. And, according to statistics presented to the Congress of the Union of Youth of Serbia in 1968, only every fifth child of secondary school age whose parents earned less than 500 new dinars per month attended secondary school, while all children of parents earning more than 1,000 new dinars per month were enrolled.[19] Furthermore, the overwhelming majority of workers' children attending secondary schools—as many as 85 per cent—were enrolled in trade and vocational secondary schools rather than the more academically oriented gymnasium.[20] That the former category of school was of lower status and standard is readily apparent; in 1964, for example, the per capita expenditure was 66 per cent higher in the gymnasiums than in the trade schools.[21] Writing in 1973, one Yugoslav scholar went so far as to claim that the entire educational system was 'adapted to suit the children of the "middle" and "upper" social levels'. It is most significant that he even suggested that these differences within Yugoslav society might be described as class differences.[22]

Clearly, then, the problem of ensuring equality of opportunity could not be solved simply by changes in the broad strategy of student aid programmes at the university level. However, for the present purpose the important fact is that not even these changes were made.[23]

FINANCIAL AID

Cynicism and frustration also seem to have been evoked by the policy concerning scholarships and loans to students. Again much was promised and little delivered. Indeed, towards the close of the period under review, it was apparent that most students were having increasing difficulty in securing sufficient income to cover their basic expenses. This increased hardship, especially when coupled with accounts of inefficiency and injustice in the operation of the student aid scheme, could only have had a negative impact on student perceptions of the total system.

During the 1960s, as Table 10 indicates, there was a sharp decline in both the number and proportion of students receiving scholarships; in 1960/61, for example, three students in ten received a scholarship, but by 1967/68 this proportion had declined to a little more than one in ten.[24]

TABLE 10
UNIVERSITY STUDENT SCHOLARSHIPS

	Full-time University Students	Scholarship Recipients	Percentage of Full-time Students Receiving Scholarships
1959/60	69,489	20,472	29.5
1960/6i	76,462	23,320	30.5
1961/62	81,321	22,459	27.6
1962/63	80,764	18,536	22.9
1963/64	76,292	15,428	20.2
1964/65	75,653	14,819	19.6
1965/66	84,891	14,431	17.0
1966/67	90,675	12,266	13.5
1967/68	97,814	10,400	10.6

Sources: Federal Council for Statistics, *Jugoslavija 1945-1964, Statistički Pregled* (Yugoslavia 1945-1964, Statistical Review), p. 307; and *Statistički Godišnjak SFRJ 1969* (Statistical Yearbook 1969), p. 299.

Further, the value of the scholarships failed to keep pace with increased costs. In 1960, the average monthly scholarship was only 86.67 per cent of the estimated minimum living costs;[25] the average scholarship in 1963 was only 85.46 per cent of the monthly cost of bed and board alone at a student hostel. In that year the hostels accommodated scarcely more than one-fifth of the full-time students; the average scholarship was only 67.76 per cent of the minimum expenses of those forced to find private accommodation.[26]

An article in *Politika* in 1964 pointed to the sharp increases in student expenses and at the same time the serious decline in the number and relative value of scholarships. The writer concluded that as the number of students increased, so the concern for their well-being decreased.[27] Similarly, in August 1965 the Rector of Belgrade University stressed that scholarships were not keeping pace with rising costs; the average scholarship at his university was just 77.78 per cent of the costs of food and lodging. In his view the situation was very serious and becoming more so each day.[28] In November 1965 a *Politika* article claimed that student costs were rising far more rapidly than scholarship payments and that for most students the basic question was simply how to 'subsist'.[29]

In the academic year of 1965/66 the average scholarship was only between 33.75 and 38.57 per cent of what the Secretary of the Central Committee of the Union of Students estimated as the minimum monthly costs (including bed, board, clothes, transportation, books and recreation).[30] He stated bluntly that student living standards were 'sharply declining'. And just prior to the 'June events' it was reported in *Politika* that scholarships at the technical departments were only 60 per cent of minimum monthly costs while at other university departments they ranged from 20 to 60 per cent.[31]

The dramatic increase in costs was linked with the avowed trend toward the 'withering' of the state, which was seen as being necessary on both ideological and practical grounds. Concerning the former, it will be recalled that in justifying the break with the Soviet Union the Yugoslav leaders had referred to the power of the state in the Soviet Union as leading to the development of a situation in which the interests of a bureaucratic caste assumed precedence over the interests of socialism and the working class; the logic of their ideological position demanded a reduction in the role of the state apparatus. Concerning the latter, it was urged that political interference in the economy and society had restricted and distorted healthy development.

One expression of this trend was the decision made in 1962 to cease the payment of subsidies to student facilities, the aim being to ensure a more economic and responsible use of society's resources. Of course, it was denied that this burden should be thrust on the students without them being in a position to assume it; a corollary of the scheme to reduce subsidies was the plan to encourage growth in both the number and value of scholarships.[32] However, scholarships declined rather than increased, and republican authorities were forced to reintroduce subsidies to avert the total collapse of these institutions.[33]

The rationale behind the reduction in the number of scholarships paid from state funds was also linked with the goal of the withering of the state. It was urged that the state should drastically reduce its role in providing scholarships from the state budget, and that the individual economic enterprises and local communities should expand their scholarship programmes. That is, the withering of the state would be accompanied by an increase in the responsibilities of the organs of self-management. The costs of educating future academics would still be borne by general state and university funds, but the cost of educating future doctors, school teachers and the like was henceforth to be borne primarily by local communities based on their assessments of future needs. Similarly, the education of the future engineers, scientists, managers and so on was to be financed by the separate economic enterprises, again based on their plans for the future.[34]

. Such a scheme was described as having several positive attributes. Individual citizens, whether through the workers' council or through their representatives in local organizations, would have a closer involvement in these decisions. Second, the number and type of scholarships would not be set out in what was termed some arbitrary central plan but, rather, would be determined by each particular enterprise or community on the basis of its real needs. The scholarship fund would simply be one part of their investment in the future. Third, the close and direct contact between the scholarship donor and recipient would mean that the student would no longer be just one among thousands at the university; rather, there would be a group of people directly interested in his education and welfare. Further, this close link to his future colleagues meant that the recipient would be made more aware of his responsibilities to prepare himself diligently for his profession. It was confidently asserted that the sum of all these factors would mean a strengthening of self-managing rights together with a reconciliation of the interests of the individual student, of the particular enterprise or community organization, and of the total socialist society.[35]

This view assumed that it was reasonable to expect the beginning student to know exactly where his talents and interests lay and that investment in education was something that could be left to the market place. On this point it must be remembered that the typical Yugoslav enterprise or community was operating in financial circumstances that made it difficult for them to look beyond short-term problems. Nevertheless, the main thrust of the 1955 *Basic Law on Scholarships* reflected the desire of the leadership to encourage this fundamental reorientation and reflected the apparent confidence that such a reorientation was practicable.

Several articles of the 1955 *Law* had obviously been designed to protect the scholarship donor's investment so as to encourage potential donors to provide scholarships. For example, it was stipulated that the student could not change his particular course of study without the approval of responsible officials of the donor organization.[36] That is, in return for its investment the donor organization was entitled to receive the type of expert it needed. Further, the scholarship agreement could require the recipient to spend a specified period of time following graduation in the service of the donor of the scholarship. This period could equal the duration of the scholarship. The law also specified that the contract could provide that the recipient must return the full amount of his scholarship if he failed to meet his obligation. As a further safeguard, the law provided that a student who accepted employment contrary to his obligation to the donor could be fined from 10,000 to 50,000 dinars.[37] (The severity of this penalty may be illustrated by remembering that the average scholarship at this time was approximately 5,500 dinars per

101

month.)[38] Similarly, those who provided the alternative employment could also receive heavy fines if they were aware of the recipient's obligations; an individual official could be fined between 10,000 and 50,000 dinars while the actual organization could be fined between 100,000 and 500,000 dinars. In presenting the scholarship bill to the Education Committee of the Federal Council of the Federal People's Assembly, Rodoljub Čolaković, the responsible minister, observed that such measures were necessary to cope with the serious violations of what were at least the moral obligations of students to the donors of the scholarships.[39]

What was reflected in these provisions was an effort to persuade the potential scholarship donor to regard scholarship payments as a wise investment which would assure the continued supply of necessary experts. However, as the statistics showed, this effort met with little and ever decreasing success. The number of scholarships paid by the state 'withered' as planned but the economic and social collectives simply failed to make up the decrease. Indeed, towards the close of this period a marked diminution in their efforts was apparent. The statistics in Table 11, relating to scholarships paid to students at all tertiary educational institutions, clearly show the trend.[40] The decline in the number of scholarships is even more startling when set against the dramatic rise in student numbers. Thus from 1958/59 to 1967/68 the number of scholarships decreased by 49 per cent while the number of students in these institutions rose by 45 per cent; consequently, as noted earlier, this meant that the proportion of students receiving a scholarship dropped from approximately one-third to approximately one-tenth.

TABLE 11

TERTIARY STUDENT SCHOLARSHIPS

Donors of Scholarships	1958/59	1962/63	1967/68
State	14,830	10,112	4,563
Educational institutions	2,003	320	395
Economic organizations	7,865	10,853	7,160
Social organizations	1,213	834	208
Others	—	2,330	888
Total number of scholarships	25,911	24,449	13,222*
Number of full-time students	78,911	106,439	143,430
Percentage of full-time students with scholarships	32.8	23.0	9.2

* Correct total of this column is 13,214. Error in the original.
Source: Miodrag Milenović, 'Dinamika razvoja visokog školstva i zapošljavanja diplomiranih studenata' (The dynamics of the development of higher education and the employment of graduates), *Ideje,* vol. i, no. 2 (1970), p. 255.

There were several obvious reasons for this failure on the part of the potential donors to play their part towards realizing the hopes of the Yugoslav leadership. First, following the logic of the market place, it was preferable to offer employment to those already graduated. This meant that the organization did not have to cover all possible contingencies in planning its scholarship programme. In particular, it was not necessary to provide for the probability that the prospective expert would take significantly more time than prescribed before graduating or even fail outright. Thus, some enterprises did not 'invest' in scholarship funds but preferred to use their money to recruit the personnel they needed, when needed, by offering housing, a higher salary and other material inducements. The serious employment situation for young experts at the end of this period, particularly following the introduction of the 'economic reforms', meant that it often made little sense for the enterprise to 'invest' money on scholarships. In the first place, they could choose from among the large group of unemployed graduates and, second, many firms at this particular time were reducing staff rather than expanding.[41]

Thus, some organizations were described as seeing scholarship payments not as a wise investment but rather as a heavy tax in a difficult period,[42] or as a 'burden' which they might be prevailed on to assume, but which they would tend to regard as a charitable contribution to education and 'even as a kind of socialist tip' given out of feelings of 'pity'.[43] Sadly it was observed that spokesmen for other enterprises sought to excuse their failure to provide scholarships by maintaining that binding the recipients was repugnant, since it represented the 'immoral, brutal and legalized purchase of experts'.[44] These spokesmen certainly did not appear to share the confident assumption underlying the scholarship system that the links and mutual obligations between donor and recipient would become close and mutually satisfying.

That close ties between donor and recipient did not always develop is further illustrated by the fact that many enterprises had little interest in the students they were supporting. On occasions they had to be reminded to send the money, they paid little attention to the student's choice of courses or his work, and when the student finally graduated it was not unknown for the enterprise to discover that it had no use for a person with his particular skills.[45]

Unpleasant experiences with past scholarship recipients also encouraged the tendency on the part of many enterprises to look askance at scholarship schemes. Numerous cases were reported of graduates failing to report to the enterprise to which they were obligated.[46] In most cases this was due to the reluctance of the young expert to leave a major urban centre;[47] in a few cases, rival enterprises even wooed a graduate or near graduate away from the enterprise to which he was obligated by offering a higher salary and by offering to reimburse the scholarship payments on his behalf.[48] Even when the employment situation deteriorated towards the close of this period, there were still reports to the effect that some scholarship holders were evading their obligation; apparently they took advantage of the opening of the borders to seek employment in foreign countries.[49]

The press and the Yugoslav leadership continued to preach and plead that the solution of the scholarship problem lay primarily in the hands of the enterprises and local organizations, emphasizing that the provision of scholarships to support the future experts must be the responsibility of the organizations which needed these experts.[50] Yet, these attempts at persuasion appeared to have limited impact. Once again the reconciliation of diverse interests (in this case students, social and economic collectives and the total society) proved to be far more difficult than the glib official rhetoric had indicated. In particular, economic enterprises and local organizations were not persuaded that it was in their vital interest to support a vigorous scholarship scheme. The drastic decline in the number and value of scholarships reflected this simple fact.

Inevitably, the contraction of the scholarship system, especially when set against the expectations which the pronouncements of the leadership had aroused, led to considerable bitterness. This was compounded by the widespread realization of the serious abuses in the system; the nine-tenths of the student body without scholarships was acutely aware that the fortunate few were not invariably chosen according to the prescribed rules.

The fundamental principles by which students were to be selected for scholarships were clearly stated in the *Basic Law on Scholarships* of 1955. The basic principle of this law was that the successful applicant should be one 'who shows success in his studies or . . . who distinguishes himself by his qualifications and capacity for . . . improvement'.[51] It provided that preference was to be given to candidates of limited means or to those who had lost their parents in the 'War of National Liberation' or as the result of 'fascist terror'. When the donor of a scholarship was the district people's committee, preference could be given to applicants from that district or ward, and when the donor of the scholarship was an economic organization, preference could be given to the children of the members of the particular organization.[52]

In an effort to ensure the implementation of these principles, the law provided that notice of at least thirty days must be given of the scholarship competition and that the award should be made by an 'independent' commission. Further, any unsuccessful applicant had the right to appeal if he felt that improper procedures had been observed or if he felt that the selected applicant did not fulfil the conditions established in the law. The appeal body had the power to overturn decisions of the selection committee.[53]

University departments were required to keep a record of scholarships held by students and, at the end of each school year, they were required to submit a report on each recipient's progress to the donor of his scholarship and to the appropriate scholarship commission. And if the donor or scholarship commission ascertained that the recipient was not progressing satisfactorily, then they were obliged to stop further payment of the scholarship. Only prolonged illness or other justified causes could prevent the application of that rule.[54]

In brief, the law sought to ensure that scholarships were awarded to the deserving. In practice, however, the scholarship system frequently served only to enhance the privileges of a select group. In the first section of this chapter it was stated that children from worker or peasant families found it difficult to enrol at university in part because there were simply so few scholarships. In addition, however, it is clear that they frequently found themselves the victims of discrimination in the competition for the scholarships available.

A *Borba* article in 1957 frankly acknowledged that the small proportion of students from workers' families was partly due to the method of granting stipends, but asserted that the situation was improving. This claim was supported by statistics for Zagreb University in 1955/56 which showed that students from workers' families were about twice as likely to be scholarship recipients as children of 'white-collar' workers.[55] However, the figures on which this optimism was based also showed that only 10 per cent of enrolled students were from workers' families and 53 per cent from white-collar families. Therefore, rather than conclude that the scholarship policy favoured the children of workers, one might as readily conclude that the figures only showed that it was substantially more difficult for the child of a worker to study at the tertiary level without a scholarship.

Certainly, towards the end of the period there was general acknowledgement that many scholarships were secured, in the words of a 1964 *Komunist* article, on the basis of 'connections, favouritism and "knowing the right people"', and that as a consequence, children of less influential parents had great difficulty in obtaining scholarships.[56] A *Borba* article in 1965 outlined abuses in the scholarship system of the district of Niš, claiming that scholarships were granted on the basis of ties of family and friendship: the competitions for scholarships were a farce since no attention was given to an applicant's success at school or the financial status of his parents. Thus, of the scholarships awarded in this particular district, only 12 per cent had been received by students from a worker or peasant background, while the bulk of the remaining scholarship holders came from either 'white-collar' families or from what were termed 'rich families'. Further, the scholarship commissions were not always independent: the members of one scholarship commission were threatened that they would lose their jobs if a certain applicant were denied a scholarship.[57]

Similarly, Tito, in his address to the Eighth Congress of the League in 1964, pointed out that only a 'very few' scholarships were received by young people from working-class families while a larger number was received by the children of white-collar workers, and that the difficulty faced by students from low-income families was reflected in the social composition of the intelligentsia.[58] Veljko Vlahović, Secretary of the Central Committee of the League, developed this theme in his address to the Congress. He urged that the League of Communists must seek to correct the condition which determined the composition of the student body for there was 'a danger that certain sections' of the community 'will have a monopoly of training for intellectual occupations'. He bluntly stated that the present scholarship system did not select out the 'capable and industrious', that it neglected those from working-class families, and that it had inherent in it 'elements of subjectivity and privilege'.[59]

In the same vein an article in *Komunist* in 1966 stated that it was a

> well-known fact that children of doctors, engineers, public workers and artists often have priority when scholarships are distributed. There too we find the well-known system—'I will give to you and you will give to me'. Thus many capable young people without financial resources and without necessary 'connections' cannot proceed.[60]

Indeed, in another article in the same year, the charge was levelled that on occasion scholarships were granted to the children of highly skilled experts as an inducement to these experts to move to that particular provincial town.[61]

According to the President of the Central Committee of the Union of Youth, the young people of Yugoslavia were 'revolted' by the method of settling such matters through the system of 'personal links and connections'; in his view, this constituted a system which was more powerful than that of self-management.[62] Inevitably, then, as the proportion of students receiving scholarships declined, so there was a commensurate rise in the number of students who felt that they had been unjustly treated and who were angered by the bias and injustice of the scholarship system.

It was urged that far greater publicity must be given to the competitions.[63] (Obviously, the less publicity given to an award the better were the chances for the children whose parents were members of the local 'in' group.)[64] In this connection, it was emphasized that there must be greater involvement of the Union of Students, the Union of Youth and other community organizations.[65]

In addition, it was insisted that those provisions of the law designed to ensure that the scholarship system was 'stimulative' should be observed. Reports revealed that often no effective check was kept on the progress of scholarship recipients; for example, an article published in 1966 indicated that officials at Belgrade University were unable to provide even the names of scholarship recipients.[66] And numerous articles protested the fact that payments were continued to those many students whose work was unsatisfactory.[67]

Resentment was widespread. Most students were bitter either because they did not receive a scholarship or because the scholarship payments were so low. Only a small number appeared to have no financial worries. There were even those with money to spare: often their life was one of expensive clothes, frequent foreign trips, special tutors, expensive cars, and the like.[68] Naturally, this only exacerbated the resentments and frustrations of the less fortunate students.

As the number of scholarships declined, so efforts were made to expand the student loan programme. A system of student loans had first been introduced in 1952 to assist those who had completed the required number of courses but who had not completed all of their examinations. Later, loans were made available to recipients of scholarships to help them bridge the gulf that developed between the scholarship payments and basic costs.[69] In both cases, therefore, loans were intended only to supplement the basic scheme for student aid, namely, scholarships. However, by 1965 it was clear that it was intended to develop the system of student loans into the basic form of student support.[70]

Initially, the expansion of the loan programme was advocated primarily on the grounds that it was essential, but, as is often the case, a virtue was made of necessity. For example, a member of the Executive Committee of the League even claimed in 1965 that the principal reason for changing from the system of scholarships to the system of loans was not financial, but was designed to develop more positive attitudes towards work. In the first place, the student would be stimulated to complete his studies on schedule since the sooner he graduated the less he would have to repay. Second, the scheme would help students to realize that their success at university and in finding employment was dependent on the system of education. Hence, the students would become motivated to exert pressure in order to secure changes in instructional programmes. In other words, the students would now join in the struggle for educational reform.[71]

By the close of this period, loans had indeed become the major source of student aid but this was due more to the contraction of the scholarship programme than to the expansion of the system of loans.[72] In 1967/68, 17 per cent of the total full-time university enrolment received support from the loan fund while only 10.6 per cent received scholarships. However, it must be remembered that the proportion of scholarship holders alone had been as high as 27.6 per cent in 1961/62.[73] As for the amount of money lent to each student, it was acknowledged to be far from adequate. An analysis issued by the Serbian Republican Secretariat for Education and Culture in 1970 calculated that the average monthly loan payments covered only half of the student's basic costs.[74] And, of course, there were reports that many loans were also obtained on the basis of connections rather than merit or need.[75]

Thus, at the close of the period under review, three-quarters of the student body received no direct financial aid from the community while the remainder received aid at a level which can only be described as generally inadequate.

STUDENT HOSTELS AND RESTAURANTS

Earlier chapters of this study have, in passing, indicated something concerning the unsatisfactory conditions at student hostels and restaurants. The aim in the present section is to give some actual examples of the difficult situation in these facilities.

The general picture in student hostels was one of gross overcrowding. One article, published in *Mladost* in 1964, noted that the pressure of numbers had led to a situation where in one hostel there was an average of eleven students to a room.[76] In this barracks-type situation, even sleeping would be difficult, and studying in one's room would be impossible. Similarly, in 1965 the four student hostels at Novi Sad in Serbia had a capacity of 776 persons but almost double that number was accommodated there; beds were crowded into all available spaces, including the study and recreation rooms. Inevitably, the *Politika* article concluded, the hostel was no more than a place to spend the night.[77]

In May 1968 an article in *Student* reported that the hostels at the Belgrade Student City which had been planned for 4,609 students, in fact contained some 5,829 beds. Even more startling, the hostels actually accommodated approximately 7,000 residents. Thus, five beds were squeezed into the space originally intended for four, and for each five beds there were on average slightly more than six occupants; these 'illegal' or unofficial tenants were for the most part simply unable to secure official admission to the hostel and unable to afford private accommodation. The extra residents (both official and unofficial) meant that actual occupancy was more than 50 per cent above the planned capacity.[78]

Sanitary facilities were far below a satisfactory standard. For example, in 1968, to serve the 5,829 'legal' residents of hostels in the Belgrade Student City, there were only 52 showers (and of these, 'many' were described as needing repair). That is, there were approximately 112 students per shower; the student was well advised to take along a book to while away the time waiting in line.[79]

Similarly, there were reports that conditions at some hostels were poor and, indeed, dangerous. Thus, an article in 1967 described how the residents of one hostel had been without heat, water and electricity for two days and that the official inspectors had warned that unless substantial repairs were made, the hostel would have to close down.[80]

Study facilities were often non-existent—as noted earlier, what were planned as reading-rooms frequently became bedrooms. An article in *Student* in 1966 reported that in the Belgrade Student City hostels there was not a single reading-room or library.[81]

Nor were recreational facilities any better. Again, conditions at the Student City in Belgrade indicate the extent of the problem: at one hostel two television sets were available to serve some two thousand students.[82] In 1966 it was reported that there was no student hall, gymnasium or playing field. Students played football on the asphalt paths. Further, each building at the Student City had only one small club room; in 1966 it was estimated that altogether these club rooms could accommodate some two hundred of the approximately six thousand residents.[83]

In this situation of gross overcrowding and grossly inadequate facilities it was scarcely surprising to learn that morale among students was low, that often bitterness concerning conditions was expressed, and that most appeared to abandon the effort to use the hostel as a place in which to work.[84] In 1963 the retiring Rector of Belgrade University singled out the persistent singing and shouting in student hostels as something which caused him great distress.[85]

Despite the unsatisfactory conditions described, there was always a strong demand for admission. Each year a significant percentage of applicants, often more than 25 per cent, was unsuccessful. The main reason for the heavy demand was its cheapness compared with private board. A survey of residents at hostels in Novi Sad, reported in 1968, showed that 71.15 per cent had decided to live in a student home for 'purely economic reasons', 9.61 per cent cited both 'economic reasons' and the desire to live with other students, while another 15 per cent referred to 'economic reasons' and, surprising as it may sound, to the fact that the hostels provided better living conditions than were available elsewhere.[86]

The student restaurants were reported to be overcrowded, and to be serving food which was often below an acceptable quality and quantity for young people. An article published in *Mladost* in 1964 reported that the average calorific value of the food served in Belgrade student restaurants was 26 per cent below the recommended level.[87] Another report quoted a Professor Miloš Bogdanović who claimed that the inadequate diet had a serious effect both on the students' health and their capacity to work.[88] And in regard to the overcrowding, several articles published in the 1960s noted that students wasted considerable time, even up to an hour, before finding a vacant seat.[89]

CONCLUSION

There can be no doubt that in the period prior to the June events, the majority of the student body could be described as living in difficult circumstances. As the President of the Belgrade University Committee of the League had commented in 1964, it was unrealistic to expect that society's future leaders could be satisfactorily educated from a social and cultural point of view without the allocation of greater financial resources; a proper climate could not be achieved 'where there are no sports playgrounds, or dancing halls, where there are no reading rooms, no social clubs, no premises for cultural and artistic and social work, and no conference halls for serious discussions'.[90]

The blunt truth was that the Yugoslav leadership had encouraged university enrolments to grow at a rate and to a level far beyond the capacity of society to support. The only rational explanation for the leaders' attitude towards growth in student numbers seems to be that, as observed in chapter IV, it enabled them to disguise and minimize at least the short-term effects of widespread unemployment among the young.

Not only was it generally felt that student standards were inadequate and declining compared to general living standards but, more importantly, it was felt that the assistance they received fell far short of the proclaimed ideals.[91] In particular, the constant official emphasis on equality of opportunity inevitably implied a programme of student support far different from the actual situation. Throughout this period, there were frequent expressions of official concern, frequent promises that the basic problems would be tackled and frequent occasions when the aid finally extended fell short of what the students felt was essential. The consequence of the discongruity between the rhetoric and the daily reality was often cynicism, or anger.[92] To some extent this was similar to the consequences described as deriving from the discongruity between the ideal and actual role of students in university self-management. However, in marked contrast to the situation at student hostels and restaurants, the self-managing system was something which the student could for the most part ignore, but every time the student tried to sleep, take a shower, have a meal, watch television, play a game or study, he was brought face to face with the harsh realities of his material position.

Chapter VI

YOUTH ORGANIZATIONS AND THE IDEOLOGICAL
EDUCATION OF THE YUGOSLAV YOUTH

This chapter endeavours to survey and note the assessments by Yugoslav officials, scholars and journalists of the work of the youth organizations in the ideological education of the Yugoslav youth and, in particular, of the university student. The chapter touches on the entire post-war period up until the June events, and relates to a vast topic—these organizations were concerned with a wide range of activities, they were frequently subjected to critical examination by the press and by the League, and their basic forms of work were sometimes modified and even on one occasion drastically altered. All of this took place within the matrix of various changes in the broad political system and often, therefore, reflected changes and developments in Yugoslav society as a whole. Inevitably, therefore, this chapter simplifies a very long and complex story. Nonetheless, it is hoped that it brings out the major themes with sufficient clarity and persuasiveness.

In particular, it is hoped that it demonstrates the aims, methods and essential nature of these organizations, the fundamental contradiction inherent in their methods as well as something of the broad obstacles impeding the realization of their ambitious goals.

The principal aim of these organizations was what Tito described as the creation of the 'new socialist man'.[1] In this vein, the Report of the 1953 Congress of the People's Youth stressed that the entire activity of the People's Youth organization 'must be permeated by [the] deep moral education of the young people'; 'it should nurture . . . all those most humane and noble traits' which should characterize the citizens of a socialist society.[2] Similarly, the several statutes which governed the work of the Union of Students reveal a strong political spirit. Thus the 1956 Statute described the Union as a 'political and educational organization'[3] which was entrusted with the task of developing student interest in the study of Marxism, raising the 'consciousness' and strengthening the ideological and political unity of the 'socialist intelligentsia'[4] who would be 'good experts and active social workers'.[5]

According to the Conclusions of the Fourth Congress of the Union of Students, held in 1959, the 'basic task' of the organization was the ideological education of the socialist intelligentsia; the Yugoslav Union of Students 'should, to a greater extent, be a school' in which students would be prepared for their future responsibilities in society; the political and educational work of the Union should be directed towards such

111

objectives as increasing student interest in social and political activities and developing their feelings of social responsibility toward the community. In this regard, it was observed that since the programme of the League was the 'programme of our socialistic development', it should be the basis of ideological work, and the content of ideological work should be oriented toward a 'deeper study of a socialistic development'. A deep knowledge of Marxism should also be developed because this was a 'prerequisite for understanding . . . contemporary social needs; in this way students [would] become capable of following the contemporary development[s] independently'. Students should be familiarized 'as realistically and directly as possible with the economic, social and other problems of our development and especially with the communal system of self-management'; they should be acquainted with the weaknesses of the capitalist society and familiarized 'with our revolutionary past'.[6]

Comments made in 1952 by Čolaković, a member of the Central Committee of the League of Communists and President of the Federal Council of Education, Science and Culture, further illustrate official goals concerning the political education of students. He stressed that a sense of responsibility for the fate of the country and the people must be developed among them, they must be educated to be bold and persistent, they must be men who would place the socialist community above everything else, and they must be capable of keeping, in the face of all the difficulties of the present times, a bright spirit and a confident faith in the future.[7]

This 'new socialist man' would thus be one who had been imbued with the attitudes and values regarded as appropriate to the system of self-management. A vital question is to evaluate the success of these organizations in realizing these bold aims, or rather, to note and endeavour to explain their widely acknowledged failure. According to the official Yugoslav view, these organizations had failed principally because the methods of work were inappropriate, due largely to the fact that the primary concern of the youth leaders was the advancement of their own careers.

The principal youth organization was the broad umbrella organization known as the People's Youth, and from 1963 as the Union of Yugoslav Youth. An important part of this larger body was the Union of Students, which was formed as a distinct section of the People's Youth in 1951; until that time, working youth and students at both the secondary and tertiary levels were organized within a common framework. What was stressed in the discussions concerning this change was that the old undifferentiated form had failed to produce satisfactory results. The view was expressed that a body specifically catering for students at the tertiary level would arouse greater interest and thus prove a more effective instrument of political education. However, it is impossible to study the Union of Students without considering the larger organization. From the first it was insisted that the student organization was to remain an integral part of the larger body, since one of the essential attributes of the 'new socialist intelligentsia' was that it would have close links with other elements in Yugoslav society, including, of course, the non-student youth.[8]

There are, however, other and more compelling reasons for examining the part in the context of the whole. In the first place, the leadership of the student body and the broader youth organization persistently overlapped, the most significant example being, of course, Mika Tripalo. From 1950 to 1953 he was the Secretary of the People's Youth in Croatia. He then held the presidency of that body from 1953 to 1955 and at the *same time* was President of the Union of Students for the whole of Yugoslavia.[9] To take another example, in 1968 fourteen of the twenty-member Presidium of the Union of Youth were either graduates or students, that is, either former or present members of the Union of Students.[10]

And while the officials of these two organizations moved back and forth from one to the other or held high office in both simultaneously, it must also be remembered that the ordinary members of the Student Union were almost invariably former members of the Youth Union and that consequently their attitudes to the student organization could be expected to reflect at least in part their experiences with the Union of Youth.

The final reason for considering the Union of Students within the larger organization is that official analyses of ideological work among the young for the most part did not distinguish between students and non-students. The part and the whole were described as having the same broad aims, both were offered the same prescriptions for success and when the ineffectiveness of both organizations became impossible to ignore, their failure was attributed to the same causes.[11]

YOUTH ORGANIZATIONS IN SELF-MANAGING YUGOSLAVIA
PRESCRIBED METHODS OF WORK

In the immediate post-war period there was general official satisfaction with developments among the young. Many were described as strong supporters of the regime and confidence was expressed that the bulk of the remainder would be won over. Indeed, seen in retrospect, this was the period of greatest enthusiasm for the communist system among at least a significant section of youth. Several factors accounted for this. Many were naturally attracted by the heroic role which had been played by the new leaders in what was described as the War of National Liberation. A basic theme of this struggle had been the need to put aside ethnic differences in the face of the common enemy. To the young, more than any other section of the community, the slogan of 'brotherhood and unity', which described this policy, had great appeal. Many of them were readily convinced that their futures could not be secure unless the force of what were seen as petty and parochial groups was defused. Again, this strengthened the position of the communist leadership which stood alone as the symbol of a united Yugoslavia. Linked with this was the propaganda which condemned the backward-

113

ness, poverty and injustice of old Yugoslavia and held out the promise of a new, industrialized, egalitarian society. Again such a theme was especially attractive to the young.

Therefore, a significant section of youth welcomed the leaders of the National Liberation Struggle as the harbingers of a new order and thus, often with genuine enthusiasm, thousands of young people responded to the call to participate in work drives. These massive projects provided the young with an opportunity to throw themselves into the struggle for change; although acting according to the leadership's plan, the youth experienced the important satisfaction which stemmed from their belief that they were playing a central role in what was described as a heroic battle. This belief was deliberately fostered by Yugoslav leaders who showered praise on the strength, selflessness, patriotism and revolutionary fervour of the young.[12] An integral facet of these work drives was that youth from all parts of the country and from all ethnic groups were brought together in a common struggle. In addition, efforts were made to teach the illiterate to read, to enable many to acquire certain basic technical skills and the like. All this contributed to the apparent success, from the ideological point of view, of the work projects.

However, this revolutionary fervour was not as widespread as official comments often suggested and indeed was beginning to wane rather than to grow. No clear evidence is available concerning the strength of these negative feelings in the immediate post-war period—the problem was only acknowledged in the period following the break with the Soviet Union and then only in general terms.

As was noted in chapter I, the rupture with the Soviet Union threw the Yugoslav leaders into a state of confusion. Out of this confusion, and in an effort to justify themselves, emerged a defiant critique of the Soviet system and the bold enunciation of a new path to socialism.

As far as the People's Youth was concerned, the major significance of these developments was a frontal attack on what was termed formalism and bureaucracy within the organization. The previous work of the organization was criticized as involving manipulation of the membership towards the achievement of goals dictated by the state apparatus; the consequence of this manipulation was seen as leading to a decline in interest and activity. Tight control was now described as self-defeating in that it did not and could not lead to enthusiastic commitment, but at best to external conformity.[13]

What is significant concerning these explanations is that they described the problems among the youth as deriving almost entirely from faults in the organization of youth work. There was no suggestion that the waning of revolutionary enthusiasm might be inescapable or that it might stem at least in part from factors quite outside the youth organization.

The fact that there were some five thousand professional youth leaders was particularly criticized as leading inexorably to 'bureaucracy in work and ideas'.[14] These young and not-so-young professional politicians had been trained at special schools for a period of up to four or even twelve months.[15] They had the knowledge, power and status to dominate the organization. And as was pointed out, their primary loyalty was to their bureaucratic superiors rather than to the membership of the People's Youth; inevitably, it was claimed, the organization had begun to serve the interests of the leaders, rather than of the members.[16]

Certain features of the old organizations were described as suitable only for the early years of socialist construction, while other features, described as deriving from the Soviet Komsomol model, were adjudged generally inappropriate to prepare the young to take their place in a self-managing society. It was explained that in the Soviet Union the youth organization was perceived, not as an independent body in which the youth could develop their own abilities toward the construction of socialism, but rather as a 'transmission belt' through which the Party could control every activity and as an organization in which discipline was maintained through a system of subordinated relationships.[17]

The rejection of the old form of organization was exemplified by the rapid reduction in the number of full-time officers in the People's Youth from five thousand to less than a hundred.[18] Further, a new statute was adopted for the organization which marked a sharp break with the previous form. The essential change was described as involving the abandonment of 'democratic centralism' in favour of the recognition of the independence and initiative of the basic organizations.[19] The essence of the Constitution of the Union of Students, adopted in 1951, was similarly described as enabling the members of the various branches to adapt the activity of their branch to accord with their own particular interests and needs.[20]

Although clearly there were some within the League who feared the consequences of this general trend, the official League position was that democratization was essential. From this point onward the avowed emphasis was on the development, within autonomous and democratic youth organizations, of free and responsible members of the socialist community. It was insisted that education for a self-managing society could not be secured in organizations in which the young merely learnt the prescribed lessons and carried out their assigned tasks; self-management could only be learned through participation.[21] Ideological education, therefore, must not be reduced to the mere recitation of dogma. The methods of an earlier age were no longer appropriate[22]— it was a misconception to suppose that political work could be successful if kept within the 'framework of explanations and mere instructions';[23] 'slogans' and 'phrases' did not satisfy the young.[24] To be successful, ideological work among the young required 'bold answers' to 'delicate questions'. Their interest could only be aroused and maintained by the frank discussion of relevant, contemporary problems and only through free participation by the rank and file could the dangers of passivity and resignation be averted. In this vein it was insisted that the youth leaders must work with and as a part of the youth, rather than decide and organize from above,[25] and that the youth must be free of 'superfluous hierarchical relations and influences'.[26]

115

Indeed, it was largely to underline this emphasis on independence that the name of the People's Youth was changed in 1963 to the Union of Yugoslav Youth.[27] As Tripolo insisted in 1967, it was considered important that the youth organizations should not be a mere transmission mechanism for the League, but rather, organizations 'where we shall hear what the youth thinks about [League] policy and where it will influence that policy'.[28] In this vein, his successor, Badovinac, emphasized the importance of the youth movement as an active political force 'of young people' within the community rather than an organization 'for the young'.[29] The young were naturally but not inevitably a progressive force in society; this potentially progressive spirit could easily turn to cynicism, passivity and bitterness if the opportunity for real involvement in the reform of society were denied.

It was urged that these youth organizations should serve as a base from which the struggle could be organized against those who misused their power within self-managing collectives to protect their own privileges regardless of the rights of others or of the interests of the broader community;[30] as a base from which, for example, the frequent neglect and denigration of the young within particular self-managing collectives and within the community as a whole could be opposed.

Almost from the first, therefore, the official policy of the Union of Students stressed that the introduction of self-management at the university did not mean that the Union was relieved of any of its responsibilities towards resolving the problems of the students and the university; on the contrary, only vigorous activity on the part of Union associations could ensure meaningful student participation in the processes of self-management. In the first place, it was reiterated that the Union's political work could not be effectively developed in a context apart from immediate student interests and needs. Second, as the 1956 Report of the Union's Central Board observed, it was fallacious to think that 'by their mere existence' these self-managing bodies were 'a guarantee that the extant problems would be solved'. Finally, and possibly most important, it was maintained in this 1956 Report that the Union had the new responsibility of developing 'voters' meetings as a means of giving the mass of students, rather than merely a few student representatives, opportunity to participate in the process of self-management.[31]

The basic principles governing the work of youth organizations were expressed time and time again throughout the post-war period, but probably their most thorough and definitive presentation was made by Mika Tripalo in his important article published in 1961, entitled 'On the Occasion of Discussions Concerning the "Crisis" of the Younger Generation'. This article noted the basic endemic 'youth' problems in both the capitalist and communist countries and contrasted these with the situation in Yugoslavia. It boldly claimed that the problems which existed in Yugoslavia among the youth were relatively minor ones and were in the process of being eradicated through the operation of the system based on the recognition of the rights and worth of each individual or group,[32] that is, the system of self-management. According to Tripalo there was a

> crisis of democracy in the capitalist system—the youth there can achieve anything, except for one 'trifle': the ability to influence effectively the management of society and the solution of public issues.[33]

This feeling of helplessness together with the feeling of insecurity explained why the youth in capitalist countries inevitably became passive as far as politics were concerned.[34]

As for the efforts of the various political parties in the capitalist system to woo the young, it was obvious, Tripalo contended, why these efforts were doomed to failure. For example, within each social-democratic party there was probably fear that young people 'might become the most powerful opposition to its opportunist and reformist policy'. In addition, there was the 'disparaging social democratic attitude towards youth, and their conviction that young people are not mature enough to have independent organizations'.[35] On this point, Tripalo quoted Lenin's views concerning the vital necessity of allowing organizational independence for the young: 'Without full independence young people will not be able to build themselves into good socialists or to prepare to lead socialism on.'[36]

His analysis of the situation in the Soviet bloc was less trenchant, but his basic view was clear. Here passivity and uncertainty among the young often developed from the failure of the Party to respect the independence of the youth organizations which resulted in their tending to become mere instruments of the state. Tripalo expressed the opinion that, while in these countries 'many problems of youth have been evaluated more realistically', the tendency towards seeking solutions through 'stepped up pressure on young people and through administrative measures can at times be seen to be holding its ground'. 'Lacking the courage to put their finger on the real causes of many phenomena among young people . . . numerous leaders . . . emphasize that young people now have too many rights and too much freedom, and that this is the basic cause of difficulties with [the] youth.'[37]

According to Tripalo, a further reason for the radical difference between the situation in Yugoslavia and the situation in both the capitalist and the other socialist countries was that 'the system of self-management and the policy of reliance on young people make the solution of all social problems accessible to young people and to their organizations. [This also explained why] the negative phenomena found among a small number of Yugoslav youth are of secondary importance.'[38]

In this vein others urged that administrative measures were inappropriate in dealing with the fact, for example, that the young were often attracted to entertainment that might be considered harmful. Rather than ban such entertainments, it was necessary to organize and encourage social, cultural and professional activities which would attract the young away from these harmful influences.[39]

117

Similarly, it was urged that it was an error to think that the entire activity of the youth could or should take place within the ambit of the formal youth organizations. Rather, encouragement and assistance should be given to various clubs 'where the young can, *according to their own desires,* pass their free time'.[40] Such social activity was praised as an important means of fostering 'comradeship', of developing a 'liking for collective life and work' and of producing 'positive educational, working and ethical results'.[41] Of course, it was important that members of the youth organizations assist these clubs to help them broaden their focus and to eliminate certain negative features.[42]

One area of activity designed to attract the young but at the same time to have a positive effect was related to the National Liberation Struggle—by retracing the routes followed by the partisans, by visiting the war museums and by talking to former partisans the young would develop a deeper appreciation of the heroic revolution of which they were now 'enjoying the fruits'.[43]

The necessity of developing forms of work which would strengthen the links between 'intellectual' and 'working youth' was also emphasized. This was especially important because the vital aim was to see the creation of a socialist intellectual rooted in, rather than above or apart from, the working class. To secure this end it was urged that visits to factories should be encouraged, that greater attention to practical work be given in the secondary schools[44] and even that the voluntary work drives be re-introduced.

The work drives had been discontinued or drastically de-emphasized in 1952, principally because they were no longer of such economic value; it was easier and cheaper to use a man and a machine than it was to feed, house and provide facilities for hundreds of young people. Many professed to see the discontinuation of the work drives as a mistake; the youth who had neither the opportunity to fight in the War of National Liberation nor to work on the major youth projects in the early post-war period were said to feel inferior. The reintroduction of work drives was therefore welcomed because it enabled the present generation 'to experience directly its power and ability' and to participate in the process of socialist construction.[45] Furthermore, the students would be given the opportunity to experience the 'profound human value' of physical work and thus to gain greater respect for workers.[46] And finally, as Tito remarked: if we 'know how to occupy the youth ... then negative influences will not affect it'.[47]

As the preceding examples indicate, the activities of the youth organizations were to be attractive and relevant to the young but at the same time the effort should be made to ensure that they assisted in creating what was seen as the proper climate for the ideological education of the young. Only in this way would it be possible to realize the basic aim of these organizations, the socialist education of the youth.

It was consistently denied, however, that effort to ensure the maintenance of a proper atmosphere could be seen as a derogation of the real self-managing rights of the members of the various youth associ-

118

ations. Indeed, such 'positive help' would enhance the real freedom of the young—many of them were not politically mature and hence needed assistance against those hostile influences[48] which could lead them onto incorrect paths. Further, the transformation of society from the administrative-statist model to one of self-management made this ideological work of the youth organizations even more important; it was no longer a question of teaching the youth to obey directives, rather, they had to be prepared to make the 'correct' decisions for themselves.[49]

It was also insisted that this 'positive help' was not dictation. The entire system of self-management was built on the assumption that the decisions of the League were not automatically binding on all social organizations. Both the People's Youth and the Student Union were independent of the League of Communists; and communists within these organizations were no longer transmitters of instructions. Rather, they were individuals who sought to persuade and guide.[50] Therefore, the implementation of the League's policy within youth organizations depended not on directives from either leaders or rank and file communists, but, as Tripalo explained it in 1959, on the 'resourcefulness, ability and knowledge' of about a hundred thousand members of the League of Communists who were members of these organizations. The activities of these communists were naturally assisted, he added, by the 'enormous' moral authority of the League.

> The youth organization therefore is not and cannot be a transmission mechanism through which the party directives are carried out, but a place of activity of the communist among the masses of youth, one of the forms through which the youth accepts and promotes the party policy, and assesses and exerts influence on its formation.[51]

Similarly, in his major article of 1961, Tripalo emphasized the fundamental importance of the independence of youth organizations, but then went on to observe that

> to be sure, this does not mean that youth organizations can be absolutely independent in ideological and political respects. Owing to their being part of subjective socialist forces, all socialist organizations, those of youth included, seek to establish a common programme of socialist construction. In such circumstances, youth organizations accept the programme of the party and its ideological and political leadership. The implementation of this programme and the ideological-political leadership of the party among young people depend on their correctness and acceptability for youth, as well as on the skill, initiative, and organizational abilities of the tens of thousands of party members who work in the organization of youth.[52]

In other words, the youth organizations would be free to develop their own interests and own conclusions but at the same time they would be guided and inspired, largely by the activity of individual communists, to accept and work for the programme of the League.

As a 1952 article in *Borba* expressed it, the individual young communists were to transform the basic organizations of the People's Youth, as well as sports and recreation clubs,

> into collectives in which the youth will get [a] proper education, develop a sense of patriotism, fellowship, boldness, persistence and other positive human qualities . . . . By their continuous political activity, by their comradely attitudes towards the rest of the youth, without imposing and without doctrinairism . . . by their personal example, they [the young Communists] will make of them truly socialist collectives in which there will be no place for the reactionary elements which are foreign to socialism.[53]

In like manner, the article cited earlier, which contended that the young sought to be free of 'superfluous hierarchical relations and influences', at the same time claimed that they desired an organization which 'by various political influences' would develop 'positive' interest among its members; indeed, this was an essential attribute of a 'truly' political organization.[54]

The views expressed by Badovinac at the 1968 Congress of the Union of Youth are also worthy of note. He stressed the necessity for 'greater independence' and for 'enhancing the role of the membership' in the formulation of policies and in determining the activity of the particular organization. He went on, however, to maintain

> that such a democratically conceived organization cannot be an ideologically colourless association that will satisfy some mathematically computed interests of the youth at large. It could not be like that even if it wished. . . . As a political organization, the Union of Youth should express, assert and realize those interests of young people that have a socialist substance and content and that represent the aspirations of young people and of the working class. This means that the Union of Youth adopts a Marxist outlook on the world and that it acts on the basis of the Programme of the League of Communists. At any rate, without such an ideological character it would not be able to advance socialist development and to strive for the strengthening of self-government and for raising new active participants in the promotion of socialism.[55]

In short, provided the independence of these organizations was respected, provided attractive and relevant activities were offered and provided individual communists within the organizations conscientiously sought to inspire and guide their colleagues in the 'proper' direction, these organizations would ensure that the mass of the young would become effective and responsible members of the self-managing society. As the Report of the 1968 Congress of the Union of Youth grandly concluded, the youth movement was helping to raise the young in the

> spirit of socialist humanism—to be deeply humane, generous and honest, at work and in their private lives, to respect the rights and personal dignity of man, to love other peoples, to be uncompromisingly opposed to all injustice and discrimination, to be sincere and devoted friends, and to place truth above everything else . . .[56]

120

Organized in the Union of Youth, young people reach common positions and programmes of social action by means of confrontation and exchange of opinion. Within the Union of Youth they formulate in a democratic manner positions which serve as a basis for independent and direct participation in social decision-making. The Union of Youth endeavours to be the self-governing forum of all young people and to make possible through the struggle of opinions and arguments to reach the most progressive conclusions and attitudes on all social issues and matters concerning their own action.[57]

Despite the blithe statements to the effect that youth work was to be both free and correct, it is clear that at least a potential contradiction existed. The attitudes implicit in the comments concerning the immaturity of the young and their need for positive help are especially significant because they relate to the question of independence and respect for the youth and their organizations, which was, it will be recalled, the major point made by Tripalo to distinguish the local situation from that applying in both capitalist and socialist countries. In those countries the lack of respect for the views of the young and for the independence of their organizations was, he claimed, the cause of the serious and basic difficulties described as the *youth* problem; by contrast, only minor problems existed among Yugoslav youth, and these were in the process of being eradicated, because within the self-managing system there was respect for views of the young and full opportunity for them to express these views.

The vital question is whether this in fact was true and whether the twin principles, that the activities of youth organizations were to be both free and correct, proved to be reconcilable in practice.

THE FAILURE OF THE YOUTH AND STUDENT ORGANIZATIONS

Despite such ringing declarations as that just quoted from the 1968 Congress of the Union of Youth, the general consensus towards the close of the period under review was that the youth organization as a whole, and the union of students in particular, had abjectly failed to achieve the goals of involving the young and inculcating in them high ideals.

In general, the major problem was simply the inability of the youth organizations to attract the mass of young people. The Union of Students was on paper a most impressive organization, encompassing during the 1950s, for example, more than 80, or even 90 per cent of the student body.[58] Such statistics, however, were often meaningless because they did not distinguish between merely nominal and 'active' members. Many may have joined simply because, while membership was unlikely to hurt, it might possibly prove useful.[59]

Little hard data on the actual participation of university students in activities of the Union is available, but a Yugoslavia-wide survey conducted in 1960 (but not fully reported until 1966) does throw valuable light on this question.[60] Only 6 per cent of the sample were not members. However, a very large proportion (approximately 30 per cent of the total sample) claimed that for a variety of reasons (listed in Table 12), they did not participate in Union activities at all.[61]

TABLE 12

REASONS GIVEN FOR FAILURE TO PARTICIPATE
IN STUDENT UNION ACTIVITIES

	%
Do not agree with the organization's aims	0.8
Lack of time for such work	55.4
Am more interested in other matters	21.6
Present method of work is unsatisfactory	6.9
Poor previous experience in social activities	4.2
This work is not useful	1.9
Don't know	9.2

Source: Jugoslav Stanković, 'Studenti na radu, u društvu i slobodnom vremenu' (Students at work, in society and at leisure), in Janićijević and others, *Jugoslovenski Studenti i Socijalizam,* p. 347.

The researcher reporting these results noted with apparent satisfaction that only a tiny fraction indicated disagreement with the aims of the organization, and 'if we allow' that the claim of 'lack of time for such work' was genuine in most cases, then over half of the students concerned had a legitimate explanation of their failure to participate.[62] Having regard for the view of the Yugoslav leadership concerning the importance of this activity, this ready acceptance of the explanation 'lack of time . . .' is surprising. Indeed, on this line of reasoning the researcher could also have accepted the response 'am more interested in other activities' and then concluded that over three-quarters of the students concerned had an acceptable explanation for their lack of involvement. Both League and youth leaders had constantly emphasized that students were expected to view this activity as an integral and essential part of their preparation to become 'socialist experts'; for example, an article in the *Yugoslav Student News* of July 1959 roundly condemned the 'narrow-professional conception' of work and the insufficiently developed socialist consciousness of 'certain students' as evidenced 'by their passive attitude towards the Yugoslav Union of Students . . . [and] other social organizations'.[63]

As for those respondents who claimed to participate, the answers to other questions indicated that their participation was frequently only nominal. Thus, all students in the sample were asked to indicate how much time per month they actually devoted to the Union of Students; 74.6 per cent of the respondents 'did not devote even two hours per month to this work'. Among the remainder, the picture was certainly not one of great involvement; two-fifths in fact participated in the work of the Union only 'up to five hours per month'.[64] Clearly this meant no more than occasional attendance at a meeting or lecture. Responses to these and other questions (discussed below) in this survey led one of the researchers to conclude that only a minority was interested in political activity; a far larger group was either passive or at best merely outwardly conformist.[65]

A smaller, newspaper, poll, conducted amongst students at Zagreb University at approximately the same time, indicated similarly unsatisfactory results.[66] Only a third of the sample indicated that they took part 'with interest' in the work of the Union of Students. Among these results, set out in Table 13, it is interesting to note that over 10 per cent claimed to participate 'only when I have to'.

TABLE 13

ATTITUDES TOWARDS PARTICIPATION IN THE UNION
OF STUDENTS

	%
I participate with interest	33.5
I am bored sometimes	17.9
The work does not interest me	21.2
I take part only when I have to	11.7
I take no part whatever in the work of the Union of Students	11.3
No response	3.2

Source: *Komunist* 9 February 1961.

As for their actual views, a clear majority (63.5 per cent) thought Marxism was a 'true and revolutionary social theory'; some 12 per cent of the sample dismissed Marxism as dogmatic and 'somewhat obsolete', while the remainder indicated that they were not interested in such questions, or simply did not respond.[67]

Further, 71.9 per cent indicated that they endorsed official policy on religion (that is, they considered it harmful and unnecessary) while 'only' 21.8 per cent thought religion was indispensable. Less than 5 per cent of the sample indicated that they would have preferred not to live in the present period; the remainder were either 'satisfied' (61.1 per cent) or 'partly satisfied' (30.01 per cent) to be living in the present period. And despite what were termed 'foreign influences' and 'all our difficulties', only 3.55 per cent of the sample thought that they would be satisfied to live abroad. The great majority (71.7 per cent) thought that they would not be happy living abroad while 22.48 per cent 'sometimes' thought they might like to live abroad. As to whether Yugoslavia should join one of the existing military blocs, it was reported that only 3 per cent favoured such a step, while 78 per cent opposed it. It is interesting to note that almost one-fifth of the sample (19 per cent) answered that they had not considered this question or that they were not interested in politics.

Of greater significance was the fact that only 43.6 per cent thought that the Yugoslav political system was the best contemporary form of democracy. About one-fifth of the sample felt only lukewarm support for the system; this group described the Yugoslav system as 'not worse' than Western European democracy. Approximately one-quarter thought the Yugoslav system was not yet a 'genuine democracy', 9.8 per cent thought it had quite a few flaws in comparison with the democracies of Western Europe and 4 per cent did not reply. In explaining these results, an article in *Komunist* suggested that they were probably due to the fact that students still tended to be isolated from those 'deep processes' which had developed in Yugoslav practice; students obtained a more negative view because the system of self-management at the universities had not yet made a sufficient impact and because the students themselves had been insufficiently active.

A more systematic picture of student beliefs and attitudes in this period was provided by the results of the Yugoslavia-wide survey previously cited. As was noted, the overwhelming majority of the sample could not be described as 'active' in the work of the Union. Further, a majority of the sample showed a very low level of political knowledge. The students were asked to write down what they thought were the basic principles of Marxism: 37.7 per cent stated that they did not know or simply gave no answer; another 33.5 per cent gave what were termed excessively vague and general answers, or 'incorrect' ones. For example, they indicated that Marxism was 'helping others', 'personal freedom', 'the humanization of relations between people' and the like; according to the particular researcher, such attributes could not be said to be exclusively Marxist or even basic Marxist principles.[68]

A point strongly emphasized in the analysis of the responses, however, was the overwhelming approval of the general objectives of society. Thus it was stressed that more than three-quarters of the sample, as indicated in Table 14, either completely or largely endorsed the general goals of society.[69] Similarly, 80.7 per cent of the sample described the Yugoslav model of socialism as 'correct', 15.2 per cent did not know, and only 3.1 per cent thought it 'incorrect'.[70] Further, 60.3 per cent described themselves as 'supporters' of Marxism while a further 27.7 per cent described themselves as supporters 'to a certain degree'. Only 2.4 per cent said that they 'generally did not' support

TABLE 14

RANGE OF AGREEMENT OF UNIVERSITY STUDENTS WITH
GENERAL OBJECTIVES OF YUGOSLAV SOCIETY

	%
Complete	32.4
For the most part	45.8
Some	12.8
Don't know	6.7
Not at all	1.2
No answer	1.1

Source: Milosav Janićijević, 'Društveno-politički i ideološki stavovi Jugoslovenskih studenata' (Socio-political and ideological attitudes of Yugoslav students), in Janićijević and others, *Jugoslovenski Studenti i Socijalizam*, p. 16.

Marxism and only 0.9 per cent said that they 'absolutely did not'. Interestingly, over 8 per cent responded that they did not know.[71]

With some surprise it was reported that more than half of the students sampled indicated that they were prepared to place the interests of society before personal interests; the researcher observed that this was the type of response one would expect from an earlier period of socialist construction. However, it may be that the vagueness of the question and the fact that they were not being asked to make any specific commitment was at least partially responsible for this result. Table 15 gives the range of responses to one such question.

TABLE 15

RANGE OF AGREEMENT OF YUGOSLAV UNIVERSITY
STUDENTS ON THE FOLLOWING STATEMENT
The individual must be prepared to renounce certain of his rights and needs if this would aid the realization of important social goals.

	%
Yes, and for a considerable period	36.8
Yes, but it is not necessary that this should last too long	18.9
Yes, but only in particular situations	31.8
Absolutely no	2.4
No opinion	7.7
No answer	2.4

Source: Milosav Janićijević, 'Društveno-politički i ideološki stavovi Jugoslovenskih studenata' (Socio-political and ideological attitudes of Yugoslav students), in Janićijević and others, *Jugoslovenski Studenti i Socijalizam*, p. 21.

Certainly these results are important; however, it must be stressed that they relate to general and abstract questions. As many researchers have shown, there are often very significant differences between attitudes expressed in response to general questions and attitudes relating to specific questions.[72] Another question which related to this same point concerning commitment to the society, but which approached it from a different perspective, gave what appear to be significantly different results. The students were asked to rank in order of personal importance a mixed list of eleven values. This list included such values as a 'good financial position', 'to engage in socially useful work', 'possibility for creative work' and 'high social reputation'. These results, presented in Table 16 as grouped and calculated by the Yugoslav researcher, indicate that ideals of socio/political engagement ranked low in the list of preferred values while the 'greatest emphasis' was given to the ideals of material well-being and professional prospects. The researcher suggested that this emphasis on material well-being was only natural in a situation where material goods were in short supply; the consequence was that material values were often raised on a pedestal of the highest values, surpassing specific human values.[73]

125

TABLE 16

IDEALS OF PERSONAL IMPORTANCE TO YUGOSLAV UNIVERSITY STUDENTS

Ideals of material well-being	A = 3.118
Ideals of professional satisfaction and promotion	A = 3.047
Ideal of 'interesting and adventurous job'	A = 3.025
Ideal of 'to lead [a] quiet and decent life even at the price of not being well-known'	A = 2.997
Ideals of socio-political engagement	A = 2.817
Ideals of social prestige	A = 2.350

Note 1. 'Numerical values should be understood by starting from 1.00 as the lowest degree of the significance of the . . . value, and 4.00 as the highest.'
    2. The student responses on the eleven items were presented in the form of a 'pondered arithmetical mean'. Most of these reponses were then placed into kindred groupings by the original researcher and 'average magnitudes of pondered arithmetical means' calculated for these groupings.
Source: Manojlo Broćić, 'Stavovi i ocene studenata o nekim društvenim vrednostima' (Student attitudes towards and appraisals of some social values), in Janićijević and others, *Jugoslovenski Studenti i Socijalizam*, pp. 237-8.

Therefore, apart from the broad support for the general *goals* of the system, the survey as a whole demonstrated a lack of interest in social and political involvement, a low level of political knowledge and an emphasis on personal considerations.

While some satisfaction was derived from the results of these surveys, the situation in the years leading up to and including 1968 was such as to evoke a spate of articles and official statements describing the ignominious failure of the youth organizations to fulfil their goals. In the early 1960s it had been possible for leaders of the Union of Students to express broad satisfaction with their major task and to claim that interest in politics among students was constantly growing. A significant example of this was the meeting of the Presidium of the Central Committee of the Union held on 18 April 1963. The stated aim of this meeting was to show the significance and range of the political activity of the Union in recent months. Reportedly, much useful work, based principally on materials prepared by the League of Communists, had been accomplished. It was also claimed that new and more effective forms of ideological education had been developed to provide a thorough grasp of Marxist theory and contemporary social and political developments. These new forms included what were described as the many ideological and cultural tribunals and various discussion clubs.[74]

Yet, within a few years, the situation had deteriorated to such an extent that even the leaders of the Union were forced to acknowledge that ideological work within the Union was virtually non-existent. For example, the principal speaker at the Seventh Congress of the union held in 1966 noted that in the recent period the Union had not performed its role; in particular, there was stagnation in the organization's ideological political work,[75] and in 1967 the new President of the Belgrade Union of Students bluntly asserted that ideological work and cultural activities within the Union were at a 'dead stop'.[76] The actual ideological work of the various associations was described as often being limited to an occasional poorly attended lecture, and those relatively few who did attend lectures or meetings organized by the Union were, it was contended, doing so more out of a sense of obligation than out of interest or need.[77]

Instead of being a decisive factor in the socialist education of the young intellectual, the Union was described as an organization which was of little interest, relevance or significance to the mass of students. As another Belgrade student leader expressed it in December 1967, the fact was 'that as a mass organization' of students, the Union of Students did 'not exist'; the organization existed more as a gathering of leaders who were at once 'the beginning and the end of student politics'.[78] According to an article in *Vjesnik* of January 1968, so few students were involved in the activities of the Union of Students that it came to be described as the 'Union of Student Leaders'.[79]

Similarly, as an article in *Komunist* in 1966 noted, it was 'no secret' that the Union of Youth had become a narrow body isolated from the bulk of the young, that it had failed to develop as an organization which involved them or met their basic needs and interests.[80] On paper the Union of Youth still appeared to be an impressively large organization; however, as an article in *Borba* in 1965 pointed out, the membership subtotals frequently overlapped, thus the same person might be counted in two or more bodies.[81] Furthermore, as in the case of the Union of Students, membership did not signify activity. An article in *Politika* stated that most of the Marxist circles, debating clubs and the like simply did not exist, at least not in any meaningful and effective form. This, the article continued, must be stated frankly instead of talking of fictitious bodies which consisted only of their leaders.[82]

To all intents and purposes, therefore, the organizations which were intended to provide the environment for the socialist upbringing of the youth and to provide a major opportunity for the young to participate in politics, had ceased to function. And their failure had become so apparent that it could not be ignored or glossed over.

YOUTH LEADERS AND THE FAILURE OF THE YOUTH ORGANIZATIONS

What was the cause of this failure of the Union of Students and of the umbrella organization, the Union of Youth, to realize the goal of involving the young and of educating them to become responsible members of the self-managing society? Time and time again it was urged that the vitality and effectiveness of the youth organizations had been eroded by the careerism of their leaders.

As has been noted, the reorganization of the youth movement following the break with the Soviet Union emphasized the smashing of the bureaucratic apparatus and the encouragement of the basic associations of student and non-student youth to develop their own activities. Constantly it was stressed that only by allowing participation was it possible to have an effective programme of ideological education and that instruction and manipulation from above could only lead to boredom and, at best, outward conformity. However, despite this talk of freedom, and despite the fact that the number of full-time youth leaders had dropped from some five thousand down to fewer than four hundred,[83] the general consensus was that bureaucratic forms of leadership had re-emerged,[84] and that the youth organizations had failed to transform themselves into democratic bodies.[85] As the President of the Union acknowledged in 1966, even these few hundred professionals had too much influence within the organization.[86] And while the stratum of professional leaders may have been thin, it was suggested that many among the non-professional group of leaders quickly learnt to think like their superiors.[87]

Within the Yugoslav political system appointment and promotion was for the most part a process of co-option. Several articles emphasized the fact that leaders of the youth organizations were chosen from above rather than below.[88] For example, the Report of the 1958 Congress of the People's Youth noted that in a single year, one-third of the Central Committee had been 'unable' to continue and hence it was necessary to co-opt individuals to fill the gaps. (Many of the resignations were no doubt due to the fact that the particular individuals had been co-opted to higher duties.)[89] And a survey of Zagreb students in 1961 disclosed that more than half of the respondents did not feel that the best candidates were in fact chosen as office holders in the Union of Students.[90] As was brought out at a meeting of the Belgrade University Committee of the League, elections for the Union of Students were not always carried out in a democratic fashion.[91] From the first, therefore, the leaders of the various youth organizations were on a different footing from the mass membership, and from the first they were accountable to 'this or that political leader' rather than to the youth.[92]

The leaders were further separated from the membership by virtue of the fact that they were invited to special Party courses where they studied League policy and learned the direction in which they should lead their particular organization. According to the Conclusions of the Central Committee of the Union of Youth in 1966, their greater knowledge and experience meant that the feeling often developed that only these leaders were capable and indeed that they were irreplaceable. This meeting went so far as to state that many youth leaders had worked in these positions for an 'excessively long time'.[93] No actual examples were given in this particular article; however, the most significant example of length of service was, of course, Mika Tripalo, who held high office in the youth organization in the entire post-war period right up until 1962.

Many leaders were described as being too quick to condemn anything which transgressed certain narrow limits; disagreements were pushed beneath the surface and spontaneity was regarded with fear. As one Yugoslav academic expressed it, such people wanted rain, but without thunder and lightning.[94] According to an article in *Mladost* in 1967, this attitude was also reflected in the fact that many youth leaders concerned themselves primarily with external appearances and hence organized rallies and celebrations rather than promoting genuine internal activities.[95] This in turn derived from the tendency to appraise the work among the youth largely on the basis of 'reports' and 'meetings'. Yet, as one youth leader was quoted as saying in 1966, many of these meetings were simply formal rallies or demonstrations while the reports were full of generalizations such as those urging a struggle against 'negative phenomena'.[96]

The President of the Belgrade University Union of Students in 1967 acknowledged that student requests were filtered and refined as they passed through the bureaucratic apparatus of the Union and the university. Thus a request made at a student meeting of a particular department would then be processed by the departmental committee of the Union; it 'often' happened that this committee would revise the request according to its own view of what was appropriate.[97] As a participant in what was termed a round table discussion among student leaders held in January 1968 complained, it was impossible for students to express their point of view within the Union of Students.[98]

The political ambitions of the young leader were seen as being stimulated by his experience of the privileges of political life with its first-class travel, cars, entertainment and the like (the salaries and expenses of these leaders used up virtually the entire budget) and naturally a social barrier between the leadership and the youth often developed.[99] In 1965 Vladimir Bakarić, the Secretary of the Central Committee of the League of Communists in Croatia, observed that many of these leaders would feel degraded if on completion of their degree they went to work, for example, as a trainee judge. As Bakarić explained, a significant number of youth leaders had become professional politicians even while they were still students.[100] And because they intended to make their career in politics they functioned in a manner designed to secure promotion.

Others described the situation in even stronger terms. Thus an article in *Borba* in 1966 maintained that many among the youth leadership simply used the organization to further their own ambitions.[101] And referring to the Union of Youth, an article in *Politika* described it as the vehicle for the personal advancement of a few.[102]

The attitude and commitment of at least some student leaders is revealed in a report of a work drive held in 1964. Much of the money allocated for this project was apparently wasted. The organizers took taxis to travel long distances rather than a bus, they used the car purchased for the project to go on picnics or to sporting events, they were seen arriving home drunk in the early morning as the brigade members were getting ready for the day's work, they revealed a 'bad' attitude to the brigade members, their neglect of their duties meant the loss or waste of materials, and after the work drive was concluded, they arranged to transfer the car and van bought out of the funds for the project to the Belgrade University Committee of the Union of Students. Significantly, the report of this incident stressed the need to adopt tighter rules in *all* student organizations concerning the use of funds and resources.[103]

129

The net effect of the control exercised by the youth leaders was that these organizations made up of young people of varying backgrounds and with varying views often presented what one Yugoslav scholar described as a picture of basic ideological harmony.[104] As another scholar observed, the Yugoslav leadership gained a grossly incorrect impression of what was happening among the young.[105] And according to a *Borba* article of 1966, the primary function of the youth organizations was, in effect, merely to give the appearance that a particular category of citizens was represented.[106]

The more successful these leaders were in controlling their members, the more the Union of Students and the Union of Youth appeared to be instruments of the League of Communists rather than organizations of the student and non-student youth. According to a statement made by a member of the Central Committee of the Union of Students in 1967, the organization had 'no authentic political autonomy' and only on the level of broad declarations was it possible for the Union to be at all critical.[107] Less bluntly, an account in *Student* of a meeting of the Central Committee of the Union of Students held later that year observed that there were occasions when the Union was a transmission organ for 'other' social political organs and was consequently unable to develop an independent, critical stand on certain questions.[108] Or as Badovinac commented just prior to the June events, the leaders of the youth organizations 'began increasingly to address the youth in the name of society'.[109]

And the more the organizations appeared to be the instrument of the League of Communists, the more the students drifted away from them. The Union leaders took what could be termed a correct and responsible path, but this was of little consequence since the students ceased to follow.[110] The passivity and resignation of the young with respect to politics in general and to their particular youth organization was described as the direct consequence of the situation in which there was instruction rather than discussion, and of the situation in which the needs, interests and views of the membership were decided by the leaders. Above all, it was asserted that the leaders of these organizations determined too much and organized too much and that, rather than work with and as a part of the youth, they lectured to the youth from above.[111] Far from providing a basis from which the young could move to secure their rights against the denigration and conservatism in the broader society, the young felt insignificant and powerless even within what was avowedly their own organization.[112]

The role of the Union of Students within the university system of self-management provides a useful illustration of this point. As noted in chapter III of this study it was generally conceded that the students failed to realize their rights, however defined, within the university, and it would seem that much of the responsibility for this must be borne by the Union of Students. As noted above, it was agreed, at least as early as 1956, that the establishment of self-management institutions in the university required the Union of Students to develop a system of voters' meetings to ensure that the mass of students secured real opportunity to participate.[113] Despite the avowed recognition of the importance of such forms they were not developed to any significant degree. And in many cases student representatives were merely chosen by leaders of the Union of Students.[114] The net result was, as a Yugoslav professor recently observed, that the student organization drifted away from the self-management system and became merely 'some kind of political diversion'.[115]

At the close of the period it was generally acknowledged, as discussed in chapter III, that a major problem with respect to student participation in self-management stemmed from the fact that the few student representatives were isolated from the student body. According to the Report of the Central Committee of the Union published in 1968, one of the most important tasks was to strengthen the student meetings, to permit all questions of interest to students to be discussed and to make the meetings the basic institution in the system of self-management.[116] The prescription was identical to that offered at least a dozen years earlier.

Therefore, while at the close of the period Union leaders expressed regret that the students had not realized an effective voice within the system of self-management, the fact remained that much of the blame for this failure can be directed at the Union. Despite constant lip-service to the need to develop student meetings, it was generally concluded that the Union of Students failed to grasp this opportunity presented by the self-managing system to thrust the Union into the centre of activities at the university.[117] The leadership much preferred to confine itself to bemoaning the fact that the role of students in self-management was insufficiently developed. As even an article in *Student,* published some five months prior to the 'June events', pointed out, there would be no progress toward the solution of this problem while the leadership of the Union persisted in merely repeating clichés.[118]

The student meetings which were held were dull, ineffective and poorly attended. According to Professor Jovan Djordjević, the leaders of the Union in effect tended to regard self-management as something which should be the epilogue, rather than the prologue and instrument of the revolution at the university. In other words, the leaders seemed of the view that meaningful participation by the mass of students could come only when the proper climate and attitudes had been secured.[119] In the meantime, the leaders of the Union would work to ensure that only 'responsible' positions were advocated rather than permitting a full and frank exchange of ideas. It was maintained that it was patently obvious that few students were interested in this type of participation.[120]

The nature and role of the youth and student organizations can be further illustrated by considering their role concerning the material problems of the young. On this point, as seen in chapter V, there was again agreement that these organizations were regarded by the young as being irrelevant. An article in *Komunist* in 1967 reported a vigorous discussion at a meeting of youth in a 'major port city' concerning their economic situation. At the conclusion of that meeting the President of the district Union of Youth was reported to have spoken on the need for 'ideological political education'. In the words of the *Komunist* report, it was 'as though he had been deaf during the entire meeting'.[121] This article insisted that it was widely acknowledged that the young were facing a multiplicity of real problems in society. And yet the People's Youth and later the Union of Youth failed to lead or even join the struggle for reform; these organizations, the article continued, could not amount to something in the eyes of the youth until they were seen as fighting for the real interests of the young and the community.

In the same vein, a survey conducted in Croatia supported the view that the work of the Union of Youth was not relevant to the needs and wishes of the ordinary members. The answers of the young persons surveyed indicated an interest in problems of employment and advancement, and the battle for the realization of the 'ideals of our society (for example, equal treatment, payment according to work . . . opposition to connections and protections . . .)'. However, an analysis of the activities of the organization showed an emphasis on work projects, organizing trips and visits to concerts and plays.[122] In the opinion of the particular researcher, the young were being 'cared for' and had a 'learner's status'. However, in his view they appeared to be seeking an opportunity for meaningful involvement and the opportunity to seek solutions to their real problems.[123]

The President of the Central Committee of the Union of Youth of Serbia noted in December 1968 that the organization had limited itself to occasionally and 'timidly' pronouncing 'some political words'.[124] A similar view expressed in an article in *Politika* was that

> Our youth organization has managed to solve not a single problem of the young. Everything ends with discussions and conclusions which are adopted as a matter of routine, but are never really implemented.[125]

At first sight the situation within the Union of Students appeared markedly different. Certainly, like the Union of Youth, during the 1950s this organization tended to focus on ideological and political matters. Instead of supporting or leading student demands for the improvement of material conditions, the role of the Union often appeared to be to help reconcile the student body to their situation. During the 1960s, however, the leadership of the Union began to pay considerable attention to these material questions. In large part this reflected an effort on the part of the leadership to stimulate student interest in the organization. So many of the reports, recommendations and requests emanating from the Union related to these material questions that the President of the Belgrade Union of Students expressed the view in late 1967 that for a 'considerable' period the Union had given almost exclusive attention to the material problems of students.[126]

Several consequences followed. First, it was contended that this emphasis on material questions led to the neglect of other vital activities.

132

Second, and least important, it was claimed that this emphasis on material questions meant that those students who were not in straitened material circumstances were not gathered in by the Union. Third, and most important, the demonstrated failure of the Union to secure any significant improvement in the students' economic situation meant, in the opinion of the student leader cited above, that no one among the general student body continued to see the Union of Students as relevant.[127] In other words, the effort to demonstrate the significance of the Union had finally served only to confirm its irrelevance.

Although greater attention was given to student material difficulties, the Union leadership, for the most part, continued to play what might be described as a 'responsible' role. That is, student leaders were not prepared to go beyond mere requests or appeals for aid—as one student expressed it, the Union requested, and *only* requested, improvement of the students' material position.[128]

The only major exception to this pattern of behaviour was that displayed by Vesna Gudelj-Velaga, the President of the Union of Students at Zagreb University in 1967/68. One of her significant acts was to endorse a petition circulated among the residents of student hostels protesting an increase in prices,[129] when, clearly, the 'responsible' stand would have been to endeavour to explain to the disgruntled students why the increase could not be avoided. Her eventual fate is discussed in a later section of this chapter because it provides a useful illustration of the limited independence of these organizations.

The 'responsible' position in matters pertaining to student living conditions was exemplified by the leadership of the Student Union at Belgrade University. For example, an article published at this time in *Student,* the official organ of the Belgrade Association of the Union, vehemently rejected the view that the primary task of the Union should be to fight for student rights rather than to be primarily a political organization. There was no place in the system of self-management, the article continued, for the notion of splitting society into separate groups each charged with the function of protecting the rights of its members. And from whom, it was asked, would these rights be defended? The proper course was clearly to work within the present system and to recognize that student demands had to be perceived in a broader context.[130]

As the Belgrade student leader Djuro Kovačević emphasized, it was essential to have a realistic view of what could be done.[131] Part of the reason for difficulties among students was that 'we' (apparently the Union leadership) had sometimes endorsed 'moralistic' goals and therefore had to accept the consequences which stemmed 'from our failure to realize them'.[132] That is, Kovačević was suggesting that student resentments and frustrations could be lessened if the Union leadership did not forget its responsibility to explain to the students what society could afford. Further, Kovačević emphasized that significant changes in material conditions could be achieved by the more efficient use of 'internal reserves' at, for example, student hostels. Finally, he insisted that the Union should not become too preoccupied with material questions and should fight the view that failures at the university were due to poor conditions. This was indeed a reason, but not, he maintained, the only one.[133]

However, the consequence of this 'responsible' attitude was that the Union was seen by students as being ineffective, unimportant, irrelevant and even unconcerned on this question of the students' material situation. A strongly worded article in *Borba* published less than a month before the June events insisted that it was essential that the Union of Students stop 'defending and justifying' 'almost anything and everything' of which the students were critical.[134] The article maintained that the various branches of the Union had 'not always' worked for the settlement of the most essential problems of the students. 'If and when' they gave attention to these problems, the article bitingly continued, they failed to pursue the matter to the end. Indeed, as noted earlier, there was a strong tendency to filter student requests and to endorse all and any responses made by those in authority. This same article concluded that it was not uncommon for the Union leaders to have to be *asked* by responsible authorities to present their view on basic student questions such as scholarships and that often their views were expressed in only general and formal terms.[135]

Discussions and decisions within the Union of Students were described as being boringly repetitive and vague; as an article in the Belgrade student paper contended, it was obvious that the materials and reports of the union were 'post-festum' documents, that is, they merely repeated what had already been decided elsewhere.[136]

It was observed that consequently student demands were increasingly articulated outside the formal structure of the Union.[137] An article in *Borba* published just prior to the June events noted that the Union of Students was scarcely functioning, and yet in recent months there had been considerable activity among the mass of students.[138] Apart from the already mentioned petition threatening a public demonstration in support of the request for recreational facilities at the Student City, there were strong protests in Belgrade, relating to Vietnam, in December 1966. The protests were organized outside the University Committee of the Union of Students and led to vigorous clashes with the militia when the students endeavoured to march on the U.S. Embassy.[139]

Thus, the effort to increase student interest in the Union by giving greater attention to material questions had only postponed what appeared to be the inevitable decline of the Union as an organization effectively encompassing the mass of students. The Union gave greater *apparent* attention to material questions but the basic attitude of most Union leaders was unchanged; therefore, the Union leaders appeared as ineffective and even unsympathetic advocates of student claims. Certainly among a significant group of students the Union's role in this area served only to increase their cynicism concerning the functioning of the Yugoslav political system.

EXPLAINING THE FAILURE OF THE YOUTH ORGANIZATIONS

A vital question is whether the judgement that the careerism of the leaders was largely responsible for the failure of these organizations is, in fact, a reasonable one. Against this view it could be urged, first, that this careerism might be at most only one of a whole range of factors responsible for the failure of these organizations; second, that this form of careerism was not something introduced by the youth leaders, but, rather, was endemic to the system. That is, anyone other than a 'careerist' would find it difficult to win office and impossible to retain it. In short, it might be maintained that there was an air of unreality about this particular criticism of the youth leaders.

Concerning the former point, were there factors apart from the careerism of the youth leaders which might help account for the widely acknowledged failure of these organizations? As far as the Union of Students in particular was concerned, were there additional reasons for the failure of this organization to attract the overwhelming bulk of students to an intensive programme of ideological education designed to transform them into socialist experts?

It might be suggested that the expectations implicit in that question were simply unrealistic. The leadership consistently maintained that it was possible to devise programmes of work that were at once attractive *and* correct, but it might be argued that the gulf between the interests of the students and what the leadership felt was necessary to inculcate was too great to bridge. As reports in the Yugoslav press indicated, there were many students who preferred sport, 'pop' music, coffee houses and the opposite sex to yet another political lecture,[140] and many demonstrated what was termed little critical judgement in their choice of films or reading matter.[141]

As for their attitude to study, many were clearly a long way from accepting the view that they should energetically prepare themselves to become socialist experts. Like students the world over, a significant number missed lectures and laboratory classes, or failed to perform their practical training requirements at a satisfactory level, or studied only for exams, and then only to 'get through'.[142] Some were even prepared to cheat in order to do so.[143] Many appeared to believe that their work was a personal matter. Such a view was, of course, vigorously condemned: all students owed a responsibility to the wider community which was bearing the cost of their studies.[144] At the Fourth Congress of the Union of Students in 1959, for example, it was resolved that the Union had the obligation to check the work and results of each student, to assist students in difficulty, to seek to create a better atmosphere for study, to encourage regular attendance at lectures and other class periods, to publicize the success of the better students and 'to struggle resolutely against all attempts at fulfilling school tasks in a frivolous and unconscientious way'.[145]

Among the general student body there were other serious faults. A strongly worded article in *Borba* in 1957 spoke of a 'significant minority' of students who were involved in various violations of public order. The article listed fighting, shouting, singing late at night, 'uncivil behaviour', offensive remarks made to women and a contemptuous attitude towards bus conductors and law enforcement officers.[146]

Similarly, many were far from accepting what the leadership saw as their responsibilities towards the total socialist community. Many were criticized for placing an 'excessive' emphasis on personal financial considerations, whether this was a question of present scholarships and conditions or future earnings.[147] For example, some medical students were reported to have said that it would be pointless to continue their studies if private practice were abolished.[148] And in 1952, the then President of the Union, Milorad Pěsić, referred to 'unhealthy theories' held by some students who failed to understand that their economic position could not be considered apart from the general economic situation.[149] In this regard the frequent tendency for students to focus on their material situation at their meetings was also decried; it was urged that they should take a 'broad' view.[150]

In May 1959 Zagreb University students seriously embarrassed the Yugoslav leadership by demonstrating against the quality and quantity of food in student restaurants. Tito spoke bitterly of the 'excesses' committed by students who were supported by funds 'our workers' had earned for them. He acknowledged that the students had not received all that was necessary, but, he declared, more was being done for students than had been done prior to the war and the community had given the students as much as it could afford. There were other avenues through which their complaints could have been made but clearly the demonstrators had been misled by the 'class enemy'.[151]

An article in *Komunist* commenting on the same demonstrations also acknowledged that there were 'shortcomings' at some hostels and restaurants, but that most students recognized that the community was making a sincere effort. However, there were some students who waited like 'parasites for the community to peel every single potato in the restaurant, or to provide the means to pay for every single thing'. Among such students there were those who were 'forever protesting and demanding—and thus the possibility is given to hostile elements to undermine and poison the atmosphere'. In this situation, both the League of Communists and the Union of Students had the duty to intervene, to explain what the community had done, to encourage the students to study, and to involve them in the work of the student institutions so that they could help advance their own interests. Above all else should be the struggle against the 'parasitical psychology of waiting for the community to do all and give all'.[152]

There were other examples of this gulf between what the leadership saw as responsible behaviour and the attitudes of the students. It was reported that some graduates refused to leave the city[153] even if this meant working in fields unrelated or only marginally related to their training.[154] An article in *Politika* in 1952 described the thwarting of the efforts of authorities in the Republic of Bosnia and Hercegovina to remedy the acute shortage of experts. For example, of the sixty-seven district people's committees of that Republic, more than fifty were without the services of a lawyer. In many cases legal work was being performed by individuals who had not even completed secondary school. Republican authorities had extended 'considerable aid' to enable local students to attend the universities at Belgrade and Zagreb but on graduating many of these students simply refused to go to those areas where they were most needed.[155] Several press reports spoke of students who falsely claimed knowledge of a particular foreign language in order to win selection for study in a foreign country. Some of these students were described as seeking to prolong their stay instead of being anxious to bring the benefits of their learning to the community, and some, on their return, failed to share their knowledge with others.[156]

There were hypocritical students who in the classroom situation professed certain beliefs and attitudes but who by their actions demonstrated the reverse.[157] There were students who showed 'great indolence' when it came to helping the community.[158] The establishment of student clubs, in either the students' home district or at the university centre, which had been urged as a means of coordinating and organizing such activities as the teaching of illiterates, the coaching of high school students and instructing the people in better methods of cultivation or higher sanitary standards did not always achieve the desired results. Some reports noted a lack of student involvement or simply an effort to turn such clubs into student recreational clubs.[159]

Clearly these examples of what the leadership saw as undesirable attitudes and behaviour do not give a complete picture. In the first place, there is little or no attempt to explain such attitudes and behaviour; the official view seemed merely to be that they were inappropriate and harmful in a socialist society. Second, the reports give no indication of the extent of each problem described. The most that can be said is that the problem was of sufficient magnitude that it was thought necessary to attack it publicly. However, the principal purpose of citing these examples at this point is simply to show that, despite the apparent assumptions on which the debate concerning ideological education rested, Yugoslav students were not qualitatively unlike students in other parts of the world. The leadership might urge the young to involve themselves in the activities of the Union of Students, to behave in a responsible manner and to prepare themselves energetically for the onerous responsibility of becoming a socialist expert, but many students, not surprisingly, were not inclined to conduct themselves in this manner.

Another factor contributing to the difficulty faced by the youth organizations was that their programmes of ideological education could not be carried out in isolation from developments in the broader society. For example, the efforts to attract and inspire young people were often affected by their perception of deformations in contemporary Yugoslav society. The injustice, careerism and selfishness, even on the part of those who claimed to be in the forefront of the battle for the new socialist order, clearly had a negative impact on the young. One of the more dramatic accounts of abuses committed by party officials was the 'Circular Letter' prepared by the leadership of the League in 1958 and which spoke of dictatorial methods, favouritism, corruption and extravagance. This letter stated that many occupying positions of authority travelled abroad far more than their duties required and that they misused funds by extravagant entertainment or the purchase of handsome automobiles.[160] As a popular joke expressed it, some officials were in such a hurry to reach communism that each year they insisted on a bigger and faster car.

The youth began to wonder what had happened to those who had shown themselves willing to risk their lives for the sake of a greater cause but who now seemed to place the retention of their own privileges above all else. In addition to evoking cynicism, the constant reference to that glorious generation evoked boredom, resentment and even outright hostility. A significant number among the young clearly chafed at being expected constantly to express their gratitude to the partisan generation and at being made to feel inferior because they were too young to have participated in the war.[161] The efforts noted earlier, to organize activities to enable the young to appreciate the heroic nature of the revolution, of which they were now 'enjoying the fruits', were, therefore, bound to have less success than had avowedly been expected. Despite the fanfare, and despite the picnic atmosphere, relatively few seemed to have been involved; for example, a march organized in 1959 by the People's Youth and drawing representatives from all republics had only four hundred participants.[162]

As for the problem of the growing gulf between what was termed the 'intellectual' and 'working youth', it could be argued that this also reflected the reality of Yugoslav society. In 1958, to take one example, Tito had remarked that close ties between these two groups no longer existed and that the attitude of the students towards other young people was frequently one of disparagement. In his judgement, there had been insufficient effort and initiative to develop forms of work that would link university youth to the broader community in order to create a new socialist type of intellectual. What was implied in this and similar comments was that appropriate new forms *could* be found which would indeed reduce the gulf between intellectual and working youth. However, it seems obvious that the organization of such activities as a factory visit would do little toward the goal of developing student respect for the working class when more compelling facts pointed in the other direction; despite the rhetoric concerning the prime importance of the working class, it was clear that the workers were lowest in income, privilege and status in an environment in which all three were very important.[163]

An example noted in the previous chapter demonstrates something of the position of the workers and their families in Yugoslav society. In 1964, 66 per cent more per student was spent in the academically oriented secondary schools than in the trade schools, even though the latter needed far more in the way of equipment, materials and the like. One effect of this discrepancy is seen in the fact that while about three-quarters of teachers of such important subjects as chemistry, physics, biology and mathematics in the academically oriented secondary schools were university qualified, in the trade schools the proportion was less than one-tenth. Students in the trade schools were described as seeing their schools as second class. The bitter conclusion of the Yugoslav scholar who presented this data was that this injustice stemmed from the fact that the children of those in responsible positions were not students in the trade schools, hence there was no one of influence to press the case for these schools.[164]

Similarly, despite the avowed hopes, the re-introduction of youth work drives was not likely to lead to a re-creation of the enthusiastic mood of the work drives held in the immediate post-war period. Several factors militated against this. First, rather than major spectacular drives, there were often only small local projects. Second, the running debate as to whether voluntary work was cheaper or more expensive made it impossible for the youth to feel that they were making the same contribution as had their predecessors. Third, and most important, the spirit of revolutionary enthusiasm and idealism of the earlier years had declined. And the very students about whom the leadership was most concerned were those who avoided such projects.[165]

In short, it was clear that for various reasons, many among the young were becoming bored and even cynical with regard to politics. Some of the responses to the 1960 Yugoslavia-wide survey cited earlier indicate something of the cynicism among the student body. The students were asked to rank in order of importance some of the methods used by most individuals to help them advance in contemporary Yugoslav society. Almost half (42.4 per cent) gave no response. Many of the others demonstrated a cynical view; thus, 15.8 per cent of the total sample considered that 'making use of friends and acquaintances' was the most important method of advancement, 4.2 per cent thought it most important not to oppose one's superiors and 3.1 per cent chose 'emphasizing one's worth'. The remaining responses included 'securing higher qualifications' (11 per cent), diligence and hard work (8.8 per cent) and 'political and social activity' (8.6 per cent).[166]

These problems of passivity and cynicism are considered at greater length in the concluding chapter—they are mentioned here simply to demonstrate something of the difficulty faced by youth and student leaders in organizing activities which would involve and enthuse the young.

Some students were described as actively opposing the efforts to develop what was the Union's primary function, namely the social and political education of the young intelligentsia. As Milorad Pešić, President of the Union of Students, sarcastically observed in 1952, these students favoured, in the name of 'freedom and democracy', a dispersed non-political organization; however, this ignored the fact that everything in the contemporary situation was imbued with the revolutionary struggle. 'It was a serious error', Pešić continued, to discuss democracy in formal and abstract terms thus separating it from the socialist battle currently being waged. This 'petty bourgeois and anarchist approach' led to passivity and a defensive attitude toward the enemies of socialism, who quickly took advantage of this situation. Besides the remnants of the pre-revolutionary order, Pešić also referred to the Cominform elements, that is, those who allegedly favoured the Soviet position in the current Soviet-Yugoslav dispute. Pešić observed that some individuals were of the opinion that the Cominform was a matter of the past, but this was a dangerous view; the Cominform elements were still actively striving to introduce a spirit of faintheartedness, ideological confusion and the like. The Student Union therefore, should lead and organize the effort to expose all appearances of 'reactionary' or 'bureaucratic' tendencies and to establish university life on the basis of 'true socialist democracy'.[167]

Despite the emphasis on greater political activity, of which Pešić's comment is an important example, and despite the thrust of the Conclusions of the Central Committee of the League of Communists in 1953 urging greater ideological cohesion and activity, the work of the youth organizations continued to be adjudged unsatisfactory.[168] For example, in 1954 Tripalo, then President of the Union of Students, attacked the concept that the Union should be simply a union of various societies and clubs. This view, he continued, must be fought; the basic organizations must discuss such issues as political problems, methods of instruction and the economic situation of students. Significantly, Tripalo stated that such discussions would recreate the essential political physiognomy of the Union.[169]

However, according to an article in *Borba* in 1956, a significant number of students continued actively to oppose the efforts by 'progressive students' to develop ideological activity. There were students who thought that ideological education was unimportant; some cynically said that a professional qualification was always useful but that ideologies were liable to change. As for those the press termed 'progressive students', some among the student body simply dismissed them as 'would-be politicians'.[170]

The organization and encouragement of social, cultural and professional activities to attract the young away from harmful activities was, it was acknowledged, important. However, it was observed that not infrequently the organization of such activities led to the tendency to overlook the less exciting tasks, such as participation in the solution of local political problems and Marxist study groups. That is, it was often forgotten that all activities must be permeated by the proper ideological atmosphere.[171]

In this vein it was contended that members of the Union of Students gave too little assistance and guidance to the various student clubs and societies which had developed outside the actual Union. It was insisted that left to their own devices these clubs developed too narrow a focus and even certain negative features. For example, in 1962 the Central Committee of the Union of Students vigorously condemned certain 'cultural' clubs which used 'cheap humour' as a means of attracting the greatest possible number of students under the motto of 'general rejoicing'.[172] The task of members of youth organizations was not to give mere lip service to the need to provide guidance, but vigorously to oppose such weaknesses. This criticism ignored a simple fact: it was unlikely that at a meeting of the Union there would be open opposition to resolutions urging the importance of developing ideological work in these various clubs, but it was clear that many were attending the same Union meeting with no great commitment to carrying out its resolutions.[173]

The young had drifted away from the youth organizations and into these various clubs because of their declining interest in politics, but the members of the youth organizations were now being urged to go out into the clubs to ensure that more suitable activities were organized and that a healthy spirit prevailed.[174] It is scarcely surprising that there were official complaints even concerning clubs where most of the committee members were communists. These young people were being asked to 'preach' to their peers about the necessity for wholesome and uplifting activities—obviously few of them even attempted to perform this duty. After all, many of them did not, and more of them did not wish to, stand apart from their contemporaries.

The role played by individual rank and file communists within the various youth organizations is worthy of some attention. It will be recalled that the abandonment of the centralized, hierarchical structure meant the imposition of enormous responsibility on the individual communists within each basic unit.

However, this increased responsibility was thrust on individual communists at a time when both their confidence and commitment were declining. The break with the Soviet Union and the embarkation on the path of self-management began a period of painful confusion for rank and file communists among the youth and within Yugoslav society as a whole.

A useful and early example of the extent of this confusion is seen in the special meeting of the Central Committee of the League of Communists, held in June 1953 at Tito's summer residence in Brioni. At this gathering, usually termed the Brioni Plenum, it was acknowledged that confusion was rampant within the League, that 'anti-Marxist' views were beginning to appear, and that many members of the League had become passive or thought even that they had the right to protest measures with which they disagreed; as a consequence the League was failing in its essential task of guiding the development of socialism. To the majority within the Central Committee, the withering of the League, of which even Tito had spoken, referred to the distant future when communism was firmly established; in the present period the withering of the League as a cohesive, guiding force would mean risking the gains of the revolution.

Despite the Brioni Plenum, the confusion within the League was not resolved; indeed, it extended to the very top ranks. To a small minority within the Central Committee, most notably Milovan Djilas, the essen-

141

tial question had now become whether the rejection of the Stalinist model was to involve the establishment of democratic or only pseudo-democratic forms; that is, whether the complete bureaucratic apparatus was to be smashed or whether the League apparatus was to retain its monopoly in the realm of ideas. His public repudiation of the essential principles on which the role of the League was based provoked another major crisis of confidence within the League and the society and led to Djilas's imprisonment.[175]

His removal from the scene did not remove the confusion concerning the appropriate role for individual communists within the basic organizations of which they were members. As was explained in chapter III, the perennial problem was to distinguish between excessive and insufficient involvement. For the individual communist it often seemed that he was always in error. If his particular collective made decisions that the League subsequently decided were incorrect, he was likely to be criticized for failing to influence the collective in the direction of correct policies. If the decisions of his particular collective were correct, he was likely to be condemned for usurping the self-managing rights of the collective and for contributing to passivity and resignation among its members. His dilemma was compounded by the fact—as even a cursory reading of the history of post-war Yugoslavia reveals—that the broad position of the League leadership itself changed depending on the general national and international situation.

Both the onerous nature and the unclear character of their responsibilities explain why individual communists were often criticized for their failures. For example, in his address to the 1956 Plenum of the Central Committee of the League, Tito declared that individual communists had failed to play their proper role among the youth, the youth had been neglected and left 'to develop by itself in the best way it knows'. The basic error, he continued, was to suppose that the socialist education of the young could occur naturally and that the daily developments and achievements within contemporary society were sufficiently educative influences. Many had taken advantage of this passivity on the part of the communists to spread dissatisfaction among the young. 'We spoke to them too little': the young should have been told more about the daily problems, more about the achievements and successes, and more about the aims of the League. The result of this neglect was that many communists were reluctant to oppose 'some dishonest man, a reactionary or a petty bourgeois who wrongly and unjustly criticizes or slanders . . . our system'. Communists still had the vital role of defending the country's 'revolutionary achievements' and they must not be afraid of offending someone 'by interfering too much in certain internal matters'. Indeed, communists had the right and duty to intervene; it was only a question, Tito asserted, of knowing the proper situation in which to do so. Only in this way could the guiding and leading role of communists be maintained. This failure on the part of communists explained the fact that the situation among the young was, in Tito's words, 'not a rosy one'. During the war, and also in the early post-war period, the young were very highly regarded and achieved enormous successes; the principal reason being that the Party carefully 'showed it the path and . . . continuously nursed and elevated it'. Later, however, 'we somehow let our youth slip out of our hand'.[176]

Similarly, in his report to this same meeting of the Central Committee, Petar Stambolić declared that the education of the youth required the 'constant, organized and deliberate activity of communists and other socialist forces', and consistent work on the 'step by step formation of a socialist personality . . . who will . . . know how to distinguish the really new and progressive from that which is obsolete and reactionary'. He reiterated Tito's argument that it was an error to assume that the socialist education of the young could be a natural and spontaneous process simply because they were living in a socialist society. Stambolić continued with a thinly veiled warning: 'In so far as such opinions are not voiced by the enemy, they derive from a complete ignorance of the nature of the period of transition' to the socialist society. In opposition to the powerful socialist tendencies, 'stubborn remnants of the past' still survived; to ignore this fact inevitably led to the under-estimation of the need for the constant development of positive influences.[177]

Referring specifically to the situation among students, it was observed that their education was too narrow—there was a great need for the all-round humanistic and cultural education of the new intelligentsia and for the development of a social and political conscience.[178]

The League leadership was claiming that lack of guidance had inevitably resulted in the failure of the People's Youth and of the Union of Students to carry out their essential task of educating the future generation of socialists. Largely as a means of securing expanded and controlled activity by the Union of Students, the decision was reached at this 1956 Plenum of the Central Committee of the League, to re-introduce party units at institutions of higher learning. In the aftermath of the Sixth Congress of the Party, held in 1952, such units had been abolished on the grounds that their continued existence did not accord with the changed role of the party from an organization of direct government to one confining itself to political and ideological education; party members were to exert their influence within the organs of self-management, not as the spokesmen for the party unit but as individuals; clearly the continued existence of such units was seen as a threat to the proposed democratization of Yugoslav society. By 1956, however, the League leadership saw passivity and confusion as greater dangers. Hence, the re-establishment of party units in the institutions of higher education was seen as a means by which activity could be revived, coordinated and directed.[179]

Despite this, the regular complaint concerned the failure of individual communists to recognize and fulfil their responsibilities. For example, it was reported that even a 'certain number' of 'active members' of the Union were heard to say that the weakening of the socio-political activity of the organization was inevitable. These 'active members' believed that the only task of the Union concerned questions of study and the material situations of students, and they considered that ideological work was not necessary as all students were politically conscious; besides, there was too little time for such work.[180] That is, even among those expected to be in the forefront of the struggle for ideological education there was passivity and resistance. The results of the 1960 survey of students showed that, by their own account, 11.7 per cent of those who were members of the League of Communists failed to participate at all in the Union of Students. There were no data reported which indicated the extent of participation by the remainder, but the data already cited concerning the total student body suggest that, for many, participation was little more than token.[181]

The available reports indicate that, toward the close of the period under review, most rank and file communists within the various youth organizations were inactive. As Tito bluntly stated in his address to the Eighth Congress of the League of Communists in 1964, communists in the Union of Students were overly concerned with their personal affairs.[182] Just how unenthusiastic some of the young communists were is illustrated by the frequent complaints that many communists were failing even to attend meetings of the basic student organization; there were even difficulties in obtaining a quorum at meetings of the student communist organization in particular departments.[183] In addition, work at these meetings was described as being marred by a lack of purpose and spirit. For example, the speakers at one meeting were described in an article in a student newspaper as appearing to be 'in a competition to see who could speak the longest and say the least'.[184] The majority of student communists in another department were reported as being quite inactive; even if they attended a League meeting they usually remained silent. When questions were voted on, they mechanically raised their hands with the majority; the majority view, the report concluded, was their sole criterion in distinguishing right from wrong.[185]

In his address to the Youth Congress held just prior to the June events, Badovinac reiterated the crucial importance of activity by communists within youth organizations in order to help create the proper climate within these bodies. He pointed out that, apart from actual office bearers within the youth organizations, 'young members of the League of Communists were almost completely inactive in the youth movement'.[186] However, as Tripalo wrote in 1967, the youth organizations could not fulfil their tasks unless there existed within each organization a group on whom the League could 'rely' and which would fight for the implementation of League policy.[187]

As the discussion in the final chapter endeavours to establish, many individual communists were passive, confused and selfish instead of being what was expected, namely, active, confident and committed. Many of them were clearly unwilling to accept any responsibility. Indeed, there was often considerable difficulty in finding individuals prepared to accept the responsibilities of office in the Union organization within particular departments. For example, in 1966 five officers of the organization within the Zagreb University Law Department were removed from their posts because they had shown little interest in their work. One of those removed was so inactive that he was known to only two of his fellow members of the Departmental Committee; another had failed even to attend the meeting at which his tenure was to be considered. It was explained that he could not attend 'because he had theatre tickets' for that evening.[188]

Clearly, the failure of individual communists to help shape the proper environment through guidance and inspiration placed a heavy burden on the leaders of these organizations. These leaders were constantly urged to organize ideological activities and they were constantly reminded that these activities should be free and frank so as to interest the youth; however, at the same time, they were subject to vigorous criticism if these activities went beyond what were seen as the correct limits. For example, an article cited earlier stressed that to be successful, ideological work among the young required 'bold answers' to 'delicate questions', and quoted with approval a series of youth forums in the Vojvodina district which had been well attended and which had evoked much interest. However, it continued, at these forums there had been lectures of 'questionable scientific or ideological worth' given by lecturers who apparently thought that the forum was a kind of 'ideological fair' at which 'everything was bought and sold'. It was reported that the young communists present felt these ideological shortcomings, but failed to deal with them; the article concluded by noting that greater help must be offered to these people for the sake of achieving better results and also because the young people deserved this help.[189]

If the 'proper' climate could not be created by the more subtle methods of guidance and inspiration from within and below, what, then, were the leaders of youth organizations to do? Allow the basic organizations to function without restraint, or impose on them 'proper' and 'responsible' policies? For them at least there was no way of glossing over the inherent contradiction in the official view that activities within youth organizations should be both free and 'correct'.

With only rare exceptions, these leaders chose a 'responsible' role—endeavouring to dissuade the rank and file from making what might be described as 'unreasonable' requests, or from participating in unapproved demonstrations or from voicing 'immature' opinions. It must be remembered that this was a very uncertain era. As is elaborated in the conclusion, the League of Communists was rent with confusion. The very pragmatism of which the Yugoslavs boasted and for which they were praised had its costs:[190] in the first place, the Yugoslav line was constantly changing; in the second place, this process of change was irregular and oscillating rather than smooth and consistent. Self-management was enunciated as the principal tenet of Yugoslav ideology, but the implementation of this system was beset with difficulties. It was challenged almost frontally by what were termed 'reactionaries' in the broad society and by adherents of bureaucratism within the League. And even to the more liberal elements within the League, self-management had a specific meaning which fell far short of implying the surrender of the League's claim to final authority. The doubts, uncertainties, oscillations and reversals all had their effect: today's brave initiative might prove to be tomorrow's serious error; therefore, it was best to be cautious.

This affected the efficacy of ideological work as well as its nature. In particular, despite the constant urging of the need to develop programmes of interest and relevance, many youth leaders thought it more prudent to avoid trouble; a dull programme of work was far safer than an exciting one that might escape control. The constant concern of the youth leader was the danger of being rebuked from above for allowing the situation within his particular area of responsibility to escape control. In such a situation his failure would be immediately apparent. However, failure on a day to day basis, as for example in a decline in interest, was less easy to perceive and hence more politic. Consequently, there developed an attitude of extreme caution among youth leaders. As one youth leader commented, 'the most dangerous thing' for him and his colleagues was to state their views publicly; the best course was to be as 'cautious and as nondescript a personality as possible'.[191]

The actual or potential pressures on the individual youth leader are well illustrated by the experience of Vesna Gudelj-Velaga. Further, her experience clearly demonstrates where the leadership actually placed the emphasis between the twin principles of insisting on complete independence for these organizations and the need for the development of a 'correct' atmosphere. It will be recalled that, while President of the Union of Students at Zagreb University in 1967/68, she had endorsed a petition circulated among the residents of students hostels protesting an increase in prices, when clearly the 'responsible' stand would have been to endeavour to explain to the disgruntled students why the increase was unavoidable.

She was promptly accused, by party leaders and the press, of ideological deviation and of having a 'trade union' mentality. In particular, it was claimed that she sought to impose a 'trade union line' on the Union with the objective of placing the student organization 'above society and its common interests' and of turning the students against society. Such behaviour served to weaken the unity of 'progressive forces'; indeed, it was contended, the problems of the students were deliberately 'exploited' in an attempt to create a rift between the League and the student body.[192] She was alleged to be operating with total disregard for, and 'even acting against', all other socio-political forces, while 'posing as the champion of student rights'. Curiously, it was even claimed that the behaviour of Gudelj-Velaga and her supporters was prompted by their political ambitions.[193]

It is important to note that Gudelj-Velaga's stance was not confined to the problem of student material conditions. On the contrary, this was only a facet of her general critique of contemporary Yugoslav developments; indeed, it may be that at least in part she sought to utilize student discontent in this area in order to build up support for her particular ideological position. She was a philosophy student and as such was clearly influenced by the *Praxis* group in that department. She described the contemporary situation as being marked by 'attractive ideas and dirty practice' and maintained that students, since they were less involved in the political and social system, constituted the only potential revolutionary force. In her view, students had the responsibility of leading the attack on deformations in society and of attacking the vested interests which thrived on these deformations.[194]

Her major official critic, Mika Tripalo, was by this stage a member of the Executive Committee of the League of Communists in Croatia. In a report to the Croatian Central Committee, he observed that at the previous annual conference of the Zagreb University Student Union, the old leadership group had been criticized for what was termed its 'opportunistic obedience' to official policy. According to Tripalo, many 'of our comrades' (that is, members of the League) came unprepared, and thus had allowed these critics of the old leadership to win power. Significantly, Tripalo excluded the representatives of the Central Committee of the League of Communists from the category of the unprepared. Of course, the sovereignty of self-managing bodies had to be respected, but, continued Tripalo, the 'substance and quality' of their decisions depended on the influence of the League among the members of these bodies; without a clear orientation on the part of communists there would be massive confusion. The present difficulties were described as stemming from this failure on the part of individual communists.[195]

The leadership of the Union of Students at Zagreb University was reported as having persisted on its mistaken course despite what were described as numerous attempts on the part of the League of Communists at the university to link up with the Union.[196] Finally, at a special meeting of the Zagreb University Committee of the League of Communists, Gudelj-Velaga and one of the members of the Union's Executive Committee were expelled from the League. Some days later, the University Committee of the Student Union, after a 'long noisy session', rejected a motion expressing confidence in the President. Two days later, when Gudelj-Velaga sought to open the Annual Assembly of the Zagreb Union of Students, a delegate rose to protest that since she had failed to win the vote of confidence at the meeting of the University Committee of the League she 'had no moral right to open [the] assembly'. According to the *Borba* account, a 'great majority' supported this protest and subsequently elected a new committee.[197]

This press report further noted that a 'great majority' of the delegates present expressed a 'decisive' determination to end 'negative' practices. Interestingly, some of the statistics quoted in the same article do not support a conclusion of overwhelming opposition to the former President. In the vote on the motion to expel Gudelj-Velaga from the Union, only 91 of the 165 accredited delegates were even in attendance. Of these, only 50 (that is, less than a third of the total number of delegates) supported her expulsion, 37 were opposed while 4 abstained. Not only did the vote fall short of the required two-thirds majority, but there was not a quorum present.[198]

In commenting on these events, an account in *Politika* approved the fact that there had been a 'more lively political activity' within the Union during the past year, but criticized the expression of 'controversial and even unacceptable standpoints'. Again it was implied that political activity which was at once 'lively' *and* 'correct' should be the aim.[199]

The oft-repeated claim that the vitality and effectiveness of the youth organizations had been eroded by the careerism of their leaders, therefore, is only a partial and indeed secondary explanation.

Those who condemned this careerism usually failed to point out that, having regard for the nature of the broad Yugoslav political system, both the careerism observed and its consequences were inescapable. As in any political system, the choice for the young politician was not simply between being or not being a careerist; just to survive in the political sense he had to be aware of what was practicable or possible. And in the Yugoslav political system the young leader's future career clearly depended on his ability to influence the ordinary members of his particular organization away from 'trouble'. In particular, this meant stifling any potentially 'dangerous' forms of ideological activity and persuading the young to be 'realistic' in their demands. As the experience of the President of the Zagreb Union of students in 1967/68 demonstrated, anyone other than a 'careerist' could at best expect to have only a limited term of office. Thus, while youth leaders made general statements condemning the failure of individuals and organizations in society to respect the young and to recognize their rights, the attitude of these same leaders towards the members of their organization can only be described as amounting in practice to condescension and denigration.

In the Yugoslav system it was not merely expedient and necessary for the politically ambitious to work to keep their particular organization within certain limits, it was also their duty as communists. Therefore, it is important to note that their behaviour came to be condemned as 'careerism' only when the collapse of the Union of Students and of the Union of Youth as effective organizations could no longer be ignored. Student leaders and youth leaders in general behaved as required by their duty as communists and the practical realities of the Yugoslav political system. After having acted in this way they found themselves blamed for the consequences.

One article in *Borba* in 1966 did, however, acknowledge that youth leaders were merely performing the role imposed on them by others.[200] And the analysis of the problem of youth organization by Crvenkovski in July of 1968 at least conceded that the youth leaders were not solely to blame. After criticizing the fact that these leaders constantly felt the need to 'co-ordinate their standpoints' with their superiors, he went on to observe that at the same time the reaction of the latter group was excessively cautious when faced with anything 'unusual'. However, one might argue that in fact the youth leaders were only being realistic, and further, that the caution of their superiors only reflected the fact that they themselves were only performing the role imposed on them by those in the next level in the hierarchy who in turn might be seen as playing their required role, and so on. In other words, as an article in *Komunist* of December 1966 conceded, the careerism and bureaucratism of the youth organizations were merely a reflection of the bureaucratism within the League of Communists.[201]

The Yugoslav leadership, however, for the most part, continued to maintain that such behaviour and attitudes were contrary to the essence of the Yugoslav system. Thus, regarding the situation among the young, Crvenkovski insisted that on 'numerous' occasions the League had urged that the transmission relationship between the League and the young should be discarded.[202] In practice, however, these statements were of little import. The basic fact was that the youth leader inevitably looked to his political superiors for guidance and approval because he looked to them for promotion.[203]

CONCLUSION

The frank assessment made even by leaders of the Union of Students in the period prior to the June events was that the Union was a resounding failure—it was an organization of a few 'leaders' rather than the mass of students; internal relations were hierarchical rather than democratic, the Union had failed to assist in the development of self-management, it had little independence, power or significance and was therefore ignored by other socio-political organizations, and above all else, it had failed to achieve its principal aim of the socialist upbringing of the young.

Three points should be made concerning this frankness. First, it was something forced on the leaders when the crisis within the Union of Students and the broader Union of Youth was such that it could no longer be hidden or overlooked. As a group, the youth leaders had sought to present the impression that all was well. When the actual situation was exposed, the leaders of the organization simply joined in the acknowledgement of that failure.[204]

Second, despite this frankness concerning the situation within the Union, the leaders were unable or reluctant to make the effort to turn the organization over to the rank and file and to make it relevant and important to them. This was graphically illustrated by the Congress of the Union of Students held just one month before the June events. The assembled delegates considered a variety of important topics such as the material position of students, the problem of employment, the question of student participation in self-management and educational reform. Yet the debates merely seemed to repeat the familiar phrases and slogans. For example, it was noted that the present material situation of the university should be 'improved' and that it was necessary to link education and science to the basic goals and tasks of societal development.[205] According to a report in *Politika* the debates were 'far from lively'; indeed they were brief and casual.[206]

149

Third, this frankness tended to be concentrated on results and peripheral reasons, rather than being applied to a consideration of the fundamental causes of the 'failure'. As noted in the introduction of this chapter, the constantly reiterated official view was that the failure of these organizations stemmed from the careerism of the youth leaders which prevented the adoption of appropriate methods of work; it was strongly implied that if only these leaders had behaved differently and if only suitable methods of work had been adopted the young would have become active, enthusiastic and committed. It could be contended, however, that this was much too facile an explanation.

In particular, the failure of these organizations cannot be considered apart from the realities concerning both their membership and the broader society. Thus, while it was stressed that the activities of these organizations were to be both free and correct, it is clear that in practice these twin principles were irreconcilable. There was too great a gulf between the interests, attitudes and beliefs of the youth and what the Yugoslav leadership would have considered appropriate. And these interests, attitudes and beliefs were to a large degree the inevitable consequence of the realities of Yugoslav society. For example, it was difficult to persuade the young that they should develop a deep and selfless commitment to the socialist community when most adult models in Yugoslav society, including those holding high office, offered an example of selfish concern for their own position and privilege. Similarly, it was difficult to persuade the students to show respect for the working class when it was clear that within the system as a whole there was little respect or concern for the workers. Therefore, any effort to teach the 'correct' attitudes would be promptly contradicted by the realities of Yugoslav society—consequently, such an effort would be at best ineffectual, at worst it could lead to the development of cynicism among the youth.

As for the careerism of the leaders of the youth organizations, these leaders generally behaved as they were obliged to behave. Incidentally, it is a revealing commentary on the Yugoslav system that one's career was best served by behaviour which violated the basic rights of the members of the particular collective and which inexorably led to the failure of the organization to achieve its goals. Clearly, this sin of careerism was not something brought into one corner of the total socio-political system by a small isolated group; as the previously cited *Komunist* article acknowledged, the situation within the youth organization was merely a reflection of the situation in the League of Communists.[207]

As noted in chapter II, the irrelevance of the Union was also affirmed by the fact that the June demonstrations entirely by-passed it.[208] This was only partly due to the fact that many officials of the Union thought it prudent to lie low when the protests erupted. Another cause was the rejection by the protesters of the bureaucratic form of organization typified by the Union of Students. This is reflected in the fact, for example, that the membership of the Action Committees changed each day. The aim, as expressed by the articulate minority among the protesters, was to have the students participate on terms of equality in the decision-making process, rather than to have a continuation of the situation in which a small, separate group claimed the right to speak for the 'real' interests of the student body as a whole.[209]

The view expressed by this radical minority during these June events was that the Action Committees and the mass meetings should be retained as permanent forms of political activity outside both the League of Communists and the Union of Students. Naturally, however, the official League response was one of vehement opposition, and this demand was condemned as tending toward the development of a multi-party system. According to an article in *Politika,* 'most' young people and communists at Belgrade University had rejected this notion of a 'new movement', not merely because they perceived the seeds of a multi-party system, but because they saw in it a new opportunity for the institutionalization and the limitation of their political activities.[210] Thus, the intended cure for the complaint of bureaucracy was itself described as the disease.

Chapter VII

CONCLUSION

If I am incapable of solving these questions, then I should no longer be in this place. I think that not one of our senior communists, whoever he may be . . . should insist on keeping his place but should make room for those who are capable of solving problems.

(Tito, 9 June 1968)

YUGOSLAV EXPLANATION OF THE JUNE EVENTS

The Yugoslav student protests of June 1968 are of vital importance, as concerns the study both of the attitudes and beliefs of the protesters and the functioning of the broad Yugoslav political system. The vital task is to determine the principal causes of these events and then to endeavour to determine exactly what they signify. As was outlined in chapter II, there are various explanations of student unrest, and various views of the nature of student feelings and motives.

The first point emphasized was that the effort to explain student feelings and motives obviously required a consideration of the students' immediate environment and problems, but it also demanded a consideration of some of the difficulties in the broader society. It must also be stressed that while the most significant disturbances occurred in Belgrade, the possibility of them spreading to the other university centres was very real because the students at these universities shared many of the grievances and frustrations of the Belgrade students.[1]

This possibility explains, in part, the care with which the Yugoslav leadership sought to handle the Belgrade demonstrations. But also important in this regard was the size and strength of the Belgrade protest—the Yugoslav leadership had already endured the embarrassment of violent and large clashes between students and militia; tough measures, though urged by some in the leading circles, were clearly not regarded as an appropriate solution. And, finally, the prospect of links being established between students and workers could not be discounted, especially in view of the fact that the recent 'economic reforms' had placed a heavy burden on the workers. In this situation it seemed that the most appropriate course for the Yugoslav leadership was to try to prevent the demonstrations from spreading, while trying to cool the mood of the Belgrade students.

As is explained in the second chapter, despite the very skilful tactics that were adopted, the strength of the protest was such that it took some seven days before it could be said that the demonstrations were over. In that period some very bitter words were spoken at the many mass meetings held in the Student City. And it required the massive intervention of Tito finally to seal the issue. Significantly, Tito—the one who was presented to the students as the hero of the revolution— lauded their idealism and motives, and humbly acknowledged that the solution to many of the problems they had raised was long overdue. Tito's final act of obeisance to the students was to offer to step down if he proved incapable of overcoming these difficulties.

Tito's speech is important not only because it ended this particular crisis, but also because of the interpretation he gave of the protests. He claimed that he did not see the demonstrations as stemming essentially from the frustrations caused by the students' particular difficulties; nor, at the other extreme, did he see the demonstrators as being motivated by the desire to overturn the present political system. He was prepared to acknowledge that the students' material and academic situation gave rise to some dissatisfaction, but he maintained that the students were not exclusively concerned with their own selfish interests. And, while acknowledging that some protesters urged drastic modification of the existing political order, he insisted that the thrust of the students' protest was merely aimed at making the *present* system work more effectively.

According to Tito, the present difficulties of which the students justifiably complained did not indicate a breakdown of the system as a whole nor the failure of the League leadership, but rather, the failure of responsible officials and individuals to strive for the implementation of League policies. All these difficulties had been recognized and appropriate remedies had been devised; however, 'bureaucratic' forces had failed to give effect to these remedies. Tito claimed this was recognized by the student body, and that therefore the students were not to be seen as either hostile or indifferent to the League leadership, but rather as the allies of the leadership in the struggle for socialist development. He also observed that, far from the students being apolitical, as had previously been feared,[2] these eventful days had demonstrated their deep political interest and commitment.

Tito's address drew together some of the more significant strands of official statements on the student protest into a coherent whole and stamped this view with all of his authority. Not surprisingly, the subsequent discussions of these events by various Yugoslav officials and scholars were generally consistent with this view.

An article in *Politika* emphasized Tito's point concerning the relationship between the young and the League of Communists: the young had not attacked the League but were, on the contrary, inspired by it. Indeed, all positive trends in Yugoslav society

> are inspired by the revolutionary action and program of the League of Communists, even when they appear outside of its . . . ranks. It is the League of Communists which . . . introduced a creative

153

restlessness into our society. The restlessness of the young is, in essence, an echo of that restlessness.[3]

A similar point was made in an article in *Komunist,* which emphasized the links between the League leadership and the young and, in particular, the 'powerful linking of . . . the revolutionary ideas of the League and the revolutionary will and wishes' of the youth.[4]

Even Svetozar Stojanović agreed that the student movement was a progressive force. It is important to note, however, that he rejected the 'most popular view' that the student protest was merely a reaction against specific 'socio-political "deformations"' and urged that the 'fundamental significance' of the protest 'should be seen in the resistance to the entropy of the social revolution'; as he saw it, the students had recognized that Yugoslav society had basic rather than particular or superficial difficulties.[5]

Other accounts noted the existence of a minority of 'extremists' on both the 'left' and the 'right' who had attacked the Yugoslav self-managing system. These extremists were variously described as 'Stalinist', 'bourgeois', 'hippies', supporters of Marcuse, supporters of Che Guevara, or supporters of Mao; some were described as supporters of a 'statist' concept of socialism while others were seen as advocates of 'primitive' egalitarian communism. However, most of these accounts reiterated Tito's judgement that these alleged extremists constituted only a tiny minority, and that the overwhelming thrust of the student protest reflected the deep-seated desire to hasten the process of socialist development and a desire to attack not the system as a whole nor the League leadership, but rather particular deformations,[6] and that the protests were a significant event in maintaining the revolutionary spirit in Yugoslavia.[7] (On this point it is worth remembering that similar protests in the West had been interpreted by the media in Yugoslavia as indicating that the very foundations of the system of these particular countries was under severe challenge.)

In general terms, such was the Yugoslav analysis of the causes and significance of the June events. Certainly there is evidence, not least of which was the student response to Tito's speech, which indicates that the official assessment is not without foundation. However, it could be argued that the case for this interpretation is by no means incontrovertible. For example, one could urge that the reported enthusiasm among the students following Tito's address demonstrated his great skill in persuasion, the affection and awe with which he was still regarded, and finally, the fact that his explanation provided both the League leadership and the students with an acceptable way of bringing the particular crisis to a close. Concerning this last point—Tito had maintained that the League leadership was not at fault and at the same time had lauded the idealism and sincerity of the protesters. The students were showered with praise—who were they to contradict this assessment? That is, it could be suggested that the enthusiasm with which Tito's analysis was received is no guarantee of its accuracy. It seems unlikely for example, that the students would insist, 'No, you are wrong—we really don't care about politics—all we care about is obtaining, with the minimum discomfort and effort, a piece of paper from the University which will guarantee us a comfortable niche in the establishment.' In particular, Tito's claim that these events demonstrated the idealism and commitment of the present generation must be set against the background described in the present study, a background which appears to reveal widespread disenchantment and passivity.

THE YUGOSLAV UNIVERSITY—FAITH, FAILURE AND FRUSTRATIONS

As far as the Yugoslav leadership was concerned, faith in the benefits of the expansion of university enrolments had seemed boundless. It was frequently observed that the number of graduates was still below that of the economically advanced societies and great pride was taken in the yearly increase in student enrolments. However, little attention was given to some of the harsh realities described earlier; the prevailing belief seemed to be that merely increasing the number of university students would automatically and inevitably have a marked, positive effect on economic development.

Apart from seeing the expansion of student enrolments as the key to progress, it seems clear that the Yugoslav leaders also saw the political significance of this increase in educational opportunity. To them this was a graphic symbol of the new era. In this connection, it is important to remember that many in the middle and top ranks in Yugoslav society had come to these positions via the revolution rather than via the university. Prior to the war, many of them had seen no future for themselves or their children other than as a peasant or worker; the opportunity to continue their education and to move up the socio-economic scale hardly existed.

The communist revolution changed all this. Suddenly, many such men were catapulted from the farm or work bench into an office; from using a hoe or hammer to using a fountain pen; from travelling by horse or tram to travelling in a chauffeur-driven automobile. Many of them, by virtue of their direct experience, were deeply cognizant of the significance of 'education'; but more than concern for their competence in a particular area, they were anxious that their social behavior should not earn them the dreaded label of 'nekulturan'.* Despite their present status, they knew and felt the importance of 'education'.

In the old order, education was for the privileged few; in the new order, educational opportunity was to be for all. The leadership urged this and an increasing proportion of the people sought this for their children. For the leadership, education was the key to progress for the entire society; for the people, education was, even as it had been before the war, the key to upward mobility. In this general situation it was very difficult to be rational about university expansion; tertiary institutions were opened in various areas for various specialities and for various reasons and often these reasons had little to do with the real

* plebeian, boorish.

needs and resources of the Yugoslav community as a whole. Even when the problems of excessive, rapid, fragmented and unplanned expansion became apparent, no significant efforts were made to remedy the situation.

While the official explanation of the protests did acknowledge student grievances concerning their particular situation, it failed to reflect either the seriousness of this situation or the bitterness felt by the students on this question. It has been demonstrated that in a variety of areas the students had experienced a marked gulf between rhetoric and reality. The rhetoric concerning the system of material support for students promised meaningful aid, offered in such a way as to provide for greater equality of opportunity and to encourage conscientious study. In fact, the number and value of scholarships was grossly inadequate; further, the scholarships were often distributed according to personal connections, rather than on fair and rational principles. Similarly, the living conditions of the students fell far short of what the rhetoric implied the conditions should be, and indeed, far short of even a reasonable level. Less than a month before the June events, Tito was reported as saying that in the Yugoslav system the care for youth received the highest priority, but went on to acknowledge that 'we have not always carried out our promises'.[8]

The students were dissatisfied with their material situation, but, more importantly, their dissatisfaction was greatly aggravated by those official statements which described what must be done; the expectations which were aroused always exceeded what was or could be provided. Their resentment was further increased by the examples of conspicuous wealth among a minority of their fellow students. Inevitably, the presence of such students served to sharpen the feelings of dissatisfaction within the student body and to highlight the discrepancy between the proclaimed ideals of equality of opportunity and the actual situation.

Similarly, the situation within the university itself was far from satisfactory. In general terms the staff could not be described as being of a high standard—this was due to a variety of factors, some 'objective', such as salary rates, and some 'subjective', such as the selection and promotion of staff for reasons other than superior ability. Further, teaching, research and library facilities generally fell far short of an acceptable level. These factors, together with the gross overcrowding and the poor preparation of the incoming students, help explain the extraordinarily high failure rate. As was emphasized in chapter IV, the overwhelming majority of students had to endure the frustrations of taking several additional years to complete their basic degree and, indeed, the prospect of not graduating at all.

This particular problem of the university was not merely something discussed casually among the students, but rather, was a frequent major issue in the speeches of Yugoslav leaders and in the pages of the daily newspapers. This constant public analysis of the problem and the constant official criticism of the fact that little had been done to rectify it, could only have accentuated student fears and frustrations. This was especially so in view of the fact that these official analyses and prescriptions tended not to blame the students themselves for their poor examination results. The official view blamed the staff for failing to implement a meaningful programme of educational reform; the staff was described as refusing to delete 'superfluous' material from curricula so as to ensure that the average student could graduate on schedule and become a useful, practical expert and not what was described as an over-educated generalist.

Rather than acknowledge that many of the university's problems stemmed from the enormous burdens imposed on it, and rather than implement measures to ease this burden (such as providing greater resources, reducing overall enrolments and rationalizing the educational network), the Yugoslav leadership demanded that the staff should remedy the appalling failure rate by lowering standards. To many faculty members this involved nothing less than changing the university into something akin to a technical institute. That little progress was made toward this concept of 'educational reform' cannot be blamed, therefore, entirely on what the leadership described as the narrowness, conservatism and selfishness of the staff. To many among the staff, greater 'efficiency', in the sense of a significant reduction of the failure rate, inevitably meant the preparation of only narrowly qualified graduates, by methods involving rote learning, over-simplification and the like; that is, it meant a drastic retreat from the ideals of the university so as to save, or so it might be suggested, the Yugoslav leadership from assuming the responsibility for resolving the problems which its own deliberate policy had created.

But, as was emphasized in chapter IV, regardless of the merits of this particular debate, the important point was simply the general acknowledgement that the universities had serious problems, that the average student could not hope to graduate on schedule and, finally, that despite frequent discussion and exhortation nothing was done to remedy the situation.

The official rhetoric also emphasized the vital importance of upgrading the qualifications of the work force by increasing the number of university trained personnel. However, there was no real attempt by responsible authorities to plan university expansion to accord with even an estimate of society's particular needs. The consequence was that many graduates found themselves unemployed. Part of this unemployment problem was also due to the fact that many of the older generation, though often inadequately qualified, jealously guarded their positions against the young graduates. While this was often condemned, little was done to remedy it, and the official emphasis on what was desirable and necessary in this area again served only to heighten student frustration.

Student cynicism was strengthened by other features of university life. It has been demonstrated in chapter III that as far as students were concerned, self-management within the university was virtually non-existent. By itself this may have had limited significance, but it assumed considerable importance against the background of the sweeping rhetoric concerning the right of all to participate, coupled with the frequent official and press criticism of the resistance of the university staff to the development of genuine self-managing relations.

But was there a strong desire on the part of the students to participate? It is clear that, in the period prior to the June events, no significant efforts seem to have been made by the students to organize student life and activities on the campus or in the hostels and no significant pressure for the exercise and the expansion of their present rights was apparent; indeed, it seems that most of them remained preoccupied with their own personal affairs and future. Does this therefore mean that the demand for participation articulated during the protests did not reflect a genuine and widespread feeling? Or did this passivity stem from a feeling that the opportunity for meaningful participation simply did not exist?[9] It is, of course, impossible to assess the real desire for participation among the students. How, for example, could one determine that there existed a genuine desire to participate but that the circumstances were so daunting and hopeless that this desire was stifled? What *can* be said with some certainty, however, is that whatever the cause or causes of this passivity they were unlikely to be removed. That is, the vast majority had been and would remain overwhelmingly preoccupied with personal interests, but, as noted earlier, the official and press criticism of the existing situation again served to persuade the students that they were being deprived of something which was their right.

A similar conclusion might be drawn with respect to the Yugoslav Union of Students and the Union of Youth. Neither of these organizations could observe the limitations imposed by the system and at the same time manage to attract the young. These limitations inevitably led to programmes which the young, no matter how great their interest in politics, could not long endure. Inevitably, these organizations came to be regarded as organizations which to all intents and purposes consisted only of their office bearers. This led to official and press criticism of the youth leaders for their failure to develop appropriate and attractive forms of work and for turning the organizations into vehicles for their own personal advancement. But, as was explained in the previous chapter, it was impossible for these leaders, in the existing political situation, to develop alternative forms of work. The youth leader who sought to do so risked allowing his group to stray from the 'correct' narrow path and consequently of being removed from his position. It was easy for the Yugoslav leadership and press to condemn careerism among the youth leaders, but it was scarcely fair—these leaders were only behaving as they were obliged to behave.

Again however, this analysis of the causes of the difficulties in these organizations may be somewhat beside the point as far as the mass of students was concerned. For them, a most significant aspect was the acknowledgement that these organizations had failed to realize their objectives of representing the particular interests of the young and of giving them the opportunity to join together to discuss League policy and to express their views on current problems of socialist development. Thus, the students were again persuaded that the situation in yet another area was grossly unsatisfactory, again persuaded that they were being deprived of something which was their right and again persuaded that they were blameless. In other words, the rhetoric concerning the youth organizations did little more than strengthen student feelings that they were discriminated against, neglected and under-valued.

Through all of this there is apparent on the part of the Yugoslav leadership a pattern of short-term expediency—each time a particular problem forced itself to prominence, official spokesmen sought to blame someone for failing to implement those policies which had been avowedly designed to eliminate such difficulties and insisted that immediate and decisive action be taken. But these spokesmen seemed to give little attention to the question of whether the past or proposed solutions were either relevant or feasible.

To reiterate, as far as the student was concerned it was not merely a question of his 'objective' situation being unsatisfactory; of vital importance were the official comments on his plight. These stressed that problems existed, and that students were deprived of their rights and opportunities largely because of the resistance of those responsible for the implementation of League policies. Feelings of frustration and dissatisfaction concerning their immediate situation were thus strengthened rather than assuaged. These feelings were exacerbated by developments beyond the immediate university environment—indeed the problems within the university reflected and were an integral part of the problems of the system as a whole: the simple fact was that the Yugoslav model of self-managing socialism had run into considerable difficulties.

THE CRISIS OF AUTHORITY AND STUDENT BELIEFS

Much had been made of the significance of the system of self-management; in particular, it had been proudly presented as the alternative to both bourgeois democracy and 'statist communism'.[10] On the one hand, self-management gave the members of a particular collective the vital right to help formulate the basic decisions directly affecting their life and work. On the other hand, the inspiration and guidance of League policies and of individual League members within the particular collective would ensure that the decisions of each self-managing collective would be in accord with the interests of the total socialist community.

However, in practice the system of self-management bore little resemblance to this model. As has been emphasized throughout this study, the decisions of each particular collective often showed scant regard for the interests of the total community or even for the long-term interests of the particular collective. And often those within the collective who were expected to provide the guidance toward the consideration of broader interests were those who sought to use the device of

159

self-management to protect their own personal privileges and position. To many of the students, self-management was often, to take an example directly relevant to them, a means by which those currently occupying responsible posts in the economy zealously sought to protect their own positions despite the proclaimed policy of employing and promoting younger individuals with greater qualifications.

The confidence and pride with which the self-managing model had been presented to the world and to the Yugoslav community had built up high expectations, especially among the young. In this regard it must be appreciated that the model of self-management, compared, for example, with 'liberal democracy', stipulates extraordinary standards. In the case of a liberal democracy it is possible to argue that the notion of direct popular control over governmental policies is largely a fiction but one which is widely believed by the people themselves; merely the opportunity to vote at periodic elections enables the individual citizen 'to enjoy a sense of involvement'.[11] By contrast, the maintenance of the 'myth' of self-management requires far more than an occasional vote for a particular candidate at a general election. At the very least, it entails regular meetings of each collective, full discussion of the many, varied issues, and finally a vote on each of these issues by the members present.

Inevitably, as the young observed both the functioning and the results of the system of self-management, any feelings of confidence or enthusiasm they may have had were not infrequently displaced by feelings of uncertainty and even pessimism. In this situation, the constant reiteration of the virtues of the self-managing system seemed only to drive the young away from politics.

Even among those who remained formally involved, the mood did not seem to be one of enthusiasm and idealism. As has been noted in chapter VI, many of those who held leading positions within the youth organizations were those who were prepared to behave so as to maintain and advance their own careers. And among young communists in general, among those who had the responsibility of guiding and inspiring their fellows, it was clear that there was little self-confidence or activity. As for their confidence in the ideals of communism, some young communists were even reported as having turned to religion as a way of finding some meaning to life. Thus, more than half of the communist students at Ljubljana University included in a survey were attending church and 'worshipping God' because, in their words, contemporary society had not 'offered . . . ideals to them'.[12]

The articulated policies of the League tended to exacerbate rather than to help overcome this mood of confusion and doubt. As the guidelines published following the June events graphically illustrated, League policy tended to be vague and ambiguous rather than a clear guide to action.[13] This was the inevitable consequence of the fact that the League was far from being a monolithic organization; its policies reflected the fact that the League as a whole, and the League leadership itself, encompassed individuals and groups of varying attitudes and interests.

As important as these differences in outlook was the *nature* of the problems facing the League. Few matters called for simple solutions; rather, it was usually necessary to endeavour to balance conflicting aims. To take one example: on the one hand, it was desirable to allow each basic organization of the Union of Students the maximum freedom to determine its own activities, but on the other hand, it was necessary to ensure that these activities were such as to provide the 'proper' climate for the ideological education of the young.

Instead of giving an impression of confidence, the League often gave the impression that it was confused and divided, and that it sought to hide this confusion and division with loud, sanctimonious declarations.

The vagueness of these declarations provided the opportunity for various members and sections of the League to continue in their own way with little risk of being accused of contravening League policy. And, in turn, this led once again to complaints from the leadership that the desired changes had not been secured, that responsible authorities were paying only lip-service to League policies and that the time had come for action.[14]

This uncertainty was especially apparent in the area of economic policy. In place of the earlier firm confidence in the inevitability of continued rapid growth, there were now anxious discussions on unemployment, inflation, low productivity and inequality of incomes.[15] Some suggested a tightening of economic controls to overcome these problems, but this suggestion was opposed by others who claimed this would mean the abandonment of self-management and the return to the 'administrative' or 'statist' model. Some even talked of the encouragement of private investment and ownership, but this suggestion was opposed by those who felt such a step would threaten the very existence of socialism.[16]

Looking back over the post-war years it is clear that the League has tended to lurch from crisis to crisis rather than to march inexorably toward the goal of socialism; the path is littered with abandoned policies and discredited former brothers-in-arms. For example, no lesser figures than Djilas and Ranković have been stripped of their power (at different times and in different circumstances). Somehow the party never managed to reconcile the various strands of belief which existed within the party, and, indeed, within the minds of most individual members: to take the most obvious example, the party which had once seemed more Stalinist than Stalin's own had suddenly become the bitterest critic of the Soviet model. It is not surprising, therefore, that there was oscillation and confusion in matters of policy.

The communist organization had begun its rule with considerable political credit in the eyes of many citizens; above all else a significant number had seen it as the party of courageous idealists and the party which would lead the people to a life of new opportunity. However, by the mid-1960s it was obvious that much of this political credit had evaporated. Instead of setting an example of selfless enthusiasm and instead of working to persuade and inspire members of their particular

161

collective to adopt League policies, many communists gave the impression of being concerned only with their own personal interests and indeed as having joined the League for primarily selfish reasons. On this point it is worth noting that a survey of the opinions of secondary school children conducted in Croatia showed that approximately half of those surveyed felt that half of the League members saw the organization 'primarily as a means of advancing one's career rather than as an organization for the struggle for progressive ideals'. Indeed, just over one-third of those surveyed felt this was true of all or most members of the League.[17]

As was frequently acknowledged in both the press and in academic journals, the reputation of communists among the young in particular was often very low;[18] a schoolboy's letter in *Vjesnik* asked where were all the 'real, sincere revolutionaries? . . . Have they all been killed?'[19] The harking back to the glories of the revolutionary struggle inevitably became less effective as a means of arousing support and enthusiasm. Indeed, many young people simply brushed aside such references with the comment that the particular struggle was in the past and that it was now necessary to concentrate on the present and the future. The young clearly resented the condescension and arrogance of many among this 'great' generation and they resented the fact that they were expected to show this generation 'everlasting gratitude'.[20] From time to time there was a bemoaning of the fact that the young were not attracted to the League, but it was also acknowledged that often there was considerable justification for their lack of enthusiasm.

It was admitted that many basic organizations of the League showed what was described as excessive tolerance for the mistakes and faults of certain of their members. They were seen as organizations which 'at times' did not reach decisions on a 'principled' basis or which were often inconsistent in the implementation of their decisions,[21] in which there was much talk of democracy but in which power was in the hands of a few,[22] as organizations in which the young were regarded with little respect or enthusiasm and in which the young were expected to listen and defer,[23] in which the young were treated as objects and whose problems were described as 'youth problems' rather than as matters of concern to the entire society,[24] and as organizations which were careful to admit only 'well disciplined' young people rather than those who might have greater idealism and enthusiasm.[25]

Even the 'highest party and government leaders' were regarded with little confidence by many students. Thus a survey, reported not long after the June events, showed that 40 per cent of the students polled felt that 'most of these top leaders should step down', and only 25 per cent felt that the leaders led the country 'in the best manner'. The remainder endorsed the alternative which stated that 'some new leaders would not be any better or worse than today's'.[26] Of course, it could be urged that as critical a response might be obtained in our own society. It must be remembered, however, that the moral authority of the League is seen as being vital to the proper functioning of the self-managing system. In our own society the authority of the law, of the electoral arrangements and the like counts for much more than the moral authority of a particular group of leaders. And the role of our leaders is vastly different from the role of the leaders in the Yugoslav system—at the risk of over-simplification, it could be maintained that in the former system the leaders' task is seen as being to serve the people; in the latter, the leaders have the far more onerous and awesome task of teaching and guiding, as well as inspiring the people.

In this context several writers stressed that the problem of persuading a greater number of young people to join the League would not be solved by recruiting drives. Rather, what was required was a change within the League itself which would serve to raise the reputation of the League in the eyes of the young and at the same time increase its influence over them. It was asserted that youth 'sensed' the League through its activities rather than through its policies and therefore it must be seen as mounting an effective struggle for the realization of its proclaimed ideals.[27] However, as has been emphasized, this was easier said than done—even on the fundamental question of the role of the League within the system of self-management there remained doubt and disagreement.

The easy confidence with which the self-management model had been elaborated had now vanished. In particular, grave doubts were voiced in various circles concerning the avowed claim that the present system inevitably and naturally led towards the strengthening of socialism. Most notable among these critics of the prevailing practice were, of course, those associated with the journal *Praxis*. Many of these critics acknowledged what they described as the real achievements of Yugoslavia in the development of socialist theory and practice which had ensued from the break with the Stalinist pattern; however, they warned that there were dangerous trends which needed careful, frank and urgent attention.

Yet, despite all the obvious and serious difficulties, the Yugoslav leadership continued to insist that these were only temporary setbacks or problems. Instead of a full, frank discussion of basic problems, the Yugoslav leadership tinkered with some of the details, adopted short-term expedients and claimed once again that all was well, or that a particular problem was receiving attention, or that the measures adopted to cope with a certain crisis were beginning to show positive results or that the problems were only in the minds of critics. Even at the height of the student demonstrations, the League leadership in Serbia issued a statement noting that the 'crisis of contemporary capitalism . . . as well as the crisis of the administrative-statist' system in socialist countries demonstrated the correctness of the path Yugoslavia had chosen. 'Workers and students throughout the world [were] proclaiming on their banners the ideals of self-management and socialist democracy. . . . Our country has taken its place in the vanguard of those social forces in the contemporary world' which were seeking to realize the human content of socialism.[28]

The decision reached by the League in each crisis was always presented as a bold step forward and as a victory over the foes of socialism, but as one member of the *Praxis* group bitingly remarked, there were 'many such . . . victories'.[29] Similarly, an article published in *Rad* at the height of the June crisis condemned the smug tone of the pronouncements of 'our socio-political forums' concerning the students' demands. These bodies calmly maintained that the problems were well known and that they were already 'in the process of being settled', but, the article continued, if this were the case, why had no effective action been taken? The article concluded by questioning the sincerity of some of the members of these organizations: it noted that the first criticisms of the gross social inequalities had been denounced by 'certain forums' as unnecessary witch hunts, yet these same bodies were now claiming that they had recognized the seriousness of this problem and were giving it their close attention.[30]

These harsh comments, together with the various strong criticisms cited in the body of the present work drawn from official speeches, the media and scholarly articles and books, give the impression of extraordinary freedom of speech in the Yugoslav system. However, such an impression is inaccurate because for the most part these criticisms have fitted within the limits (albeit often vague and unclear) laid down by the Yugoslav leadership. As Stane Dolanc, the Secretary of the Executive Bureau of the Presidium of the LCY, recently remarked concerning the media:

> In our self-management socialist society, information media are not only a means for informing the working people . . . . The press, radio, and television are first of all instruments of the working class itself, and of their struggle for socialism, and self-management, for the pursuit of their current goals and interests, and their long-term historical goals and interests.[31]

Using the media 'irresponsibly' on directly political matters is fraught with danger. Thus the criticisms from *Rad,* quoted just above, resulted in the dismissal of several members of the paper's staff.[32] It must be emphasized, however, that on matters not directly relating to the principles of the Yugoslav system or to the role of the Yugoslav leadership, there are few restrictions. Hence there is a plethora of papers, magazines, books, films and television programmes which cannot be distinguished from those of the 'decadent West'. Despite the claim that the media must remain an instrument of the working class in the struggle for socialism, in all but the one area the principles of the market place appear to reign supreme—if it sells or can help something else to sell, it is acceptable.

Concerning the academic community, the experience of the *Praxis* group is most instructive. They have been consistently criticized and harassed, their journal has been starved of funds, particular issues have been banned and, finally, they have been forced to cease publication. Eight staff members at the University of Belgrade's Philosophy Department, several of them such as Svetozar Stojanović and Zagorka Pešić-

Golubović frequent contributors to *Praxis,* were recently dismissed from their teaching posts by a special act of the Serbian parliament for activities described as being 'contrary to the aims and practices of Yugoslavia's socialist society, basic constitutional principles and policies of the Communist Party'.[33]

As far as the work of scholars is concerned, the League leaders have persistently maintained that only constructive criticism can be permitted and, of course, that they and not individual scholars should decide what is constructive and what is not. Thus particular problems may be discussed, but again it is unwise to criticize directly principles of self-management or the Yugoslav leaders or to discuss certain more delicate problems. Concerning the latter, it is important to note that the study of the June events is taboo.[34]

For the most part it could be urged, therefore, that these apparently forthright criticisms represent the effort of the leadership to stop or limit particular abuses, to allow the safety valve of criticism on less significant aspects of the system and to promise or suggest the prospect of reform. Quite clearly, as Tito himself has acknowledged, a double standard exists within Yugoslav society, one standard applying to those in higher positions and another for those below.[35] However, despite his condemnation of this double standard, the situation, as far as the potential critic is concerned, has become even more difficult in recent times.

Inevitably, therefore, the explanation presented in official speeches, the media and so on, may owe more to considerations of expediency than to the facts. If, for example, all officials and commentators in a Westminster system were obliged to accept the explanation of the result of a by-election offered by a spokesman for just one of the parties, we would have a situation analogous to that which prevails in Yugoslavia. As Tito expressed it in 1966,

> Comrades, let us put our hands on our hearts and acknowledge that all is not always as we describe it. For example, when we began the economic reform [of 1964, aimed at giving greater weight to market forces] we said that this was the result of the buoyant development of our economy and our society as a whole, however, in that buoyant development there were a whole series of negative signs and tendencies. Let us take, for example, the exceeding of our material capabilities, the unnecessary investments, the building of factories in every republic and every commune and so on. It goes without saying in the main it was the political leaders who insisted on that.[36]

In these two comments it is clear that Tito has highlighted the basic difficulty in using these Yugoslav sources. Consequently, one is obliged to examine very carefully the official view that the student protest reflected the strength of progressive forces within the community and the strength of support for the League leadership.

Often the youth were described as *inevitably* enthusiastic, active and idealistic, and as the major force for progress in society. It seems that such a view stemmed from the experience of the war and the immediate post-war period when there was ample evidence to support the idea of the young as enthusiastic and selfless supporters of the revolution. The spirit and role of the young in that period had been exceptional, but the Yugoslav leadership often talked as if it were the norm. Indeed, one could argue that until relatively recent times Yugoslav society had not had a distinct and significant group which could be termed 'the youth'. In pre-revolutionary Yugoslavia most children went directly from child-hood to adulthood, becoming peasants or workers like their parents. There was little hope, and even less opportunity, for them to secure significant change in their role or status.

The war, however, changed that. The young were the major force in the struggle against the Nazi invaders and their local allies. Gradually, under the leadership of the Communist Party, the thrust of this struggle broadened beyond the mere expulsion of the invaders to include the hope of a new order. Many of these young men and women were easily persuaded that the old regime was unjust and that it must be replaced. Part of the process of persuasion was, of course, lavish praise: the communist leadership described these young fighters as the heroic creators of the revolution who were willing to sacrifice even their lives in order to bring a better life to their own and succeeding generations. The commitment and courage of the partisans justifiably earned them enormous, world-wide respect. However, in order to understand some of the views concerning the youth propagated by the Yugoslav leader-ship, this brave struggle must be seen in its particular context. While no one can deny the achievement of this generation, it is important to remember that the initial motivation to join this struggle might not have been as selfless and as idealistic as Yugoslav spokesmen have implied; many young people, especially in the villages, had come to feel that there was little chance of avoiding involvement in this increasingly brutal struggle and that it was better to die fighting than to be shot as a victim of reprisal. In other words, these acts of selflessness and courage were in large part the direct consequence of the anger and fear engen-dered by the occupation forces and their local allies.

The immediate post-war period also was marked by particular cir-cumstances. In place of the former enemy of fascism there was a new but equally obvious enemy, that of backwardness. And in the apparent enthusiasm of this period it seemed inevitable that this enemy would also be decisively conquered.

The rhetoric concerning the importance of the youth remained the same, but gradually, almost imperceptibly, the circumstances began to change. At first many among the youth were caught up in the revolu-tionary fervour—they toiled valiantly and enthusiastically on massive voluntary work projects and assumed, or prepared themselves to assume, new positions in the new society. The son of the peasant or worker no longer saw himself as following in his father's footsteps—opportunity was open to all.

In this period, the struggles to create a new society and a new life for oneself seemed largely intertwined. However, gradually the two aims began to become distinct as revolutionary enthusiasm waned, as it became obvious that the struggle to build a new society was far more difficult than had been thought[37] and as it was realized that the problems faced were not as identifiable or as personally threatening as had been the enemy during the war.[38] Clearly it was becoming more difficult to be a revolutionary than it had been during the war: for the most part the partisans had known who were their allies and who were their enemies and they knew what had to be done, but that assurance no longer existed.[39] As Tito remarked at the Eighth Congress of the Union of Youth, 'we are facing many complex tasks in the present phase of our revolution. Many people are losing their bearings and are falling behind.'[40] Finally, the simple fact was that society could not remain at a fever pitch indefinitely. After the rigours of the war and immediate post-war years, an increasing number of people, beginning at the very top, began to look for a little more personal pleasure and security.[41]

Most notable in this regard was Tito himself. Throughout his life, even during the difficult days of the partisan struggle, he showed a love for handsome clothes. In the post-war period he 'had numbers of houses, powerful cars, yachts, aeroplanes' and the like.[42] According to Phyllis Auty in her biography of Tito, 'these were no more than were available to most heads of state, though perhaps they were more luxurious than those that the heads of other communist states allowed themselves'. But it was her opinion that for every Yugoslav who criticized Tito's lifestyle, 'there was another who considered it fitting for their President'.[43] Even this mild comment makes clear that there are many Yugoslavs critical of Tito on this question. And further, one could urge that, regardless of the number who approved or disapproved of his mode of life, his example was a powerful one. His subordinates seemed quick to learn the need for cars, houses and clothes appropriate to their new status.

Increasingly and especially since the 'economic reforms', the primary preoccupation of many Yugoslav citizens seemed to be money and the pleasures that money could buy, and conversations often concentrated on such matters as fashion, cars, holidays and income. According to a student member of the Belgrade University Council of the Union of Students, Yugoslav society was in danger of disintegration because of the lack of a social conscience on the part of many individuals and organizations.[44] Or as one writer observed in 1972, the swing to the market economy was accompanied by the 'victory of the consumer mentality of petty-bourgeois values . . . [an] enormous increase in social differentiation, unjustified accumulation of wealth, economic crime, bribes and corruption'.[45] The Yugoslav leadership had endeavoured to present the dramatic, further swing towards the market as a great impetus to efficiency and productivity, as increasing the real freedom of the particular collectives and, above all else, as a decisive step towards self-managing socialism. Many clearly had a different view.

Often politics were mentioned only when jokes were being told, and these jokes revealed a deep cynicism. One popular story described a Yugoslav official showing his peasant mother through his splendid new home. To his surprise her admiration was tinged with concern: 'Aren't you worried, my son, that when the Communists come they will take all this?' One version of the story even has Tito describing to the spirit of his late mother how well her boy had done for himself.

As far as the young were concerned, then, the basic fact for many of them seemed to be that they were growing up in a society in which the total 'cake' was relatively small, but also in a society of rapidly rising expectations and one in which many of the adult models gave an example of conspicuous consumption.[46] In such a situation it made little sense to call for anything resembling selfless commitment. Such calls sounded increasingly faint alongside the music of foreign and local 'pop' stars; the model of the idealistic, determined, lean partisan paled into insignificance alongside the example of the contemporary function- ary who sat sleek and comfortable in his Mercedes, his handsome residence or his grand office; and the popular newspapers, magazines, television programmes and films all sounded a note very different from that heard in the ideological education programme. The workers' society was one which in fact scorned physical labour and rewarded it meagrely. In general, the message was often one of extravagant con- sumption and selfish pleasure rather than sacrifice or even reasonably fair conditions for all.[47]

The changes in the model of self-management appeared to acknow- ledge the weakening of non-material incentives. Thus, a greater emphasis was placed on profit for the particular collective as a means of increas- ing productivity. (In turn, of course, these changes served to strengthen the trend on the part of individuals and groups to give primary attention to their own interests.)

And yet the Yugoslav leadership often sought to suggest, for example, that the contemporary youth was or could be essentially the same as that youth which had showed such a spirit of self-sacrifice in those proud days of the revolution. Or in criticizing negative attitudes among the young, the Yugoslav leadership might say that the youth ought to model themselves on those heroes of an earlier generation.[48] The blunt truth, however, was that the present generation was largely the product of the forces of *its* era, just as the young partisans were the product of the different forces of theirs.

Despite what the Yugoslav leaders hoped for or claimed to expect, it was clear that most of the students were interested primarily in them- selves and, in particular, in securing high material rewards.[49] The mass desire for higher education was seen not as a means of preparing oneself to serve the community but as reflecting the desire for a piece of paper which would unlock the doors to personal economic security and social prestige.[50] In fairness to the students, it must be reiterated that such attitudes were not unrelated to the policies of the leadership and the realities of Yugoslav society such as the neglect of vocational education and the low status of workers. As the employment prospects for young graduates deteriorated, so the students' preoccupation with their own future became even more intense and increasingly many came to feel that they would have to make their futures in the capitalist West rather than in their homeland.

They were told how vitally important they were to the cause of socialist construction and at the same time told by particular collectives that there were no vacancies. They were told how the youth had to be involved in all facets of community life because youth was a major force for progress, and yet in practice the young were expected to listen, to defer and to wait their turn. It was widely agreed that in all areas of society, whether in employment, within bodies of self-management or within the League, the young were having increasing difficulty in gaining recognition.[51]

Not surprisingly, the young often became bitter and angry and came to believe that a system of 'connections' and of clannishness far more powerful than the system of self-management had evolved.[52] Similarly, many came to believe that individual communists often were concerned only with their personal interests and privileges rather than their responsibility to set an example.[53] Some even came to believe that the policies of the League as a whole were inappropriate and harmful.[54]

If all this is borne in mind, then the nature of the problems faced by those responsible for the ideological education of the young become much clearer. As has been emphasized in chapter VI, this period was marked by a deliberate and comprehensive effort to inculcate the young with the 'correct' values and attitudes. Thus the student organization was to involve the students in a programme of activities appropriate to their interests but also appropriate to the goal of creating socialist experts. However, while in theory these aims were reconcilable, in practice they proved to be contradictory; it was quite false, therefore, to insist that the failures of the youth organizations could be solved simply by the adoption of more 'relevant' methods. The more the particular youth or student organization provided for the interests of its members, the more that particular organization departed from the objective of providing the 'proper' climate for the ideological upbringing of the young and the more likely it was that responsible authorities would intervene to 'help' the organization back on to the correct path. Usually of course, there was no need for direct intervention because the youth leaders understood what was expected of them. Thus, the youth were denied the opportunity to discuss their own problems and those of the broader society and, instead, were offered a programme of lectures characterized by vagueness and moral exhortation. However, while the pursuance of the 'correct' line avoided any embarrassment, it inevitably meant that little interest was aroused. This was especially serious in view of the nature and extent of the competing attractions. Inevitably, then, these youth and student organizations became elaborate but empty shells.

In a situation of rising expectations, of limited resources, of uncertainty regarding the future and, above all, in a situation in which the adult models gave the example of being primarily concerned for themselves, it is scarcely surprising that many students withdrew into their personal concerns and showed little idealistic fervour. Therefore, the programme of ideological education was largely irrelevant. Indeed, one might even argue that from the point of view of the Yugoslav leadership the effort was dysfunctional. In other words, if the young gained anything from these programmes, it was often only a greater disdain for political activity, and even in some cases a complete rejection of society's achievements. In this regard it is worth noting the view expressed in a *Borba* editorial of 13 June 1968: Yugoslav society had reached the point where the 'long standing habit' of simply expressing verbal support for broad policy was not only useless but also extremely harmful.[55]

But if the majority was indeed cynical and apathetic regarding politics, how was it that the rhetoric of the demonstrators demanded the expansion of student rights in the area of self-management and, in general, urged the more rapid development of socialism? And how was it that these apathetic students bothered to participate in these political demonstrations?

Concerning the first question it seems that while the mass of students was indeed apathetic and cynical with respect to politics, it was not surprising that those who spoke at the student rallies should emphasize broad socialist values. Nor was it surprising that the mass of students should applaud such speeches.

It seems only natural that the small group of 'idealists' within the student body should come to the fore in this time of crisis. It could be urged that these were students who had been socialized 'too well'. That is, they had absorbed the prescribed values and then went on to demand that others in society, including the League itself, should conform to these values. Their response to the realization that their society fell far short of its grand ideals was not to withdraw, but rather to think, discuss and even read about what had gone wrong and why. These were the students who talked of Mao or Marcuse, and these were the students to whom the trenchant criticisms of Yugoslav developments made by the *Praxis* group had considerable appeal. The overwhelming majority of the demonstrating students may have felt considerable frustration at various times, but this small minority was better able to articulate a coherent critique. That is, the disturbances gave this small minority its opportunity.

But why were they applauded rather than ignored or jeered? It could be suggested that this was because their analysis provided a legitimization of the protests. Most students were able to persuade themselves, and to seek to persuade the broader community, that they were not being selfish but rather that their own difficulties were merely a part of the general problem of socialist development in Yugoslavia. That is, they were able to couch their demands in terms of the public interest.

The rhetoric of the demonstrators is important but, in my view, it cannot be taken to represent the real beliefs and feelings of more than a small minority. Similarly, I disagree with the claim that the June demonstrations disproved earlier conclusions concerning student apathy; the rhetoric and activity of those few days stand out as an extraordinary exception to the general pattern of passivity and cynicism.

CONCLUDING REMARKS

The focus of this particular study has been to endeavour to explain the causes and significance of the student protests of June 1968. However, even to begin this task demanded a consideration of more than merely the particular environment of the university student. That is, the scope of this study has inevitably been broad and general rather than narrow and specific. Only in this way, for example, was it possible to explain the failure of the deliberate and comprehensive programme of ideological education and only in this way was it possible to explain the difficulties experienced in the implementation of the principles of self-management.

In chapter II consideration was given to a variety of explanations of the phenomenon of student unrest in the West. The distilled wisdom of these various explanations was that student protest stemmed from a crisis of authority in the particular society. However, as to what caused this crisis of authority poses a most difficult question—in its simplest form, some observers saw the problem as lying within the individual protesters while others saw these protesters as reacting to problems in their society. The discussion also showed the difficulty of seeking to apply any one explanation to all situations and, conversely, emphasized the need to seek the explanation for the crisis of authority in the context of each society.

In my view a considerable part of the responsibilty for the crisis of authority which existed within Yugoslavia must lie with the leadership of the League of Communists. As has been emphasized throughout this study, the leadership has persistently gone, or been forced to go, too far, too fast, too erratically and, more important, often in the wrong direction. The problems of the universities considered at some length in the previous chapters is merely one illustration of this tendency. And when particular problems could no longer be ignored the leaders sought to obscure them with rhetoric or to shift the responsibility onto particular groups or individuals.

Time and time again, eloquent calls for action and vigorous criticism of the failures of others managed to stave off a major confrontation. However, these declamations and criticisms only increased expectations still further, emphasized the particular difficulties and highlighted the persistent failure to secure meaningful change. The end result was that the gulf between the rhetoric and the reality widened so much that it could no longer be obscured by more rhetoric.

The students were not an idealistic group of young socialist experts, but rather they were closer to being a cynical mass of individuals, each primarily interested in satisfying his personal hopes and needs. In the

171

situation of deepening personal frustration and fears, a tiny spark—the barring of several hundred students from a concert—was enough to provoke a major eruption. This is not to suggest, however, that the mass of students was anti-communist; as in any society, passivity or even contempt for political activity are a far cry from determined opposition to the fundamentals of the system. And further, it would be a grave error to deny the pride of many Yugoslavs concerning the level of economic development achieved or concerning the manner in which Yugoslavia to date has managed to preserve its independence.

The ideals of self-management are admirable. However, it may be that, at least at the present stage of development in Yugoslavia, the standards required to enable it to function effectively are too demanding, and, therefore, reality falls so far short of these ideals that individuals inevitably become defeatist, despairing and apathetic. It must be remembered that Yugoslavia is not an affluent society, and the combination of high personal expectations and limited opportunities accentuates the concern for one's own situation. It must also be remembered that the level of education among the population as a whole is very low and that many of the members of the various self-managing collectives have extremely little knowledge or experience of commercial or industrial life, being scarcely one remove from an insular, traditional, peasant background.

Alternatively, it could be argued, as those associated with *Praxis* endeavoured to, that the gross inequalities, injustice and irrationality which characterized the system were largely responsible for the creation of attitudes which proved to be so uncongenial to the development of a self-managing, socialist society. In this regard it is worth reiterating the comments of Svetozar Stojanović: in his view the existing model of self-management in the area of economic and social policy placed too much reliance on the market as the regulator and determinant of investment, pricing, income distribution and the like—the resultant system was best described as 'anarcho-liberal' rather than socialist because it assumed that the antagonistic interests of self-managing groups would, through the device of the market, *'spontaneously* mingle harmoniously to form the social interest'; in fact, all this brought to mind the concept of the 'invisible hand' associated with the work of early theoreticians of liberal capitalism such as Adam Smith. In Stojanović's opinion, the market was an important tool, at least at this stage of development, but he insisted that 'in order to preserve a given society's socialist character', the market 'must be placed within the framework of serious planning, regulation and coordination'.[56] In other words, he appeared to believe that many of the problems of the type discussed in the present work stemmed from the fact that the League leadership pinned too much faith in the free operation of market forces and failed to press for the imposition by the community of standards and rules to correct some of the worst abuses and some of the more serious irrationalities.

Despite the facile assumptions of the model, experience had shown that the independent interactions of the various self-managing collectives did not inevitably result in policies which, according to any reasonable measure harmonized the interests of the individual of the particular collective and of the total socialist community. In theory, the guidance and inspiration of the individual communists and the moral authority of the League of Communists as a whole would ensure that the individual collectives exercised their powers responsibly. As the foregoing has demonstrated, neither individual communists nor the League as a whole have shown the desire, capacity or authority to persuade particular collectives to look beyond their own short-term interests.

To return to the example of university education, no serious effort was made to end the waste, irrationality and injustice inherent in the existing system—all was left to the actions of independent self-managing collectives within the university system. Inevitably, the problems continued. And no effort was made to induce the self-managing collectives within the economy and society to accept their responsibilities to provide greater support, for example, to education. In the case of scholarship policy the most that was done was to set guidelines for the contracts between donors and recipients. As was noted in chapter V, it was assumed that this would inevitably lead to the harmonization of the interests of the student, the collective and society: the student would receive a scholarship, the collective would receive the expert it needed, the community would benefit from the fact that a rational cadre plan built up from the real needs of society would emerge and so on. As that chapter demonstrated, collectives showed little willingness to offer scholarships because in economic terms there was simply no need for them to do so. This strengthened the tendency for education to remain the preserve, for the most part, of the more privileged.

It had similarly been assumed that financing of higher education could be removed from the state budget and provided by a special Education Fund of which only a relatively minor proportion was to be drawn from the state; the bulk was to be provided by industrial and communal bodies in accord with their own views of their needs and capabilities. In practice, this change, introduced in 1961, remained little more than a change in form—the various collectives were not persuaded that they could or should support such a fund and thus their contributions to the fund remained miniscule. In 1965, for example, the contribution of all collectives to the Education Fund amounted to only 6.5 per cent of the total.[57]

Despite such examples of the low and indeed decreasing commitment to interests outside of one's immediate collective, the persistent trend in the development of constitutional forms has been away from the setting of limits, guidelines, responsibilities and the like by representative state organs, towards a system in which policies and responsibilities are increasingly set by the independent decisions of separate collectives.

How can this trend be explained? Why have the representative bodies of the state not made specific rules and directives, as in our own society, to limit some of the worst abuses of unchecked activity by groups to ensure that all groups accept some responsibility to contribute to the long-term well-being of the whole community?

The trend is to a considerable extent linked with the problems arising from the marked imbalance in economic development between the various regions. As Deborah Milenkovitch has explained it,

> Centrally planned investment may have become impossible in Yugoslavia because of the absence of political agreement about such planning. It appears that the interests of the six republics differed so sharply that no consensus about the objectives of planning or development strategy was possible . . . . The developed regions saw investment planning as a burden which transferred resources from their areas, cut seriously into economic incentives and created errors of allocation. At the same time the less developed regions were convinced that without investment planning they were doomed to remain under-developed.[58]

Spokesmen for the more developed regions urged that much of Yugoslavia's economic difficulties were caused by investments which had been made on political rather than economic grounds and which then required large and continual subsidy. Economic development, they insisted, was being hampered by political interference and further, this political interference violated what they described as the rights of particular collectives under the system of self-management. In other words, in the debate between what have been described as the economic liberals and conservatives, the former were able to buttress their argument by reference to the actual economic problems as well as to the rhetoric of self-management and the 'withering' of the state; their own economic self-interest in the context of the model of self-management led them to argue for a greatly diminished role for government.[59]

Therefore, the many economic 'reforms' and the four different constitutions since the war, all of which have tended in the direction of allowing the separate collectives independently to determine their duties towards the wider community, do not demonstrate the diffusion of a sense of commitment and responsibility throughout society and do not reflect a growing maturation which would justify another significant step to be taken towards self-management. Even amongst the avowedly most advanced section of society, namely the membership of the League, there is considerable evidence that such a commitment is lacking. Rather, each change, although presented as yet another victory in the struggle for socialism, in fact represented a desperate effort to stave off or cover up a crisis.

But why have these changes been accepted, why does the system still hold together, why does it still work, even if far from satisfactorily? Why, for example, was Tito able to end the crisis of the June events with grand rhetoric which promised much but which many, on the basis of their past experience, must have suspected as being empty words?

A major reason why his eloquent and clever, but only temporary, partial and vague, solutions are accepted is that there simply does not appear to be any alternative. Better the inadequate solution which at least staves off the crisis than one aimed directly at the problem but which might lead to open conflict and even civil war with the consequent risk of Soviet intervention—the memories of Hungary in 1956 and Czechoslovakia in 1968 are extremely vivid. An additional reason for Tito's success in papering over some cracks on this and similar occasions is the respect and affection with which many Yugoslavs still regard him. The importance of Tito's role in maintaining the stability of the system can be inferred from the increasing and grave concern in Yugoslavia regarding the viability of a post-Tito regime. His authority is still considerable but it must be stressed that it is not so great as to enable him to force real change; his authority is analogous to that of the weak father who by yelling at his quarrelling children may temporarily, but only temporarily, quell the clamour and stifle the more overt signs of their disagreement.

This account of some of the difficulties experienced in the self-managing system, relating principally to the university and the university students and focussing on the causes of the demonstrations of June 1968, is inevitably only a part of the larger story. To assess adequately both the record and prospects of the system would require a more detailed examination of such questions as the difficult economic situation, the nature and strength of the armed forces and internal security organizations, the influence of external factors on domestic developments, the problems caused by the marked regional disparities in economic development as well as the grave ethnic tensions. (Something of the strength of the latter was seen in the massive protests in Croatia in 1970 and 1971 which led to a purge of many of the leaders of the League within Croatia.)[60] Nonetheless, on the basis of the evidence concerning the causes and significance of this one major event, the student protests of June 1968, I am prepared to argue that neither the past record nor the future prospects of the system can be described as good.

It must be emphasized that the examples of particular shortcomings and abuses presented in this work were derived in most cases from official or officially endorsed sources, and furthermore, that the conclusions regarding the existence of grave problems in various areas derive almost entirely from such sources. Where the present work differs from the official or officially endorsed sources is in its explanation of the causes and significance of these major problems. The official Yugoslav line has persistently urged that the system and the theory on which it is based are essentially sound and widely supported, that the various problems stem from the failure of individuals or groups, and that these individuals and groups can be guided to recognize their own 'real' interests. That is, while the Yugoslav leaders have acknowledged that there is often resistance to the implementation of League policies and to the principles of self-management, they have insisted that this resistance was only of secondary importance. It might be urged, however, that these persistent failures and this growing gulf between rhetoric and reality cannot be dismissed so readily and, indeed, that they bring into question the efficacy of the total system. Rather than seeking to cajole and persuade reality to fit the theory it might

175

make more sense to recognize that the commitment and sense of responsibility on which the system is theoretically based scarcely exists—unless, as suggested earlier, it is believed that there is no point in attempting to devise substantially clearer and less equivocal policies to overcome this lack of responsibility because such an attempt is bound to fail.

Within Yugoslavia, however, there is little debate concerning the viability of the present model. While in most areas the Yugoslav leadership espouses what might be described as a *laissez-faire* position, it has adopted a strict, indeed harsh, line in the area of political freedom. Those who venture to point up the difficulties which in their view *stem* from the present system of self-management, those whose arguments imply a questioning of whether the present system is indeed socialist or is tending towards socialism are, as has been noted earlier in this chapter, vigorously criticized and harassed. Indeed, those who point out the problems are not infrequently castigated as their cause. It is, in my view, a significant indication of the degree of confidence of the Yugoslav leadership in the viability of the system that they have in the last few years adopted an increasingly hard line towards internal debate.

Returning to the question of the student protests of June 1968 it is obvious that, contrary to the view expressed by the Yugoslav leadership, they do not represent a major turning point as far as the university or the university students or indeed the entire society is concerned. The universities remain severely overcrowded, under-financed, un-'reformed' and with appalling examination results.[61] The students still endure grossly inadequate living conditions,[62] the programme of material support remains inadequate and biased,[63] their prospects for employment remain dismal[64] and, far from becoming the allies of the League in the struggle for the reform of society as a whole, they seem passive and cynical as far as politics is concerned.[65] As for the League of Communists, society's self-proclaimed vanguard, it remains an organization plagued by deep division, selfishness, careerism, apathy and doubt; that is, there is no reason to suspect that the League is any more able than it was in the period under review to play the vital role envisaged for it.[66] That these events do not represent a dramatic turning point is most readily demonstrated by an examination of the 'ideological and political offensive' mounted by the Yugoslav leadership in 1972 to overcome what it described as a fundamental crisis in Yugoslav society.[67] This 'offensive' is discussed in the postscript to the present work.

The Yugoslav leaders sought to present the June events as the desire of an overwhelmingly 'socialist' student body to join them in the struggle to secure the more rapid development of socialism, and as a vote of confidence in the system and the League. But these students were not, nor could they be, a generation cast in the mould of the 'glorious generation' of the War of National Liberation. The official rhetoric may have urged the need for selfless commitment, but this call was drowned out by the message trumpeted throughout society. To repeat the point made earlier: as far as the young were concerned, the basic fact was that they were growing up in a society in which the total 'cake' was relatively small, but also in a society of rapidly rising expectations and one in which many of the adult models gave an example of conspicuous consumption.

Other parts of the official rhetoric did, however, appear to impinge on the students. There was the part which spoke of equality of opportunity for all in the sphere of education and which implied an adequate and fair system of financial support. There was also the part which spoke of the need for university reform and which strongly suggested that the difficulties experienced by students within the university were largely the fault of the staff. There was also that part which spoke of the right of all to participate as equals in the decision-making process within their own organizations and within the organs of self-management. There was also that part which insisted on the vital importance of the new graduates to the cause of socialist construction. Finally, it was all these put together—a rhetoric which presented the system of self-management as one in which the interests of individuals, collectives and of the total socialist community could be harmonized under the guidance and inspiration of dedicated individual communists and the farsighted League of Communists as a whole. All this rhetoric served only to arouse unrealizable expectations, to highlight the widespread weaknesses and abuses, and finally to demonstrate the system's inefficacy. Rather than confidence in authority or in the system, there appeared to be a crisis of authority—the students seemed to have been exploded out of their political apathy by their anger at the frustration of their needs and of the hopes which had been aroused.

The Yugoslav leadership, most notably Tito himself, succeeded in quelling these particular disturbances but, particularly with the benefit of hindsight, it is clear that this was a 'victory' that would ultimately strengthen negative feelings and become merely another entry on that long list of 'decisive' victories in the struggle for socialism.[68] The helplessness and cynicism which appear to stem from such 'victories' can have only serious consequences as far as the functioning of any system is concerned but is especially detrimental to one which assumes the existence of widespread commitment and confidence. One is forced to ask how many more such victories can the system afford.

POSTSCRIPT

The Yugoslav leadership had insisted that the system was essentially sound, that only particular difficulties needed to be overcome and that the support of what the June events had shown was an enthusiastic and socialist youth would ensure the successful resolution of these difficulties. That is, this student protest was presented as a decisive event in the struggle for socialism. One of the conclusions of the present work is that such a claim could not then be justified; this postscript seeks to show that not even the Yugoslav leadership could readily repeat that claim.

In the early 1970s, that is, not long after these events, there was what the Yugoslav leadership described as a grave crisis in the League and the country as a whole. It is not the present purpose to describe this new crisis in any detail but simply to note something of its seriousness and implications. In bald terms, the policies which had been pursued by the League leadership in the Croatian republic and which avowedly aimed at ensuring appropriate recognition for the rights of the Croatian people ultimately led to a situation which even Tito described as tending inexorably toward civil war.[1]

The nature of this crisis and the prospect for an effective solution are indicated in the principal documents of the League's so-called 'ideological and political offensive' of 1972, such as Tito's speech to 'leading functionaries' in Serbia and the letter to all League members from the Executive Bureau of the LCY. Most of what the letter described and prescribed constitutes a familiar litany.[2] For example, it emphasized that the conclusions adopted within the League were often 'generalized and insufficiently clear, that after their adoption different interpretations are made and that behaviour in practice is contrary to them'. Among the many weaknesses within 'the organizations and leading organs of the League' were:

>   the presence and influence of interests and ideas opposed to the interests of the working class and socialist self-management;
>
>   the influence of a bureaucratic mentality, a rise in uncontrolled private-ownership tendencies and petty-bourgeois psychology, which is reflected in the substitution of political demagogy for principled policy and in political intrigues often inspired by hostile elements at home and abroad;
>
>   established and widespread opportunism; tolerance of views and political behaviour which are contrary to the ideology and policy of the League of Communists;
>
>   unequal criteria and varying degrees of activity to implement the political stands of the LCY in various social settings;
>
>   occurrences of disunity in political ideology and actions and even attempts to renew and strengthen, in old or new forms, sectarian-

178

ism, factional activity and a struggle of cliques for positions of power.

The letter urged that within the League there should be regular and critical assessment of how conclusions were being applied; it sought the 'more resolute elimination' from the League of 'corrupt individuals, petty-bourgeois elements, advocates of bureaucratic self-will, opportunists [and] careerists'; it insisted on determined opposition to the tendencies for democracy within the League 'to be reduced to inconclusive discussions' but at the same time warned against 'bureaucratic centralism'; it condemned 'any tendency' which might lead to the conversion of the League 'into a loose coalition of republican and provincial organizations and to the division of the working class' on ethnic and republican criteria; it urged greater attention to ideological work; it spoke of the 'urgent' need for action to eliminate abuses in the economic sphere and of the need to stem those currents conducive to a division of society into poor and rich; and it concluded that the essential question at this 'decisive moment' was nothing less than whether the working class would secure the major role or whether those forces opposed 'to the interests of the working class, socialism and self management will gain strength'.

Less than one month later President Tito attended a meeting of 'leading functionaries of socio-political organizations' of Serbia. At the end of this four-day gathering he made a speech in which he expressed fear that there might be a repetition of 'the old practice of simply reading [the letter] and then filing it'.[3] In this vein he noted that from the 'very start' the discussion at this particular gathering had taken 'a different direction from what I wished and which I thought it should take'; 'not a small number of comrades to whom I listened, I am thinking primarily of leaders, lack virtues such as self-criticism'. Tito then went on to urge the vital significance of criticism and self-criticism in overcoming the present unsatisfactory situation.

Significantly, he then noted that the question had been raised as to why 'individual cases, particular mistakes and weaknesses' had not been raised. He answered this by referring to his own speech at the opening session of this gathering in which he had expressed the view that the deliberations should not 'get bogged down in . . . minor matters, since this would take up too much time, and probably the discussion . . . would assume an undesired character'. Tito claimed to possess considerable material, culled from speeches and statements of those present, which indicated that many of them held views contrary to his own but that he had decided not to mention these matters in his opening address since he had felt certain that there would 'be comrades who would themselves raise these matters, that is to say, would take a self critical approach. . . . But this did not happen, to my very great regret.'

What these texts make abundantly clear is that there was official concern regarding the disunity in the League, concern regarding the character and ambitions of members of the League (that is, of those who were expected to guide and inspire the broad mass of citizens),

179

and concern for the growing cynicism in the community as a whole.

However, while the top leadership raised and condemned these matters, it showed itself unwilling and unable to initiate substantial action against specific problems or persons. It railed only in general terms against individual selfishness and irresponsibility and called on those who had failed to observe the professed standards to confess their sins and mend their ways. The next level of leaders simply made similar general statements and so it went down through the League. It was one thing to arouse support for the general proposition that the situation was serious and that the existing policies, at least as presently implemented, were grossly unsatisfactory; however, it was quite another matter to attempt to specify what was required because this would immediately destroy the fragile consensus and lead to vigorous factional struggles. The ideological offensive was therefore unlikely to have any substantial effect except on a relatively small number. Some of those affected were individuals not in positions of authority who raised fundamental questions concerning the nature and efficacy of the Yugo-slav system (e.g. the small group of philosophers, several of whom were regular contributors to *Praxis*, who lost their teaching positions at Belgrade University in 1975 in circumstances which can, at best, only be described as being of doubtful legality).[4] These individuals were punished because they were convenient scapegoats, but, more importantly, be-cause they questioned the Yugoslav leadership's persistent claim that the problems faced were only of a secondary nature and did not reflect on the efficacy of the system as a whole.

Another category of affected individuals is exemplified by those officials of the League in Croatia who lost their positions following the crisis of 1971-72. The behaviour of these officials seemed to be going beyond the bounds of the existing broad, vague and unsatisfactory consensus to the point where it threatened to destroy it. That is, what might have been described as an agreement to differ was, in Croatia at least, coming perilously close to an insistence on a new and unequivocal policy.

Ultimately this particular crisis was resolved principally because a majority of the League leadership in Croatia proved unwilling to ride the wave of nationalist feeling to the end, an end which as noted earlier may have been civil war. In other words, the members of this majority grudgingly endorsed the existing arrangements and forced the resignation of those identified with the profoundly different policies. Once again the intervention of Tito was crucial and again the resolution of the crisis was presented as a 'victory' for socialism. However the nature and extent of this victory are convincingly demonstrated by the prescriptions urged to seal it, and by the response these prescriptions seem to have been accorded. Officials in other areas have also been forced from their posts and there has been a general effort towards the tightening of control,[5] but the fundamental weaknesses, which the events of 1968 and of 1970-71 most graphically revealed, do not appear to have been seriously confronted, let alone overcome.

NOTES

I. INTRODUCTION

1. *After the Revolution? Authority in a Good Society* (New Haven: Yale University Press, 1970), p. 130.
2. (London: Cambridge University Press, 1970), p. 88.
3. Statements attributed to Tito in this paragraph and the succeeding two are all to be found in (Josip Broz) Tito, 'Our Youth Has Proved Mature', address delivered on 9 June 1968, translated in *Socialist Thought and Practice,* no. 30 (April/June 1968), pp. 4-8.
4. M. George Zaninovich, *The Development of Socialist Yugoslavia* (Baltimore: Johns Hopkins Press, 1968), pp. 146-9.
5. Tito, 'Our Youth Has Proved Mature', pp. 6-9.
6. Jelko Žagar, 'Reform of the University Education', *Yugoslav Student News,* no. 20 (1956), p. 2.
7. See discussion of education reform in chapter IV.
8. See chapter VI.
9. Miodrag Milenović, 'Dinamika razvoja visokog školstva i zapošljavanja diplomiranih studenata' (The dynamics of the development of higher education and the employment of graduates), *Ideje,* vol. i, no. 2 (1970), p. 240 (hereinafter cited as 'Dinamika razvoja').
10. Vladimir Dedijer, *The Battle Stalin Lost: Memoirs of Yugoslavia 1948-1953* (New York: The Viking Press, 1971), p. 98.
11. A useful review of this rupture is provided by George W. Hoffman and Fred Warner Neal, *Yugoslavia and the New Communism* (New York: Twentieth Century Fund, 1962), especially pp. 112-13, 136; and Woodford McClellan, 'Postwar Political Evolution', in *Contemporary Yugoslavia: Twenty Years of Socialist Experiment,* ed. Wayne S. Vucinich (Berkeley and Los Angeles: University of California Press, 1969), pp. 119-53.
12. Dedijer, *The Battle Stalin Lost,* repeated on pp. 41, 43, 147, 168.
13. *Tito Speaks* (London: Weidenfeld and Nicolson, 1954), especially pp. xiv, xv, 341, 375. See also Hoffman and Neal, *Yugoslavia and the New Communism,* pp. 140, 142.
14. *Yugoslavia's Way: The Program of the League of Communists of Yugoslavia,* translated from the Serbo-Croatian by Stoyan Pribichevich (New York: All Nations Press, 1958), pp. 43-4 (hereinafter cited as *Yugoslavia's Way*).
15. Ibid.; and Vladimir Gligorov, 'Polivalentnost kulture i revolucije' (The polyvalence of culture and revolution), *Univerzitet Danas,* vol. x, no. 2/3 (1969), p. 73; and Veljko Cvjetičanin, 'Sveučilište i samoupravno društvo' (The university and the self-managing society), in *Sveučilište i Revolucija,* ed. Ema Derosi-Bjelajac and others (Zagreb: Sveučilišni komitet SKH-Zagreb, 1970), p. 234.
16. Svetozar Stojanović, *Between Ideals and Reality: A Critique of Socialism and its Future,* translated by Gerson S. Sher (New York : Oxford University Press, 1973), p. 126.

17. *Yugoslavia's Way,* pp. 130, 151.
18. *JTS,* 4924, p. 50: *Vjesnik* 15 January 1968.
19. *Between Ideals and Reality,* pp. 125-6. (Emphasis in the original.)
20. Ibid. See discussion on pp. 126-8.
21. Ibid., p. 132.
22. For an excellent account of this, see Paul Shoup, *Communism and the Yugoslav National Question* (New York: Columbia University Press, 1968).
23. For a view concerning some of the differences, see Ivan Kuvačić, 'Additional Thoughts on Synchrony and Diachrony', *Praxis* (Int. ed.), no. 3/4 (1971), pp. 434-6.

II. Student Unrest

1. See for example, *Youth Life,* vol. xiv, no. 46 (September 1965), p. 2 (editorial); and *Šesti Kongres Narodne Omladine Jugoslavije* (Sixth Congress of the People's Youth of Yugoslavia) (Belgrade: Kultura, 1958), especially p. 232 (hereinafter cited as *Šesti Kongres NOJ*).
2. See in particular, *Borba, Komunist* and *Politika* regarding events in France in May 1968.
3. See *Student* 14 May 1968, p. 8 re support for students in Berlin, Bonn and Paris.
4. *Komunist* 13 June 1968, p. 6; and *Borba* 8 June 1968, p. 1.
5. See for example, the Conclusions of the Meeting of the Presidium and Executive Committee of the CC LC Serbia, *Komunist* 6 June 1968, pp. 3, 14; Tito, 'Our Youth Has Proved Mature', pp. 3-9; and the Guidelines announced by the Presidium and Executive Committee of the CC LCY, *Borba* (Z) 14 June 1968, pp. 5-6.
6. *Borba* 5 June 1968, p. 7.
7. (Nataša Dizdarević), *JTS* 5048, pp. 49-51: *Odjek* 15 June 1968. See also Slavko Miloslavlevski, 'Anketa' (Inquiry), *Ideje,* vol. i, no. 2 (1970), p. 25; and (Mika Tripalo, Secretary of the Executive Committee CC LC Croatia), *Studentski List* 26 November 1968, p. 4.
8. Vladimir Goati, 'Razlike i sličnosti studentskih gibanja u Jugoslaviji sa gibanjima u zapadnoevropskim zemljama' (Differences and similarities between the Yugoslav student movement and movements in Western European countries), in *Društvo, Revolucija, Omladina* (Society, Revolution and Youth), ed. Veljko Cvjetičanin and others (Zagreb: Centar za Kulturnu Djelatnost Omladine Zagreba, 1969), pp. 115-16.
9. *JTS* 5062, p. 5: *Svet* 15 June 1968; also (Mika Tripalo), *Mladost,* no. 634 (5-12 December 1968), p. 1.
10. *Borba* 12 June 1968, p. 4.
11. Ibid., 4 June 1968, p. 5.
12. Ibid., 12 June 1968, p. 4; and *Student* 4 June 1968, p. 2.
13. *Borba* (Z) 4 June 1968, pp. 1, 7; and *Politika* 4 June 1968, p. 1.
14. *Borba* 4 June 1968, p. 5.
15. Ibid., p. 4.
16. *Student* 4 June 1968, p. 2, and 11 June 1968, p. 3.
17. *Borba* 4 June 1968, p. 1.
18. (Toma Bunuševac), *Student* 4 June 1968, p. 3.
19. (Radojica Klajić), ibid.
20. *Borba* 4 June 1968, p. 4.
21. Ibid., pp. 1, 4.

22. Ibid., pp. 4, 5; and *JTS* 5040, p. 42: *Rad* 7 June 1968.
23. *Student* 4 June 1968, pp. 1, 4.
24. *Borba* 4 June 1968, p. 5.
25. See Conclusion of the Meeting of the Presidium and Executive Committee of the CC LC Serbia, *Komunist* 6 June 1968, p. 3.
26. *Politika* 19 June 1968, p. 4; and *Borba* (Z) 7 June 1968, p. 6; also *Komunist* 13 June 1968, p. 9; (Mika Tripalo), *Mladost*, no. 634, 5-12 December 1968, p. 1; *Borba* 6 June 1968, p. 6, and 7 June 1968, p. 6.
27. *Borba* 6 June 1968, p. 6, and 8 June 1968, p. 5; *Komunist* 13 June 1968, p. 9; and *Student* 8 June 1968, p. 3.
28. *Borba* 4 June 1968, p. 5; and *Vjesnik* 4 June 1968, p. 4.
29. Ibid.; and *Politika* 6 June 1968, p. 8.
30. *Borba* (Z) 8 June 1968, p. 4; and *Komunist* 13 June 1968, p. 9.
31. *Komunist* 13 June 1968, p. 9.
32. *Politika* 6 June 1968, p. 8.
33. *JTS* 5040, p. 42: *Rad* 7 June 1968; and Svetozar Stojanović, 'Junski studentski pokret i socijalna revolucija u Jugoslaviji' (The June student movement and social revolution in Yugoslavia) (hereinafter cited as 'Junski studentski pokret'), in Cvjetičanin and others, *Društvo, Revolucija, Omladina*, p. 125.
34. *Student* 4 June 1968, p. 3.
35. George Klein, 'Yugoslavia—the Process of Democratization', in *The Changing Face of Communism in Eastern Europe*, ed. Peter A. Toma (Tucson, Arizona: University of Arizona Press, 1970), p. 226.
36. This contrast is conveniently and clearly illustrated in the Editorial, *Borba* 10 June 1968, p. 1, and in Tito's speech reported on the front page of the same issue.
37. *Borba* 8 June 1968, p. 1; and (Š. Zatezalo), *Borba* 26 June 1968, p. 4.
38. (Zatezalo), *Borba* 6 June 1968, p. 4.
39. *Borba* 10 June 1968, p. 1.
40. See chapter VI.
41. *Komunist* 6 June 1968, pp. 3, 14.
42. *Borba* 4 June 1968, p. 6.
43. Ibid., p. 4.
44. Ibid., p. 5.
45. *Komunist* 6 June 1968, pp. 3, 14.
46. *Borba* 4 June 1968, p. 6.
47. (Mirko Popović), *Politika* 18 June 1968, p. 5. Details of the provisions were given in *Borba* 4 June 1968, p. 6.
48. *Komunist* 6 June 1968, p. 1.
49. See for example the communique of the Serbian Executive Council, *Borba* 5 June 1968, pp. 1, 6; *Komunist* 6 June 1968, p. 1, and 13 June 1968, pp. 2, 5.
50. *Borba* 8 June 1968, p. 4; and (Mika Tripalo) *Studentski List* 26 November 1968, p. 1.
51. *Borba* 4 June 1968, p. 5.
52. *Borba* (Z) 4 June 1968, p. 6.
53. Alex M. Dragnich, 'Students Shake Tito Regime' (unpublished paper, Department of Political Science, Vanderbilt University, 1969), pp. 8, 11.
54. *Borba* 5 June 1968, p. 5, and 10 June 1968, p. 4; also *Komunist* 6 June 1968, p. 1.
55. *Borba* 5 June 1968, p. 5. See also television address by Veljko Vlahović, published in *Borba* 4 June 1968, p. 6.

56. *Borba* 8 June 1968, p. 5.
57. *Komunist* 6 June 1968, p. 3. See also Editorial, *Borba* (Z) 5 June 1968, p. 1; and (Djurica Jojkić, President of the Serbian Executive Council), *Borba* (Z) 4 June 1968, p. 6.
58. *Komunist* 6 June 1968, p. 14.
59. *Borba* 4 June 1968, p. 6.
60. Ibid., 5 June 1968, p. 1.
61. (Janez Kocijančić), *Borba* 18 June 1968, p. 4.
62. *Politika* 8 June 1968, p. 7. See also *JTS* 5040, pp. 41, 43: *Rad* 7 June 1968.
63. S. Stojanović, 'Junski studentski pokret', p. 125. Note also student comments in *Komunist* 13 June 1968, p. 7.
64. *Borba* 5 June 1968, p. 5.
65. (Miloš Minić), *Borba* 5 June 1968, p. 7; and *Komunist* 6 June 1968, p. 1. For other reports of worker opposition to student methods see *Borba* (Z) 4 June 1968, p. 7; and *Borba* 6 June 1968, p. 5.
66. *Borba* 4 June 1968, p. 7. See also *Vjesnik* 4 June 1968, p. 4, and 9 June 1968, p. 4.
67. *JTS* 5040, p. 42: *Rad* 7 June 1968. See also *Student* 8 June 1968, p. 2.
68. S. Stojanović, 'Junski studentski pokret', p. 125.
69. *Politika* 9 June 1968, p. 8; and *Borba* 9 June 1968, p. 4.
    The response of the *Rad* editorial board was published in *Borba* (Z) 14 June 1968, p. 11.
70. *Borba* 8 June 1968, p. 1.
71. Goati, 'Razlike i sličnosti studentskih gibanja u Jugoslaviji sa gibanjima u zapadnoevropskim zemljama', p. 114.
72. (Dr Žarko Bulajić), *Borba* 22 June 1968, p. 5. See also *Borba* 4 June 1968, p. 5; and *New York Times* 5 June 1968, p. 4.
73. The Programme was published in *Politika* 8 June 1968, p. 7.
74. 8 June 1968, p. 4. See also *Komunist* 6 June 1968, p. 1.
75. *Borba* 8 June 1968, p. 4.
76. *Politika* 9 June 1968, p. 8.
77. Ibid. Also S. Stojanović, 'Junski studentski pokret', p. 126; and *JTS* 5146, p. 21: *Politika Expres* 20 October 1968.
78. *Borba* 8 June 1968, p. 4, and 9 June 1968, p. 1.
79. e.g. *Borba* 9 June 1968, p. 1.
80. Ibid., 10 June 1968, p. 5.
81. Ibid.
82. Ibid., 14 June 1968, p. 1.
83. Tito, 'Our Youth Has Proved Mature', p. 6.
84. *Komunist* 20 June 1968, p. 1.
85. *Borba* 14 June 1968, p. 1.
86. *JTS* 5054, p. 42: *Borba* 27 June 1968.
87. (Bora Pavlović), *Politika* 19 June 1968, p. 5.
88. Noted by Kenneth Keniston, *Young Radicals: Notes on Committed Youth* (New York: Harcourt Brace Jovanovich, 1968), p. 339.
89. Bruno Bettelheim, 'Obsolete Youth', *Encounter,* vol. xxxiii, no. 3 (September 1969), pp. 32-3.
90. Daniel Bell, 'Columbia and the New Left', in *Confrontation,* ed. Daniel Bell and Irving Kristol (New York: Basic Books, 1969), p. 92; and Nathan Glazer, ' "Student Power" in Berkeley', in *Confrontation,* p. 21. See also Zbigniew Brzezinski, *Between Two Ages: America's Role in the Technotronic Era* (New York: The Viking Press, 1970), p. 108.

91. For comment on this point, see 'Report on the Fact-finding Commission Appointed to Investigate the Disturbances at Columbia University in April and May 1968', *Crisis at Columbia* (New York: Vintage Books, 1968), p. 6.
92. Max Beloff, 'Universities and Violence', *Survey*, no. 69 (October 1968), p. 39.
93. Lewis Feuer, *The Conflict of Generations* (New York: Basic Books, 1969), p. 45.
94. Lewis Feuer, 'Patterns of Irrationality', *Survey*, no. 69 (October 1968), pp. 47-8.
95. Ibid., p. 51.
96. Christian Bay, 'Political and Apolitical Students: Facts in Search of a Theory', *Journal of Social Issues*, no. 23 (July 1967), pp. 76-91.
97. Keniston, *Young Radicals*, p. 339.
98. Ibid., p. 238.
99. Richard M. Abrams, 'The Student Rebellion at Berkeley—An Interpretation', in *The Berkeley Student Revolt: Facts and Interpretations*, ed. Seymour Martin Lipset and Sheldon S. Wolin (New York: Anchor Books, 1965), pp. 387-8; and Sheldon S. Wolin and John H. Schaar, 'The Abuses of the Multiversity', in ibid., p. 362.
100. Theodore Roszak, *The Making of a Counter Culture: Reflections on the Technocratic Society and its Youthful Opposition* (London: Faber and Faber, 1970), pp. xii-xiii.
101. *The Conflict of Generations*, and 'Patterns of Irrationality'.
102. 'Patterns of Irrationality', p. 48.
103. *The Conflict of Generations*, pp. 83-4.
104. On this point see Seymour Martin Lipset, 'University Student Politics', in Lipset and Wolin, *Berkeley*, pp. 3-4.
105. *Young Radicals*, pp. 308-9.
106. Ibid., p. 309.
107. *The Conflict of Generations*, p. 199.
108. *From Generation to Generation* (Glencoe, Illinois: Free Press, 1956).
109. 'Social and Cultural Meanings of Student Revolt', in *Student Activism and Protest*, ed. Edward E. Sampson, Harold A. Korn and Associates (San Francisco: Jossey-Bass, 1970), p. 121.
110. Ibid., p. 132.
111. 'Academic Freedom and Academic Anarchy', *Survey*, no. 69 (October 1968), p. 62. See also Trevor Fisk, 'The Nature and Causes of Student Unrest', in *Protest and Discontent*, ed. Bernard Crick and William A. Robson (Middlesex: Penguin, 1970), p. 80.
112. 'Columbia and the New Left', p. 68.
113. *Young Radicals*, pp. 299-300.
114. Seymour L. Halleck, 'Why Students Protest: A Psychiatrist's View', in *Student Protest*, ed. Gerald F. McGuigan with George Payerle and Patricia Horrobin (Toronto: Methuen, 1968), p. 170.

III. Self-Management in the Yugoslav University

1. Mika Tripalo, Secretary of the People's Youth of Yugoslavia, 'Social Management of Schools', *Youth Life*, no. 11 (Autumn 1954), pp. 12-13.
2. *Komunist* 16 April 1964, p. 4.
3. *JTS* 1220, pp. 31-2: *Nin* 18 April 1954; Vladimir Serdar, 'Simpozij

"Društveni i ekonomski aspekti obrazovanja" ' (A symposium on 'Social and economic aspects of education'), *Univerzitet Danas,* vol. x, no. 7/8 (1969), p. 3; Mihailo Mitić, 'O izmenama u sistemu samoupravljanja na fakultetima' (Concerning changes in the system of self-management in university departments), *Univerzitet Danas,* vol. ix, no. 2 (1968), p. 53; Aleksandar Bazala and Ante Vukasović, 'Sistem samoupravljanja na sveučilištu' (The system of self-management at the university), *Univerzitet Danas,* vol. ix, no. 7 (1968), p. 7; and *JTS* 4771, p. 3: *Borba* 3 August 1966.

4. Tripalo, 'Social Management of Schools', pp. 12-13; and Bora Pavlović, 'Social Management in the Field of Culture and Education', *Youth Life,* vol. v (Spring 1956), p. 19.

5. Bogdan Pilić, 'Uslovi ostvarivanja socialističkog odnosa izmedju nastavnika i studenata' (Conditions for creating socialist relations between staff and students), in Derosi-Bjelajac and others, *Sveučilište i Revolucija,* p. 287 (hereinafter cited as 'Uslovi socialističkog odnosa'). Also *JTS* 4658, p. 34: *Borba* 11 March 1967.

6. Dušan Stanković, 'Neki zanemareni suštinski aspekti reforme univerziteta' (Some neglected essential aspects of university reform), *Univerzitet Danas,* vol. xi, no. 7/8 (1970), p. 35 (hereinafter cited as 'Reforma univerziteta').

7. Danilo Ž. Marković, 'Principi organizacije samoupravnog društva i oblici samoupravljanja na univerzitetu' (Organizational principles of a self-managing society and forms of self-management at the university), in Derosi-Bjelajac and others, *Sveučilište i Revolucija,* p. 291; also Pilić, 'Uslovi socialističkog odnosa', p. 287.

8. Vojislav Stojanović, 'Reforma univerziteta u teoriji i praksi' (The reform of the university in theory and practice), *Univerzitet Danas,* vol. xi, no. 1 (1970), pp. 19-20 (hereinafter cited as 'Reforma univerziteta').

9. Aleksandar Bazala, 'Samoupravljanje kao osnova reforme sveučilišta' (Self-management as the basis for university reform), *Univerzitet Danas,* vol. x, no. 7/8 (1969), p. 30; Petar Ignjatović, 'Razgovor tek počinje' (The discussion is only beginning), *Ideje,* vol. i, no. 2 (1970), p. 94; and *Politika* 16 June 1968, p. 10.

10. Budimir Košutić, 'Neke dileme o samoupravljanju na univerzitetu' (Some dilemmas concerning self-management at the university), *Arhiv,* vol. xli, no. 1 (January/March 1971), p. 143 (hereinafter cited as 'Neke dileme'); and Krsto S. Kilibarda, 'Za socialističke odnose na univerzitetu' (For socialist relations at the university), *Naše Teme,* vol. viii, no. 4 (1964), p. 509 (hereinafter cited as 'Za socijalističke odnose'). See also *Borba* (Z) 18 June 1967, p. 10; *Student* 14 May 1968, p. 4; Stevan K. Vračar, 'Neizbežne promene na univerzitetu' (Unavoidable changes at the university), *Gledišta,* vol. viii, no. 3 (March 1967), p. 323; Dag Strpić, 'Studenti, revolt, revolucija' (Students, revolt, revolution), *Pitanja,* no. 1 (1969), p. 10; Ivan Kuvačić, 'Teorijski pristup za shvaćanje suvremene omladine' (A theoretical approach to the study of contemporary youth), *Sociologija,* vol. x, no. 1 (1968), p. 52; and Kiro Hadži-Vasilev, 'Za samoupravni sistem obrazovanja' (For the self-managing system in education), *Socijalizam,* vol. xv, no. 10 (1972), p. 1079.

11. Bazala and Vukasović, 'Sistem samoupravljanja na sveučilištu', p. 6.

12. Ibid., pp. 6-7.

13. Ibid., pp. 7, 9, 11.

14. Ibid., pp. 7, 9.

15. Ibid., pp. 7, 9, 11.

16. Ibid., p. 7.
17. *JTS* 735, pp. 9-10: *Borba* 15 September 1952; and V. Stojanović, 'Reforma univerziteta', p. 13.
18. e.g. *Borba* (Z) 18 June 1967, p. 10.
19. Eugen Pusić, 'Samoupravljanje i sveučilište' (Self-management and the university), in Derosi-Bjelajac and others, *Sveučilište i Revolucija,* p. 231.
20. V. Stojanović, 'Reforma univerziteta', p. 12; also Krste Crvenkovski, 'Reforma visokoškolskog obrazovanja u FNRJ' (The reform of higher education in the FPRY), *Univerzitet Danas,* vol. i, no. 5/6 (1960), p. 165; Branislav Šoškić, 'Reforma univerziteta i izbor naučno-nastavnih radnika' (The reform of the university and the selection of scientific-educational staff), *Univerzitet Danas,* vol. xi, no. 6 (1970), p. 5; and Vojislav Stojanović, 'Nauka, naučno stvaralaštvo i naučna kritika' (Scholarship, scholarly creativity and scholarly criticism), *Univerzitet Danas,* vol. xi, no. 6 (1970), p. 32; and *Student* 20 February 1968, p. 1.
21. D. Stanković, 'Reforma univerziteta', p. 37; *Borba* (Z) 8 July 1967, p. 1; *Komunist* 7 May 1964, p. 9, and 12 May 1966, p. 3; and Vračar, 'Neizbežne promene na univerzitetu', pp. 326-7.
22. Kilibarda, 'Za socijalističke odnose', p. 511.
23. V. Stojanović, 'Reforma univerziteta', p. 12. Also *Borba* 8 July 1967, p. 1; *Student* 28 March 1964, p. 14, and 7 January 1964, p. 3.
24. Milorad Bertolino, 'Mehanizam izbora i reizbornosti' (The mechanics of election and re-election), *Univerzitet Danas,* vol. xi, no. 7/8 (1970), p. 23; and Šoškić, 'Reforma univerziteta i izbor naučno-nastavnih radnika', pp. 5, 6.
25. *Komunist* 28 May 1964, p. 6; also *Borba* (Z) 8 July 1967, p. 1; *Student* 10 December 1963, p. 3; Šoškić, 'Reforma univerziteta i izbor naučno-nastavnih radnika', p. 5; and *Studentski List* 9 March 1965, p. 5.
26. *JTS* 4392, p. 4: *Borba* 23 April 1966. See also *Komunist* 30 September 1965, p. 5; *Borba* 8 July 1967, p. 8; and D. Stanković, 'Reforma univerziteta', p. 35.
27. Institute for Social Research, University of Zagreb, *Innovation in Higher Education: Reforms in Yugoslavia* (Paris: OECD, 1970), p. 110.
28. *Borba* 1 February 1966, p. 7; Djoko Stojičić, 'Način glasanja pri izboru nastavnika' (Voting procedure in electing staff), *Univerzitet Danas,* vol. vi, no. 2 (1965), pp. 9-11.
29. *JTS* 4324, p. 16: *Politika* 6 February 1966; and *JTS* 743, appendix pp. a-d: *Nova Makedonija* 9 March 1952.
30. V. Stojanović, 'Reforma univerziteta', p. 12; and Kilibarda, 'Za socijalističke odnose', pp. 513, 516.
31. *JTS* 1943, p. 21: *Borba* 5 September 1956.
32. D. Stanković, 'Reforma univerziteta', p. 37. Also Grujica Žarković, 'O materijalnom položaju nastavnika i naučnih radnika SR BiH' (On the material situation of teachers and scientific workers in the Socialist Republic of Bosnia and Hercegovina), *Univerzitet Danas,* vol. xii, no. 1 (1971), p. 26; Dubravka Plećaš, 'Neki sociološki problemi i problemi samoupravljanja u visokom školstvu' (Some sociological problems and problems of self-management in higher education), *Univerzitet Danas,* vol. xii, no. 1 (1971), p. 50 (hereinafter cited as 'Problemi samoupravljanja'); and Budimir Lazović, 'Položaj, funkcije i odgovornost studenata u samoupravljanju univerzitetom' (The status, functions and responsibilities of students in university self-management), *Univerzitet Danas,* vol. x, no. 9/10 (1969), p. 110 (hereinafter cited as 'Odgovornost studenata').

33. Tone Klemenčić, 'Reforma visokog školstva sa gledišta društveno-privrednog razvoja' (The reform of higher education from the viewpoint of social and economic development), *Univerzitet Danas,* vol. x, no. 7/8 (1969), pp. 12-13; and *Komunist* 4 February 1965, p. 6.

34. Jovan Ristović, 'Ambivalentna socijalizacija ličnosti asistenta' (The environment for the socialization of the assistant), *Univerzitet Danas,* vol. x, no. 6 (1969), p. 101 (hereinafter cited as 'Socijalizacija asistenta'). Also *JTS* 5067, p. 29: *Vjesnik* 25 June 1968; and *Borba* (Z) 27 June 1967, p. 8.

35. Ristović, 'Socijalizacija asistenta'. Also see Kilibarda, 'Za socijalističke odnose', p. 516; and *Student* 20 February 1968, p. 1.

36. (Milosav Prelić), *Komunist* 12 May 1966, p. 3.

37. Ristović, 'Socijalizacija asistenta', pp. 92-3.

38. Ibid., p. 95. See also *Borba* (Z) 18 June 1967, p. 10.

39. *JTS* 4756, p. 25: *Borba* 8 July 1967; *JTS* 5067, p. 29: *Vjesnik* 25 June 1968; *Borba* 8 July 1967, p. 1; Branko Pribićević, 'Sprovodjenje reforme sistema visokoškolskog obrazovanja i zadaci saveza komunista' (The realization of the reform of the system of higher education and the tasks of the League of Communists), *Univerzitet Danas,* vol. xi, no. 5 (1970), p. 57 (hereinafter cited as 'Zadaci komunista').

40. For details see chapter IV.

41. Institute for Social Research, *Innovation in Higher Education,* p. 51.

42. *JTS* 4754, p. 35: *Borba* 5 July 1967.

43. *JTS* 669, pp. 4-6: *Borba* 20 July 1952.

44. 'Yugoslav Union of Students in 1953', *Yugoslav Student News,* no. 9 January 1954), pp. 24-5.

45. 'Implementation of New University Law', ibid., no. 13 (Apr. 1955), pp. 1-3.

46. e.g. *JTS* 2296, p. 19: *Borba* 3 November 1957.

47. *JTS* 2297, p. 36: *Borba* 5 November 1957.

48. 'Conclusions of the Fourth Congress of the Yugoslav Union of Students', *Yugoslav Student News,* no. 28/29 (July 1959), pp. 69-70; 'Implementation of New University Law', ibid., no. 13 (April 1955), pp. 1-3.

49. (Jovan Veselinov), *JTS* 2296, p. 19: *Borba* 3 November 1957.

50. *Borba* 14 October 1959; see also *Yugoslav Student News,* no. 27 (December 1958), p. 45.

51. *JTS* 2560, p. 23: *Borba* 17 September 1958.

52. (Miloš Minić), *JTS* 2482, p. 32: *Borba* 18 June 1958.

53. Nerkez Smailagić, 'Sveučilište i demokratija' (The university and democracy), in Derosi-Bjelajac and others, *Sveučilište i Revolucija,* p. 135; *JTS* 743, appendix pp. a-d: *Nova Makedonija* 9 March 1952; Pribićević, 'Zadaci komunista', p. 61.

54. Jakov Sirotković, 'O radu sveučilišta s posebnim osvrtom na uvjete i probleme reforme visokog školstva' (Concerning the work of the university, with particular regard to the conditions and problems of the reform of higher education), *Univerzitet Danas,* vol. ix, no. 9/10 (1968), p. 24 (hereinafter cited as 'O radu sveučilišta'); Veljko Mratović, 'Razvijanje samoupravnih odnosa u sveučilištu' (The development of self-managing relations at the university), *Univerzitet Danas,* vol. xi, no. 4 (1970), p. 18; and Dragoslav Mirković, 'Aktuelna pitanja organizacije univerziteta i fakulteta' (Some current questions on the organization of universities and departments), *Univerzitet Danas,* vol. ix, no. 9/10 (1968), pp. 4, 5.

55. Institute for Social Research, *Innovation in Higher Education,* p. 101.

56. Ibid., pp. 101-2; see also speech by Professor Božo Težak, *Sveučilišni Vjesnik* (Zagreb), vol. xii, no. 222 (1966), p. 411.

57. Slavko Macarola, speech to University Council, *Sveučilišni Vjesnik* (Zagreb), vol. xii, no. 222 (1966), pp. 393, 394, 399, 402.
58. 'Conclusions of the Fourth Congress of the Yugoslav Union of Students', p. 69; Žagar, 'Reform of university education', pp. 1-10.
59. Djordje Lazarević, 'Reforma univerziteta' (The reform of the university), *Univerzitet Danas,* vol. xi, no. 4 (1970), p. 7; Miodrag Čekić, 'Specijalizacija i opšte obrazovanje' (Specialized and general education), *Univerzitet Danas,* vol. xi, no. 4 (1970), p. 56; and Ivan Jurković, 'Uloga sveučilišta i nauke u našoj zemlji u svijetlu savremene naučno-technološke revolucije' (The role of the university and science in our land in light of the contemporary scientific-technological revolution), *Univerzitet Danas,* vol. xi, no. 1 (1970), p. 55.
60. 'Conclusions of the Fourth Congress of the Yugoslav Union of Students', p. 69; and Pribićević, 'Zadaci komunista', p. 61.
61. (Mika Špiljak), *Borba* 4 December 1965, p. 7.
62. (Milosav Prelić), *JTS* 4392, p. 4: *Borba* 23 April 1966.
63. *General Law on Universities* proclaimed 15 June 1954, *JTS* 1295, pp. 4-22.
64. Omer Ibrahimagić, 'Prilog pitanju izgradnje samoupravnog univerziteta' (On the subject of building the self-managing university), in Derosi-Bjelajac and others, *Sveučilište i Revolucija,* p. 277. Also *Studentski List* 14 May 1968, p. 5; *The Eighth Congress of the Union of Yugoslav Youth* (Belgrade: Youth Life, 1968), p. 177.
65. Article 20.
66. Articles 34 and 35.
67. Articles 39 and 40.
68. *JTS* 982, p. 14: *Borba* 8 July 1953.
69. (Z. Midžić), *Youth Life,* no. 9 (1953), p. 6.
70. Article 46.
71. (Midžić), *Youth Life,* no. 9 (1953), p. 6.
72. See Articles 43, 42, 35 and 56.
73. Lazović, 'Odgovornost studenata', p. 112.
74. *General Law on Faculties [Departments] and Universities in Yugoslavia* (Belgrade: Union of Jurists Association of Yugoslavia, [1960]), proclaimed 2 July 1960.
75. Articles 45 and 58.
76. Articles 69 and 70.
77. Esad Pašalić, 'Sadržaj rada samoupravnih organa' (The nature of the work of the self-managing bodies), *Bilten Univerziteta u Sarajevu,* vol. vii, no. 25 (1967), p. 4; and *Komunist* 6 June 1968, p. 9.
78. *Student* 11 April 1967, p. 8; *Komunist* 23 May 1968, p. 13; Zoran Pjanić, 'Univerzitet—nekad i sad' (The University—then and now), *Univerzitet Danas,* vol. x, no. 9/10 (1969), p. 27; 'Osvrt na XIV interfakultetsku konferenciju pravnih fakulteta Jugoslavije' (Review of the XIV interdepartmental conference of Yugoslav law departments), *Univerzitet Danas,* vol. xi, no. 2/3 (1970), p. 116; Milorad Bertolino, 'O kompetencijama na reformisanom univerzitetu' (On 'competence' at the reformed university), in Derosi-Bjelajac and others, *Sveučilište i Revolucija,* p. 279.
79. Božo Težak, 'Diskusija' (Discussion), in Derosi-Bjelajac and others, *Sveučilište i Revolucija,* p. 316; and V. Stojanović, 'Reforma univérziteta', p. 19. Also *Student* 17 May 1966, p. 3; and *Komunist* 12 October 1967, p. 6.
80. *Studentski List* 19 May 1964, p. 4.
81. Quoted in *Student* 12 November 1968, p. 9.

82. Quoted in *Studentski List* 24 May 1966, p. 4.
83. Pilić, 'Uslovi socialističkog odnosa', p. 288; also see 'Osvrt na XIV inter-fakultetsku konferenciji pravnih fakulteta Jugoslavije', p. 116.
84. Makso Šnuderl, 'Prilagodjavanje fakultetskih i univerzitetskih statuta novom ustavu' (Adapting the departmental and university statutes to the new constitution), *Univerzitet Danas,* vol. iv, no. 9/10 (1963), p. 371; Vladimir Serdar, 'Organizacija i financiranje fakulteta i univerziteta' (The organization and financing of departments and universities), *Univerzitet Danas,* vol. v, no. 1/2 (1964), p. 2; and Pašalić, 'Sadržaj rada samoupravnih organa', p. 5.
85. 'Samoupravljanje, dohodak i organizacione osnove univerziteta' (Self-management, income and the organizational basis of the university), *Bilten Univerziteta u Sarajevu,* vol. vii, no. 24 (1967), p. 95.
86. F. Pivec and C. Ribičič, 'Razvoj ideje i zakonodavstva o studentu radniku samoupravljaču' (The development of ideas and legislation concerning the student as worker and self-manager), *Ideje,* vol. i, no. 2 (1970), p. 100.
87. Milojko Drulović, 'Report on the current problems and future tasks of the Yugoslav Union of Students', *Yugoslav Student News,* no. 21 (October 1956), p. 56.
88. *Komunist* 13 April 1967, p. 8 (Report of meeting of CC LCY); Ivo Bojanić, 'Election of students to various bodies of social management at the Zagreb University', *Yugoslav Student News,* no. 19 (May 1956), p. 1; and *Student* 15 November 1966, p. 3.
89. Pilić, 'Uslovi socialističkog odnosa', p. 287.
90. Borisav Džuverović, 'Studenti i samoupravljanje' (Students and self-management), *Gledišta,* vol. viii, no. 5 (1967), p. 708; Jovan Djordjević, 'Društvena osnova prava studenata na samoupravljanje' (The basic self-management rights of students in our society), *Ideje,* vol. i, no. 2 (1970), p. 16.
91. *JTS* 5016, p. 8: *Politika* 12 May 1968.
92. Džuverović, 'Studenti i samoupravljanje', p. 795, *JTS* 5062, p. 5: *Svet* 15 June 1968; *JTS* 5003, p. 35: *Borba* 26 April 1968; Vladimir Milanović, 'Sociološki aspekti transformacije uloge škole' (Sociological aspects of the transformation of the role of the school), *Univerzitet Danas,* vol. xi, no. 2/3 (1970), p. 31.
93. Krešimir Bezić, 'Stavovi studenata o vaspitnoj ulozi u samoupravnim organima visokoškolskih ustanova' (Views of students on the educational role of self-managing bodies of schools for higher education), *Univerzitet Danas,* vol. ix, no. 7 (1968), p. 78 (hereinafter cited as 'Stavovi studenata'). Also Plećaš, 'Problemi samoupravljanja', p. 51.
94. *Student* 8 March 1966, p. 5; Ibrahimagić, 'Prilog pitanju izgradnje samoupravnog univerziteta', p. 277; and *Student* 15 March 1966, p. 3.
95. Lazović, 'Odgovornost studenata', p. 111; *JTS* 5078, p. 17: (Borisav Džuverović), *Nin* 21 July 1968; *Student* 8 March 1966, p. 5; Košutić, 'Neke dileme', p. 146; and Kosta Čavoški, 'Studenti i samoupravljanje' (Students and self-management), *Arhiv,* vol. xli, no. 1 (January/March 1971), p. 156.
96. Bezić, 'Stavovi studenata', pp. 77-8.
97. Zvonimir Cviić, 'Stavovi visokoškolskih nastavnika o ulozi studenata u organima samoupravljanja' (Views of teachers in tertiary institutions on the role of students in self-managing bodies), *Univerzitet Danas,* vol. ix, no. 7 (1968), p. 67.
98. Bezić, 'Stavovi studenata', p. 75.

99. Cviić, 'Stavovi visokoškolskih nastavnika o ulozi studenata u organima samoupravljanja', pp. 68, 69; Bezić, 'Stavovi studenata', p. 79. See also discussion by Plećaš, 'Problemi samoupravljanja', especially p. 50.

100. Bezić, 'Stavovi studenata', p. 72.

101. Mustafa Heremić, 'Studentski centar sveučilišta u Zagrebu' (The Zagreb University student centre), *Univerzitet Danas,* vol. i, nos. 7-10 (1960), p. 250; 'Upravljanje ustanovama studentskog standarda' (The management of student service institutions), *Univerzitet Danas,* vol. ix, no. 8 (1968), especially pp. 98-102; *Studentski List* 9 April 1968, p. 4; 'Novi zakon o studentskim ustanovama u SR Srbiji' (New law on student institutions in SR Serbia), *Univerzitet Danas,* vol. ix, no. 9/10 (1968), pp. 122-3.

102. S. Resulović, 'Upravljanje ustanove studentskog standarda' (The management of student service institutions), *Bilten Univerziteta u Sarajevu,* vol. viii, no. 28 (1968), pp. 81-104, especially pp. 81, 100.

103. *Politika* 20 April 1968, p. 6. Meeting of Belgrade University Committee of the LC. See also *Student* 26 April 1966, p. 3.

104. *Student* 24 March 1964, p. 9.

105. Resulović, 'Upravljanje ustanove studentskog standarda', p. 99.

106. e.g. *Student* 14 May 1968, p. 4; and Lazović, 'Odgovornost studenata', p. 111.

107. Bojanić, 'Election of students to various bodies of social management at the Zagreb University', pp. 1-3.

108. Ibid., p. 32.

109. (Tripalo), *Studentski List* 16 April 1968, p. 1.

110. 23 May 1968, pp. 12-13.

111. *Borba* 26 May 1968, p. 5; see also *Borba* (Z) 8 May 1968, p. 1.

112. Bezić, 'Stavovi studenata', pp. 77-8; see also *Studentski List* 29 October 1968, regarding unsuccessful efforts to hold meetings of student representatives.

113. 14 July 1966, p. 6; see also *Komunist* 12 November 1964, p. 3.

114. 'Some current tasks in the political and ideological activities of the Yugoslav Union of Students', *Yugoslav Student News,* no. 26 (July 1958), p. 9 (hereinafter cited as 'Some current tasks').

115. See chapter V.

116. Lazović, 'Odgovornost studenata'; see also *Politika* 20 April 1968, p. 6; 'Some current tasks', p. 9; and Pivec and Ribičič, 'Razvoj ideje i zakonodavstva o studentu radniku samoupravljaču', p. 100.

117. e.g. *Student* 15 November 1966, p. 3; and Košutić, 'Neke dileme', p. 146.

118. 'Social self-government at Yugoslav universities', *Youth Life,* no. 45 (1965), p. 8.

119. Mika Tripalo, 'Social Management of Schools', *Youth Life,* no. 11 (Autumn 1954), p. 13; and Pilić, 'Uslovi socialističkog odnosa', pp. 288, 290.

120. *Komunist* 9 January 1964, p. 9, and 25 May 1967, p. 1; *The Eighth Congress of the Union of Yugoslav Youth,* pp. 137, 177; Drulović, 'Report on the current problems and future tasks of the Yugoslav Union of Students', p. 42; and *Student* 15 March 1966, p. 3.

121. Ivo Bojanić, 'Participation of students in the management of universities', *Yugoslav Student News,* no. 24 (July 1957), p. 18. Also see discussion in the following: Bertolino, 'O kompetencijama na reformisanom univerzitetu', p. 279; J. Djordjević, 'Društvena osnova prava studenata na samoupravljanje', p. 18; *Politika* 16 June 1968, pp. 8, 9; Džuverović,

'Studenti i samoupravljanje', pp. 707-10; Košutić, 'Neke dileme', p. 147; *Student* 11 April 1967, p. 8; (Midžić), *Youth Life,* no. 9 (1953), p. 6; *Komunist* 23 May 1968, p. 13; *JTS* 5207, p. 45: *Politika* 25 December 1968. For a different view, see Slavko Milosavlevski, 'Aktuelni momenat reforme Skopskog Univerziteta' (The reform of the University of Skoplje—the current moment), *Univerzitet Danas,* vol. xiii, no. 1/2 (January/February 1972), p. 10.

122. Lazar Nikodimovski, 'Neki aspekti nove uloge univerziteta u savremenom društvu' (Some aspects of the new role of the university in contemporary society), *Univerzitet Danas,* vol. xi, no. 1 (1970), p. 33; also Šnuderl, 'Prilagodjavanje fakultetskih i univerzitetskih statuta novom ustavu'; Jovan Djordjević, 'The case for a new modern university', *Socialist Thought and Practice,* no. 36 (October/December 1969), p. 155.

123. See discussion in the following: Bertolino, 'O kompetencijama na reformisanom univerzitetu', p. 279; J. Djordjević, 'Društvena osnova prava studenata na samoupravljanje', p. 18; *Politika* 16 June 1968, pp. 8, 9.

124. See remarks by Milosav Prelić (Secretary of Belgrade University Committee LC), quoted in *JTS* 4392, p. 4: *Borba* 23 April 1966; *Student* 26 April 1966; also *Yugoslavia's Way,* pp. 121, 165, 230; *Borba* (Z) 6 July 1968, p. 5; *JTS* 4835, p. 5: *Borba* 7 October 1967; 'Resolution of the Eighth Congress on the future responsibilities of the League of Communists of Yugoslavia', *Yugoslav Survey,* vol. vi, no. 20 (1965), pp. 2900-16.

125. (R. Čolaković), *JTS* 774, pp. 24-5: *Borba* 4 November 1952.

126. *JTS* 1680, pp. 14-15: *Borba* 16 October 1955.

127. Ibid.

128. Tito to the Sixth Plenum of CC LCY, *JTS* 1798, p. 38: *Borba* 14 March 1956.

129. Ibid.; and *JTS* 1802, pp. 13, 14: *Politika* 17 March 1956.

130. *JTS* 2018, p. 23: *Borba* 25 November 1956.

131. (Vida Tomšić), *JTS* 1813, p. 14: *Komunist,* nos. 1-2 (1956).

132. *Yugoslavia's Way,* p. 255.

133. Ibid., p. 141.

134. (Djoko Stojičić), *Student* 7 January 1964, p. 1, 16 January 1968, p. 1, 17 May 1966, p. 3, and 5 October 1965, p. 1; and *Studentski List* 26 April 1966, p. 5.

135. (Marko Bulc), *Borba* (Z) 2 June 1967, p. 4; and *Student* 17 January 1967, unnumbered supplement.

136. *Borba* (Z) 8 May 1967, p. 4; *Komunist* 1 June 1967, p. 3.

137. *JTS* 4713, p. 22: *Borba* 19 May 1967; see also *Borba* (Z) 8 May 1967, p. 4; *Komunist* 1 June 1967, p. 3.

138. *Borba* 31 June 1967, pp. 1, 4.

139. *Borba* (Z) 28 June 1967, p. 4.

140. (C. Mijatović), *Borba* (Z) 25 May 1967, p. 4.

141. *JTS* 4722, p. 43: *Oslobodjenje Nedelje* 28 May 1967.

142. Milan Kangrga, 'Praksa i kritika' (Practice and criticism), *Praxis,* vol. ii, no. 2 (1965), especially pp. 280-1; and Gajo Petrović, 'O našoj filozofiji' (About our philosophy), *Praxis,* vol. ii, no. 2 (1965), pp. 249-55.

143. Gajo Petrović, 'Kritika u socijalizmu' (Criticism in socialism), *Praxis,* vol. ii, no. 3 (1965), p. 475; and 'O našoj filozofiji', pp. 249, 254; *JTS,* Magazine supplement, no. 4 (March 1966), pp. 10-17: Svetozar Stojanović, 'Morality of the revolutionary vanguard as a historical presupposition of socialism', translated from *Praxis,* no. 1 (1966); and Predrag Vranički,

'O nekim problemima odnosa u komunizmu' (Concerning some problems of relations in Communism), *Praxis,* vol. ii, no. 4/5 (1965), p. 679.

144. 'Još jednom o alternitivi: Staljinistički pozitivizam ili stvaralački Marksizam?' (Once again on the alternatives: Stalinist positivism or creative Marxism?), *Praxis,* vol. ii, no. 6 (1965), p. 892; see also Kangrga, 'Praksa i kritika', p. 269.

145. Petrović, 'Kritika u socijalizmu', p. 469. See also Mihailo Marković, 'Društvena uloga univerzitetskog nastavnika' (Social role of the university teacher), *Univerzitet Danas,* vol. ix, no. 3/4 (March/April 1968), pp. 99-103, especially pp. 101, 102.

146. *Yugoslav Survey,* vol. vii, no. 25 (1966), p. 3577.

147. See for example, comments by Kiro Hadži-Vasilev, member of the Executive Committee CC LCY, *Politika* 30 June 1968, p. 9; also *Komunist* 13 August 1964, p. 3, 20 February 1964, p. 1, and 21 January 1965, p. 6.

148. *JTS* 5069, p. 12: *Politika* 14 July 1968; *Komunist* 16 July 1964, p. 8, and 4 July 1968, p. 3.

149. (Tripalo), *JTS* 4920, p. 4: *Mladost* 28 December 1967.

150. *JTS* 4419, p. 22: *Vjesnik* 15 May 1966; *Borba* 18 July 1968, pp. 5, 6, and 14 June 1968, p. 12; Resolutions of the Belgrade City Committee LC and the Serbian Executive Committee CC LC, *Borba* 14 June 1968, p. 7; *Politika* 19 June 1968, p. 4; see also Supek, 'Još jednom o alternativi: Staljinistički pozitivizam ili stvaralački Marksizam?' p. 892, for a brief review of the types of attack.

151. *Borba* 17 July 1968, p. 5, and 24 November 1967, p. 4. Note discussion and denial of this criticism in an editorial entitled 'U povodu nekih najnovijih kritika *Praxisa'* (On the occasion of some of the newest criticisms of *Praxis*), *Praxis,* vol. v, no. 4 (1968), pp. 449-58, especially p. 456.

152. *JTS* 4419, p. 24: *Vjesnik* 15 May 1966.

153. M. George Zaninovich, 'The Yugoslav Variation on Marx', in *Contemporary Yugoslavia: Twenty Years of Socialist Experiment,* ed. Wayne S. Vucinich (Berkeley and Los Angeles: University of California Press, 1969), p. 309; and *JTS* 5075, p. 48: *Politika* 22 July 1968.

154. See for example, Vranički, 'O nekim problemima odnosa u komunizmu', p. 680; Rudi Supek, 'Robno-novčani odnosi i socijalistička ideologija' (Material-monetary relations and socialist ideology), *Praxis,* vol. v, no. 1/2 (1968); and editorial preface to *Praxis,* vol. viii, no. 3/4 (1971), pp. 309-11, especially p. 311.

155. *Borba* 17 July 1968, p. 5.

156. *JTS* 5053, p. 7: *Borba* 22 June 1968.

157. *JTS* 5081, p. 9: *Ekspres Politika* 21 July 1968.

158. *JTS* (Magazine supplement), no. 4 (March 1966), pp. 12, 13.

159. 'Kritika u socijalizmu', pp. 471-2.

160. Ibid., pp. 479, 481; and *Studentski List* 2 March 1965, p. 5.

161. 'Kritika u socijalizmu', p. 473.

162. 'Još jednom o alternativi: Staljinistički pozitivizam ili stvaralački Marksizam?', p. 892.

163. *JTS* 2094, p. 19: *Student* 4 March 1957.

164. (Djoko Stojičić), *JTS* 3822, p. 7: *Borba* 17 June 1964.

165. *Borba* 18 May 1968, p. 5; see also *Student* 26 April 1966, p. 1, 7 December 1965, p. 1, and 16 April 1963, p. 3.

166. *Komunist* 14 July 1966, p. 6; also *Borba* 8 July 1967, p. 8.

167. Veljko Cvjetičanin quoting O. Davić, *Studentski List* 6 December 1966, p. 1.

168. *Student* 16 April 1963, p. 3.
169. 'Work and development of the League of Communists of Yugoslavia (LCY) between the Seventh and Eighth Congress', *Yugoslav Survey,* vol. v, no. 19 (1964), p. 2725.
170. Ibid. See also *Student* 16 January 1968, p. 1, 26 April 1966, p. 1, and 1 January 1964, p. 3.
171. (Milosav Prelić), *Student* 13 December 1966, p. 4.
172. *Komunist* 14 July 1966, p. 6.
173. *JTS* 4474, p. 15: *Borba* 6 August 1966.
174. *Student* 19 March 1963, p. 4; 'Work and development of the League of Communists of Yugoslavia (LCY) between the Seventh and Eighth Congress', p. 2725; *JTS* 5050, pp. 12-13: *Mladost* 20 June 1968; Muhamed Nuhić, member of the Executive Committee CC LC Bosnia and Hercegovina, *Komunist* 30 September 1965, p. 5.
175. *JTS* 4533, p. 45: *Borba* 12 October 1968; *Komunist* 1 May 1968, p. 13; *JTS* 4588, p. 1; *Borba* 18 December 1966.
176. *Student* 19 March 1963, p. 4; Pavle Novosel, *Organizacije Saveza Komunista i Mladi Komunisti* (The Organization of the League of Communists and Young Communists) (Zagreb: Naše Teme, 1969), p. 5; and *Student* 26 April 1966, p. 1.
177. *JTS* 4474, p. 15: *Borba* 6 August 1966; Vračar, 'Neizbežne promene na univerzitetu', pp. 323, 326.
178. Note discussion on this point, e.g. Novosel, *Organizacije Saveza Komunista i Mladi Komunisti,* pp. 5-8; and *Borba* (Z) 18 June 1967, p. 10.
179. *Politika* 16 June 1968, p. 7; and Lazović, 'Odgovornost studenata', p. 110. See also *JTS* 2094, p. 19: *Student* 4 March 1957; and *Komunist* 16 April 1964, p. 4.
180. 'Work and development of the League of Communists of Yugoslavia (LCY) between the Seventh and Eighth Congress', p. 2725; Milorad Muratović, 'Političko organizovanje i djelovanje omladine' (The political organization and activity of youth), in Cvjetičanin and others, *Društvo, Revolucija, Omladina,* p. 159; see also Bazala and Vukasović, 'Sistem samoupravljanja na sveučilištu', p. 7; *Student* 1 January 1967, unnumbered supplement; and Dragomir Drašković, 'Neformalno grupisanje u osnovnoj organizaciji saveza Komunista' (Informal grouping in the basic organizations of the League of Communists), *Gledišta,* vol. vii, no. 1 (January 1966), pp. 43-53.
181. (Stanko Pekeć), *Studentski List* 26 May 1964, p. 3.
182. *JTS* 2094, p. 19: *Student* 4 March 1957; see also *Komunist* 10 June 1965, p. 5; and Vladimir Bakarić, 'Omladina i savez komunista Jugoslavije' (The Young and the League of Communists of Yugoslavia), *Gledišta,* vol. vii, no. 6/7 (June/July 1966), pp. 859-61.
183. *Komunist* 13 October 1966, p. 4, and 7 May 1964, p. 9; and (T. Badovinac), *JTS* 4676, p. 43: *Mladost* 22 March 1967.
184. *Komunist* 29 April 1965, p. 8, 12 May 1966, p. 3, and 12 October 1967, p. 6; and *Student* 7 January 1964, p. 3.
185. *Politika* 20 April 1968, p. 6; *JTS* 3810, p. 3: *Borba* 25 September 1964.
186. (Žarko Bulajić), *Politika* 20 April 1968, p.6.
187. *Student* 24 May 1966, p. 3; see also *Komunist* 12 May 1966, p. 3.
188. Branko Pribićević, 'Politička situacija na univerzitetu' (Political situation at the university), *Univerzitet Danas,* vol. x, no. 7/8 (1969), pp. 78-9.
189. Pribićević, 'Zadaci komunista', p. 57.
190. 'Politička situacija na univerzitetu', p. 79.

191. 'Zadaci komunista', pp. 52-7.
192. Ibid., pp. 52-3.
193. Ibid., p. 54.
194. Ibid.
195. Ibid., p. 56.
196. Branko Caratan, 'Studentski lipanj—uzroci i konsekvence' (The students' June—causes and consequences), in Cvjetičanin and others, *Društvo, Revolucija, Omladina,* p. 167; see also Dag Strpić, 'Studenti i revolucija' (Students and revolution), in Derosi-Bjelajac and others, *Sveučilište i Revolucija,* pp. 169-70.

IV. THE ACADEMIC ENVIRONMENT

1. e.g. Crvenkovski, 'Reforma visokoškolskog obrazovanja u FNRJ', pp. 157, 158, 162; 'Reform of Higher Education', speech made to the Federal People's Assembly, 2 June 1960, and published as the preface in *General Law on Faculties [Departments] and Universities in Yugoslavia,* pp. 2-3; and Vladimir Bakarić, 'Razgovor na univerzitetu', *Univerzitet Danas,* vol. x, no. 6 (1969), p. 4.
2. e.g. *JTS* 1295, p. 5: *General Law on Universities* (1954), Federal People's Assembly, FPRY, Article 5; see also 'Notebook', *Youth Life,* no. 9 (1953), p. 25; and Djuro Takalić, 'Neka pitanja nove uloge sveučilišta u samoupravnom društvu' (Some questions concerning the new role of the university in a self-governing society), in Derosi-Bjelajac and others, *Sveučilište i Revolucija,* p. 271 (hereinafter cited as 'Nove uloge sveučilišta').
3. Federal Council for Statistics, *Jugoslavija 1945-1964, Statistički Pregled* (Yugoslavia 1945-64, Statistical Review) (Belgrade, n.d., [1965], p. 299; *Statistički Godišnjak SFRJ, 1969* (Statistical Yearbook FPRY, 1969) (Belgrade, 1969), p. 292; and *Statistički Godišnjak SFRJ, 1975* (Statistical Yearbook FPRY, 1975) (Belgrade, 1975), p. 330.
4. Borisav Džuverović, *Omladina u Jugoslovenskom društvu* (Youth in Yugoslav Society) (Belgrade: Mladost, 1974), p. 44.
5. Vladimir Serdar, 'Reformski zahvati u dodiplomskoj nastavi' (Reform undertakings in undergraduate education), *Univerzitet Danas,* vol. x, no. 2 (1971), p. 14; Sirotković, 'O radu sveučilišta', p. 24; and Mratović, 'Razvijanje samoupravnih odnosa u sveučilištu', p. 18.
6. Institute for Social Research, *Innovation in Higher Education,* p. 100.
7. Milorad Mladjenović, 'Neki problemi univerziteta u zemljama u razvoju' (Some problems of universities in developing countries), *Univerzitet Danas,* vol. x, no. 2/3 (1969), p. 109; Jovan Veselinov, 'Aktuelni problemi generacije mladih' (Actual problems of the young generation), *Gledišta,* vol. vii, no. 6/7 (June/July 1966), p. 811; *Student* 5 March 1968, p. 3; and Tihomir Vasiljević, 'Naša visokoškolska politika' (Our higher education politics), *Gledišta,* vol. vii, no. 4 (April 1966), p. 502.
8. V. Stojanović, 'Reforma univerziteta', p. 23.
9. Blagoj Popov, '20 godina univerziteta u Skoplju' (20 years of the university in Skoplje), *Univerzitet Danas,* vol. x, no. 4 (1969), p. 3.
10. Predrag Ignjatović, 'Prilog diskusiji o reformi univerziteta' (Some points for discussion concerning the reform of the university), *Univerzitet Danas,* vol. xi, no. 1 (1970), p. 58 (hereinafter cited as 'Reforma univerziteta'); Hamdija Čemerlić, 'Dvadeset godina rada univerziteta u Sarajevu'

(Twenty years' work of the Sarajevo University), *Univerzitet Danas*, vol. xi, no. 5 (1970), p. 92; J. A. Spakarev, 'Stanje i tendencije u nastavno-obrazovnom procesu Skopskog univerziteta' (The present situation and trends in the process of teaching and education at the University of Skoplje), *Univerzitet Danas*, vol. x, no. 7/8 (1969), pp. 89-95 (hereinafter cited as 'Skopski univerzitet').

11. Vojislav Stojanović, 'Problemi u procesu visokoškolskog obrazovanja i naučnog rada' (Problems in tertiary education and research work), *Univerzitet Danas*, vol. xiii, no. 5/6 (May/June 1972), p. 24.

12. Jovan Gligorijević, 'Univerzitet u Beogradu: Rad na reformi univerziteta' (Belgrade University: Work on university reform), *Univerzitet Danas*, vol. xii, no. 9/10 (1971), p. 36.

13. Šefkija Žuljević, 'Materijalni položaj univerzitetskih nastavnika i mogućnost vrednovanja naučnog i nastavno-pedagoškog rada na univerzitetu' (The material situation of university teachers and the possibility of measuring the value of research work and teaching at the university), *Univerzitet Danas*, vol. xi, no. 9/10 (1970), pp. 92-3; Predrag Ignjatović, 'Reforma univerziteta', p. 59; Jovan Jovanović, 'Učešće federacije u izgradnji univerziteta u SFR Jugoslaviji' (Federal participation in university building in the SFR of Yugoslavia), *Univerzitet Danas*, vol. vi, no. 2 (1965), pp. 21-30; *Politika* 13 February 1955; and Jugoslav Rajković, 'Planiranje kadrova i prijem studenata—osnova saradnje univerziteta i srednjih škola' (Cadre planning and student enrolment—the basis of co-operation between the universities and secondary schools), *Univerzitet Danas*, vol. xi, no. 3/4 (1973), especially pp. 21, 23, 24 (hereinafter cited as 'Planiranje kadrova').

14. *Borba* 15 October 1966, and 23 December 1966; see also Rajković, 'Planiranje kadrova', p. 21.

15. Institute for Social Research, *Innovation in Higher Education*, p. 148.

16. *Student* 1 January 1967, p. 3.

17. *JTS* 4570, p. 19: *Borba* 26 November 1966; see also *JTS* 4392, p. 4: *Borba* 23 April 1966; and *Student* 4 April 1967, p. 1.

18. Crvenkovski, 'Reform of Higher Education', p. 13.

19. (Milojko Drulović), *JTS* 2008, p. 24: *Politika* 18 November 1956; see also 'Selekcija po znanju ili prostoru' (Selection according to knowledge or space), *Ekonomska Politika*, no. 661 (1964), pp. 1661-2; Sirotković, 'O radu sveučilišta', pp. 22-3; Ivan Božić, 'Društvene potrebe kao uticajan činilac u procesu univerzitetske nastave' (Social needs as an influencing factor in the process of university education), *Univerzitet Danas*, vol. xi, no. 9/10 (1970), p. 32.

20. D. Milanović, 'Universities Open to All', *Youth Life*, no. 30 (1959), p. 9; Miroslav Ravbar, 'Povodom pedesetogodišnjice slovenačkog univerziteta u Ljubljani' (On the occasion of the fiftieth anniversary of the Slovenian University in Ljubljana), *Univerzitet Danas*, vol. xi, no. 2/3 (1970), pp. 81-2; R.J., 'Enrolment at Faculties and Art Academies', *Yugoslav Survey*, vol. i, no. 1 (1960), pp. 83-5.

21. Institute for Social Research, *Innovation in Higher Education*, p. 89; and Jakim Sinadinovski, 'Slobodan upis studenata i njegove posledice na univerzitetu "Kiril i Metodij" u Skoplju' (Free enrolment and its consequences at the 'Kiril and Metodij' university in Skoplje), *Univerzitet Danas*, vol. xiv, no. 1/2 (1973), pp. 51-62 (hereinafter cited as 'Slobodan upis').

22. Vasiljević, 'Naša visokoškolska politika', p. 499.

23. Federal Council for Statistics, *Jugoslavija 1945-1964, Statistički Pregled*, p. 299; and *Statistički Godišnjak SFRJ, 1969*, p. 292.

24. B.D.-D.P., 'The System of Higher Education', *Yugoslav Survey*, vol. ii, no. 4 (1961), p. 530.

25. Mladjenović, 'Neki problemi univerziteta u zemljama u razvoju', p. 109; and Crvenkovski, 'Reforma visokoškolskog obrazovanja u FNRJ', p. 158.

26. Tomislav Badovinac, speech to *The Eighth Congress of the Union of Yugoslav Youth*, p. 46.

27. Hadži-Vasilev, 'Za samoupravni sistem obrazovanja', pp. 1080-1.

28. Miodrag Milenović and Vera Gavanski, 'Razvoj visokog školstva 1939-1968' (The development of tertiary education 1939-1968), paper prepared for the Presidium of YUS, Belgrade, 1969, p. 38 (mimeographed).

29. Something of the difficulty of accurately determining the numbers in these categories is illustrated by Antun Petak, 'Motivi zapošljavanja u inozemstvu' (Motives for working abroad), *Naše Teme*, vol. xiii, no. 3 (1969), p. 397.

30. Miloš Bogdanović, 'Problem zapošljavanja mladih kadrova u zemljama u razvoju kao posledica priraštaja stanovnistva' (The problem of employment of young cadres in the developing countries as an effect of the growth of population), *Univerzitet Danas*, vol. x, no. 1 (1969), pp. 37, 39; see also *JTS* 4943, p. 49: *Komunist* 14 February 1968.

31. *JTS* 4744, p. 5: *Borba* 23 June 1967; see also Petar Kobe, 'Efikasnost studiranja na Jugoslovenskim univerzitetima' (The effectiveness of study in Yugoslav universities), *Univerzitet Danas*, vol. ix, no. 9/10 (1968), p. 48 (hereinafter cited as 'Efikasnost studiranja'); Joze Konc, 'Osipanje studenata' (Student drop-out), *Univerzitet Danas*, vol. xi, no. 9/10 (1970), p. 89. Also *Student* 23 May 1967, p. 4.

32. (T. Badovinac), *JTS* 4937, p. 44: *Borba* 9 February 1968.

33. *JTS* 5027, p. 22: *Borba* 26 May 1968.

34. (Bora Pavlović), *Politika* 19 June 1968, p. 7.

35. V. Milanović, 'Sociološki aspekti transformacije uloge škole', p. 23.

36. Miroslav Radovanović, 'Problem "prekobrojne" generacije u savremenom Jugoslavenskom društvu' (The problem of the 'superfluous' generation in contemporary Yugoslav society), *Sociologija*, no. 1 (1968), pp. 63-78; Ivan Lučev, 'Položaj mladih prema stepenu otvorenosti društva i njegovoj pokretljivosti' (Stance of the young towards the level of openings and the degree of mobility in society), *Sociologija*, vol. x, no. 1 (1968), pp. 55-61; and Branko Horvat, 'Marksistička analiza društvenih klasa suvremenog Jugoslavenskog društva' (Marxist analysis of social class in contemporary Yugoslav society), *Gledišta*, vol. viii, no. 10 (October 1967), pp. 1279-92.

37. Vladimir Serdar, 'Sistem upisa studenata u prvu godinu studija na univerzitete u Jugoslaviji 1967/68' (The system of enrolling students in the first year of study at Yugoslav universities 1967/68), Zagreb, 1968, p. 3 (mimeographed, Institut za Društvena Istraživanja Sveučilišta u Zagrebu). See also *Student* 24 May 1966, p. 1.

38. See discussion later in chapter.

39. *Studentski List* 26 May 1964, p. 1.

40. Milan Netkov and Georgi Stardelov, 'Savremeni aspekti demokratizacije jugoslovenskog univerziteta' (The present-day aspects of the democratization of the Yugoslav universities), *Univerzitet Danas*, vol. x, no. 9/10 (1969), p. 50.

41. 'Some questions regarding studies at Belgrade University', pp. 4, 5; and Sirotković, 'O radu sveučilišta', pp. 23-4.
42. Yugoslav Union of Students, 'Neki statistički podaci', n.d. [1971] (mimeographed).
43. Sirotković, 'O radu sveučilišta', p. 14.
44. Milenović, 'Dinamika razvoja', p. 240.
45. Petar Ignjatović, 'Razgovor tek počinje', p. 58; see also Božidar Jakšić, 'Sedam teza o temi: promene na univerzitetu i društvu', in Derosi-Bjelajac and others, eds, *Sveučilište i Revolucija,* p. 267 (hereinafter cited as 'Univerzitet i društvo'); Vojislav Stojanović, 'Perspektive u razvoju visokoškolskog obrazovanja i nauke' (Perspectives in the development of higher education and learning), *Univerzitet Danas,* vol. xv, no. 1/2 (1974), pp. 31-2 (hereinafter cited as 'Perspektive'). Also *Student* 24 March 1964, p. 3.
46. Crvenkovski, 'Reform of Higher Education', p. 17; and Article 34 of *General Law on Faculties and Universities* (1960).
47. Mladjenović, 'Neki problemi univerziteta u zemljama u razvoju', pp. 108-9.
48. Popov, '20 godina Univerziteta u Skoplju', pp. 7-8; see also Jakšić, 'Univerzitet i društvo', p. 267; and Cemerlić, 'Dvadeset godina rada univerziteta u Sarajevu', p. 92.
49. *Vjesnik* 7 June 1956; J. Djordjević, 'The Case for a New Modern University', p. 145.
50. e.g. Djordje Lazarević, 'Reforma univerziteta', p. 6; *Komunist* 6 June 1968; *Student* 3 March 1964; V. Stojanović, 'Perspektive', p. 32; and *Student* 24 March 1964, p. 3.
51. e.g. *Studentski List* 19 May 1964, p. 4.
52. Quoted by Zoran Pjanić, 'Socijalni i materijalni položaj univerziteta' (The social and material position of the university), *Univerzitet Danas,* vol. viii, no. 2 (1967), p. 8; Božidar Jelčić, 'Materijalni položaj visokoškolskog obrazovanja' (The material position of higher education), in Derosi-Bjelajac and others, *Sveučilište i Revolucija,* p. 259 (hereinafter cited as 'Materijalni položaj'); Andrija Čolak, 'Privredna reforma i visoko školstvo' (Economic reform and higher education), *Mladost* (Belgrade), no. 477 (1965); Milan Zjačić, 'Privredna reforma i reforma sveučilišta' (Economic reform and the reform of the university), *Studentski List* (Zagreb), no. 19, 1965. For a similar comment by Tito, see *Studentski List* 15 December 1964, p. 3.
53. Institute for Social Research, *Innovation in Higher Education,* p. 152; Jelčić, 'Materialni položaj', pp. 260-1. See also Pavle Dimitrijević, 'O ličnim dohodcima univerzitetskih nastavnika i saradnika' (On the personal incomes of university teachers and assistants), *Gledišta,* vol. vii, no. 12 (December 1966), pp. 1530-2.
54. Pjanić, 'Socialni i materijalni položaj univerziteta', p. 8.
55. *Borba* 15 October 1966.
56. Žarkovic, 'O materijalnom položaju nastavnika i naučnih radnika SR BiH', p. 27. See also *Student* 6 December 1966, p. 1, and 22 November 1966, p. 1.
57. *JTS* 743, appendix pp. a-d: *Nova Makedonija* 9 March 1952.
58. D. Stanković, 'Reforma univerziteta', p. 35.
59. Vladimir Serdar, address to University Council, *Sveučilišni Vjesnik* (Zagreb), vol. ix, 'A' Supplement, no. 154-55 (1962), pp. 116-17; *Studentski List* 14 May 1968; and *Borba* 30 June 1967.

60. e.g. (Radomir Lukić), *Borba* (Z) 29 July 1967, p. 6; and *Studentski List* 12 May 1964, p. 3, and 24 May 1966, p. 4.
61. *Borba* (Z) 27 June 1967, p. 8; see also Professor Pavle Savić's comments reported in *Borba* (Z) 6 July 1967, p. 6.
62. Grujica Žarković, 'O materijalnom položaju nastavnika i naučnih radnika SR BiH', p. 26; V. Stojanović, 'Perspektive', p. 31; and *Studentski List* 16 February 1965, p. 4.
63. *JTS* 4724, p. 33: *Borba* 31 May 1967; *JTS* 4399, p. 39; *Borba* 27 April 1966; *Borba* 30 June 1967, p. 6.
64. Jelčić, 'Materijalni položaj', p. 262.
65. *JTS* 4754, p. 35: *Borba* 5 July 1967.
66. Comment by Professor Jovan Marjanović, *Borba* (Z) 30 June 1967, p. 6; see also Plećaš, 'Problemi samoupravljanja', p. 50.
67. *Borba* 1 June 1966; *Komunist* 27 May 1965; Drago Grdelić, 'Univerzitet i naučno istraživanje' (The university and academic research), *Univerzitet Danas,* vol. vi, no. 5 (1965), pp. 33-42; Zoran Pjanić, 'Univerzitet—nekad i sad', especially p. 26.
68. J. Djordjević, 'The case for a new modern university', p. 153; *JTS* 1736, pp. 12-13: *Vjesnik* 6 December 1955; *JTS* 3974, p. 20: *Borba* 15 December 1964; D. Stanković, 'Reforma univerziteta', p. 35.
69. V. Milanović, 'Sociološki aspekti transformacije uloge škole', p. 31. Concerning the attitude of assistants to their discipline, note report of Conference of LC Belgrade University, *Komunist* 14 February 1965, p. 6.
70. Jakšić, 'Univerzitet i društvo', p. 267.
71. *Politika* 3 December 1965, and see earlier discussion in *Politika* 12 March 1965.
72. Predrag Ignjatović, 'Reforma univerziteta', p. 59.
73. *Vjesnik* 5 November 1957.
74. Joint Publication Research Service, 'Education in Yugoslavia', Report no. 658, New York, 20 August 1958, p. 51 (mimeographed).
75. 'Some data on post-war development and problems of Yugoslav Universities', *Yugoslav Student News,* no. 27 (December 1958), p. 76.
76. Joint Publication Research Service, 'Education in Yugoslavia', p. 52.
77. Institute for Social Research, *Innovation in Higher Education,* p. 51.
78. Ibid., pp. 36, 37.
79. *JTS* 3718, p. 41: *Borba* 13 February 1964; see also *Komunist* 18 June 1964, p. 4; *Student* 19 March 1963, p. 3.
80. *JTS* 3992, p. 11; *Politika* 9 January 1965; Konc, 'Osipanje studenata', p. 84; see also *JTS* 4321, p. 17: *Borba* 4 February 1966; *JTS* 5067, p. 53: *Borba* 12 July 1968.
81. Based on Milenović, 'Dinamika razvoja', p. 245; Institute for Social Research, *Innovation in Higher Education,* p. 175; and Federal Council for Statistics, *Statistički Godišnjak SFRJ, 1975.*
82. Based on statistics cited by Milenović, 'Dinamika razvoja', p. 251.
83. Kobe, 'Efikasnost studiranja', p. 46; see also Jugoslav Rajković, 'Rezultati nastave i učenja na Beogradskom univerzitetu u školskoj 1964/65 godini' (Results of instruction and learning at Belgrade University in 1964/65), *Univerzitet Danas,* vol. vii, no. 1 (1966), pp. 29-42; *JTS* 4321, p. 17: *Borba* 4 February 1966.
84. Branko Borčić, 'Reforma univerziteta u jugoslovenskoj samoupravnoj zajednici' (University reform in the Yugoslav self-managing society), *Univerzitet Danas,* vol. xiv, no. 1/2 (1973), p. 23 (hereinafter cited as 'Reforma univerziteta').

85. e.g. *JTS* 2294, p. 9: *Oslobodjenje* 6 October 1957.
86. *Borba* (Z) 30 June 1967.
87. V. Stojanović, 'Reforma univerziteta', p. 10; *Borba* 3 December 1965.
88. 'Obrazovni procesi u reformiranoj univerzitetskoj nastavi (prikaz IV simpozija "Društveni i ekonomski aspekti obrazovanja", Zagreb 1970 godine)' (Educational methods in the reformed university's teaching [survey of the IV symposium 'Social and economic aspects of education']), *Univerzitet Danas,* vol. xi, no. 6 (1970), p. 105 (hereinafter cited as 'Obrazovni procesi').
89. e.g. Jovan Gligorijević, 'Prijem novih studenata na univerzitet' (Admission of new students to the university), *Univerzitet Danas,* vol. xiv, no. 1/2 (1973), p. 49. Note also his criticism of the reliability of entrance exams. See discussion for and against in *Student* 10 March 1964, p. 3; *Studentski List* 1 January 1966, p. 6, and 8 December 1964, p. 3.
90. *Borba* 21 February 1965; V. Stojanović, 'Perspektive', p. 31.
91. *Student* 11 January 1966, p. 5.
92. V. Stojanović, 'Reforma univerziteta', p. 11.
93. e.g. *Borba* 28 November 1953; V. Mirković, 'Solving student problems', *Youth Life,* no. 9 (1953), p. 5; Zdravko Midžić, 'Students and Professors', *Youth Life,* no. 9 (1953), p. 6.
94. Kobe, 'Efikasnost studiranja', p. 47; Mirković, 'Solving student problems', *Youth Life,* no. 9 (1953), p. 5; Lazarević, 'Reforma univerziteta', p. 5; Petar Kozić, 'Sociografija nekih studentskih zapažanja o učenju, ispitima i dokolici' (A socio-graph of some student observations concerning studying, exams and leisure), *Univerzitet Danas,* vol. xi, no. 2/3 (1970), p. 37; and *Student* 30 April 1968, p. 3.
95. e.g. *Šesti Kongres NOJ,* p. 169; Borislav Blagojević, 'Neka pitanja reforme visokog školstva i neposredni politički zadaci na pravnom fakultetu u Beogradu' (Some questions on the reform of higher education and the immediate political tasks at the faculty of law in Belgrade), *Univerzitet Danas,* vol. x, no. 4 (1969), p. 21.
96. Serdar, 'Reformski zahvati u dodiplomskoj nastavi', p. 15.
97. e.g. *Borba* 13 February 1964.
98. Stanoje Ivanović, 'Opterećenost nastavnog osoblja nastavnim radom i efikasnost završavanja studija na visokoškolskim ustanovama u SR Srbiji' (The teaching burden of the staff and the effectiveness of completing studies at tertiary institutions in the Serbian Socialist Republic), *Univerzitet Danas,* vol. xiii, no. 3/4 (March/April 1972), p. 53.
99. 18 October 1966, p. 5.
100. e.g., see Crvenkovski, 'Reform of higher education', especially p. 7; 'Reforma visokoškolskog obrazovanja u FNRJ', p. 158; and Borivoj Samolovčev, 'Nastavni planovi i programi i modernizacija visokoškolske nastave' (Teaching plans and programmes and the modernization of tertiary teaching), *Univerzitet Danas,* vol. iv, no. 9/10 (1963), pp. 375-85.
101. Quoted in *Youth Life,* nos 22-23 (1957), p. 6; see also Tito's statement to teachers in *Komunist* 25 February 1965, p. 1.
102. Crvenkovski, 'Reform of higher education', p. 529; and *Studentski List* 11 January 1966, p. 3.
103. Pribićević, 'Zadaci komunista', pp. 56-7; Božidar Djordjević, 'Univerzitet i privreda' (The university and the economy), *Univerzitet Danas,* vol. viii, no. 1 (1967), pp. 5-9.
104. *Borba* 27 September 1952; Dragiša Ivanović, 'O nekim praktičnim pitanjima reforme univerziteta' (On some practical questions concerning

university reform), *Univerzitet Danas,* vol. x, no. 9/10 (1969), pp. 10-11; J. A. Spakarev, 'Skopski univerzitet', p. 90; and Hadži-Vasilev, 'Za samoupravni sistem obrazovanja', pp. 1082-3.

105. e.g. *Borba* 19 May 1964.

106. Bertolino, 'Mehanizam izbora i reizbornosti', p. 32; and V. Stojanović, 'Problemi u procesu visokoškolskog obrazovanja i naučnog rada', p. 24.

107. *JTS* 3755, p. 51: *Vjesnik* 25 March 1964.

108. Milosavlevski, 'Aktuelni momenat reforme Skopskog Univerziteta', p. 9.

109. Nerkez Smailagić, 'Sveučilište i demokratija', p. 135; and Pribićević, 'Zadaci komunista', p. 61.

110. Ivan Supek, Rector of Zagreb University, *Studentski List* March 1969; Borčić, 'Reforma univerziteta', pp. 25-6; and Jakšić, 'Univerzitet i društvo', pp. 268-9.

111. Grgo Gamulin, 'Uloga sveučilišta u kulturi socijalističkog društva' (The role of the university in the culture of the socialist society), in Derosi-Bjelajac and others, *Sveučilište i Revolucija,* pp. 148-51; see also Borčić, 'Reforma univerziteta', p. 26.

112. J. Djordjević, 'The case for a new modern university', p. 143; Report of University Council meeting, *Sveučilišni Vjesnik* (Zagreb), vol. xi, 'A' Supplement, no. 199 (May 1965), p. 282; Miodrag Čekić, 'Specijalizacija i opšte obrazovanje', p. 56; and Takalić, 'Nove uloge sveučilišta', p. 273.

113. Crvenkovski, 'Reform of higher education', pp. 9-11; *General Law on Faculties and Universities* (1960), Articles 13 and 14; Institute for Social Research, *Innovation in Higher Education,* p. 33; *Borba* 20 March 1964; Dolfe Vogelnik, 'Značenje studija u ciklusima' (The significance of organizing separate levels of study), *Univerzitet Danas,* vol. i, no. 3/4 (1960), pp. 89-92.

114. See for example, report of meeting of University Council, *Sveučilišni Vjesnik* (Zagreb), vol. xi, 'A' Supplement, no. 199 (May 1965), p. 281.

115. See for example, Spakarev, 'Skopski univerzitet', p. 89; Kobe, 'Efikasnost studiranja', p. 54.

116. Mirjana Milojković, 'Studenti Beograda 1945-1969 godine' (Students at Belgrade 1945-1969), *Univerzitet Danas,* vol. x, no. 5 (1969), p. 60.

117. 'Zašto: stepenasta nastava' (Why: separate levels of study), *Ekonomska Politika,* no. 668 (1965), p. 99; and *Studentski List* 23 March 1965, p. 7, and 19 May 1964, p. 3.

118. Spakarev, 'Skopski univerzitet', p. 94; Institute for Social Research, *Innovation in Higher Education,* pp. 84-5; and Kobe, 'Efikasnost studiranja', p. 54.

119. Jakšić, 'Univerzitet i društvo', p. 266; Jovan Djordjević, 'O značaju i ulozi univerziteta danas' (On the significance and role of the university today), *Univerzitet Danas,* vol. vi, no. 4 (1965), pp. 15-23.

120. See (Tito), *Komunist* 25 February 1965; and Crvenkovski, 'Reform of higher education', pp. 15-16.

121. Vogelnik, 'Značenje studija u ciklusima', pp. 89-92.

122. Institute for Social Research, *Innovation in Higher Education,* p. 36; see also Edhem Čamo, 'Jugoslavenski univerziteti pred novim zadacima' (Yugoslav universities face new tasks), *Univerzitet Danas,* vol. i, no. 3/4 (1960), p. 79.

123. On this point, see the bitter comment by Svetozar Stojanović, 'Univerzitet i etatistička struktura' (The university and the state structure), *Gledišta,* vol. vii, no. 12 (December 1966), pp. 1526-7. Also *Student* 6 December 1966, p. 4.

124. Rajković, 'Planiranje kadrova', p. 19; and Sinadinovski, 'Slobodan upis', pp. 51-62.

125. *Student* 8 March 1966, p. 1; Plećaš, 'Problemi samoupravljanja', p. 52; 'Obrazovni procesi', p. 105; *JTS* 5137, p. 45: *Borba* 2 October 1968; *Komunist* 21 October 1965, p. 1.

126. Blagojević, 'Neka pitanja reforme visokog školstva i neposredni politički zadaci na pravnom fakultetu u Beogradu', pp. 17-18; Takalić, 'Nove uloge sveučilišta', p. 272; Borislav Blagojević, 'Nužnost jasnog razgraničenja odnosa izmedju društva i univerziteta (fakulteta) pri rešavanju pitanja visokoškolske nastave' (The necessity of drawing clear lines in the relations between society and university [faculties] when solving the questions of higher education), *Univerzitet Danas,* vol. x, no. 9/10 (1969), pp. 20, 22 (hereinafter cited as 'Rešavanje pitanja'). See also *Šesti Kongres NOJ,* p. 176; Veselinov, 'Aktuelni problemi generacije mladih', p. 8111; and Rajković, 'Planiranje kadrova', p. 19.

127. Radovan Lukić.

128. Reported in *Student* 1 January 1967. See also *Student* 1 January 1966, p. 5, 24 October 1967, p. 4, and 31 October 1967, p. 1.

129. *Komunist* 22 September 1966; *Borba* 3 July 1967; *Studentski List* 27 February 1968.

130. Milenović, 'Dinamika razvoja', p. 258.

131. Presidium of CC Youth Federation (Serbia), *JTS* 4607, p. 32: *Borba* 13 January 1967; *Studentski List* 27 February 1968, p. 3.

132. *JTS* 4836, p. 26: *Komunist* 5 October 1967; see also *JTS* 4494, p. 31: *Politika* 27 August 1966; *JTS* 5035, pp. 45-6: *Borba* 5 June 1968; 'Prijedlog rezolucije o problemima zapošljavanja diplomiranih studenata' (Draft resolution concerning the problems of employment for graduates), prepared for the Eighth Congress YUS, *Studentski List,* Supplement, 9 April 1968, p. 7. Also see Veselinov, 'Aktuelni problemi generacije mladih', p. 142.

133. Useful reviews on this question are contained in *The Eighth Congress of the Union of Yugoslav Youth,* pp. 24, 178-9; and Conclusions of the Presidium and Executive Committee of the CC LC Serbia, *Komunist* 6 June 1968; Predrag Ignjatović, 'Reforma univerziteta', p. 60; see also Bogdanović, 'Problem zapošljavanja mladih kadrova u zemljama u razvoju kao posledica priraštaja stanovništva', p. 39; and *Student* 1 January 1966, p. 5.

134. *JTS,* Special supplement, 3 December 1965, translation of interview reported in *Svet* 14 November 1965, p. 6; see also Stipe Šuvar, 'Društveni položaj i aspiracije omladine' (The social position and aspirations of the young), in Cvjetičanin and others, *Društvo, Revolucija, Omladina,* p. 226; *The Eighth Congress of the Union of Yugoslav Youth,* pp. 168-9.

135. Sirotković, 'O radu sveučilišta', pp. 25-6; *Komunist* 6 June 1968.

136. Bogdan Pilić, 'Uzajamna zavisnost optimalne veličine fakulteta i visokog kvaliteta univerzitetske nastave i naučnog rada' (The interdependence of the optimal size of a faculty and the quality of university teaching and scientific work), *Univerzitet Danas,* vol. x, no. 7/8 (1969), p. 49.

137. Rodoljub Čolaković, 'Usvojen je opšti zakon o školstvu' (The general law on schools is passed), *Prosvetni Pregled,* no. 26 (June 1958), pp. 1-6; Rodoljub Jemuović, *Društveno Upravljanje u Prosveti* (Social Management in Education) (Belgrade: Kultura, 1959).

138. *General Law on Universities* (1954), Article 33, translated in *JTS,* 1295, pp. 4-22.

139. Article 35.
140. Articles 39 and 37.
141. Article 34.
142. Article 46.
143. *JTS* 752, p. 8: *Politika* 4 October 1952.
144. Žagar, 'Reform of the University Education', p. 3; see also Crvenkovski, 'Reform of Higher Education', pp. 15, 16; Miloš Nikolić, 'The New University Law', *Youth Life*, no. 10 (1954), p. 10. This general question of social management in education is considered at length in the following: Čolaković, 'Usvojen je opšti zakon o školstvu', pp. 1-6; and Jemuović, *Društveno Upravljanje u Prosveti*.
145. *JTS* 743, appendix pp. a-d: *Nova Makedonija* 9 March 1952; (Veljko Vlahović), *Komunist* 29 April 1965, p. 8; Bojanović, 'Participation of Students in the Management of Universities', p. 19; Milan Mesić, 'Diskusija' (Discussion), in Derosi-Bjelajac and others, eds, *Sveučilište i Revolucija*, p. 207.
146. *JTS* 3920, p. 4: *Vjesnik* 23 May 1964; Nikolić, 'The New University Law', *Youth Life*, no. 10 (1954), p. 10.
147. Tripalo, 'Social Management of Schools', *Youth Life*, no. 11 (1954), p. 13.
148. (Čolaković, then Vice-President of the Federal Executive Council), *JTS* 1972, p. 32: *Borba* 9 October 1956; *JTS* 1220, pp. 31-2: *Nin* 18 April 1954; Mesić, 'Diskusija', p. 210; Pašalić, 'Sadržaj rada samoupravnih organa', p. 6.
149. Tripalo, 'Social Management of Schools', *Youth Life*, no. 11 (1954), p. 13; Pašalić, 'Sadržaj rada samoupravnih organa', p. 5; 'Social Self-government at Yugoslav Universities', *Youth Life*, no. 45 (1965); Žagar, 'Reform of the University Education', p. 7.
150. Ibid.
151. Article 2.
152. Article 4.
153. Žagar, 'Reform of the University Education', pp. 6-7; Drulović, 'Report on the Current Problems and Future Tasks of the Yugoslav Union of Students', pp. 54-5.
154. Božo Težak, 'Prilozi problematici Jugoslovenskih univerziteta' (Concerning some problems of Yugoslav universities), *Univerzitet Danas*, vol. i, no. 1/2 (1960), p. 7; also remarks by Težak to University Council meeting, *Sveučilišni Vjesnik* (Zagreb), vol. xii, no. 222 (July 1966), p. 411.
155. Ivo Puhan, 'Normativno regulisanje i savremeni društveni odnosi na univerzitetu' (Normative regulation and contemporary social relations at the university), *Univerzitet Danas*, vol. x, no. 7/8 (1969), pp. 82-3; *JTS* 3933, p. 46: *Borba* 27 October 1964.
156. Blagojević, 'Rešavanje pitanja', p. 21.
157. Milenović and Gavanski, 'Razvoj visokog školstva 1939-1968', p. 78.

V. THE MATERIAL SITUATION OF STUDENTS

1. Toša Tišma, 'Naše visoko školstvo u svetlu nekih statističkih podataka' (Our higher education in the light of some statistical data), *Univerzitet Danas*, vol. viii, no. 5 (1967), p. 33.
2. *Student* 10 January 1967, p. 5. The writer was referring to Article 44 of *The Constitution of the Socialist Federal Republic of Yugoslavia* (1963), translated by Petar Mijusković (Belgrade: Sekretarijat Saveznog

Izvršnog Veća za Informacije [Secretariat for Information of the Federal Executive Council], 1963); see also 'Opšti zakon o školstvu' (General Law on Education), *Službeni List FNRJ* (Official Gazette of the FPRY), Belgrade, 16 July 1958, pp. 746-61, especially Articles 7, 9, 10; Toša Tišma, 'Osnovni problemi i nesporazumi samoupravljanja' (The basic problems and misunderstandings arising from self-government), *Univerzitet Danas,* vol. ix, no. 1 (1968), p. 12.

3. Žagar, 'Reform of the university education', p. 5.
4. *Šesti Kongres NOJ,* p. 75.
5. *JTS* 2626, p. 17: *Borba* 5 December 1958.
6. Žagar, 'Reform of the university education', p. 5.
7. *Komunist* 21 September 1967, p. 3, and 4 February 1965, p. 6; *Student* 13 December 1966, p. 4; 'Some current tasks', p. 14; V. Milanović, 'Sociološki aspekti transformacije uloge škole', p. 26; T. Badovinac (President of Union of Yugoslav Youth), *JTS* 4676, p. 43: *Mladost* 22 March 1967.
8. Plećaš, 'Problemi samoupravljanja', p. 52; Vladimir Pezo, 'Društvena pitanja afirmacije omladine' (Social questions concerning the recognition of the young), *Naše Teme,* no. 9 (September 1972), p. 1293.
9. On this point see Milenović, 'Dinamika razvoja', p. 252; Jakšić, 'Univerzitet i društvo', p. 266; and *Student* 27 February 1968, p. 4.
10. Velimir Tomanović, *Socijalna struktura učenika i studenata u Srbiji* (Social structure of pupils and students in Serbia) (Belgrade: Institut Društvenih Nauka, 1970), quoted in Miloš Nikolić, *Omladina i Društvo* (Youth and Society) (Belgrade: Komunist, 1972), p. 56.
11. Milenović, 'Dinamika razvoja', p. 253; see also 'Nacrt rezolucije o materijalnom položaju studenata' (Draft resolution concerning the material situation of students), prepared for the Eighth Congress of YUS, *Studentski List,* Supplement, 9 April 1968, p. 6 (hereinafter cited as 'Nacrt rezolucije').
12. Mihailo Popović, 'Društveni uslovi i mogučnosti školovanja omladine u Jugoslaviji' (Social conditions and educational opportunity for the youth in Yugoslavia), *Sociologija,* vol. x, no. 1 (1968), pp. 93-4; see also Jakšić, 'Univerzitet i društvo', p. 266; Konc, 'Osipanje studenata', pp. 85-6; and Mladen Bošnjak, 'Društveni položaj omladine: socijalne razlike i njihov uticaj na obrazovanje i kulturu mladih' (The social position of the young: social differences and their influence on the education and culture of the young), *Lica* 10 December 1973, p. 10.
13. *JTS* 1497, pp. 10-11: *Politika* 20 February 1955.
14. Dragoslav Mirković, 'Problemi materialnog obezbedjenja studenata' (Problems concerning the material security of students), *Bilten Univerziteta u Sarajevu,* vol. vi (January 1966), pp. 75-6; see also *JTS* 2118, p. 23: *Borba* 4 April 1957; *JTS* 4170, p. 4: *Politika* 16 August 1965; and *Studentski List* 24 March 1964, p. 6.
15. 'Analiza problema studenata' (An analysis of the problems of students), a report prepared for the Republican Secretariat for Education and Culture (Serbia), reprinted in *Student* 12 May 1970.
16. *Studentski List* 26 October 1965, p. 4.
17. Joint Publication Research Service, 'Education in Yugoslavia', p. 55.
18. Velimir Tomanović, 'Problemi socijalne diferencije u oblasti obrazovanja' (Problems of social differences in the area of education), *Sociologija,* vol. x, no. 1 (1965), pp. 111-34; Konc, 'Osipanje studenata', p. 85; *Komunist* 28 October 1965, p. 7; *The Eighth Congress of the Union of Yugoslav*

Youth, p. 136; Plećaš, 'Problemi samoupravljanja', p. 51; and *Student* 20 May 1965, p. 7.

19. *Student* 27 February 1968, p. 2; Milan Zjalić, 'VIII Kongres Saveza Komunista Jugoslavije i' problemi omladine' (The VIII Congress LCY and youth problems), *Naše Teme,* vol. ix, no. 1 (1968), p. 26; Dušan Čalić, 'Omladina kao revolucionarni subjekt' (The youth as a revolutionary subject), in Cvjetičanin and others, *Društvo, Revolucija, Omladina,* p. 174; 'Resolution on education and on the possibilities of acquiring education', *The Eighth Congress of the Union of Yugoslav Youth,* p. 172; Vlado Obradović, 'Gledanje učenika na obrazovanje' (Students' views on education), *Naše Teme,* vol. xi, no. 2 (1967), p. 169.

20. Ibid.

21. Tomanović, 'Problemi socijalne diferencije u oblasti obrazovanja', pp. 123-6.

22. Bošnjak, 'Društveni položaj omladine: socijalne razlike i njihov uticaj na obrazovanje i kulturu mladih', p. 10; see also p. 9.

23. Jelčić, 'Materijalni položaj', p. 263.

24. Calculated from the following publications of the Federal Council for Statistics: *Jugoslavija 1945-1964, Statistički Pregled,* p. 307; and *Statistički Godišnjak SFRJ 1969,* p. 299. See also Ivo Cecić, 'Kreditiranje studenata sa aspekta reforme visokog školstva' (Student loans from the viewpoint of the reform of higher education), *Univerzitet Danas,* vol. x, no. 7/8 (1969), pp. 51, 52 (hereinafter cited as 'Kreditiranje studenata').

25. *JTS* 2532, p. 12: *Borba* 27 March 1960.

26. *Student* 29 October 1963, p. 4; also *JTS* 3734, p. 28: *Komunist* 27 February 1964.

27. *JTS* 3734, p. 27: *Politika* 27 February 1964; *JTS* 3921, p. 51: *Mladost* 23 September 1964; also *Studentski List* 17 November 1964, p. 3.

28. *JTS* 4170, p. 4: *Politika* 16 August 1965; D. Mirković, 'Problemi materialnog obezbedjenja studenata', pp. 67, 78, 79; and *Studentski List* 16 March 1965, p. 7.

29. *JTS* 4267, p. 1: *Politika* 25 November 1965.

30. *Student* 11 October 1966, p. 4. See also *Studentski List* 17 January 1967, p. 3.

31. *JTS* 5016, p. 8: *Politika* 12 May 1968; see also Konc, 'Osipanje studenata', p. 88; 'Materialni položaj studenata' (The material position of students), *Mladost,* no. 469 (1965), p. 4; and *Borba* 1 July 1967, p. 4.

32. *JTS* 3921, p. 51: *Mladost* 23 September 1964.

33. Katica Marendić and Vlastimir Čolić, 'Financial Aid to Pupils and Students', *Yugoslav Survey,* vol. x, no. 2 (1969), p. 148; *JTS* 3921, p. 55: *Večernji List* 1 October 1964; *JTS* 4232, p. 12: *Borba* 17 October 1965.

34. Marendić and Čolić, 'Financial Aid to Pupils and Students', p. 143; *JTS* 3734, p. 27: *Politika* 27 February 1964; Plećaš, 'Problemi samoupravljanja', p. 48.

35. Marendic and Čolić, 'Financial Aid to Pupils and Students', p. 143; *JTS* 3734, p. 27: *Politika* 27 February 1964; Plećaš, 'Problemi samoupravljanja', p. 48.

36. *JTS* 1617, pp. 3-15: 'Decree Proclaiming the Basic Law on Scholarships', *Official Gazette,* no. 32 (13 July 1955), Item 349, Article 41.

37. Articles 36 and 44.

38. e.g. figure for 1958/59 cited in *Student* 29 October 1963, p. 4.

39. *JTS* 1587, p. 11: *Borba* 29 June 1955; see also Joint Publication Research Service, 'Education in Yugoslavia', p. 26.

40. Milenović, 'Dinamika razvoja', p. 255.
41. *JTS* 3734, p. 27: *Politika* 27 February 1964; *Student* 29 October 1963, p. 4; Marendić and Čolić, 'Financial Aid to Pupils and Students', p. 144; *Student* 8 October 1963, p. 4; *Borba* 1 July 1967, p. 4; and *Student* 1 January 1966, p. 4.
42. *JTS* 4267, p. 1: *Politika* 25 November 1965; *Student* 1 January 1967, p. 5.
43. *JTS* 3734, p. 27: *Politika* 27 February 1964; *Komunist* 9 July 1964, p. 4; *Student* 29 October 1963, p. 4; *Student* 11 October 1966, p. 4.
44. *JTS* 3729, p. 10: *Borba* 26 February 1964.
45. Ibid., and *JTS* 2745, p. 19: *Borba* 9 December 1960. See also *Studentski List* 18 February 1964, p. 5.
46. *JTS* 2745, p. 19: *Borba* 9 December 1960; *JTS* 2206, pp. 42-3: *Borba* 21 July 1957; *Komunist* 1 September 1966, p. 7.
47. *JTS* 3799, p. 33: *Borba* 19 May 1964.
48. *Komunist* 13 August 1964, p. 4; *JTS* 1450, p. 27: *Borba* 19 January 1955.
49. *Komunist* 13 August 1964, p. 4; *JTS* 4178, p. 16: *Borba* 18 August 1965; see also *Komunist* 1 September 1966, p. 7.
50. *JTS* 3734, p. 27: *Politika* 27 February 1964; Vladimir Bakarić, 'Diskusija' (Discussion), in Derosi-Bjelajac and others, *Sveučilište i Revolucija,* p. 87; *Student* 4 January 1963, p. 1; *JTS* 4013, p. 6: *Borba* 24 January 1965; *JTS* 4170, p. 4: *Politika* 15 August 1965.
51. 'Decree Proclaiming the Basic Law on Scholarships', *Official Gazette,* no. 32 (13 July 1955), Item 349, Article 2.
52. Articles 30 and 26.
53. Articles 7, 31 and 32.
54. Article 32.
55. *JTS* 2118, pp. 23-4: *Borba* 4 April 1957.
56. *JTS* 3734, p. 27: *Komunist* 27 February 1964; see also Kiril Penušliski, 'Stipendije ili kreditiranje studenata' (Scholarships or loans for students), *Univerzitet Danas,* vol. i, no. 5/6 (1960), p. 183; Cecić, 'Kreditiranje studenata', p. 52.
57. *JTS* 4030, p. 16: *Borba* 20 February 1965.
58. *Youth Life,* no. 44 (March 1965), p. 5; *Student* 14 December 1965, p. 1, and 16 November 1965, p. 1.
59. *Youth Life,* no. 44 (March 1965), p. 7; also D. Mirković, 'Problemi materialnog obezbedjenja studenata', p. 77.
60. *Komunist* 1 September 1966, p. 7; see also Cecić, 'Kreditiranje studenata', p. 51; *Komunist* 13 August 1964, p. 4. Also *Student* 22 March 1966, p. 9.
61. *JTS* 4298, p. 31: *Borba* 8 January 1966.
62. (Tomislav Badovinac), *JTS* 4533, p. 44: *Borba* 12 October 1966; see also *Student* 15 March 1966, p. 9.
63. *Politika* 9 July 1968, p. 4; *Komunist* 29 April 1965, p. 8.
64. *JTS* 2532, p. 12: *Borba* 27 March 1960.
65. *JTS* 3734, p. 27: *Komunist* 27 February 1964.
66. *Komunist* 1 September 1966, p. 7; 'Excerpts from the Report of the YUS Central Board submitted at the III Congress of the YUS', *Yugoslav Student News,* no. 21 (October 1956), pp. 1-39.
67. 'Treća plenarna sjednica Zajednice Jugoslavenskih Univerziteta' (Third plenary meeting of the Association of Yugoslav Universities), *Univerzitet Danas,* vol. i, no 3/4 (1960), p. 117; Report of proceedings at Congress of Union of Yugoslav Youth, *JTS* 4938, p. 16: *Borba* 10 February 1968; *Politika* 9 July 1968, p. 4; and *Studentski List* 25 May 1965, p. 5.
68. *JTS* 4965, p. 38: *Borba* 12 March 1968; *Borba* 5 June 1968, p. 6;

V. Stojanović, 'Reforma univerziteta', p. 16; see also *JTS*, Supplement, 3 December 1965, p. 5, for report of interview with V. Bakarić, Secretary of CC LC (Croatia) *Svet* 5 September 1965; and *Student* 22 March 1966, p. 9.

69. Cecić, 'Kreditiranje studenata', p. 51; 'Treća plenarna sjednica Zajednice Jugoslavenskih Univerziteta', p. 117.
70. *JTS* 4218, p. 3: *Komunist* 30 September 1965.
71. (M. Špiljak), *JTS* 4277, p. 9: *Borba* 4 December 1965; see also Cecić, 'Kreditiranje studenata', pp. 50-3; Remarks by Professor Vladimir Serdar to the University Council, *Sveučilišni Vjesnik* (Zagreb), vol. xii, no. 222 (July 1966), pp. 421-3.
72. *Student* 18 February 1964, p. 4.
73. See above, Table 10, p. 99.
74. *JTS* 4509, p. 9: *Borba* 14 September 1966; see also 'Nacrt rezolucije', p. 6; also *JTS* 3921, p. 51: *Mladost* 23 September 1964; *Borba* (Z) 1 July 1967, p. 4; *Student* 29 October 1963, p. 4; *Studentski List* 5 November 1968, p. 3; and *Student* 18 February 1964, p. 4.
75. *JTS* 4636, p. 25: *Borba* 16 February 1967.
76. *JTS* 3921, p. 51: *Mladost* 23 September 1964; also Miloš Nikolić, 'Economic Problems concerning Students and International Student Co-operation', *Yugoslav Student News,* no. 20 (August 1956), p. 65.
77. *JTS* 4019, p. 33: *Politika* 11 February 1965. See also *Student* 10 May 1966, p. 1, and 18 October 1966, p. 4.
78. *Student* 21 May 1968, p. 11; see also *Student* 19 April 1966, p. 9; Blažo Zec, 'Deset godina rada ekonomskog fakulteta u Titogradu' (Ten years work of the economics department in Titograd), *Univerzitet Danas,* vol. xii, no. 1 (1971), p. 73.
79. *Student* 21 May 1968, p. 11; see also *JTS* 3921, p. 51: *Mladost* 23 September 1964.
80. *Student* 21 February 1967, n.p.; 'Excerpts from the Report of the YUS Central Board submitted at the III Congress of the YUS'.
81. On this point see 'Nacrt rezolucije', p. 6; Joža Šlander, 'Socijalna struktura studenata i jedinstvo njihove društvene akcije' (The social structure of the student body and the unity of their social action), *Ideje,* vol. i, no. 2 (1970), p. 42.
82. *Student* 7 April 1970, p. 6.
83. *Student* 18 October 1966; D. Mirković, 'Problemi materialnog obezbedjenja studenata', pp. 65-7; 'Nacrt rezolucije', p. 6.
84. *Student* 14 May 1968, p. 5.
85. (Borislav Blagojević), *Student* 24 September 1963, p. 3.
86. Radoslav Ćurić, 'Neki stavovi studenata o disciplini u studentskim domovima' (Some student views on discipline in student hostels), *Univerzitet Danas,* vol. ix, no. 1 (1968), pp. 24-32.
87. *JTS* 3921, p. 51: *Mladost* 23 September 1964; Milojković, 'Studenti Beograda 1945-1969 godine', p. 58.
88. *Student* 22 November 1966, p. 4. Also *Student* 20 February 1968, p. 5.
89. See, for example, report of conditions at Novi Sad, *JTS* 4019, p. 33: *Politika* 11 February 1965.
90. (Milan Dragović), *JTS* 3822, p. 7: *Borba* 19 June 1964; see also *Student* 10 October 1966, p. 4; and 'Nacrt rezolucije', p. 6.
91. Report of the meeting of the Fifth Plenum of CC YUS, *Student* 29 October 1963, p. 4.
92. *Student* 18 October 1966, 10 January 1967, 1 November 1966, p. 4, and 11 October 1966, p. 5.

VI. Youth Organizations and the Ideological Education
of the Yugoslav Youth

1. Tito's address to the Eighth Party Congress, *Youth Life,* no. 44 (March 1965), p. 1.
2. *Youth Life,* no. 8 (1953), p. 7; and Mirko Bolfek, 'Razvoj i uloga omladinskog pokreta poslije kongresa ujedinjenja' (The development and role of the youth movement after the Congress on Unification), in Cvjetičanin and others, *Društvo, Revolucija, Omladina,* p. 31 (hereinafter cited as 'Omladinski pokret').
3. 'Statute of the Union of Yugoslav Students (1956)', *Yugoslav Student News,* no. 22 (October 1956), Article 1.
4. Ibid., Article 5.
5. Ibid., Article 7.
6. 'Conclusions of the Fourth Congress of the Yugoslav Union of Students', pp. 62-4; see also 'Report of Central Board YUS', *Yugoslav Student News,* no. 21 (October 1956), pp. 2-3.
7. *JTS* 739, p. 9: *Borba* 10 March 1952; see also *JTS* 868, p. 13: *Borba* 21 February 1953.
8. e.g. 'Students at the rostrum', *Youth Life,* vol. i, no. 6 (1952), p. 4; see also Milojković, 'Studenti Beograda 1945-1969 godine', p. 54; *JTS* 888, pp. 4-8: *Omladina* 18 March 1953.
9. *Jugoslovenski Savremenici—Ko je Ko u Jugoslaviji* (Contemporary figures in Yugoslavia—Who's Who in Yugoslavia) (Belgrade: Hronometar, 1970).
10. *The Eighth Congress of the Union of Yugoslav Youth,* p. 17.
11. See the section titled 'Explaining the failure of the youth organizations' below, p. 135 ff.
12. e.g. Tito's speech of 27 September 1946, to youth building the Brčko-Banovići railway, in Josip Broz Tito, *Selected Speeches and Articles 1941-1961* (Zagreb: Naprijed, 1963), pp. 72-4; (*Četvrti*) *IV Kongres SKOJ-a* (Fourth Congress of the League of Communist Youth of Yugoslavia) (Belgrade, 1948), especially pp. 89-95; *Peti Kongres Narodne Omladine Jugoslavije* (Fifth Congress of the Yugoslav People's Youth) (Belgrade: Central Committee Yugoslav People's Youth, 1953), pp. 13-15 (hereinafter cited as *Peti Kongres NOJ*); and *The Eighth Congress of the Union of Yugoslav Youth,* p. 131.
13. *Youth Life,* no. 8 (1953), p. 7; Mika Tripalo, 'To prepare and adapt young people for participation in the system of social self-government', *Youth Life,* no. 25 (1958), p. 10 (hereinafter cited as 'To prepare young people'); *JTS* 742, p. 20: *Politika* 14 March 1952; and *JTS* 857, p. 7: *Borba* 9 February 1953.
14. *Youth Life,* no. 8 (1953), p. 7; and Tripalo, 'To prepare young people', pp. 10-11.
15. *JTS* 1470, pp. 8-9: *Omladina* 2 February 1955.
16. e.g. Tripalo, 'To prepare young people', pp. 10-11.
17. e.g. Jakša Bučević, 'Komsomol today', *Youth Life,* no. 8 (1953), p. 15; and *Peti Kongres NOJ,* pp. 30, 36.
18. *Youth Life,* no. 8 (1953), p. 7; and Tripalo, 'To prepare young people', pp. 10-11.
19. *Youth Life,* no. 8 (1953), p. 8; and *Peti Kongres NOJ,* especially p. 37.
20. 'Constitution of the Yugoslav Union of Students', *Yugoslav Student News,* no. 1 (April 1952), pp. 6-7.

21. T. Badovinac, 'To be a revolutionary', *Youth Life,* no. 44 (March 1965), pp. 12-13.
22. (Saša Mikić), Keynote address to the 1966 Congress of YUS, *Student* 15 March 1966, p. 1.
23. T. Badovinac, 'To be a revolutionary', *Youth Life,* no. 44 (March 1965), pp. 12-13.
24. *Komunist* 5 June 1959; also *JTS* 1799, p. 27: *Borba* 15 March 1956.
25. *JTS* 4579, p. 12: *Komunist* 8 December 1966; Velimir Tomanović, 'O menjanju položaja, uloge i odnosa u omladinskom pokretu u novije vreme' (On changing the position, role and relations in the youth movement in newer times), in Cvjetičanin and others, *Društvo, Revolucija, Omladina,* p. 45 (hereinafter cited as 'Omladinski pokret'); and Pavle Novosel, 'Omladinska organizacija danas' (The youth organization today), in ibid., p. 206.
26. *JTS* 4726, p. 1: *Politika* 1 June 1967.
27. Dušan Plenča, ed., *The Yugoslav Youth Movement* (Belgrade: Mladost, 1969), p. 173.
28. *JTS* 4920, p. 4: *Mladost* 28 December 1967; see also Bolfek, 'Omladinski pokret', p. 35; and *JTS* 4918, p. 46: *Mladost* 21 December 1967.
29. (Badovinac), *JTS* 4831, p. 14: *Borba* 4 October 1967; Tomanović, 'Omladinski pokret', p. 44; Radoš Smiljković, 'Transformacija odnosa Saveza Komunista—omladina u samoupravljanju (Changes in the attitude of the League of Communists—the youth in the system of self-management), in Cvjetičanin and others, *Društvo, Revolucija, Omladina,* pp. 230-1; and *JTS* 4654, p. 27: *Borba* 9 March 1967.
30. 'Komisija za organizaciono-politički razvoj' (Commission for organizational-political development), paper prepared for VI Congress YUS, pp. 10-11 (mimeographed); *Komunist* 1 September 1966, p. 7; Nikolić, *Omladina i Društvo,* p. 12; and T. Badovinac, address to *The Eighth Congress of the Union of Yugoslav Youth,* pp. 65-6.
31. 'Report of Central Board YUS', p. 17.
32. Mika Tripalo, 'On the occasion of discussions concerning the "crisis" of the younger generation', *Socialist Thought and Practice,* no. 2 (August 1961), pp. 89-103 (hereinafter cited as 'Crisis').
33. Ibid., p. 91.
34. Ibid., p. 93.
35. Ibid., p. 94.
36. Ibid., pp. 95-6.
37. Ibid., p. 97.
38. Ibid., p. 100.
39. *JTS* 1013, pp. b, c: *Nova Makedonija* 16 July 1953; *Yugoslav Student News,* no. 28-29 (July 1959), p. 9; and 'Commentary on the decisions adopted at the Third Congress of the Yugoslav Union of Students', *Yugoslav Student News,* no. 21 (October 1956), p. 61.
40. *Peti Kongres NOJ,* pp. 25-6. My emphasis.
41. *The Eighth Congress of the Union of Yugoslav Youth,* p. 185.
42. *Šesti Kongres NOJ,* p. 135, also pp. 65, 134, 209. Also see *Peti Kongres NOJ,* pp. 25-6; 'Komisija za organizaciono-politički razvoj', p. 1.
43. *Yugoslav Student News,* no. 28-29 (July 1959), pp. 16-17; and 'Some current tasks', pp. 5-17.
44. e.g. *JTS* 2315, p. 37: *Borba* 26 November 1957.
45. 'Resolution of the Eighth Congress on the future responsibilities of the League of Communists of Yugoslavia', p. 2912.

46. 'Yugoslav youth at work drives', *Yugoslav Student News,* no. 27 (December 1955), p. 17; and Tito to *Eighth Congress of the Union of Yugoslav Youth,* p. 20.
47. *Youth Life,* no. 22-23 (1956), p. 7.
48. *JTS* 701, pp. 25-6: *Borba* 3 August 1952.
49. See for example, *Peti Kongres NOJ,* pp. 32-3; and *Šesti Kongres NOJ,* p. 146, also pp. 58, 59, 89.
50. e.g. L.P., 'The People's Youth Organization', *Yugoslav Survey,* vol. i, no. 3 (1960), p. 315; see also 'Speech by Milovan Djilas', *Youth Life,* no. 8 (1953), p. 10.
51. 'What is [the] "revisionism" of the People's Youth Leaders?', *Youth Life,* vol. viii, no. 29 (1959); also L.P., 'The People's Youth Organization', *Yugoslav Survey,* vol. i, no. 3 (1960), p. 315.
52. 'Crisis', p. 96.
53. *JTS* 701, pp. 25-6: *Borba* 3 August 1952.
54. *JTS* 4726, p. 1: *Politika* 1 June 1967.
55. *The Eighth Congress of the Union of Yugoslav Youth,* pp. 71-2.
56. Ibid., p. 143.
57. Ibid., p. 145.
58. e.g. Vukašin Stambolić (president of YUS), 'The role and basic tasks of the Yugoslav Union of Students in the socialist upbringing and speedier vocational qualification of students', *Yugoslav Student News,* no. 28-29 (July 1959), p. 4 cites a percentage of 82.3; see also *Yugoslav Student News,* no. 14 (June 1955), p. 10, which cites a percentage of 95.
59. *Studentski List* 18 May 1965, p. 5.
60. Milosav Janićijević and others, *Jugoslovenski Studenti i Socijalizam* (Yugoslav Students and Socialism) (Belgrade: Institut Društvenih Nauka, 1966) (hereinafter cited as *Studenti i Socijalizam*).
61. Jugoslav Stanković, 'Studenti na radu, u društvu i slobodnom vremenu' (Students at work, in society and at leisure), in Janićijević and others, *Studenti i Socijalizam,* pp. 338, 347 (hereinafter cited as 'Studenti na radu').
62. Ibid., p. 347.
63. No. 28/29, p. 13.
64. J. Stanković, 'Studenti na radu', pp. 346, 347.
65. Manojlo Broćić, 'Stavovi i ocene studenata o nekim društvenim vrednostima' (Student attitudes towards and appraisals of some social values), in Janićijević and others, *Studenti i Socijalizam,* p. 221.
66. *Komunist* 9 February 1961.
67. Source for this and following three paragraphs is *Komunist* 9 February 1961.
68. Milosav Janićijević, 'Društveno-politički i ideološki stavovi Jugoslovenskih studenata' (Socio-political and ideological attitudes of Yugoslav students), in Janićijević and others, *Studenti i Socijalizam,* p. 99.
69. Ibid., p. 16.
70. Ibid. The remaining 1 per cent gave no answer.
71. Ibid., p. 104.
72. e.g. James W. Prothro and Charles M. Grigg, 'Agreement on fundamentals', in *The American Political System: Notes and Readings,* ed. Bernard E. Brown and John C. Wahlke (Homewood, Illinois: The Dorsey Press, 1967), especially p. 156.
73. Broćić, 'Stavovi i ocene studenata o nekim društvenim vrednostima', p. 220.

74. *Student* 23 April 1963, p. 3; also *Studentski List* 18 February 1964, p. 5.
75. (Saša Mikić), *Student* 15 March 1966, p. 1; also *Studentski List* 1 March 1966, p. 2 (editorial).
76. *Student* 17 January 1967, p. 1.
77. e.g. *Student* 8 March 1966, pp. 2, 3.
78. *Student* 19 December 1967, p. 1.
79. *JTS* 4924, p. 50: *Vjesnik* 15 January 1968; *Studentski List* 22 November 1966, p. 3, and 18 October 1966, p. 3. See also *Student* 14 January 1964, p. 11.
80. *JTS* 4579, p. 12: *Komunist* 8 December 1966; see also *JTS* 4534, p. 15: *Komunist* 13 October 1966; *JTS* 4533, p. 45: *Borba* 12 October 1966; and Muratović, 'Političko organizovanje i djelovanje omladine', p. 158.
81. *JTS* 4059, p. 16: *Borba* 26 March 1965.
82. *JTS* 4494, p. 21: *Politika* 29 August 1966; see also Tomanović, 'Omladinski pokret', p. 45; *JTS* 4570, p. 4: *Borba* 25 November 1966; and Tito's speech to the Eighth Party Congress, *Youth Life,* no. 44 (1965), p. 4.
83. (T. Badovinac), *Komunist* 10 March 1966, p. 3.
84. *JTS* 4470, p. 4: *Politika* 1 August 1966.
85. *JTS* 4847, p. 10: *Mladost* 12 October 1967.
86. (T. Badovinac) *Komunist* 10 March 1966, p. 3; also *Student* 8, November 1966, p. 4.
87. See for example, *Komunist* 21 September 1967, p. 3.
88. *JTS* 4390, p. 1: *Borba* 26 April 1966; and *Studentski List* 8 November 1966, p. 3. See also Veselinov, 'Aktuelni problemi generacije mladih', p. 819.
89. *Šesti Kongres NOJ,* p. 196.
90. *Komunist* 9 February 1961; also *JTS* 4607, p. 23: *Komunist* 12 January 1967.
91. *Student* 23 March 1965, p. 1.
92. *JTS* 4607, p. 23: *Komunist* 12 January 1967.
93. *JTS* 4564, p. 36: *Borba* 19 November 1966.
94. Muratović, 'Političko organizovanje i djelovanje omladine', p. 160; also *Studentski List* 25 October 1966, p. 3.
95. *JTS* 4847, p. 10: *Mladost* 12 October 1967; *Student* 8 March 1966, p. 2; and Želimir Žilnik, participant in round table discussion, 'Diskusija: društveno angažovanje i organizovanje omladine' (Discussion: public involvement and organization of the youth), *Gledišta,* vol. vii, no. 5 (May 1966), p. 685 (hereinafter cited as 'Diskusija').
96. Veselinov, 'Aktuelni problemi generacije mladih', p. 819; see also Bolfek, 'Omladinski pokret', p. 31; and Tomanović, 'Omladinski pokret', p. 44.
97. (Radovan Lukić), *Student* 1 January 1967, p. 5.
98. *Student* 9 January 1968, p. 4.
99. *JTS* 3916, p. 48: *Borba* 6 October 1964; *Komunist* 21 September 1967, p. 3; Interview with Vladimir Bakarić, *JTS* (special supplement), 3 December 1965, p. 4: *Svet* 5 September 1965; and *Student* 30 April 1968, p. 5.
100 *JTS* (special supplement), 3 December 1965, pp. 7, 8.
101. *JTS* 4570, p. 4: *Borba* 25 November 1966; Novosel, 'Omladinska organizacija danas', p. 206; and Žilnik, 'Diskusija', p. 684.
102. *JTS* 4489, p. 1: *Politika* 23 August 1966; see also Oleg Mandić, 'Suvremeni problemi omladine' (Problems of today's young generation), in Derosi-Bjelajac and others, *Sveučilište i Revolucija,* p. 179; and Mesić, 'Diskusija', p. 208.

103. *Student* 26 April 1966, p. 9; see also *Student* 1 November 1966, p. 9. For another example of the attitude of the activists, see *Student* 16 March 1965, p. 1.

104. Bolfek, 'Omladinski pokret', p. 33.

105. Tomanović, 'Omladinski pokret', p. 44.

106. *JTS* 4570, p. 4: *Borba* 25 November 1966.

107. (Mufid Memija), *Student* 18 April 1967, p. 1; see also Petar Vodopivec, 'O razlozima za više vidova reorganizacije studentskog udruživanja na Ljubljanskom univerzitetu' (The reasons for multiform reorganization of student associations at Ljubljana University), *Univerzitet Danas,* vol. x, no. 9/10 (1969), p. 122; and *Studentski List* 22 November 1966, p. 3.

108. *Student* 23 May 1967, p. 3; also (T. Badovinac), *JTS* 4831, p. 14: *Borba* 4 October 1967; Tomanović, 'Omladinski pokret', p. 44; and Smiljković, 'Transformacija odnosa Saveza Komunista—omladina u samoupravljanju', pp. 230-1.

109. *The Eighth Congress of the Union of Yugoslav Youth,* p. 65.

110. *Student* 9 January 1968, p. 4; Manojlo Broćić, 'Omladina i politika' (Youth and politics), *Gledišta,* vol. viii, no. 2 (1967), pp. 167-8; and Bolfek, 'Omladinski pokret', p. 33.

111. *JTS* 4579, p. 12: *Komunist* 8 December 1966; Tomanović, 'Omladinski pokret', p. 45; and Novosel, 'Omladinska organizacija danas', p. 206.

112. (T. Badovinac), *JTS* 4831, p. 14: *Borba* 4 October 1967; Tomanović, 'Omladinski pokret', p. 44; Smiljković, 'Transformacija odnosa Saveza Komunista—omladina u samoupravljanju', pp. 230-1; *JTS* 4654, p. 27: *Borba* 9 March 1967; and Novosel, 'Omladinska organizacija danas', p. 207.

113. 'Report of Central Board YUS', p. 17; *Student* 19 April 1966, p. 1.

114. *Studentski List* (editorial) 1 March 1966, p. 2.

115. Konc, 'Osipanje studenata', p. 87; and Bezić, 'Stavovi studenata', p. 80.

116. *Studentski List* 23 April 1968, p. 3; see also *Student* 8 March 1966, p. 5; and *JTS* 4353, p. 15: *Politika* 13 March 1966.

117. Konc, 'Osipanje studenata', p. 87; and *Studentski List* 23 April 1968, p. 3.

118. *Student* 19 December 1967, p. 4. See also Žilnik, 'Diskusija', p. 685.

119. J. Djordjević, 'Društvena osnova prava studenata na samoupravljanje', pp. 14-15.

120. *Student* 1 January 1967, p. 5; and Žilnik, 'Diskusija', p. 685.

121. *Komunist* 21 September 1967, p. 3.

122. Novosel, 'Omladinska organizacija danas', p. 209.

123. Ibid., p. 211; *Student* 14 March 1967, p. 3; Radomir Lukić, 'Osnovni problemi omladine: podruštvljenje, usvajanje kulture, vaspitanje' (Basic problems of the youth: socialization, identification with the culture, education), *Sociologija,* vol. x, no. 1 (1968), pp. 41-2; and T. Badovinac, 'To be a revolutionary', *Youth Life,* no. 44 (March 1965), pp. 12-13.

124. *JTS* 5201, p. 35: *Politika* 18 December 1968.

125. (P. Popović), *JTS* 4470, p. 4: *Politika* 1 August 1966.

126. (Djuro Kovačević), *Student* 19 December 1967, p. 1; see also *Student* 29 March 1966, p. 3.

127. (Djuro Kovačević), *Student* 10 January 1967, p. 4; *Student,* 10 January 1967, p. 1, and 1 September 1966, p. 4; and Srećko Mihailović, 'Drugo savetovanje studenata sociologije' (Second council of sociology students), *Sociologija,* vol. ix, no. 1 (1967), p. 89.

128. Danica Mojsin, participant in a symposium on youth questions reported in *Gledišta,* vol. viii, no. 3 (1967), p. 393.

129. *Studentski List* 9 January 1968, p. 3, and 7 November 1967, p. 2.

130. *Student* 1 January 1968, p. 2.
131. Ibid., 17 January 1967, p. 1.
132. Ibid., 1 September 1966, p. 4.
133. Ibid., 17 January 1967, p. 1.
134. *JTS* 5020, p. 9: *Borba* 18 May 1968.
135. Ibid.; and *JTS* 4505, p. 27: *Komunist* 1 September 1966.
136. *Studentski List* 18 October 1966, p. 3.
137. *JTS* 4998, p. 45: *Politika* 20 April 1968. On this point concerning the possibility of demonstrations, see *Studentski List* 13 December 1966, p. 4.
138. *JTS* 5020, p. 9: *Borba* 18 May 1968; and *JTS* 4997, p. 47: *Borba* 19 April 1968.
139. *Student* 1 January 1967, p. 4.
140. e.g. *JTS* 2018, p. 19: *Borba* 25 November 1956; *JTS* 743, pp. 24-30: *Borba* 16 March 1952; *JTS* 1514, p. 5: *Politika* 2 April 1955; and *Studentski List* 29 March 1966, p. 7.
141. *JTS* 1514, p. 5: *Politika* 2 April 1955.
142. e.g. *JTS* 2018, p. 19: *Borba* 25 November 1956; and *JTS* 1972, pp. 30-4: *Borba* 9 October 1956.
143. *Yugoslav Student News*, no. 28/29 (July 1959), p. 22.
144. Ibid.; and 'Some current tasks', pp. 5-17.
145. 'Conclusions of the Fourth Congress of the Yugoslav Union of Students', pp. 68-9.
146. *JTS* 2051, pp. 10-11: *Borba* 14 January 1957; see also Drulović, 'Report on the current problems and future tasks of the Yugoslav Union of Students', p. 50; and *Student* 2 March 1965, p. 1, 16 January 1968, p. 11, and 20 February 1968, p. 9.
147. *Yugoslav Student News*, no. 28/29 (July 1959), pp. 12-13; and *JTS* 743, pp. 24-30: *Borba* 16 March 1952.
148. *JTS* 2106, p. 11: *Student* 11 March 1957.
149. *JTS* 739, p. 13: *Borba* 10 March 1952.
150. *Yugoslav Student News*, no. 24 (July 1957), pp. 24-5.
151. Josip Broz Tito, *Tito Omladini* (Tito to the Youth) (Belgrade: Mlado Pokolenje, 1961), pp. 239f.
152. *Komunist* 21 May 1959.
153. *JTS* 2118. p. 24: *Borba* 4 April 1957; *JTS* 3316, p. 29: *Borba* 20 October 1962; and Borislav J. Dimković, 'Gdje je i kuda će diplomirani sociolog?' (Where is the sociology graduate and where will he go?), *Gledišta*, vol. viii, no. 1 (January 1967), p. 91.
154. *JTS* 3316, p. 29: *Borba* 20 October 1962; and *Yugoslav Student News*, no. 28/29 (July 1959), pp. 12-13.
155. *JTS* 601, pp. 4-5: *Politika* 27 April 1952; see also *JTS* 586, p. 4: *Politika* 11 April 1952.
156. e.g. *JTS* 650, p. 13: *Borba* 28 June 1952; and *JTS* 599, p. 24: *Borba* 27 April 1952.
157. *JTS* 747, p. 3: *Politika* 16 March 1952.
158. *JTS* 1926, p. 6: *Naš Glas* 4 August 1956.
159. *Politika* 2 November 1959; *JTS* 702, pp. 4-6: *Borba* 5 August 1952; and 'Some current tasks'.
160. Hoffman and Neal, *Yugoslavia and the New Communism*, p. 201; see also comments by Tito re decline in reputation of communists, *JTS* 743, pp. 23-4: *Borba* 16 March 1952.
161. e.g. *JTS* 4459, p. 1: *Komunist* 4 July 1966; and *Studentski List* 16 March 1965, p. 5.

162. *Borba* 12 May 1959; and *Studentski List* 13 May 1969, p. 3.
163. Tito's address to Eighth Party Congress, *Youth Life*, no. 44 (March 1965), p. 4; *JTS* 4018, p. 1: *Komunist* 4 February 1965; and *JTS* 4011, p. 12: *Politika* 1 February 1965.
164. Tomanović, 'Problemi socijalne diferencije u oblasti obrazovanja', p. 123-6.
165. 'Conclusions of the IV Congress of the Yugoslav Union of Students', *JTS* 1926, p. 6: *Naš Glas* 4 August 1956; *JTS* 4051, p. 35: *Politika* 19 March 1965; *Youth Life*, no. 12 (1955), p. 5; 'Voluntary youth camps—schools of comradeship', *Youth Life*, no. 45 (1965), p. 19; Nikolić, *Omladina i Društvo*, p. 12; Pavle Novosel, 'Omladina u savremenom svijetu' (Youth in the contemporary world), *Sociologija*, vol. x, no. 1 (1968), p. 20; *Student* 19 April 1966, p. 9, and 23 April 1968, p. 5; and *Studentski List* 24 May 1966, p. 2.
166. Janićijević, 'Društveno-politički i ideološki stavovi jugoslovenskih studenata', pp. 72-3.
167. *JTS* 739, pp. 10-11: *Borba* 10 March 1952.
168. See Fred Warner Neal, *Titoism in Action: The Reforms in Yugoslavia after 1948* (Berkeley and Los Angeles: University of California Press, 1958), especially pp. 47, 49, 64-9 (hereinafter cited as *Titoism in Action*).
169. *JTS* 1189, p. 11: *Borba* 10 March 1954.
170. *JTS* 2018, pp. 19-20: *Borba* 25 November 1956.
171. See Tito's address to the Sixth Plenum CC LCY, *JTS* 1798, p. 38: *Borba* 14 March 1956: and 'Commentary on the decisions adopted at the Third Congress of the Yugoslav Union of Students', p. 61.
172. *JTS* 3218, p. 47: *Politika* 21 June 1962; see also *JTS* 2634, p. 9: *Politika* 13 December 1958.
173. *Šesti Kongres NOJ*, p. 135, also pp. 65, 209. See also 'Conclusions of the Fourth Congress of the Yugoslav Union of Students', p. 65; and J. Stanković, 'Studenti na radu', p. 341.
174. e.g. *Peti Kongres NOJ*, pp. 25-6; 'Komisija za organizaciono-politički razvoj', p. 1; and *Šesti Kongres NOJ*, p. 134.
175. A useful discussion of the confusions and contradictions of this period and of the Brioni Plenum is contained in Neal, *Titoism in Action*, especially pp. 47, 49, 64-9.
176. *JTS* 1798, pp. 37, 38: *Borba* 14 March 1956; see also *JTS* 1802, p. 13: *Politika* 17 March 1956.
177. *JTS* 1799, p. 27: *Borba* 15 March 1956.
178. See for example, (Edvard Kardelj), *JTS* 1800, p. 29: *Borba* 15 March 1956.
179. Hoffman and Neal, *Yugoslavia and the New Communism*, p. 200.
180. *Yugoslav Student News*, no. 28/29 (July 1959), p. 14.
181. J. Stanković, 'Studenti na radu', pp. 345, 346.
182. *Youth Life*, no. 44 (March 1965), p. 6.
183. *JTS* 4972, p. 12: *Politika* 17 March 1968; *Student* 19 December 1967, p. 1.
184. *Student* 29 October 1963, p. 4.
185. Ibid., 9 April 1966, p. 5.
186. *The Eighth Congress of the Union of Yugoslav Youth*, p. 67.
187. *JTS* 4918, p. 46: *Mladost* 21 December 1967.
188. *Student* 22 March 1966, p. 3.
189. *Komunist* 5 June 1959; also *JTS* 1799, p. 27: *Borba* 15 March 1956; and Drulović, 'Report on the current problems and future tasks of the Yugoslav Union of Students', pp. 46, 48.

190. e.g. Neal, *Titoism in Action,* pp. 13, 30.
191. *JTS* 4570, p. 4: *Borba* 25 November 1966; Žilnik, 'Diskusija', pp. 686-7; and *JTS* 5061, p. 16: *Borba* 5 July 1968.
192. *Studentski List* 9 January 1968, p. 1, and 14 November 1967, p. 1.
193. Ibid., 9 January 1968, p. 1; and *JTS* 4219, p. 26: *Politika* 19 January 1968.
194. *Studentski List* 9 January 1968, pp. 1, 3, and 17 January 1967, p. 3.
195. Report by Mika Tripalo (Secretary of the Executive Committee CC LC Croatia), *Vjesnik* 8 February 1967, p. 2; and *Studentski List* 17 January 1967, p. 1.
196. *Studentski List* 9 January 1968, p. 1.
197. *JTS* 4917, p. 14: *Borba* 17 January 1968; see also *JTS* 4910, p. 27: *Borba* 9 January 1968.
198. *Studentski List* 7 May 1968, p. 4.
199. *JTS* 4919, p. 26: *Politika* 19 January 1968; also *Student* 16 January 1968, p. 4.
200. *JTS* 4570, p. 4: *Borba,* 25 November 1966.
201. *Komunist* 8 December 1966, p. 1.
202. *JTS* 5061, p. 16: *Borba* 5 July 1968.
203. e.g. *JTS* 4494, p. 16: *Politika* 26 August 1966.
204. e.g. Compare Conclusions of VI Congress of the Union of Students (*Studentski List* 18 February 1964, p. 5) with editorial in *Studentski List* (1 March 1966, p. 2). The latter post-dates Tito's criticisms of the youth organizations (see *Studentski List* 15 December 1964, p. 3, also 23 March 1965, p. 4).
205. 'Stavovi predsedništva saveza studenata Jugoslavije o reformi univerziteta' (Positions of the Presidium of the Yugoslav Union of Students on university reform), *Univerzitet Danas,* vol. x, no. 1 (1969), pp. 3, 7.
206. *JTS* 5016, p. 8: *Politika* 12 May 1968; also 'Stavovi predsedništva saveza studenata Jugoslavije o reformi univerziteta', p. 3. For a similar account of the Union of Youth Conference see *Student* 20 February 1968, p. 3, report by Alija Hodžić.
207. *Komunist* 8 December 1966, p. 1.
208. *Student* 14 April 1970, p. 2; and Mesić, 'Diskusija', p. 208.
209. *JTS* 5046, p. 16: *Politika* 9 July 1968.
210. *JTS* 5076, p. 17: *Politika* 23 July 1968.

VII. CONCLUSION

1. It is important to note that they also had somewhat *different* (or were persuaded by responsible officials that they had different) grievances. It was pointed out to me in interviews on several occasions that the Zagreb students stopped short of complete support of the Belgrade protesters because they believed or were told that part of the Belgrade students' demands involved the adoption of policies which would bear more heavily on the more developed areas of the country such as Croatia. See above, p. 22.
2. On this point see *JTS* 4944, p. 25: *Komunist* 15 February 1968; *JTS* 4939, p. 36: *Borba* 11 February 1968; Nikolić, *Omladina i Društvo,* p. 163; and *Komunist* 13 June 1968, pp. 5, 9.
3. *Politika* 16 June 1968, p. 7.
4. *Komunist* 13 June 1968, p. 2; see also same issue p. 5.

5. Svetozar Stojanović, 'The June student movement and social revolution in Yugoslavia', *Praxis* (Int. ed.), no. 3/4 (1970), p. 397.
6. *Politika* 25 June 1968, p. 5; Goati, 'Razlike i sličnosti studentskih gibanja u Jugoslaviji sa gibanjima u zapadnoevropskim zemljama', p. 116; Netkov and Stardelov, 'Savremeni aspekti demokratizacije jugoslovenskog univerziteta', p. 46; and Petar Ignjatović, 'Razgovor tek počinje', p. 89.
7. Noted in Caratan, 'Studentski lipanj—uzroci i konsekvence', p. 165.
8. *JTS* 5027, p. 22: *Borba* 26 May 1968; see also *Eighth Congress of the Union of Yugoslav Youth,* p. 20. See also chapter V above.
9. See Nikolić, *Omladina i Društvo,* pp. 163-4.
10. e.g. Dušan Bilandžić, *Social Self-Government* (Belgrade: Medjunarodna Politika, 1965), especially pp. 8-23.
11. Murray Edelman, *The Symbolic Uses of Politics* (Urbana, Illinois: The University of Illinois Press, 1964), p. 3.
12. *JTS* 4969, p. 18: *Politika* 13 March 1968.
13. See p. 33.
14. Note comments on this point by Zoran Malenica, 'Zapreke, mogućnosti i perspektive socijalističkog pokreta mladih' (The socialist youth movement: obstacles, opportunities and perspectives), *Naše Teme,* no. 9 (September 1972), p. 1296 (hereinafter cited as 'Zapreke').
15. Ibid.
16. See discussion in S. Stojanović, 'The June student movement and social revolution in Yugoslavia', p. 399; and Kuvačić, 'Additional thoughts on synchrony and diachrony', p. 428.
17. Centralni Komitet Saveza Komunista Hrvatske i Centralni Komitet Saveza Omladine Hrvatske (Central Committee of the LC Croatia and Central Committee of the Union of Youth, Croatia), 'Omladine i Savez Komunista (Rezultati Empirijskog Istraživanja)' (The Youth and the League of Communists [Results of an empirical investigation]) (Zagreb, 1968), p. 24 (second of two pages numbered 24) (mimeographed); *Komunist* 20 June 1968, p. 6; *JTS* 4329, p. 15: *Komunist* 10 February 1966; *JTS* 4442, p. 31: *Borba* 26 June 1966; and *JTS* 4655, p. 39: *Borba* 10 March 1967.
18. e.g. *JTS* 4655, p. 39: *Borba* 10 March 1967; *JTS* 4870, p. 4: *Komunist* 15 October 1967; and Stanko Milošević and Dragan Miljanić, 'Neka razmatranja o današnjem položaju i ulozi omladine u SKJ i društvu' (Some observations on the contemporary position and role of the youth in the LCY and society), *Sociologija,* vol. x, no. 1 (1968), pp. 231-40.
19. *JTS* 4674, p. 30: *Vjesnik* 19 March 1967.
20. *JTS* 4459, p. 1: *Komunist* 4 July 1966.
21. *JTS* 4407, p. 46: *Komunist* 19 May 1966; Lovro Lisičić, 'Savez komunista i stvaralaštvo mladih' (The League of Communists and the creativity of the young), *Naše Teme,* no. 9 (September 1972), p. 1371.
22. *JTS* 4651, p. 17: *Komunist* 23 February 1967; see also Novosel, *Organizacije Saveza Komunista i Mladi Komunisti,* p. 6.
23. *JTS* 4836, p. 26: *Komunist* 5 October 1967; *JTS* 4835, p. 59: *Borba* 7 October 1967; *JTS* 4943, p. 49: *Komunist* 14 February 1968; and Tomanović, 'Omladinski pokret', p. 45.
24. *JTS* 4836, p. 26: *Komunist* 5 October 1967; and Tomanović, 'Omladinski pokret', p. 45.
25. *JTS* 4835, p. 5: *Borba* 7 October 1967; Muratović, 'Političko organizovanje i djelovanje omladine', p. 159; *JTS* 5086, p. 34: *Večernje Novosti* 1 August 1968; *Eighth Congress of the Union of Yugoslav Youth,* p. 60;

Nikolić, *Omladina i Društvo,* p. 27; and (Kocijančić), *JTS* 5011, p. 23: *Komunist* 1 May 1968.

26. Ivan Magdalenić and Ivan Siber, 'Idejno-političke tendencije medju omladinom i studentima' (Ideological-political tendencies among the youth and the students), *Naše Teme,* vol. ii, pp. 135-6, quoted in Nikolić, *Omladina i Društvo,* p. 199.

27. Muratović, 'Političko organizovanje i djelovanje omladine', p. 159; *JTS* 4870, p. 4: *Komunist* 15 October 1967; *JTS* 4998, p. 45: *Politika* 20 April 1968; Stipe Šuvar, 'Naš komunistički pokret i novi naraštaji' (Our communist movement and the new generation), *Naše Teme,* no. 9 (September 1972), p. 1284 (hereinafter cited as 'Naš komunistički pokret').

28. Report of joint meeting of Presidium and Executive Committee of the CC LC (Serbia), *Komunist* 6 June 1968, p. 3.

29. S. Stojanović, 'Junski studentski pokret', p. 123.

30. *JTS* 5040, p. 43: *Rad* 7 June 1968, p. 3.

31. Stane Dolanc, Secretary of the Executive Committee of the Presidium of the CC, 'Concerning the tasks of the information media in the struggle for new social relationships', *Yugoslav Information Bulletin,* vol. ii, no. 1 (January 1975), p. 11.

32. *Politika* 9 June 1968, p. 8; and *Borba* 9 June 1968, p. 4.

33. A convenient English language summary of these events is provided in *The Times* (London) 28 January 1975, p. 6, and 22 February 1975, p. 4; and *The Times Higher Education Supplement* 7 February 1975, p. 13.

34. S. Stojanović, 'The June student movement and social revolution in Yugoslavia', p. 397.

35. *Student* 1 March 1966, p. 1.

36. Ibid.

37. *JTS* 4459, p. 1: *Komunist* 4 July 1966.

38. Badovinac, address to the *Eighth Congress of the Union of Yugoslav Youth,* p. 35; Šuvar, 'Naš komunistički pokret', p. 1285.

39. Something of the difficulty of being a revolutionary in post-war Yugoslavia is sensitively discussed by Branko Horvat, *An Essay on Yugoslav Society* (White Plains, N.Y.: International Arts and Science Press, 1969), p. 210.

40. *Speech to Eighth Congress of the Union of Yugoslav Youth,* p. 22.

41. Neal, *Titoism in Action,* p. 39.

42. Phyllis Auty, *Tito* (London: Longmans, 1970), p. 287, also p. 290.

43. Ibid., p. 287.

44. (Alija Hodžić), *Komunist* 13 June 1968, p. 6.

45. Malenica, 'Zapreke', p. 1296.

46. Šuvar, 'Naš komunistički pokret', p. 1285; and Tomanović, 'Omladinski pokret', p. 45.

47. Šuvar, 'Naš komunistički pokret', p. 1285; Malenica, 'Zapreke', p. 1296; *Eighth Congress of the Union of Yugoslav Youth,* p. 37.

48. Celestin Sardelić, 'Mladi i savez komunista' (The young and the League of Communists), *Naše Teme,* vol. viii, no. 6 (1969), pp. 975-80; and *JTS* 4870, p. 4: *Komunist* 15 October 1967.

49. See discussion on this point by Šuvar, 'Naš komunistički pokret', pp. 1284-5; V. Milanović, 'Sociološki aspekti transformacije uloge škole', p. 31; Komisija za Delovanje Studenata u Reformi Visokog i Višeg Školstva Presedništva SSJ, 'Društveno-Ekonomski Položaj Univerziteta i Razvoj Samoupravljanja na Visokom Školstvu u Uslovima Društvene Reforme' (Belgrade, July 1972), p. 25 (mimeographed).

50. Pusić, 'Samoupravljanje i sveučilište', p. 231; and V. Milanović, 'Sociološki aspekti transformacije uloge škole', p. 23.
51. e.g. *Student* 27 February 1968, p. 4; Danica Mojsin, 'Sociolozi o omladini' (Sociologists on the young), *Gledišta,* vol. ix, no. 4 (1968), pp. 609-15.
52. (T. Badovinac), *JTS* 4533, p. 44: *Borba* 12 October 1966.
53. *JTS* 4674, p. 30: *Vjesnik* 19 March 1967.
54. *Studentski List* 9 January 1968, pp. 1, 3, and 17 January 1967, p. 3.
55. *Borba* 13 June 1968, p. 1.
56. S. Stojanović, *Between Ideals and Reality,* p. 126. A very useful account of the ideas of the *Praxis* group is provided by Oskar Gruenwald, 'Marxist Humanism', *Orbis,* vol. xviii, no. 3 (Fall 1974), pp. 888-916.
57. Institute for Social Research, *Innovation in Higher Education,* p. 150.
58. Deborah D. Milenkovitch, 'Which Direction for Yugoslavia's Economy?', in *Comparative Communism,* ed. Gary S. Bertsch and Thomas W. Ganschow (San Francisco: W. H. Freeman and Company, 1976), p. 354.
59. Ibid.; and Barbara Jancar, 'Yugoslavia: The Case for a Loyal Opposition under Communism', in ibid., p. 211.
60. For a convenient English language summary of these events see *The Times* (London) 13 November 1971, p. 4, 14 November, p. 5, 20 November, p. 4, 3 December, p. 8, and editorials of 8 November, p. 13, and 15 December, p. 15.
61. e.g. *Student* 16 October 1973, p. 10, 1 May 1973, p. 10, 23 May 1974, p. 10, and 26 December 1974, p. 5; also *Studentski List* 7 November 1975, p. 3, 9 April 1974, p. 2, 22 December 1976, p. 2, and 19 March 1976, p. 2.
62. e.g. *Student* 26 December 1974, pp. 4, 5, 7, and 28 March 1974, p. 2; and *Studentski List* 21 May 1974, pp. 8, 9.
63. e.g. *Studentski List* 21 May 1974, pp. 8, 9; and *Student* 9 January 1975, p. 5.
64. e.g. *Student* 25 December 1973/8 January 1974 (Double issue), p. 5.
65. e.g. *Vjesnik u Srijedu* 15 January 1975, p. 4; and *Studentski List* 19 March 1976, pp. 2, 3, and 20 January 1976, pp. 2, 3.
66. *Student* 16 October 1973, pp. 3, 4; *Studentski List* 22 December 1976, p. 2; Tito, 'Letter of the Executive Bureau of the Presidium of the LCY and President Tito', sent to members of the League of Communists of Yugoslavia on 29 September, and published on 18 October 1972 in Tito and others, *Ideological and Political Offensive of the League of Communists of Yugoslavia: Speeches by Tito, Kardelj and Dolanc* (Belgrade: The Secretariat for Information of the Federal Executive Council, 1972), pp. 96-104 (hereinafter cited as 'Letter of the Executive'). Also see Tito, 'Speech of the President of the Republic, Josip Broz Tito, to leading functionaries of socio-political organizations of the Socialist Republic of Serbia, on October 16, 1972', in Tito and others, *Ideological and Political Offensive,* p. 90 (hereinafter cited as 'Speech of the President of the Republic').
67. Tito, 'Speech of the President of the Republic', pp. 84-95; and 'Letter of the Executive', pp. 96-104.
68. e.g. *Borba* 12 June 1974, p. 1; *Studentski List* 22 November 1966, p. 2 (editorial); see also Tito's Speech to the Ninth Congress of the Socialist Youth Union held 21-23 November 1974, in *Yugoslav Information Bulletin,* no. 11 (1974), pp. 5-8. One might add that there have also been a number of 'historical gatherings' and dramatic 'turning points' as well as numerous occasions on which it was resolved that communists must immediately switch from 'words to deeds'.

POSTSCRIPT

1. See Dennison Rusinow, *The Yugoslav Experiment 1948-1974* (London: C. Hurst and Company for the Royal Institute of International Affairs, 1977), p.311. This new work provides a convenient and excellent account of these events.
2. Quotations in this and the succeeding paragraph are drawn from 'Speech of the President of the Republic'.
3. Quotations in this and the succeeding paragraph are drawn from 'Letter of the Executive'.
4. See pp. 164-165 above, and Rusinow, *The Yugoslav Experiment,* p. 318.
5. Rusinow, *The Yugoslav Experiment,* especially chapter 8.

BIBLIOGRAPHY

ABBREVIATIONS

Berkeley   Lipset, Seymour Martin, and Sheldon S. Wolin, eds. *The Berkeley Student Revolt: Facts and Interpretations.* New York: Anchor Books, 1965.
Confrontation   Bell, Daniel, and Irving Kristol, eds. *Confrontation.* New York: Basic Books, 1969.
DRO   Cvjetičanin, Veljko, and others, eds. *Društvo, Revolucija, Omladina.* Zagreb: Centar za Kulturnu Djelatnost Omladine Zagreba, 1969.
Protest   Crick, Bernard, and William A. Robson, eds. *Protest and Discontent.* Middlesex: Penguin, 1970.
SiR   Derosi-Bjelajac, Ema, and others, eds. *Sveučilište i Revolucija.* Zagreb: Sveučilišni Komitet SKH-Zagreb, 1970.
UD   *Univerzitet Danas.*

I
JOURNALS AND NEWSPAPERS

Bilten Univerziteta u Sarajevu
Borba
Gledišta
Ideje
Joint Translation Service, Belgrade
Komunist
Mladost
Naše Teme
Politika
Praxis
Socialist Thought and Practice
Sociologija
Student
Studentski List
Sveučilišni Vjesnik (Zagreb)
Univerzitet Danas
Youth Life
Yugoslav Student News
Yugoslav Survey

II
BOOKS, ARTICLES, THESES

Abrams, Richard M. 'The student rebellion at Berkeley—an interpretation.' *Berkeley.*
Anderson, Stephen Sanford. 'The political role of youth organizations in Com-

munist Yugoslavia.' Ph.D. dissertation, Department of Government, Harvard University, 1962.

Andrijašević, Jovan. 'Socijalistički tip integracije naučnog progresa i društvene reprodukcije.' *UD* XI, 4 (1970), 38-49.

Auty, Phyllis. *Tito.* London: Longmans, 1970.

Bakarić, Vladimir. 'Diskusija.' *SiR.*

―――. 'Omladina i Savez Komunista Jugoslavije.' *Gledišta* VII, 6/7 (June/ July 1966), 859-861.

―――. 'Razgovor na univerzitetu.' *UD* X, 6 (1969), 3-23.

Bartoš, Milan. 'Regrutovanje nastavnika univerziteta.' *UD* VI, 2 (1965), 3-9.

Bay, Christian. 'Political and apolitical students: facts in search of a theory.' *Journal of Social Issues* 23 (July 1967), 76-91.

Bazala, Aleksandar. 'Samoupravljanje kao osnova reforme sveučilišta.' *UD* X, 7/8 (1969), 30-40.

―――, and Ante Vukašović. 'Sistem samoupravljanja na sveučilištu.' *UD* IX, 7 (1968), 3-15.

Bell, Daniel. 'Columbia and the New Left.' *Confrontation.*

Beloff, Max. 'Universities and Violence.' *Survey* 69 (October 1968), 39-41.

Bertolino, Milorad. 'Mehanizam izbora i reizbornosti.' *UD* XI, 7/8 (1970), 22-33.

―――. 'O kompetencijama na reformisanom univerzitetu.' *SiR.*

Bertsch, Gary S., and Thomas W. Ganschow, eds. *Comparative Communism.* San Francisco: W. H. Freeman and Company, 1976.

Bettelheim, Bruno. 'Obsolete youth.' *Encounter* XXXIII, 3 (1969), 29-42.

Bezić, Krešimir. 'Stavovi studenata o vaspitnoj ulozi u samoupravnim organima visokoškolskih ustanova.' *UD* IX, 7 (1968), 73-81.

Bilandžić, Dušan. *Social Self-Government.* Belgrade: Medjunarodna Politika, 1965.

Blagojević, Borislav. 'Neka pitanja reforme visokog školstva i neprosredni politički zadaci na pravnom fakultetu u Beogradu.' *UD* X, 4 (1969), 14-23.

―――. 'Nužnost jasnog razgraničenja odnosa izmedju društva i univerziteta (fakulteta) pri rešavanju pitanja visokoškolske nastave.' *UD* X, 9/10 (1969), 17-23.

Bogdanović, Miloš. 'Problem zapošljavanja mladih kadrova u zemljama u razvoju kao posledica priraštaja stanovništva.' *UD* X, 1 (1969), 35-40.

Bojanić, Ivo. 'Election of students to various bodies of social management at the Zagreb University.' *Yugoslav Student News* 19 (May 1956), 1-3.

―――. 'Participation of students in the management of universities.' *Yugoslav Student News* 24 (July 1957), 18-20.

Bolfek, Mirko. 'Razvoj i uloga omladinskog pokreta poslije kongresa ujedinjenja.' *DRO.*

Borčić, Branko. 'Reforma univerziteta u jugoslovenskoj samoupravnoj zajednici.' *UD* XIV, 1/2 (1973), 22-35.

Bošnjak, Mladen. 'Društveni položaj omladine: socijalne razlike i njihov uticaj na obrazovanje i kulturu mladih.' *Lica,* 10 December 1973, 5-12.

Božić, Ivan. 'Društvene potrebe kao uticajan činilac u procesu univerzitetske nastave.' *UD* XI, 9/10 (1970), 31-36.

Božović, Ljubomir. 'Neki problemi upisa studenata na univerzitet.' *UD* VI, 6 (1965), 81-83.

Broćić, Manojlo. 'Omladina i politika.' *Gledišta* VIII, 2 (1967), 161-178.

―――. 'Stavovi i ocene studenata o nekim društvenim vrednostima.' *Jugoslovenski Studenti i Socijalizam.* Milosav Janićijević and others. Belgrade: Institut Društvenih Nauka, 1966.

Brown, Bernard E., and John C. Wahlke, eds. *The American Political System: Notes and Readings.* Homewood, Illinois: The Dorsey Press, 1967.

Brzezinski, Zbigniew. *Between Two Ages: America's Role in the Technetronic Era.* New York: The Viking Press, 1970.

Čalić, Dušan. 'Omladina kao revolucionarni subjekt.' *DRO.*

Čamo, Edhem. 'Jugoslavenski univerziteti pred novim zadacima.' *UD* I, 3/4 (1960), 79-88.

Caratan, Branko. 'Studentski lipanj—uzroci i konsekvence.' *DRO.*

Čavoški, Kosta. 'Studenti i samoupravljanje.' *Arhiv* XLI, 1 (January/March 1971), 151-160.

Cecić, Ivo. 'Kreditiranje studenata sa aspekta reforme visokog školstva.' *UD* X, 7/8 (1969), 50-63.

Cekić, Miodrag. 'Specijalizacija i opšte obrazovanje.' *UD* XI, 4 (1970), 53-56.

Ćemerlić, Hamdija. 'Dvadeset godina rada univerziteta u Sarajevu.' *UD* XI, 5 (1970), 89-97.

Centralni Komitet Saveza Komunista Hrvatske i Centralni Komitet Omladine Hrvatske. 'Omladina i Savez Komunista (Rezultati Empirijskog Istraživanja).' Zagreb, 1968. Mimeographed.

(Četvrti) IV Kongres Saveza Studenata Jugoslavije. Beograd: Centralni Odbor SSJ, 1959.

(Četvrti) IV Kongres SKOJ-a. Beograd: Omladina, 1949.

Čobeljić, Dušan. 'Neki problemi nastavnih planova i osvrt na pitanje dvostepene nastave na ekonomskim fakultetima.' *UD* VI, 6 (1965), 31-40.

Cockburn, Alexander. 'Introduction.' *Student Power: Problems, Diagnosis, Action,* edited by Alexander Cockburn and Robin Blackburn. Middlesex: Penguin, 1969.

———, and Robin Blackburn, eds. *Student Power: Problems, Diagnosis, Action.* Middlesex: Penguin, 1969.

Čolaković, Rodoljub. 'Usvojen je opšti zakon o školstvu.' *Prosvetni Pregled* 26 (June 1958), 1-6.

'Commentary on the Decisions Adopted at the Third Congress of the Yugoslav Union of Students.' *Yugoslav Student News* 21 (October 1956), 61-65.

'Conclusions of the Fourth Congress of the Yugoslav Union of Students.' *Yugoslav Student News* 28-29 (July 1959), 61-89.

'Constitution and membership of the Yugoslav Union of Students.' *Yugoslav Student News* 14 (June 1955), 3-5.

Constitution of the Socialist Federal Republic of Yugoslavia (1963), The. Translated by Petar Mijusković. Belgrade: Sekretarijat Saveznog Izvršnog Veća za Informacije, 1963.

'Constitution of the Yugoslav Union of Students.' [Excerpts] *Yugoslav Student News* 1 (April 1952), 6-7.

Crvenkovski, Krste. 'Reforma visokoškolskog obrazovanja u FNRJ.' *UD* I, 5/6 (1960), 155-165.

———. 'Reform of higher education.' Speech to Federal People's Assembly, FPRJ. Published as preface to *General Law on Faculties and Universities in Yugoslavia.* Belgrade: Union of Jurists Association of Yugoslavia, [1960].

Čurić, Radoslav. 'Neki stavovi studenata o disciplini u studentskim domovima.' *UD* IX, 1 (1968), 24-32.

Cviić, Zvonimir. 'Neki faktori racionalizacije visokoškolske nastave.' *UD* VII, 7 (1966), 43-48.

———. 'Stavovi visokoškolskih nastavnika o ulozi studenata u organima samoupravljanja.' *UD* IX, 7 (1968), 65-72.

Cvjetičanin, Veljko. 'Sveučilište i samoupravno društvo.' *SiR.*

Dahl, Robert A. *After the Revolution? Authority in a Good Society.* New Haven: Yale University Press, 1970.

D., B., and D.P. 'The system of higher education.' *Yugoslav Survey* II, 4 (1961), 528-530.

'Decree on Proclamation of the General Law on Universities.' Belgrade, 1954. Translated in *JTS,* 1295, 4-22.

'Decree proclaiming the Basic Law on Scholarships.' *Official Gazette* 32 (13 July 1955).

Dedijer, Vladimir. *The Battle Stalin Lost: Memoirs of Yugoslavia 1948-1953.* New York: The Viking Press, 1971.

―――. *Tito Speaks.* London: Weidenfeld and Nicolson, 1954.

Dimitrijević, Pavle. 'O ličnim dohodcima univerzitetskih nastavnika i saradnika.' *Gledišta* VII, 12 (December 1966), 1530-1532.

Dimković, Borislav J. 'Gde je i kuda će diplomirani sociolog?' *Gledišta* VIII, 1 (January 1967), 89-93.

Djordjević, Božidar. 'Univerzitet i privreda.' *UD* VIII, 1 (1967), 5-9.

Djordjević, Jovan. 'The case for a new modern university.' *Socialist Thought and Practice* 36 (October/December 1969), 141-155.

―――. 'Društvena osnova prava studenata na samoupravljanje.' *Ideje* I, 2 (1970), 11-22.

―――. 'O značaju i ulozi univerziteta danas.' *UD* VI, 4 (1965), 15-22.

Dolanc, Stane. 'Concerning the tasks of the information media in the struggle for new social relationships.' *Yugoslav Information Bulletin* II, 1 (January 1975), 9-12.

Dragnich, Alex M. 'Students shake Tito regime.' Unpublished paper, Department of Political Science, Vanderbilt University, 1969.

Drašković, Dragomir. 'Neformalno grupisanje u osnovnoj organizaciji Saveza Komunista.' *Gledišta* VII, 1 (January 1966), 43-53.

Drulović, Milojko. 'Report on the current problems and future tasks of the Yugoslav Union of Students.' *Yugoslav Student News* 21 (October 1956), 40-58.

'Društvena uloga Saveza Studenata Jugoslavije.' *UD* VII, 6 (1966), 3-25.

Džuverović, Borisav. *Omladina u Jugoslovenskom društvu.* Belgrade: Mladost, 1974.

―――. 'Studenti i samoupravljanje.' *Gledišta* VIII, 5 (1967), 707-710.

'Economic care of the students of Yugoslavia.' *Yugoslav Student News* 1 (April 1952), 13-14.

Edelman, Murray. *The Symbolic Uses of Politics.* Urbana, Illinois: The University of Illinois Press, 1964.

Eighth Congress of the Union of Yugoslav Youth, The. Belgrade: Youth Life, 1968.

Eisenstadt, S. M. *From Generation to Generation.* Glencoe, Illinois: Free Press, 1956.

'Excerpts from the Report of the YUS Central Board submitted at the III Congress of the YUS.' *Yugoslav Student News* 21 (October 1956), 1-39.

Federal Council for Statistics. *Jugoslavija 1945-1964, Statistički Pregled.* Belgrade, n.d. [1965].

―――. *Statistički Godišnjak SFRJ 1969.* Belgrade, 1969.

―――. *Statistički Godišnjak SFRJ 1975.* Belgrade, 1975.

Feuer, Lewis. *The Conflict of Generations.* New York: Basic Books, 1969.

―――. 'Patterns of Irrationality.' *Survey* 69 (October 1968), 43-51.

Fisk, Trevor. 'The nature and causes of student unrest.' *Protest.*

Flacks, Richard. 'Social and cultural meanings of student revolt.' *Student*

Activism and Protest, edited by Edward E. Sampson, Harold A. Korn and Associates. San Francisco: Jossey-Bass, 1970.

Gamulin, Grgo. 'Uloga sveučilišta u kulturi socijalističkog društva.' *SiR.*

General Law on Faculties [Departments] and Universities in Yugoslavia. Belgrade: Union of Jurists Association of Yugoslavia, [1960].

'General Law on Universities.' *JTS,* 1295, 4-22.

'A general survey of student economic and health questions in Yugoslavia.' *Yugoslav Student News* 14 (June 1955), 14-18.

Glazer, Nathan. ' "Student power" in Berkeley.' *Confrontation.*

Gligorijević, Jovan. 'Univerzitet u Beogradu: Rad na reformi univerziteta.' *UD* XII, 9/10 (1971), 17-40.

Gligorov, Vladimir. 'Polivalentnost kulture i revolucije.' *UD* X, 2/3 (1969), 70-74.

Goati, Vladimir. 'Razlike i sličnosti studentskih gibanja u Jugoslaviji sa gibanjima u zapadnoevropskim zemljama.' *DRO.*

Grdelić, Drago. 'Univerzitet i naučno istraživanje.' *UD* VI, 5 (1965), 33-42.

Gruenwald, Oskar. 'Marxist Humanism.' *Orbis* XVIII, 3 (Fall 1974), 888-916.

Hadži-Vasilev, Kiro. 'Za samoupravni sistem obrazovanja.' *Socijalizam* XV, 10 (1972), 1078-1098.

Halleck, Seymour L. 'Why students protest: a psychiatrist's view.' *Student Protest,* edited by Gerald F. McGuigan with George Payerle and Patricia Horrobin. Toronto: Methuen, 1968.

Hanson, A. H. 'Some literature on student revolt.' *Protest.*

Heremić, Mustafa. 'Studentski Centar sveučilišta u Zagrebu.' *UD* I, 7-10 (1960), 245-250.

Hoffman, George W., and Fred Warner Neal, *Yugoslavia and the New Communism.* New York: Twentieth Century Fund, 1962.

Hook, Sidney. 'Academic freedom and academic anarchy.' *Survey* 69 (October 1968), 62-75.

Horvat, Branko. 'Analysis of the economic situation and proposal for a program of action.' *Praxis* (Int. ed.). 3/4 (1971), 533-562.

———. *An Essay on Yugoslav Society.* White Plains, N.Y.: International Arts and Science Press, 1969.

———. 'Markesistička analiza društvenih klasa suvremenog jugoslavenskog društva.' *Gledišta* VIII, 10 (October 1967), 1279-1292.

Ibrahimagić, Omer. 'Prilog pitanju izgradnje samoupravnog univerziteta.' *SiR.*

Ignatović, Predrag. 'Prilog diskusiji o reformi univerziteta.' *UD* XI, 1 (1970), 58-67.

Ignjatović, Petar. 'Razgovor tek počinje.' *Ideje* I, 2 (1970), 89-96.

'Implementation of New University Law.' *Yugoslav Student News* 13 (April 1955), 1-3.

Institute for Social Research, University of Zagreb. *Innovation in Higher Education: Reforms in Yugoslavia.* Paris: OECD, 1970.

Ivanović, Dragiša. 'O nekim praktičnim pitanjima reforme univerziteta.' *UD* X, 9/10 (1969), 3-12.

Ivanović, Stanoje. 'Opterećenost nastavnog osoblja nastavnim radom i efikasnost završavanja studija na visokoškolskim ustanovama u SR Srbiji.' *UD* XIII, 3/4 (1972), 41-55.

Jancar, Barbara. 'Yugoslavia: The Case for a Loyal Opposition under Communism.' *Comparative Communism,* edited by Gary S. Bertsch and Thomas W. Ganschow. San Francisco: W. H. Freeman and Company, 1976.

J., R. 'Enrolment at faculties and art academies.' *Yugoslav Survey* I, 1 (1960), 83-85.

Jakšic, Božidar. 'Sedam teza o temi: promene na univerzitetu i društvu.' *SiR.*

Janićijević, Milosav. 'Društveno-politički i ideološki stavovi jugoslovenskih studenata.' *Jugoslovenski Studenti i Socijalizam.* Milosav Janićijević and others. Belgrade: Institut Društvenih Nauka, 1966.

————, and others. *Jugoslovenski Studenti i Socijalizam.* Belgrade: Institut Društvenih Nauka, 1966.

Jelčić, Božidar. 'Materijalni položaj visokoškolskog obrazovanja.' *SiR.*

Jemuović, Rodoljub. *Društveno Upravljanje u Prosveti.* Belgrade: Kultura, 1959.

Joint Publication Research Service. 'Education in Yugoslavia.' Report No. 658, New York, 20 August 1958, 1-63. Mimeographed.

Jovanović, Jovan. 'Učešće federacije u izgradnji univerziteta u SFR Jugoslaviji.' *UD* VI, 2 (1965), 21-30.

Jugoslovenski savremenici—ko je ko u Jugoslaviji, Belgrade: Hronometar, 1970.

Jupp, James. 'The discontents of youth.' *Protest.*

Jurković, Ivan. 'Uloga sveučilišta i nauke u našoj zemlji u svijetlu savremene naučno-tehnološke revolucije.' *UD* XI, 1 (1970), 50-57.

Kangŕga, Milan. 'Praksa i kritika.' *Praxis* II, 2 (1965), 269-281.

Keniston, Kenneth. *Young Radicals: Notes on Committed Youth.* New York: Harcourt Brace Jovanovich, 1968.

————. *Youth and Dissent: The Rise of a New Opposition.* New York: Harcourt Brace Jovanovich, 1971.

Kilibarda, Krsto S. 'Za socijalističke odnose na univerzitetu.' *Naše Teme* VIII, 4 (1964), 509-519.

Klein, George. 'Yugoslavia—the process of democratization.' *The Changing Face of Communism in Eastern Europe,* edited by Peter A. Toma. Tucson, Arizona: University of Arizona Press, 1970.

Klemenčić, Tone. 'Reforma visokog školstva sa gledišta društveno-privrednog razvoja.' *UD* X, 7/8 (1969), 7-14.

Kobe, Petar. 'Efikasnost studiranja na jugoslovenskim univerzitetima.' *UD* IX, 9/10 (1968), 39-55.

Komisija za delovanje studenata u reformi visokog i višeg školstva, presedništva SSJ. 'Društveno-ekonomski položaj univerziteta i razvoj samoupravljanja na visokom školstvu u uslovima drustvene reforme.' Belgrade, July, 1972. Mimeographed.

'Komisija za organizaciono-politički razvoj.' Paper prepared for VI Congress YUS. Mimeographed.

Konc, Joze. 'Osipanje studenata.' *UD* XI, 9/10 (1970), 84-90.

Košutić, Budimir. 'Neke dileme o samoupravljanju na univerzitetu.' *Arhiv* XLI, 1 (January/March 1971), 143-150.

Kozić, Petar. 'Sociografija nekih studentskih zapažanja o učenju, ispitima i dokolici.' *UD* XI, 2/3 (1970), 36-42.

Kristol, Irving. 'A different way to restructure the university.' *Confrontation.*

Kuvačić, Ivan. 'Additional thoughts on synchrony and diachrony.' *Praxis* (Int. ed.) 3/4 (1971), 423-437.

————. 'Teorijski pristup za shvaćanje suvremene omladine.' *Sociologija* X, 1 (1968), 45-52.

Lang, Rikard. 'Sveučilište i ekonomski razvoj u samoupravnom društvu.' *SiR.*

Lazarević, Djordje. 'Reforma univerziteta.' *UD* XI, 4 (1970), 3-16.

Lazović, Budimir. 'Položaj, funkcije i odgovornost studenata u samoupravljanju univerzitetom.' *UD* X, 9/10 (1969), 108-112.

Leko, Ivan. 'Idejni problemi školstva i obrazovanja danas.' *Naše Teme* XIII, 6 (1969), 865-893.

Lipset, Seymour Martin. 'University student politics.' *Berkeley.*

———, and Paul Seabury. 'The lesson of Berkeley.' *Berkeley.*

Lisičić, Lovro. 'Savez komunista i stvaralaštvo mladih.' *Naše Teme* 9 (September 1972), 1357-1373.

Lubell, Samuel. 'That "generation gap".' *Protest.*

Lučev, Ivan. 'Položaj mladih prema stepenu otvorenosti društva i njegovoj pokretljivosti.' *Sociologija* X, 1 (1968), 55-61.

Lukić, Radomir. 'Osnovni problemi omladine: podruštvljenje, usvanjanje kulture, vaspitanje.' *Sociologija* X, 1 (1968), 27-42.

Macarola, Slavko. 'Neki problemi organizacije nastave i naučnog rada na sveučilištu. *UD* VIII, 1 (1967), 10-15.

———. Speech to University Council. *Sveučilišni Vjesnik* (Zagreb) XII, 222 (1966), 387-426.

McClellan, Woodford. 'Postwar political evolution.' *Contemporary Yugoslavia: Twenty Years of Socialist Experiment,* edited by Wayne S. Vucinich. Berkeley and Los Angeles: University of California Press, 1969.

McGuigan, G. F., George Payerle and Patricia Horrobin, eds. *Student Protest.* Toronto: Methuen, 1968.

Malenica, Zoran. 'Zapreke, mogućnosti i perspektive socijalističkog pokreta mladih.' *Naše Teme* 9 (September 1972), 1295-1302.

Mander, John. 'An indispensable activity.' *Survey* 69 (October 1968), 52-55.

Mandić, Oleg. 'Suvremeni problemi omladine.' *SiR.*

Marcuse, Herbert. *An Essay on Liberation.* Middlesex: Penguin, 1972.

Marendić, Katica, and Vlastimir Čolić. 'Financial aid to pupils and students.' *Yugoslav Survey* X, 2 (1969), 143-148.

Marković, Danilo Z. 'Principi organizacije samoupravnog drustva i oblici samoupravljanja na univerzitetu.' *SiR.*

Marković, Mihailo. 'Društvena uloga univerzitetskog nastavnika.' *UD* IX, 3/4 (March/April 1968), 99-103.

Mesić, Milan. 'Diskusija.' *SiR.*

Mihailović, Srečko. 'Drugo savetovanje studenata sociologije.' *Sociologija* IX, 1 (1967), 89-91.

Milanović, Vladimir. 'Sociološki aspekti transformacije uloga skole.' *UD* XI, 2/3 (1970), 20-35.

Milenkovitch, Deborah D. *Plan and Market in Yugoslav Economic Thought.* New Haven: Yale University Press, 1971.

———. 'Which Direction for Yugoslavia's Economy?' *Comparative Communism,* edited by Gary S. Bertsch and Thomas W. Ganschow. San Francisco: W. H. Freeman and Company, 1976.

Milenović, Miodrag. 'Dinamika razvoja visokog školstva i zapošljavanja diplomiranih studenata.' *Ideje* I, 2 (1970), 225-274.

———, and Vera Gavanski. 'Razvoj visokog školstva 1939-1968.' Paper prepared for the Presidium of YUS, Belgrade, 1969. Mimeographed.

Milojković, Mirjana. 'Studenti Beograda 1945-1969 godine.' *UD* X, 5 (1969), 51-62.

Milošević, Stanko, and Dragan Miljanić. 'Neka razmatranja o današnjem položaju i ulozi omladine u SKH i društvu.' *Sociologija* X, 1 (1968), 231-239.

Miloslavlevski, Slavko. 'Anketa.' *Ideje* I, 2 (1970), 23-34.

———. 'Aktuelni momenat reforme Skopskog Univerziteta.' *UD* XIII, 1/2 (January/February 1972), 9-14.

227

Mirković, Dragoslav. 'Aktuelna pitanja organizacije univerziteta i fakulteta.' *UD* IX, 9/10 (1968), 3-13.

———. 'Problemi materialnog obezbedjenja studenata.' *Bilten Univerziteta u Sarajevu* VI (January 1966), 65-87.

Mitić, Mihailo. 'O izmenama u sistemu samoupravljanja na fakultetima.' *UD* IX, 2 (1968), 53-68.

Mladjenović, Milorad. 'Neki problemi univerziteta u zemljama u razvoju.' *UD* X, 2/3 (1969), 107-113.

Mojsin, Danica. 'Sociolozi o omladini.' *Gledišta* IX, 4 (1968), 609-615.

Mratović, Veljko. 'Razvijanje samoupravnih odnosa u sveučilištu.' *UD* XI, 4 (1970), 17-31.

Muratović, Milorad. 'Političko organizovanje i djelovanje omladine.' *DRO*.

'Nacrt rezolucije o materijalnom položaju studenata.' [Prepared for the Eighth Congress SSJ]. *Studentski List,* Supplement, 9 April 1968, 1-8.

Neal, Fred Warner. *Titoism in Action: the Reforms in Yugoslavia after 1948.* Berkeley and Los Angeles: University of California Press, 1958.

'Neki problemi daljeg razvoja univerziteta u Sarajevu.' *Bilten Univerziteta u Sarajevu* VIII, 22 (1967).

Netkov, Milan, and Georgi Stardelov. 'Savremeni aspekti demokratizacije jugoslovenskog univerziteta.' *UD* X, 9/10 (1969), 46-52.

'New Curricula.' *Yugoslav Student News* 23 (March 1957), 25-26.

Nikodimovski, Lazar. 'Neki aspekti nove uloge univerziteta u savremenom društvu.' *UD* XI, 1 (1970), 29-34.

Nikolić, Miloš. 'Economic problems concerning students and international student cooperation.' *Yugoslav Student News* 20 (August 1956), 61-70.

———. *Omladina i Društvo.* Belgrade: Komunist, 1972.

'Novi zakon o studentskim ustanovama u SR Srbiji.' *UD* IX, 9/10 (1968), 122-123.

Novosel, Pavle. 'Diskusija.' *DRO.*

———. 'Omladina u savremenom svijetu.' *Sociologija* X, 1 (1968), 7-25.

———. 'Omladinska organizacija danas.' *DRO.*

———. *Organizacije Saveza Komunista i Mladi Komunisti.* Zagreb: Naše Teme, 1969.

Obradović, Vlado. 'Gledanje učenika na obrazovanje.' *Naše Teme* XI, 2 (1967), 161-191.

'Obrazovni procesi u reformiranoj univerzitetskoj nastavi (prikaz IV simpozija "Društveni i ekonomski aspekti obrazovanja," Zagreb, 1970 godine).' *UD* XI, 6 (1970), 103-114.

'Opšti zakon o školstvu.' *Službeni List FNRJ.* Belgrade, 16 July 1958, 746-761.

'Osvrt na XIV interfakultetsku konferenciju pravnih fakulteta Jugoslavije.' *UD* XI, 2/3 (1970), 110-118.

P., L. 'The People's Youth Organization.' *Yugoslav Survey* I, 3 (1960), 315-324.

Pašalić, Esad. 'Sadžraj rada samoupravnih organa.' *Bilten Univerziteta u Sarajevu* VII, 25 (1967), 3-11.

Pateman, Carole. *Participation and Democratic Theory.* London: Cambridge University Press, 1970.

Pavlović, Milovan. 'Položaj asistenata i neka pitanja samoupravljanja na univerzitetu.' *UD* X, 6 (1969), 82-86.

Penušliski, Kiril. 'Stipendije ili kreditiranje studenata.' *UD* I, 5/6 (1960), 182-185.

Pešić-Golubović, Zagorka. 'Socialist ideas and reality.' *Praxis* (Int. ed.) 3/4 (1971), 399-421.

Petak, Antun. 'Motivi zapošlavanja u inozemstvu.' *Naše Teme* XIII, 3 (1969), 395-418.

Petersen, William. 'What is left at Berkeley.' *Berkeley.*

Peti Kongres Narodne Omladine Jugoslavije. Belgrade: Centralni Komitet NOJ, 1953.

Petrović, Gajo. 'Kritika u socijalizmu.' *Praxis* II, 3 (1965), 468-481.

———. 'O našoj filozofiji.' *Praxis* II, 2 (1965), 249-255.

Pezo, Vladimir. 'Društvena pitanja afirmacije omladine.' *Naše Teme* 9 (September 1972), 1291-1294.

Pilić, Bogdan. 'Uslovi ostvarivanja socialističkog odnosa izmedju nastavnika i studenata.' *SiR.*

———. 'Uzajamna zavisnost optimalne veličine fakulteta i visokog kvaliteta univerzitetske nastave i naučnog rada.' *UD* X, 7/8 (1969), 41-49.

Pivec, F., and C. Ribičič. 'Razvoj ideje i zakonodavstva o studentu radniku samoupravljaču.' *Ideje* I, 2 (1970), 99-108.

Pjanić, Zoran. 'Socijalni i materijalni položaj univerziteta.' *UD* VIII, 2 (1967), 7-11.

———. 'Univerzitet-nekad i sad.' *UD* X, 9/10 (1969), 24-28.

Plećaš, Dubravka. 'Neki sociološki problemi i problemi samoupravljanja u visokom školstvu.' *UD* XII, 1 (1971), 47-54.

Plenča, Dušan, ed. *The Yugoslav Youth Movement.* Belgrade: Mladost, 1969.

Popov, Blagoj. '20 godina univerziteta u Skoplju.' *UD* X, 4 (1969), 3-13.

Popović, Dušan. 'Samoupravljanje na Beogradskom Univerzitetu.' *UD* VII, 3 (1966), 7-11.

Popović, Mihailo. 'Društveni uslovi i mogučnosti školovanja omladine u Jugoslaviji.' *Sociologija* X, 1 (1968), 81-101.

Popović, Milentije. 'Changes in the balance of forces of direct socialist democracy and bureaucracy.' *Socijalizam* (October 1966). Translated in *JTS, Magazine Supplement* X, n.d., 12-22.

Prelić, Milosav. 'Odgovornost komunista na univerzitetu.' *UD* VII, 6 (1966), 36-41.

Pribićević, Branko. 'Politička situacija na univerzitetu.' *UD* X, 7/8 (1969), 72-81.

———. 'Sprovodjenje reforme sistema visokoškolskog obrazovanja i zadaci Saveza Komunista.' *UD* XI, 5 (1970), 52-68.

'Principi izgradnje sistema i organizacije stručne izobraze.' Report presented by a committee of the University Council, *Sveučilišni Vjesnik* (Zagreb) X, 'A' Supplement, 184/85 (September 1964).

Programska Načela i Statut SOJ. Beograd: Komunist, 1964.

Prothro, James W., and Charles M. Grigg. 'Agreement on fundamentals.' *The American Political System: Notes and Readings,* edited by Bernard E. Brown and John C. Wahlke. Homewood, Illinois: The Dorsey Press, 1967.

Prva Konferencija Saveza Omladine Jugoslavije. Beograd: Komunist, 1965.

Prvi (I) Kongres Saveza Studenata Jugoslavije. Beograd: Narodni Student, 1952.

Puhan, Ivo. 'Normativno regulisanje i savremeni društveni odnosi na univerzitetu.' *UD* X, 7/8 (1969), 82-87.

Pusić, Eugen. 'Samoupravljanje i sveučilište.' *SiR.*

Radovanović, Miroslav. 'Problem "prekobrojne" generacije u savremenom jugoslavenskom društvu.' *Sociologija* 1 (1968), 63-78.

Rajković, Jugoslav. 'Planiranje kadrova i prijem studenata-osnova saradnje univerziteta i srednjih škola.' *UD* XI, 3/4 (1973), 16-32.

———. 'Rezultati nastave i učenja na Beogradskom Univerzitetu u školskoj 1964/65 godini.' *UD* VII, 1 (1966), 29-42.

Rapoport, David C. 'Generations in America.' *Protest.*

Raskin, A. H. 'The Berkeley Affair: Mr. Kerr Vs. Mr. Savio & Co.' *Berkeley.*

Ravbar, Miroslav, 'Povodom pedesetogodišnjice slovenačkog univerziteta u Ljubljani.' *UD* XI, 2/3 (1970), 78-84.

Reich, Charles A. *The Greening of America.* Harmondsworth, Middlesex, England: Penguin, 1972.

'Report of Central Board YUS.' *Yugoslav Student News* 21 (October 1956).

'Report on the Fact-finding Commission Appointed to Investigate the Disturbances at Columbia University in April and May 1968.' *Crisis at Columbia.* New York: Vintage Books, 1968.

'Resolution of the Eighth Congress on the future responsibilities of the League of Communists of Yugoslavia.' *Yugoslav Survey* VI, 20 (1965), 2900-2916.

Resulović, S. 'Upravljanje ustanova studentskog standarda.' *Bilten Univerziteta u Sarajevu* VIII, 28 (1968), 81-104.

'Rezolucija o pitanju trajanja studija na našim univerzitetima.' *Sveučilišni Vjesnik* (Zagreb) IV, 'A' Supplement, 61/62 (May 1958), 151-153.

Ristović, Jovan. 'Ambivalentna socijalizacija ličnosti asistenta.' *UD* X, 6 (1969), 87-104.

Roszak, Theodore. *The Making of a Counter Culture: Reflections on the Technocratic Society and its Youthful Opposition.* London: Faber & Faber, 1970.

Rusinow, Dennison. *The Yugoslav Experiment 1948-1974.* London: C. Hurst and Company for the Royal Institute of International Affairs, 1977.

Sadiković, Čazim. 'O jednoj zanemarenoj funkciji univerziteta.' *SiR.*

Samolovčev, Borivoj. 'Nastavni planovi i programi i modernizacija visokoškolske nastave.' *UD* IV, 9/10 (1963), 375-385.

'Samoupravljanje, dohodak i organizacione osnove univerziteta.' *Bilten Univerziteta u Sarajevu* VII, 24 (1967), 90-150.

Sampson, Edward E., Harold A. Korn and Associates, eds. *Student Activism and Protest.* San Francisco: Jossey-Bass, 1970.

Sardelić, Celestin. 'Mladi i savez komunista.' *Naše Teme* XIII, 6 (1969), 975-980.

Sedma Konferencija Saveza Studenata Jugoslavije. Beograd: SSJ, 1966.

Sedmi Kongres Saveza Omladine Jugoslavije, 23-26 Januara 1963 Godine. Beograd: Narodni Odbor, 1963.

Serdar, Vladimir. Address to University Council *Sveučilišni Vjesnik* (Zagreb) IX, 'A' Supplement, 154/55 (1962), 110-117.

———. 'Organizacija financiranja fakulteta i univerziteta.' *UD* V, 1/2 (1964), 1-8.

———. 'Reformski zahvati u dodiplomskoj nastavi.' *UD* X, 2 (1971), 13-16.

———. Remarks to the University Council. *Sveučilišni Vjesnik* (Zagreb) XII, 222 (July 1966), 421-423.

———. 'Simpozij "Društveni i ekonomski aspekti obrazovanja".' *UD* X, 7/8 (1969), 3-6.

———. 'Sistem upisa studenata u prvu godinu studija na univerzitete u Yugoslaviji 1967/68.' Zagreb, 1968. Mimeographed. Institut za Društvena Istraživanja Sveučilišta u Zagrebu.

Sergejev, Dimitrije. 'Mentorstvo kao princip reformirane sveučilišne nastave.' *UD* XI, 6 (1970), 50-58.

Šesti Kongres Narodne Omladine Jugoslavije. Belgrade: Kultura, 1958.

Shoup, Paul. *Communism and the Yugoslav National Question.* New York: Columbia University Press, 1968.

Sinadinovski, Jakim. 'Slobodan upis studenata i njegove posledice na univerzitetu "Kiril i Metodij" u Skoplju.' *UD* XIV, 1/2 (1973), 51-62.

Sirotković, Jakov. 'O radu sveučilišta s posebnim osvrtom na uvjete i probleme reforme visokog školstva.' *UD* IX, 9/10 (1968), 14-30.

'Skoplje university students help citizens in neighbouring villages.' *Yugoslav Student News* 19 (May 1956), 5-6.

Šlander, Joža, 'Socijalna struktura studenata i jedinstvo njihove društvene akcije.' *Ideje* I, 2 (1970), 40-43.

Smailagić, Nerkez. 'Sveučilište i demokratija.' *SiR.*

Smiljković, Radoš. 'Transformacija odnosa Saveza Komunista—omladina u samoupravljanju.' *DRO.*

Šnuderl, Makso. 'Prilagodjavanje fakultetskih i univerzitetskih statuta novom ustavu.' *UD* IV, 9/10 (1963), 369-374.

'Some current tasks in the political and ideological activities of the Yugoslav Union of Students.' *Yugoslav Student News* 26 (July 1958), 5-17.

'Some data on post war development and problems of Yugoslav universities.' *Yugoslav Student News* 27 (December 1958), 72-77.

'Some questions regarding studies at Belgrade University.' *Yugoslav Student News* 19 (May 1956), 3-5.

Šoškić, Branislav. 'Reforma univerziteta i izbor naučno-nastavnih radnika.' *UD* XI, 6 (1970), 3-9.

Spakarev, J. A. 'Stanje i tendencije u nastavno-obrazovnom procesu Skopskog Univerziteta.' *UD* X, 7/8 (1969), 89-95.

Stambolić, Vukašin. 'The foundations of social sciences as a subject at the university.' *Naša Stvarnost* 5 (May 1957). Translated in *JTS* 2185, 5-9.

———. 'The role and basic tasks of the Yugoslav Union of Students in the socialist upbringing and speedier vocational qualification of students.' *Yugoslav Student News* 28/29 (July 1959), 4-12.

Stanković, Dragiša. 'Efikasnost i kvalitet studiranja.' *UD* VI, 4 (1965), 43-51.

Stanković, Dušan. 'Neki zanemareni suštinski aspekti reforme univerziteta.' *UD* XI, 7/8 (1970), 34-37.

Stanković, Jugoslav. 'Studenti na radu, u društvu i slobodnom vremenu.' *Jugoslavenski Studenti i Socijalizam.* Milosav Janićijević and others. Belgrade: Institut Društvenih Nauka, 1966.

'Statute of the Union of Yugoslav Students (1956).' *Yugoslav Student News* 22 (October 1956), 38-45.

Statut Narodne Omladine Jugoslavije. Beograd: Centralni Komitet NOJ, 1951.

Statut Narodne Omladine Jugoslavije. Beograd: Centralni Komitet NOJ, 1956.

Statut Narodne Omladine Jugoslavije. Beograd: NOJ, Mladost, 1961.

Statut Narodne Omladine Jugoslavije. Rezolucija V Kongresa Narodne Omladine Jugoslavije. Beograd: NOJ, 1953.

Statut Saveza Studenata Jugoslavije. Beograd: Centralni odbor SSJ, 1959.

'Stavovi Predsedništva Saveza Jugoslavije o reformi univerziteta.' *UD* X, 1 (1969), 3-8.

Stojanović, Svetozar. *Between Ideals and Reality: A Critique of Socialism and its Future.* Translated by Gerson S. Sher. New York: Oxford University Press, 1973.

———. 'Junski studentski pokret i socijalna revolucija u Jugoslaviji.' *DRO.*

———. 'The June student movement and social revolution in Yugoslavia.' *Praxis* (Int. ed.) 3/4 (1970), 394-402.

———. 'Morality of the revolutionary vanguard as a historical presupposition of socialism.' Translated from *Praxis* 1 (1966), in *JTS,* Magazine Supplement 4 (March 1966), 10-17.

———. 'Social self-government and socialist community.' *Praxis* (Int. ed.) 1/2 (1968), 104-116.

——. 'Univerzitet i etatistička struktura.' *Gledišta* VII, 12 (December 1966), 1526-1527.

Stojanović, Vojislav. 'Nauka, naučno stvaralaštvo i naučna kritika.' *UD* XI, 6 (1970), 21-34.

——. 'Perspektive u razvoju visokoškolskog obrazovanja i nauke.' *UD* XV, 1/2 (1974), 31-32.

——. 'Problemi u procesu visokoškolskog obrazovanja i naučnog rada.' *UD* XIII, 5/6 (May/June 1972), 14-26.

——. 'Reforma univerziteta u teoriji i praksi.' *UD* XI, 1 (1970), 3-28.

Stojičić, Djoko. 'Način glasanja pri izboru nastavnika.' *UD* VI, 2 (1965), 9-11.

Strpić, Dag. 'Studenti i revolucija.' *SiR.*

——. 'Studenti, revolt, revolucija.' *Pitanja* 1 (1969), 10-13.

Sunjić, M. 'Savez Komunista u idejno-političkoj borbi za reformu visokog školstva.' *Bilten Univerziteta u Sarajevu* VIII, 30 (1968), 36-37.

Supek, Rudi. 'Još jednom o alternativi: Staljinistički pozitivizam ili stvaralački Marksizam?' *Praxis* II, 6 (1965), 891-915.

——. 'Robno—novčani odnosi i socialistička ideologija.' *Praxis* V, 1/2 (1968), 170-179.

——. 'Some contradictions and insufficiencies of Yugoslav self-managing socialism.' *Praxis* (Int. ed.) 3/4 (1971), 375-397.

Šuvar, Stipe. 'Društveni položaj i aspiracije omladine.' *DRO.*

——. 'Naš komunistički pokret i novi naraštaji.' *Naše Teme* 9 (September 1972), 1283-1290.

Takalić, Djuro. 'Neka pitanja nove uloge sveučilišta u samoupravnom društvu.' *SiR.*

Težak, Božo. 'Diskusija.' *SiR.*

——. 'Prilozi problematici jugoslavenskih univerziteta.' *UD* I, 1/2 (1960), 7-12.

——. Speech to University Council. *Sveučilišni Vjesnik* (Zagreb) XII, 222 (1966), 387-426.

'Theses for Discussion: Current Problems of the Struggle of the League of Communists of Yugoslavia for the Implementation of the Reform.' *Yugoslav Survey* VII, 25 (1966), 3578-3600.

Tišma, Toša. 'Finansiranje i raspodela na fakultetu.' *UD* VI, 4 (1965), 23-24.

——. 'Naše visoko školstvo u svetlu nekih statističkih podataka.' *UD* VIII, 5 (1967), 33-46.

——. 'Osnovni problemi i nesporazumi samoupravljanja.' *UD* IX, 1 (1968), 10-13.

Tito, Josip Broz. Excerpts from the opening speech of the Third Session of the Central Committee of the League of Communists of Yugoslavia. *Yugoslav Survey* VII, 25 (1966), 3569-3600.

——. 'Letter of the Executive Bureau of the Presidium of the LCY and President Tito sent to members of the League of Communists of Yugoslavia on September 29, and published on October 18, 1972.' *Ideological and Political Offensive of the League of Communists of Yugoslavia: Speeches by Tito, Kardelj and Dolanc.* Belgrade: The Secretariat for Information of the Federal Executive Council, 1972.

——. 'Our youth has proved mature.' Address delivered on 9 June 1968. Translated in *Socialist Thought and Practice* 30 (April/June 1968), 3-9.

——. *Selected Speeches and Articles 1941-1961.* Zagreb: Naprijed, 1963.

——. 'Speech of the President of the Republic, Josip Broz Tito, to leading functionaries of socio-political organizations of the Socialist Republic of Serbia, on October 16, 1972.' *Ideological and Political Offensive of the*

League of Communists of Yugoslavia: Speeches by Tito, Kardelj and Dolanc. Belgrade: The Secretariat for Information of the Federal Executive Council, 1972.

——. Speech to the Ninth Congress of the Socialist Youth Union held November 21-23, 1974, in *Yugoslav Information Bulletin* 11 (1974), 5-8.

——. *Tito Omladini.* Belgrade: Mlado Pokolenje, 1961.

—— and others. *Ideological and Political Offensive of the League of Communists of Yugoslavia: Speeches by Tito, Kardelj and Dolanc.* Belgrade: The Secretariat for Information of the Federal Executive Council, 1972.

Toma, Peter A., ed. *The Changing Face of Communism in Eastern Europe.* Tucson, Arizona: University of Arizona Press, 1970.

Tomanović, Velimir. 'O menjanju položaja, uloge i odnosa u omladinskom pokretu u novije vreme.' *DRO.*

——. 'Problemi socijalne diferencije u oblasti obrazovanja.' *Sociologija* X, 1 (1968), 111-134.

'Traditional May festival of Belgrade and Zagreb students.' *Yugoslav Student News* 13 (April 1955), 6-7.

'Treća plenarna sjednica Zajednice Jugoslavenskih Univerziteta.' *UD* I, 3/4 (1960), 115-118.

Tripalo, Mika. 'On the occasion of discussions concerning the "crisis" of the younger generation.' *Socialist Thought and Practice* 2 (August 1961), 89-103.

'U povodu nekih najnovijih kritika *Praxisa.*' Editorial, *Praxis* V, 4 (1968), 449-458.

'Upravljanje ustanovama studentskog standarda.' *UD* IX, 8 (1968), 97-105.

Vasiljević, Tihomir. 'Naša visokoškolska politika.' *Gledišta* VII, 4 (April 1966), 495-507.

Veselinov, Jovan. 'Aktuelni problemi generacije mladih.' *Gledišta* VII, 6/7 (June/July 1966), 809-820.

Vodopivec, Petar. 'O razlozima za više vidova reorganizacije studentskog udruživanja na Ljubljanskom Univerzitetu.' *UD* X, 9/10 (1969), 122-125.

Vogelnik, Dolfe. 'Značenje studija u ciklusima.' *UD* I, 3/4 (1960), 89-92.

Vračar, Stevan K. 'Neizbežne promene na univerzitetu.' *Gledišta* VIII, 3 (1967), 321-328.

Vranić, Vladimir. 'O kvalifikakacionim ispitima.' *UD* IV, 3/4 (1963), 136-139.

Vranički, Predrag. 'O nekim problemima odnosa u komunizmu.' *Praxis* II, 4/5 (1965), 676-682.

Vučenov, Nikola. 'Putevi usavršavanja univerzitetske nastave.' *Gledišta* 3 (1965), 367-378.

Vucinich, Wayne S., ed. *Contemporary Yugoslavia: Twenty Years of Socialist Experiment.* Berkeley and Los Angeles: University of California Press, 1969.

Wolin, Sheldon S., and John H. Schaar. 'The abuses of the multiversity.' *Berkeley.*

'Work and development of the League of Communists of Yugoslavia (LCY) between the Seventh and Eighth Congress.' *Yugoslav Survey* V, 19 (1964), 2721-2736.

Yugoslav Union of Students. 'Neki statistički podaci.' N.d. [1971]. Mimeographed.

Yugoslavia's Way: The Program of the League of the Communists of Yugoslavia. Translated by Stoyan Pribichevich. New York: All Nations Press, 1958.

Žagar, Jelko. 'Reform of the university education.' *Yugoslav Student News* 20 (1956), 1-10.

Zaninovich, M. George. *The Development of Socialist Yugoslavia.* Baltimore: Johns Hopkins Press, 1968.

————. 'The Yugoslav Variation on Marx.' *Contemporary Yugoslavia: Twenty Years of Socialist Experiment.* Edited by Wayne S. Vucinich. Berkeley and Los Angeles: University of California Press, 1969.

Žarković, Grujica. 'O materijalnom položaju nastavnika i naučnih radnika SR BiH.' *UD* XII, (1971), 24-37.

Zec, Blažo. 'Deset godina rada ekonomskog fakulteta u Titogradu.' *UD* XII, 1 (1971), 72-79.

Žilnik, Želimir. 'Diskusija: društveno angažovanje i organizovanje omladine.' *Gledista* VII, 5 (May 1966), 661-707.

Zjalić, Milan, 'VIII Kongres Saveza Komunista Jugoslavije i problemi omladine.' *Naše Teme* IX, 1 (1968), 24-37.

Zukin, Sharon. *Beyond Marx and Tito.* London: Cambridge University Press, 1975.

Žuljević, Šefkija. 'Materijalni položaj univerzitetskih nastavnika i mogućnost vrednovanja naučnog i nastavno-pedagoškog rada na univerzitetu.' *UD* XI, 9/10 (1970), 91-101.

INDEX

235